This book is dedicated to the memory of
Philip A. L. Brownsey,
a true son of Mount Royal and Alberta.

University of Calgary Press
2500 University Drive NW
Calgary, Alberta
Canada T2N 1N4
press.ucalgary.ca

LIBRARY AND ARCHIVES CANADA CATALOGUING IN PUBLICATION

　　Orange Chinook : politics in the new Alberta / edited by Duane Bratt, Keith Brownsey, Richard Sutherland, and David Taras.

(Arts in action ; no. 2)
Includes index.
Issued in print and electronic formats.
ISBN 978-1-77385-025-2 (softcover).—ISBN 978-1-77385-027-6 (PDF).—
ISBN 978-1-77385-028-3 (EPUB).—ISBN 978-1-77385-029-0 (Kindle).—
ISBN 978-1-77385-026-9 (open access PDF)

　　1. Alberta--Politics and government--2015-. I. Bratt, Duane, 1967-, editor II. Brownsey, Keith, 1955-, editor III. Sutherland, Richard, 1964-, editor IV. Taras, David, 1950-, editor V. Series: Arts in action (Series) ; no. 2

FC3676.2.O73 2019　　　　　971.23'04　　　　　C2018-905894-3
　　　　　　　　　　　　　　　　　　　　　　　　　　　　　　C2018-905895-1

The University of Calgary Press acknowledges the support of the Government of Alberta through the Alberta Media Fund for our publications. We acknowledge the financial support of the Government of Canada. We acknowledge the financial support of the Canada Council for the Arts for our publishing program.

This book has been published with the help of a grant from Mount Royal University Library, through the Mount Royal University Library Open Access Fund.

Canada Council　Conseil des Arts
for the Arts　　du Canada

MOUNT ROYAL
UNIVERSITY
1910

Printed and bound in Canada by Friesens
✪ This book is printed on 57lb 100 Enviro FSC paper

Copyediting by Ryan Perks
Cover image: Kanadano, *Chinook Arch*, 31 July 2016, Photograph, https://commons.wikimedia.org/wiki/File:Chinook-arch-03.jpg
Cover design, page design, and typesetting by Melina Cusano

TABLE OF CONTENTS

VI. Alberta's Future Political System

PREFACE

The term "Orange Chinook" describes the changes that have consumed Alberta politics during one of the most tumultuous periods in the province's history. Indeed, if a group of Albertans living in 1990 were to be suddenly transported to 2019, much of what they would see would be unrecognizable. They would likely be surprised to learn that the Progressive Conservative Party that governed Alberta with almost no opposition in 1990 no longer exists in 2019; that the New Democrats, who had barely survived at the margins of Alberta politics, are now in power, led by a woman premier, Rachel Notley; that the province, after many years of unbridled prosperity, is barely emerging from a devastating economic downturn caused by a crash in global energy prices and a dearth of pipelines; and that environmental politics, long ignored or considered a sideshow, is now front and centre in Alberta politics. They would see a carbon tax, bitter clashes with British Columbia over pipelines, consistent increases in the minimum wage, massive government deficits, and that what was left of the old Progressive Conservative Party has merged with what was left of the Wildrose Party—which was not even in existence in 1990—to form the United Conservative Party. In short, much of the political and economic ground has shifted in Alberta, and what many would have thought to be the unimaginable has in fact taken place.

This book's goal is to chronicle these changes and describe the forces and events that led to the New Democrats' victory in the 2015 provincial election, and to examine how the Notley government has governed the province since. In assembling the book, the editors were careful to include a variety of perspectives and ensure that a wide expanse of issues was covered. Those seeking to find a single point of view with which to agree will be disappointed. The book covers a broad policy canvas, from the perils and shocks of transition, the politics of pipelines, the oil sands and the carbon tax, the provincial government's relationships with cities and big-city mayors, the precarious nature of government finances, the changing contours of rural Alberta, and the passions that shape the province's Indigenous politics, among a host of other topics. Unfortunately, not all policies or events could be covered with the same depth in a single volume. Nonetheless, *Orange*

Chinook provides what we believe will be the essential guide to Alberta politics and to the NDP government for some time to come.

While the book features a distinguished roster of contributors from across the province and beyond, much of the expertise and indeed the financial support for this enterprise came from Mount Royal University. We are grateful to Jeff Keshen, the former dean of arts, Jeffrey Goldberg, the former provost and vice-president, and David Docherty, the current president of Mount Royal University, for their enthusiasm and unwavering support. Kim Halvorson and Sue Torres of the Faculty of Arts went beyond the call of duty in helping us with this project. David Taras would like to thank Elizabeth Evans, dean of the Faculty of Business and Communication Studies, for her encouragement and guidance.

The book benefited from an intensive workshop held at the Banff Centre in October 2016. We are grateful to the Social Sciences and Humanities Research Council of Canada and to the Department of Economics, Justice and Policy Studies Innovation Fund at Mount Royal University for their generous support. Special thanks go to Don Braid, David Docherty, Sydney Sharpe, and Christopher Waddell for their contributions. Carolina Serrano Andres, Philip Brownsey, Kent Clayton, Sam Green, Demi Okuboejo, Cordelia Snowden, and Henry Wearmouth, who were public policy students at Mount Royal University at the time, attended and helped with the preparation of materials for the workshop.

We are also grateful to Brian Scrivener and Helen Hajnoczky at the University of Calgary Press for their professionalism, encouragement, and advice, and Ryan Perks, our copyeditor, whom we would like to thank for his outstanding work. We also owe a great debt to Kathryn Brownsey and Kenzie Webber, who helped organize and prepare the volume. Lastly, we are indebted to our contributors for their wisdom and enthusiasm and to the outside readers who offered both a critical eye and sound advice.

Duane Bratt
Keith Brownsey
Richard Sutherland
David Taras

I

SETTING THE SCENE

Introduction:
Out of an Orange-Coloured Sky

Richard Sutherland

Perhaps we should not have been that surprised. For instance, Ernest Manning was right. In the late stages of the 1971 Alberta election, Manning came out of retirement to campaign on behalf of the Social Credit Party he had led from 1944 to 1968. According to historian David Watts, Manning warned, "Elect the Conservatives now and you'll have the NDP next!"[1] Sure enough, Albertans did elect the Progressive Conservatives that year, and, although it would take another forty-four years for Manning's prediction to come to pass, the PCs have indeed been succeeded by a majority NDP government. Notwithstanding Manning's prescience, the election of a left-of-centre government in 2015 (with a majority, no less) came as a shock to Canadians, including many Albertans. The province has been the ideological heartland for Canadian conservative politics for decades, the birthplace of the Reform Party and the incubator for Prime Minister Stephen Harper's political career. The Progressive Conservatives had ruled Alberta uninterrupted for forty-four years and twelve elections, always with majority governments—an unparalleled feat in Canadian politics. How could Alberta, of all places, elect an NDP government? Certainly the polls leading up to the 5 May vote had shown this might be a possibility. But the previous election, in 2012, had also seen predictions of a change of government, and the ruling Progressive Conservatives had still managed to beat the right-wing Wildrose Party at the last minute. Even then, a victory by a small-c conservative party such as the Wildrose would have been far less surprising than the election of an NDP government.

This book is about that succession. It brings together the work of scholars, journalists, and others involved in public and political life in Alberta and beyond, who discuss a range of subjects from the 2015 campaign, through subsequent government policy, to the prospects for the future of Alberta politics. The contributors also bring to bear an equally wide range of methodologies, from close reading of texts and visuals, to interviews with key actors, to survey data and statistical analysis. The book is divided into several parts, including a discussion of the 2015 campaign and an assessment of the NDP government since taking power, and it features sections focusing on energy policies, an examination of Rachel Notley's governing style, and, finally, an analysis of the future of Alberta politics in light of the NDP's rise and other recent developments. The aim is to take stock of Alberta politics at a critical juncture in its history, to understand how these changes came about and to assess what they mean for the province both now and in the future.

Orange Chinook is the first scholarly appraisal of this critical moment in the history of Alberta politics. Some measure of the significance of the book's contribution is directly a result of the pivotal nature of the events it examines: the 2015 Alberta election and its most important immediate consequence, the transfer of power from the Progressive Conservatives to the New Democrats. This collection joins a select literature dealing with transitions in government in Canada, such as *Cycling into Saigon* by David Cameron and Graham White (the latter a contributor to this volume).[2] Indeed, Cameron and White's book remains one of the few studies of this phenomenon. Most Canadian provinces have received little scholarly attention in this respect, and Alberta less than most. The reason is that such moments of transition are extremely rare in Alberta, which has opted for a change in governing party only four times in its 110 years as a province, making the 2015 transition a relatively unique event. Further, as Duane Bratt has argued in this volume, the NDP's victory ended a run of small-*c* conservative governments dating back to 1935, making the switch to a social democratic government even more remarkable.

In light of this considerable change, an assessment of the continuities and breaks in policy from the previous government is even more worthy of examination. This is particularly notable in the analysis of the new government's energy policies, where one would expect considerable change with

RICHARD SUTHERLAND

the succession of a pro-industry conservative government by a social democratic government whose platform includes a much more prominent environmental focus. This book provides one of the first examinations of the considerable change in tone in Alberta's energy policy as the government grapples with issues such as climate change and other aspects of environmental stewardship.

A substantial portion of the book deals with the 2015 election that brought about this change in Alberta's provincial government. Despite the continuing work of Clarke and his various collaborators,[3] among others, the literature on Canadian elections is not large, and as Cross, Malloy, Small, and Stephenson note in their recent book *Fighting for Votes*, studies of subnational elections in Canada are even rarer.[4] *Orange Chinook* marks a contribution to this literature by allowing for a comparison between Alberta's 2015 election and elections at both the federal level and the subnational level in other Canadian provinces. Further, it contextualizes the importance of the 2015 campaign by examining the events leading up to it, and assessing what its consequences for Alberta have actually been in the first years of the NDP government.

The Tory Fall and NDP Victory

The first section of this book examines the campaign and the events leading up to it. As its title suggests, this is not just about the election of the NDP; it is also, necessarily, about the end of the longest-running political dynasty in Canadian history. In his chapter "Politics, Alberta Style: The Rise and Fall of the Progressive Conservatives, 1971–2015," David Taras looks at the fortuitous political and economic circumstances that kept the PCs in power for so long, and at how the unravelling of these conditions exposed the party's vulnerabilities and failures in the years prior to the 2015 election. Taras's analysis of the forty-four years of Tory government alerts us to just how dependent the party's compact with Albertans was on a healthy energy industry. Indeed, the sharp downturn in the world price for oil in 2015 provided the backdrop for that year's provincial election. In June of 2014, West Texas Intermediate crude was trading at nearly $110 a barrel. By the time Jim Prentice called the provincial election in March of 2015, the price had dropped by more than 50 per cent to below $50. The effect on

Alberta's economy was staggering. Companies quickly went from having very healthy balance sheets to sharp losses, and a wave of layoffs in the sector began, driving the province's unemployment rate from one of the lowest in Canada to among the highest in a matter of months.

The first polls indicating that Albertans might end up with an NDP government came in the wake of the April 23 leader's debate, and in this they were proven correct. Yet Albertans could be forgiven for being skeptical. The PCs had been nothing if not resilient in their years in office, and the previous election, in 2012, had suggested, right up to the last minute, that the Tories were bound for defeat. In their chapter "Marginally Better," Janet Brown, an experienced pollster in her own right, with her co-author John Santos, examines some of the problems that beset pollsters trying to accurately predict not only winners, but shares of the vote—difficult but a vital task in our multi-party system. When one examines a number of recent elections in Canada, it is obvious that, in some cases, even the best pollsters can be wrong. Brown and Santos identify what seem to be some systemic biases in polling, particularly the overestimating of Albertans' desire for change in government. As the public becomes increasingly difficult for pollsters to reach or unwilling to participate in polls, critical methodological concerns have arisen around areas such as sample construction and persistence in contacting respondents.

Duane Bratt offers an analysis of the Progressive Conservatives' 2015 campaign in his chapter "Death of a Dynasty: The Tories and the 2015 Election." While much of the anger directed at the late Jim Prentice and the PCs stemmed from the sudden decline in the province's economy, the party's internal tumult from 2006 to 2015 was clearly an indication of trouble. Even so, the campaign itself showed a number of missteps and miscalculations that sealed the PCs' fate. As important as the mistakes and weakness of the Progressive Conservatives were in their downfall, had they been succeeded by the Wildrose Party this would have been a very different book. The Wildrose would have been a continuation of the right-leaning governments in Alberta that, as both Bratt and Taras note, date back to the beginning of Social Credit rule in 1935.

Bratt notes that the PCs' campaign failures do not by itself explain the NDP's success in 2015. It is apparent that the NDP benefitted from other circumstances, including the governing party's rightward turn under

Prentice, the disorganization of the Liberals, and the Alberta Party's lack of experience. However, as Melanee Thomas points out in her chapter "Ready for Rachel: The 2015 Alberta NDP Campaign," the NDP also did a lot of things right when it came to preparing and executing the campaign that brought them to power. It is clear that the party had the ambition and strategy to form a government, even if this happened sooner than they expected. As Thomas argues, much of this comes down to the skills of Rachel Notley, who had assumed leadership of the party late in 2014. Already blessed with a last name famous in Alberta politics (her father, Grant Notley, had been the well-liked and respected leader of the Alberta NDP from 1968 until his death in 1984), Rachel Notley also proved to be a more than capable campaigner. This was especially apparent in the April 23 leader's debate, which took place midway through the campaign. Whether or not this was the decisive moment, the debate was certainly a microcosm of the larger campaign—replete with stumbles by Premier Jim Prentice, particularly the "math is hard" quip directed at Notley, and Notley's adroit handling of the situation, which turned the dismissive insult to her advantage. Notley's persona was also effectively projected through the NDP's online campaign, as Peter Malachy Ryan shows in his chapter "Alberta Politics Online: Digital Retail Politics and Grassroots Growth, 2006–2016." Ryan makes the case for the continuing relevance of retail politics over social media, and examines the evolution of online campaigns and risks over the last several elections in the province.

Oil Sands, Carbon Tax, and Pipelines

No book on Alberta politics can ignore the central role of the oil and gas sector in the province's economy, and the third section focuses on this area of policy. In fact the Alberta energy sector's influence is so pervasive that there is almost no chapter in this book that does not refer, at least in passing, to some aspect of the industry and the issues it faces in respect to low commodity prices, access to markets, and both local and global environmental impact.

The NDP inherited these issues and the challenges that go with them. One of the key questions as the party assumed office was its level of continuity with or departure from the Progressive Conservatives' energy policy.

In her chapter "Betting on Bitumen: Lougheed, Klein, and Notley," Gillian Steward focuses specifically on the previous government's policies regarding the development of Alberta's oil sands, noting that the PCs' policies were by no means consistent throughout their time in power. In the 1970s, Peter Lougheed's government placed itself at the centre of the emerging oil sands industry by offering various means of support, but taking a measured approach to the development of the resource while emphasizing provincial control. In contrast, Premier Ralph Klein's hands-off approach sought to remove any and all regulatory barriers to industry in an effort to encourage rapid and unfettered development. If the Notley government's policies constitute a break with the previous government's approach, this is by no means unprecedented, and may even mark a return to the policies of the early days of Progressive Conservative government.

With regard to the energy industry and the provincial government, most attention has focused on two specific policy areas: pipelines and the carbon tax. Two chapters in this section provide an assessment of these issues, giving us a sense of precisely where we can find both change and continuity in Alberta's energy policy. The NDP's major departure from previous energy policy has been its Climate Leadership Plan, the centrepiece of which is an economy-wide carbon tax, which has served as a lightning rod for much opposition to the NDP government. One-time Alberta Liberal leader Kevin Taft offers an examination of the tax as a response to environmental concerns, and he includes an assessment of the considerable opposition it has met within the province. Taft makes a strong case for the tax, but he notes that this may not be as radical a change as it is often presented. Apparently, Jim Prentice might have contemplated a similar measure had he been re-elected, particularly with the federal government's introduction of a federal carbon tax for those provinces that did not introduce similar measures of their own.[5]

When it comes to pipelines, there is a necessary bargain to be struck, as business columnist Deborah Yedlin points out in her chapter "Notley: The Accidental Pipeline Advocate." One of the NDP's stated aims with the carbon tax was to demonstrate to environmental groups and other governments Alberta's commitment to environmental stewardship. In exchange, it is hoped that pipelines bringing oil from land-locked Alberta to tidewater might be easier for these other governments to approve or support. This

RICHARD SUTHERLAND

approach has been successful to some extent, helping to bring the federal government onside, although it has not been enough to win over the NDP-Green coalition elected in British Columbia in 2017. But the commitment to the necessity of pipelines remains, and this shows one respect in which the NDP is not significantly different from previous governments in Alberta. Even if the party attempted, at least initially, to pursue these aims in a more collaborative style, resistance from the BC government has been met with a more confrontational style, one that is highly reminiscent of the Progressive Conservatives under Lougheed, and even Klein. Nonetheless, Yedlin suggests that a pragmatic approach will continue to be necessary to ensure co-operation from other governments and regions.

The NDP in Power

In the third section we turn to the NDP's exercise of power in other policy areas over its first few years in office. This begins with the transfer of power from the Progressive Conservatives to the NDP immediately following the 5 May election. Precisely how long this transition process lasted is perhaps less straightforward than it might appear. Keith Brownsey presents a close examination of this transition and offers insights into what governmental transition consists of and how we might assess its successes or failures. Brownsey notes the considerable role of the civil service in preparing for a new government, as well as the careful planning done by Notley's senior political staff. He also notes the ineffectiveness of both the Wildrose and Progressive Conservative Parties in the immediate aftermath of the election.

It is not only businesses and jobs that have suffered as a result of the drop in oil prices; government finances in Alberta have also taken an enormous hit. Although they may be dubbed the "royalty rollercoaster," the ups and downs occasioned by price swings in volatile commodities are not nearly so pleasurable as an amusement park ride. For one thing, the fortunes of Alberta's economy and its government finances are tied to these price swings. Ron Kneebone and Jennifer Zwicker examine the difficulties this has posed for Alberta governments' fiscal situation over decades of reliance on fossil fuel royalties. This historical perspective shows that Alberta governments have long been over-reliant on the revenue from non-renewable resources. This has precluded introducing other, perhaps more sustainable revenue sources, such as a sales tax. It has also meant that little of this revenue has been saved, and that when royalties decline, these governments run substantial deficits. On the spending side, Kneebone and Zwicker assess the growth in health spending, the government's single largest area of expenditure, and they offer some ways of addressing this growth.

Expectations were high for the NDP among many communities. A new governing party unaccustomed to winning elections led many to anticipate that some long-standing areas of neglect on the part of the Progressive Conservatives might now be addressed. According to Brad Clark, much of the NDP's support in rural Alberta came from Indigenous communities. The party appears to have cultivated more dialogue with these communities, and this has been repaid with more electoral support and a more positive relationship with Indigenous media outlets, both before and after the election. However, while the NDP have a much more developed Aboriginal platform than their predecessors, its engagement with issues around environmental impacts and revenue sharing remain as problematic as ever.

It was also clear on election night that the basis of the NDP's strength was largely in urban areas. Indeed, in his chapter "Alberta's Cities under the NDP," James Wilt starts with the assumption that the NDP can be seen as "the party of cities." Yet here, again, there has been less change than many municipal governments would have liked. The NDP's record on municipal issues involving regional planning and conflicts between rural and urban governments at the local level remains a point of frustration for local leaders, despite the imminent introduction of big-city charters for Calgary and Edmonton. Nevertheless, despite the difficulties of crafting a new relationship between the province and its municipalities, the election of an NDP government can be seen as a continuation of the shift in the province's centre of gravity from the rural to the urban population. Roger Epp refers to a "post-rural politics" in his chapter, a strong claim that suggests that rural Alberta has become less of a physical place and more of a political idea, a way of referring back to the province's historical, predominantly rural past.

Notley's Governing Style

Deborah Yedlin's is clearly not the only chapter to mark Notley's political persona and style as an asset. While Melanee Thomas examined Notley's success as a campaigner, the two chapters that comprise the fourth section of this book look at how that style has influenced her performance as premier. In her chapter "A League of Their Own: Women Leaders in Alberta Politics," Lori Williams looks at Notley's persona through the lens of gender, drawing attention to the particular barriers and challenges women face in a political system that has traditionally been a masculine preserve. Drawing comparisons to two other recent provincial leaders in Alberta, Alison Redford and Danielle Smith, Williams suggests that Notley has been more successful in developing a public persona and a governing style that have allowed her to negotiate a path between the often incompatible stereotypes of femininity and political leadership.

In "Notley and the Beast," Chaseten Remillard and Sheridan McVean give us a picture of that style in action—and under duress—as they focus on Notley's performance communicating with Albertans during the Fort McMurray wildfire in the Spring of 2016. Here, too, we can find useful comparisons with other Alberta politicians during other times of crisis, notably Alison Redford and Naheed Nenshi in the wake of the floods that devastated much of Southern Alberta, particularly Calgary and High River, in 2013.

Alberta's Future Political System

In his chapter "What's Past is Prologue: Ontario 1990 and Alberta 2015," Graham White takes up a number of points that have been discussed in earlier chapters, reminding us that this is not the first time in Canadian history that an NDP government has come to power rather unexpectedly. The 1990 Ontario election delivered that province's first (and, so far, only) NDP government. The fate of the Ontario NDP under Bob Rae's leadership (one term in office) might stand as a warning to Rachel Notley and her government in Alberta, but White's aim here is not so much to find similarities (much less to suggest that Ontario has already been there and done that) than it is to alert us to the differences between the two cases, both in terms of the circumstances that brought them to power and even more the steps each government has taken during the transition. While White is rightly reticent to predict the Notley government's fortunes in relation to the Ontario example, he does suggest that Alberta has seen a surprisingly smooth transition from the Progressive Conservatives to the NDP.

Finally, one of the biggest questions that any analysis of the current NDP government must ask is what will happen in 2019 and after. Will the 2015 election mark the start of the long reign of the NDP, as happened in 1935 with Social Credit or in 1971 with the Progressive Conservatives? Alberta's history of long periods of rule by one party punctuated by sudden change is worth remembering, but in this case it is not clear whether it will offer us much of a guide to the future. Alberta seems less cohesive and monolithic than it did under the Progressive Conservatives. On top of this, a redistribution of seats will see more power for urban areas, particularly those outside of Edmonton and Calgary, and less for those rural communities that have generally been a reliable base for right-of-centre governments in the province.

Whatever party wins in 2019, we need to ask whether the dynamics of Alberta politics have shifted. We do know that the Progressive Conservatives will not be returning to power, as that party no longer exists. As Duane Bratt notes, electoral defeat has in most cases dealt a fatal blow to the fortunes of governing parties, and that is once again the case. Over the summer of 2017, the Progressive Conservatives and the Wildrose Party voted to merge, forming the United Conservative Party, and in October 2018, the party selected former federal cabinet minister Jason Kenney as leader. In their chapter "Out of the Blue? Goodbye Tories, Hello Jason Kenney," Anthony Sayers and David Stewart look at the new party's prospects under Kenney's leadership. While vote shares from the last election might suggest that the future looks positive for the United Conservatives, there is some dispute over whether unity on the right will allow the party to hold on to the centrist vote going forward. Certainly Jim Prentice's attempt to incorporate the Wildrose caucus into the Progressive Conservative Party through a secretly negotiated mass floor crossing in 2014 is widely cited as a factor that led to disillusion with his leadership and his party.

There is the possibility that the eponymous Orange Chinook will, like its namesake, fade quickly back into a Tory winter. On the other hand it could be a harbinger of a real change of season in Alberta politics. Will the centre or left-of-centre vote continue to coalesce around the NDP as it did in 2015? Or will the Liberals and the Alberta Party erode that support? If the NDP remains the alternative to the right in Alberta politics, this raises the possibility of a two-party situation in the province, different from the three-party split seen in the last election, or the tremendous gap between the Progressive Conservatives and everybody else that obtained through most of the last four decades. Some would suggest that the NDP's victory was a fluke, and that the chances of their maintaining a hold on power are slim in a province that maintains a strong conservative consensus. However, the occasion for this book, the party's victory in 2015, would have seemed even more unlikely just weeks before it happened. In what follows, we hope to offer a more informed basis for assessing both the significance of the NDP's assumption of power and what the party has done while in government.

NOTES

1   David W. Watts, "Prophecy may be coming true; 'You'll have the NDP next' said Ernest Manning," *Edmonton Journal*, 27 April 2015, A15.

2   David Cameron and Graham White, *Cycling into Saigon: The Conservative Transition in Ontario* (Vancouver: University of British Columbia Press, 2001).

3   See, for instance, Harold, D. Clarke, Allan Kornberg, John MacLeod, and Thomas Scotto, "Too Close to Call: Political Choice in Canada, 2004," *PS: Political Science & Politics* 38, no. 2 (April 2005): 247–53.

4   William P. Cross, Jonathan Malloy, Tamara A. Small, and Laura B. Stephenson, *Fighting for Votes: Parties, the Media, and Voters in an Ontario Election* (Vancouver: University of British Columbia Press, 2015).

5   Jim Prentice with Jean-Sebastien Rioux, *Triple Crown: Winning Canada's Energy Future* (Toronto: Harper Collins, 2017), 187–90.

II

THE TORY FALL
AND THE NDP VICTORY

Politics, Alberta Style: The Rise and Fall of the Progressive Conservatives, 1971–2015

David Taras

Alberta is unique in many ways. It is the only place in North America where prairies, mountains, and boreal forests meet. Few realize, in fact, that over half the province is covered by forests. Its diversity is such that one can traverse over 300 square kilometres of glacier ice, visit badlands that are so desolate and eerie that they look as if they are on another planet, plunge down ski runs that are among the most famous and challenging in the world, and look up at skies that are deeply and often endlessly majestic. There is hardly a day that goes by without a post on Reddit from someone who has photographed some aspect of Alberta's beauty and wants to share it with the world.

Until the 1960s, Alberta was Canada's most rural province. Today, it is the country's most urbanized, with almost two-thirds of the population hemmed in to the narrow and burgeoning Calgary–Edmonton corridor. Alberta is home to Canada's oil and gas industry, which until recently accounted for the highest standard of living in Canada, but also for the brutal and often unpredictable convulsions that have distorted the province's economy and can be felt in almost every pore of its political life. It is also the province that, with the exception of Quebec, has been the most alienated from and suspicious of the federal government. Indeed, Alberta's politics have been defined in no small way by a series of dramatic and painful battles for control over its natural resources and how they would be used. What also makes Alberta unique is that it is home to the political party that remained in power longer than any other in Canadian history—a party, in fact, that came close to setting the record for longevity among democratic governments across the globe.

Alberta's Progressive Conservative Party came to power in 1971 and governed Alberta with what Geo Takach has described as "King Kong" sized majorities until it was defeated by the New Democrats in 2015.[1] Only the Progressive Conservatives in Ontario, the famed "Big Blue Machine," which formed governments in that province from 1943 to 1985, has come close to matching the longevity of Alberta's Conservatives. The key to the Ontario Tories' success was a series of formidable leaders—George Drew, Leslie Frost, John Robarts, and William Grenville Davis—a growing economy, and an opposition divided between the Liberals and the NDP. As I hope to show in this chapter, the Alberta Conservatives, by contrast, were able to remain in office for so long because unlike the Conservatives in Ontario they were not a Big Blue Machine. Instead, the party maintained its hold on power by governing from the political centre. The party tent was large enough to include many shades of blue as well as those who in other places and circumstances would have been Liberals. Moreover, unlike Ontario's Progressive Conservatives, which built a formidable political apparatus, the Alberta Tories were relatively weak on the ground, and they were able to maintain a hold on government, I argue, because of identity politics on one hand and voter apathy on the other.

What makes the Alberta story even more unique is that every government in Alberta's history has been elected by an overwhelming majority. While the pendulum has swung from the Liberals (1905–21) to the United Farmers of Alberta (1921–35) to Social Credit (1935–71), and then to the Tories and finally the NDP, Albertans as a whole have never voted by half measures. Public opinion has always moved decisively from one party to another, so that, remarkably, the province has never elected a minority government.

It should also be noted that in some ways the reign of conservative politics in Alberta lasted even longer than the forty-four years of Progressive Conservative governments. This is because the Social Credit government that preceded it was also in a sense a conservative government. While Ernest Manning famously mixed religion and politics (continuing to preach on Sunday-morning radio as part of *Canada's National Bible Hour* even after he became premier), his premiership was characterized by budgetary

DAVID TARAS

frugality, a belief in small government, a close relationship with the oil industry, the notion that individual struggle was the road to redemption, and a strict moral code that included harsh film censorship and a prohibition against men and women drinking together in bars. Arguably, Social Credit was overturned by the Progressive Conservatives in 1971 because it was if anything too conservative for the changing times.

This chapter describes the economic and social forces that allowed the PCs to dominate Alberta politics for two generations. My argument is that the Tories remained in power because of a confluence of factors: identity politics, economic prosperity, the weakness of the opposition parties, and a largely conservative provincial political culture. Each of these forces reinforced the others, resulting in an almost unbreakable chain-link fence. Elections would be decided within minutes of the polls closing, with almost no need for people to watch the results for longer than half an hour at the most. The party won so easily that it almost didn't have to campaign. But while the end of this remarkable reign came suddenly and caught many observers by surprise—including Premier Jim Prentice and his team, who were convinced until the very end that they would win another majority—the Progressive Conservative dynasty had begun to unravel years earlier. Most critically, the foundations on which the party's power rested had begun to crumble. While the chapter will concentrate on the forces and strategies that allowed the Conservatives to remain in power for so long, it will also examine some of reasons for their defeat in 2015. While the end would appear to come suddenly, a slow-motion collapse has been underway for quite some time.

The Foundations of Progressive Conservative Power

Tory power in Alberta was built on a number of historic and strategic foundations. As the American frontier was closing at the turn of the nineteenth century, Alberta was seen as the "Last Best West," the final opportunity for open ranges, homesteading, and good land. Between 1898 and 1914, some 600,000 American immigrants would arrive mostly from the Midwest. By 1911, roughly a quarter of the Alberta population was born in the United States.[2] They brought with them different religious values from those held by those of British and Ontario heritage, including an adherence to smaller and more populist religious sects over established churches. The evangelical streak in Alberta politics that helped produce Social Credit governments under "Bible Bill" Aberhart and his disciple Ernest Manning arguably had its origins in the fundamentalist churches that took root in Alberta during this period.

The American influence in late-nineteenth-century Calgary was so great that what is now Mount Royal, one of the city's more elite and most posh areas, was once called American Hill. Its name was changed to Mount Royal and its streets given Canadian place names in order to Canadianize the city. A second wave of American immigrants came in the 1950s, when the oil industry began to take off. The culture subtlety changed as cowboy hats, football, and Texas accents became prominent.[3] Just as crucial was the fact that Houston became as important a financial centre as Toronto—perhaps even more important—when it came to financing large oil projects. American immigration might also explain why the cowboy culture that is showcased during the Calgary Stampede, as well as in the rodeos that are so popular in small towns across Central and Southern Alberta, came to over-shadow other aspects of Alberta's history, such as the northern fur trade and the traditions brought by immigrants from Eastern Canada and the British Isles. The consequences of immigration were felt in another critical way. In the province's mythology, in its songs and its literature, Alberta is always the place of coming and never the place of leaving. The "four strong winds" made famous by singer Ian Tyson always brought people *to* Alberta rather than away from it; if they did leave, it was assumed that they did so with regret. The province's population surged from a little over 1.5 million when the Progressive Conservatives came to power in 1971 to over 4 million when they were ousted by the NDP in 2015. This meant that new Canadians as well as immigrants from other provinces had enough electoral power to tilt the political scales in any direction they chose.

The popular wisdom is that immigrants who came with different political traditions and who had voted for liberal or socialist parties in their home societies would transplant those beliefs to Alberta, and that they would eventually by sheer force of numbers change the province's political life. The effects of immigration, however, seemed to have been counterintuitive in that they reinforced rather than altered prevailing political beliefs. And yet this is in keeping with a larger trend. Through much of Canadian history, immigrants have been attracted to the party that was in power when they first came to Canada. While the Liberals have benefited from this phenomenon at the federal level, the Alberta Tories benefited at the provincial level. In addition, as Tamara and Howard Palmer have pointed out, immigrants often self-selected; in other words, they came to Alberta precisely because of its conservative values and its much-celebrated individualistic and rugged spirit.[4] For at least some immigrants, voting for the Progressive Conservatives was a way of integrating into the larger society, part of being accepted. It was also the surest route to political power and influence.

The province is roughly divided into three separate political universes: Calgary, Edmonton, and rural Alberta. The basic math of Alberta politics has long been that the Tories would go into any election with an almost automatic majority because they could always count on winning thirty to thirty-five seats in rural and small-town Alberta. This was bloc voting par excellence. Even in the hotly contested 1993 election, when public opinion in the cities had turned against the PCs, and the Liberals under former Edmonton mayor Lawrence Decore seemed close to winning, rural Alberta remained loyal to the Progressive Conservatives. For their part, the PCs always ensured that rural Alberta was overrepresented on the electoral map, even as the cities exploded in population. They understood that keeping rural Alberta onside was the hinge on which power rested.

In chapter 13 of this volume, University of Alberta political scientist Roger Epp mourns the end of rural Alberta and the emergence of what he calls a "post-rural" province. His argument is that with a declining population, the increasing encroachments of urban life, and the loss of health and education services, the rural way of life is quickly fading or has already past. Epp claims that the NDP has added to the disenfranchisement of rural voters by failing to see this constituency through a separate and distinctive lens. This was a mistake that Premiers Peter Lougheed (1971–85) and Ralph Klein (1992–2006) never made. As rural Alberta clung to the PCs in order to ensure that it got its share of government spoils—a relationship that became ever more important as the farm economy weakened—rural party lieutenants such as Hugh Horner, Marv Moore, Ken Kowalski, and Ed Stelmach became major power brokers. When the Wildrose Party broke with the Progressive Conservatives in 2012 and 2015, the guaranteed rural majority that had sustained the PCs for close to two generations came to an end.

The party could also count on sweeping Calgary, which was Peter Lougheed and Ralph Klein's political fiefdoms. While the Liberals would always win a sprinkling of seats in the city, usually in the urban core, suburban Calgary was an impregnable Tory fortress. While the Liberals could sometimes also do well in Edmonton—winning some eighteen seats in the 1993 and 1997 elections, for instance—Edmonton would always hedge its bets by electing a sizeable number of Tories. It was simply too dangerous for the city to be seen as an opposition stronghold when the PCs had held power for so long.

The Politics of Western Alienation

In their incisive book on voting, *Democracy for Realists*, political scientists Christopher Achen and Larry Bartels contend that in the end almost all voting is based on identity.[5] While other schools of thought argue that people vote based on chequebook politics—that is, on how the economy is performing—Achen and Bartels believe that issue voting is often an illusion because it masks deeper issues of identity. In the case of Alberta, economic fortunes and identity politics have often been one in the same. This is because the politics of Western grievance has always been deeply woven into Alberta's political DNA.

Historian Doug Francis has argued that "the crucible out of which Western regional consciousness was forged was one of failure, depression and disappointed dreams. It became a defensive identity, seeking to locate blame in institutions and individuals outside the region, namely federal politicians, the Canadian Pacific Railway Company, and the people of Ontario."[6] While natural resources were given to the provinces under the British North America Act, Ottawa did not relinquish control over natural resources in the Western provinces until 1930. Thus, from the time that Alberta became a province in 1905 until 1930, Ottawa acted largely as a colonial power. In the 1920s, Calgarians could, much to their anger, turn to the night sky to see flares in nearby Turner Valley burn off and waste valuable gas.

The federal government's control over Alberta's natural resources was emblematic of the unequal economic relationship that had been imposed on the province. For many decades, high tariffs on US imports forced Westerners to buy manufactured goods from Ontario at prices far higher

DAVID TARAS

than those of manufactured products from the United States. At the same time, they had to sell their agricultural produce at the discounted Crow Rate, far below its real market value. In this "rigged" system, Albertans rightly felt powerless and exploited. These inequalities were compounded by the despair and agony of the dirty thirties. Waves of bankruptcies, mass fore-closures, and evictions produced bitter recriminations against the Eastern banks and the mythical "50 big shots" that William Aberhart claimed were controlling the economy. This explosive cauldron of festering resentment brought the Social Credit Party to power at the height of the depression, in 1935. Promises to fight the banks and control the supply of money brought the Social Credit government into headlong and continued confrontations with the federal government and with the Supreme Court of Canada, which disallowed much of Aberhart's legislation.

All of this set the stage for the energy wars fought by Peter Lougheed against the Trudeau government in the early 1980s. Lougheed believed that Pierre Trudeau's National Energy Program was an attempt to dismantle Alberta's control over natural resources and with it the very existence of the Alberta state. Ottawa's *coup de force* included an export tax on Alberta oil, changes to the tax code that would infringe on Alberta's right to set the royalty regime, incentives for companies to shift exploration away from Alberta to Canada Lands in the North, and the setting of a Canadian price instead of a global price for oil. One estimate, based on the differential be-tween the Canadian and global price for oil, puts the cost of Ottawa's pol-icies for Alberta at close to $70 billion between 1973 and 1985.[7] Lougheed responded by launching court actions and cutting back oil production. At one point he took to the airwaves to tell Albertans that their choice was ei-ther to see more of their lives "directed and controlled" by Ottawa or to opt for "decision-making determined by Albertans in Alberta." Even after the National Energy Policy was repealed by the Mulroney government in 1986, its memory haunted Alberta politics for at least a generation.

The Alberta Conservatives' defensive approach to the rest of Canada could be seen in a number of policy arenas. Lougheed was a principal ar-chitect of article 33 of the Canadian Charter of Rights and Freedoms, the so-called "notwithstanding clause," which allowed provinces to opt out of federal legislation. Premier Don Getty (1985–92) pushed Senate reform onto the constitutional agenda by sponsoring and instituting elections to the

Senate. Getty believed that a revitalized Senate would enhance the power of the regions and act as a buffer against the unbridled power of the House of Commons. Ralph Klein, who as mayor of Calgary had lashed out at the Eastern "creeps and bums" that had arrived during the boom years of the early 1980s, told Quebecers during the 1995 Quebec referendum on sovereignty, that while Canada was a "safe harbour" for Quebec, Alberta would be an ally and kindred spirit in standing up to Ottawa.

Klein was also the recipient of the famous "firewall" letter penned by, among others, future prime minister Stephen Harper, future Alberta cabinet minister Ted Morton, and campaign strategist Tom Flanagan. The letter proposed that Alberta insulate itself from "an increasingly hostile government in Ottawa" by creating its own pension plan, collecting its own income tax, replacing the RCMP with its own police force, fighting for Senate reform, and assuming exclusive jurisdiction over health care. While this was never acted on by Klein, it can be argued that as prime minister, Stephen Harper did erect a firewall of sorts. He gave the provinces wide discretion in formulating and carrying out policies and largely stepped away from a leadership role in federal-provincial relations.

There can be little doubt that one of the keys to the Tories' popularity was that they came to be seen as the great protector of Alberta's rights against encroachments by the federal government. The logic for many voters was that the province had to be unified, had to speak with a single voice, in order to stand up to Ottawa. The best way to do that was to give the Tories a strong majority. Economic interests were therefore merged with identity politics so that, for many, being a strong Albertan also meant being a strong Tory. Interestingly, Jim Prentice never played the alienation card. And in fact, as a former federal cabinet minister and then as an executive vice-president of the Canadian Imperial Bank of Commerce who also sat on a myriad of powerful corporate boards, he seemed to some the very picture of satisfied Eastern power; put simply, many Albertans may not have been sure on which team he was playing. Interestingly, Jason Kenney, the leader of the new United Conservative Party, has been more than eager to play the anti-Ottawa card. His criticism of Prime Minister Justin Trudeau have been bitter and personal and he has railed against the federal government's equalization as well climate change policies.

The Alberta Liberals, for their part, were on the wrong side of identity politics. Amid the boiling emotions that simmered and overflowed during the energy wars, the party stood little chance since most Albertans who were disgruntled with the PCs preferred to stay at home rather than vote Liberal. In some ridings, in fact, Liberal signs were virtually non-existent at election time. While, as mentioned above, the party came close to winning in 1993, they have been distant challengers in every other election. Their very weakness bred further weakness. Being far from power meant that, except in a handful of inner-city ridings in Calgary and Edmonton, the Liberals rarely attracted large donations, top candidates, or sizable numbers of volunteers.

The Liberals, along with the NDP, also received surprisingly little media coverage. Indeed, the opposition parties played such a minor role in the legislature and appeared to be so far from the decision-making process that the news media treated them as little more than an afterthought. To make matters worse, ambitious opposition politicians, realizing that they were unlikely to have careers at the provincial level, tended to vacate provincial politics entirely, with many migrating to municipal politics. In fact, one can argue that the progressive nature of city politics in Alberta owes much to politicians whose careers had been blocked at the provincial level.

Governing from the Centre

Another key to power for the PCs was that they were a big-tent party. While the political centre may be further to the right in Alberta than elsewhere, the Tories always had a keen sense of where public opinion was on any particular issue, such that the party was rarely caught on the wrong side of the public mood. Ralph Klein in particular was so adept at changing positions according to shifts in public opinion that he seemed at times to be a kind of political contortionist. One only has to recall his sensational back flip when it came to compensating the victims of government sterilization programs, his many zigs and zags on the privatization of health care, his epic reversal on electing representatives to regional health authorities, and his change of mind on government support for kindergartens, to name just a few.

Like Klein, the party itself was in reality only partially blue. The tent it constructed was wide enough to include people who in other settings would vote Liberal. In his 2009 biography of Klein, Rich Vivone, a long-time observer of Alberta politics, described this phenomenon as follows: "the Conservatives were ideologically flexible. In one era, they were social activists who interfere in the private sector; in another era they dismantle the foundations of everything done by the same party in the previous 15 years; and in yet another era, they go on another wild spending spree. In 35 years, the Conservative Government under three leaders covered the entire political spectrum."[8] Or, to put it differently, PC cabinets usually contained enough right wingers to suppress the emergence of more powerful alternatives on the right and enough moderates to dissuade Liberals from throwing in their lot with the provincial Liberal Party. This "blocking" strategy worked well until the PCs lost control of the right with the rise of the Wildrose Party.

Peter Lougheed, who began the Tory dynasty, believed that Alberta needed a "supersized" (my description) government in order to offset Ottawa's power, manage and diversify the economy, and build a strong Alberta identity. Far from viewing the economy from the sidelines, government was to be a main player. Lougheed tried to alter the economic balance in the province and indeed the country by creating the Alberta Energy Company, half of which was owned by the province and half by individual Alberta shareholders; by renegotiating royalty agreements with oil and gas producers to wring more money for the provincial coffers; by buying the country's second-largest airline, Pacific Western Airlines; by making the Alberta government a partner in oil sands development through Syncrude; and by brokering deals to ensure increased petrochemical production in the province, among other actions. Most dramatically, the Loughheed government established the Alberta Heritage Trust Fund in order to create a large pool of capital with which to diversify the economy and build infrastructure. Following an initial endowment of $1.5 billion, 30 per cent of the revenue from natural resources was to be plowed into the fund annually. Famously, the Lougheed government also invested $300 million in the Alberta Heritage Foundation for Medical Research with the goal of making Alberta a world leader in medical research.

In short, Lougheed's interventionist style mimicked federal Liberal policies far more than they did those of right-wing politicians. In fact, Allan Tupper has argued that in ideological terms there was little to distinguish

Peter Lougheed from then NDP leader Grant Notley (Rachel Notley's father), who also believed in public ownership of natural resources.[9] While his policies of government ownership and intervention worried more than a few conservatives, Lougheed made sure that right wingers in the party, such as Edmonton MLA Keith Alexander, were treated respectfully and even warmly. He liked to point out that his cabinet was made up of practical rather than ideological politicians—"doers rather than knockers." In his view, a growing Alberta, a province in a hurry to catch up, had no time for exercises in ideological purity.

Attempts to diversify the economy away from its dependency on oil and gas reached a fever pitch under Premier Don Getty. Getty had the bad fortune to be in power during a deep global recession, a severe downturn in energy prices, the disrepair brought by the federal government's National Energy Program, and a financial crisis that included the collapse of two Alberta-based banks. To make matters worse, as Mark Lisac notes, Getty was a shy person who had little interest in public relations or even in telling his side of the story, which made governing during a perfect political storm all the more difficult.[10] Nonetheless, Getty led an activist government that bailed out dozens of credit unions, offered loan guarantees to fund the expansion of the Syncrude oil sands plant, the giant Husky upgrader near Lloydminster, and pulp and paper mills in the north; he also poured hundreds of millions of dollars into a series of dubious enterprises, including the Gainers meat-packing plant, the Swan Hills waste-treatment plant, and Novatel, which manufactured cell phones. As its finances crumbled, the Getty government lurched from crisis to crisis, nearly bringing the Tory dynasty to an end.

When Getty recruited Calgary mayor Ralph Klein to join his government in 1989, some speculated that Klein had first toyed with the idea of running as a Liberal, and that Getty had shrewdly brought him into the government in order to shore up the government's centre-left credentials. While Klein would soon be venerated as a rock star of the right because of his drastic cuts to government spending, a wave of privatizations and sell-offs, and his desire to see government run like a business, by the end of his third term the government was again spending heavily. Right wingers such as Lorne Taylor, Lyle Oberg, and Steve West wielded considerable power, to be sure, but Klein also surrounded himself with centrist politicians such as

Peter Elzinga, David Hancock, Gary Mar, Iris Evans, and Ron Stevens. He was also friendly with Liberal MLA Sheldon Chumir, after whom his government named a medical centre in Calgary. Perhaps most crucially, Klein chose ex-Liberal MLA Mike Percy to chair his government's 1997 Growth Summit, which was charged with recommending new policy directions for the government's second term. While choosing Percy gave the exercise a patina of neutrality, the fact that Klein didn't choose someone from the Tory brain trust sent a signal.

As described above, Klein would often change political course with little notice. He had an instinctive sense for how "Martha and Henry"—two fictional characters that stood in his mind for ordinary Albertans, and to whom he referred in many of his speeches—were reacting to events and would like a cat on a hot tin roof know when and where to jump to avoid political disaster.

The way that leadership races were conducted also ensured that the party was open to people of different ideological stripes. The process used for the 1992, 2006, and 2011 leadership races allowed for so-called "instant Tories" to join the party right up to the last day of voting. In 2006, Ted Morton came close to pulling a first ballot upset after an extraordinary recruiting drive that mobilized tens of thousands of ultra-conservative voters. The eventual winner, Ed Stelmach, benefited from a recruiting drive among more moderate voters in Edmonton in the week leading up to the second and last ballot. In 2011, Alison Redford won the leadership by appealing to nurses and teachers, many of whom had no previous connection to the party. While this selection process would be criticized for distorting democracy and producing "surprise" leaders, it also ensured that the party remained a big tent open to diverse influences.

One can argue that one of the crucial errors that led to the Tories' downfall was that Premier Jim Prentice moved the party dramatically to the right—first by uniting the Progressive Conservatives with the Wildrose Party, and then by taking an almost fiendish delight in describing the deep cuts that he intended to make to health, education, and the size of the civil service. He also announced that the government would not match charitable donations made by companies or individuals. While he eventually reversed this decision, he sent the message to the non-profit sector that he was not its friend. Simply put, by abandoning the political centre, he gave Rachel Notley the opening that she needed to claim that territory.

In evaluating the foundations of Tory electoral success, one has to consider Kevin Taft's argument about what he calls "Oil's Deep State."[11] Taft, a former leader of the Alberta Liberal Party and a contributor to this volume, argues in a 2017 book that, at least under Klein, the government had for all intents and purposes been captured by the oil industry. According to Taft, the Tories and Big Oil enjoyed an *entente cordial*, with each supporting and acting on behalf of the other. While this certainly was not the case under Peter Lougheed, who often fought with the energy sector and squeezed it for higher royalties, the Klein government seemed to fall in line with barely a murmur or protest. Patricia Black, who was energy minister from 1992 to 1997 before being promoted to finance minister, operated through a "kitchen cabinet" that consisted of representatives of "every aspect of the [energy] industry."[12] Major oil sands projects were approved with little thought to long-term environmental impacts and few efforts were made to pressure the industry into upgrading raw bitumen before it left the province. Most critically, under Klein the royalties paid by oil sands producers were famously the lowest in the world; only 1 per cent of gross revenue was paid to the government until companies had recovered the full costs of their investment. After this period, the royalty rate rose to 25 per cent of net revenue.

In some ways, the partnership between the government in Edmonton and Big Oil paid off handsomely. In exchange for policies that did little more than allow companies to "rip and strip," hundreds of billions of dollars were invested in the province, and bitumen royalties—even at a giveaway royalty rate—created sizable surpluses for the government, especially during the Klein years. The province's prosperity was apparent. Gleaming new office towers sprung up in downtown Calgary and jobs became so plentiful that workers clambered to come to Alberta from all over Canada, and even from overseas. To complete the circle of mutual co-operation, for years energy companies gave generously to the PCs and largely ignored the opposition parties.

Interestingly, after Premier Ed Stelmach (2006–11) increased the royalty rate by roughly 20 per cent in the wake of an extraordinary and vociferous public debate, he quickly retreated, rolling the rate back to close to where it had been before the hike. His action was largely a response to the global economic crisis that began in 2008: the province wanted to help companies weather the storm. But another reason for the retreat may have been that some industry players upset with the Tories had begun to funnel donations to the new Wildrose Party. This tentative alliance between Wildrose and some players in the oil patch, combined with that party's growing war chest, may have been one reason why Prentice was so eager to merge with the Wildrose after he assumed office. The war chest would be his. As discussed elsewhere in this volume, the merger proved to be a disaster, as many Albertans saw the move as utterly cynical and manipulative, the very embodiment of old-style politics.

The problem for the PCs was that they became increasingly dependent on Big Oil. Although Lougheed was reluctant to attack Klein, by 2006—after a visit to the oil sands—the old lion had had enough. The former premier observed that, "It is just a moonscape. It is wrong in my judgment, a major wrong, and I keep trying to see who the beneficiaries are. . . . It is not the people of the province, because they are not getting the royalty return they should be getting."[13] Similarly, Allan Warrack, a former Lougheed cabinet minister, saw the non-stop development of the oil sands as "reckless" and "disorderly."[14] Other critics argued that Tory energy policies were preventing Alberta from taking the steps needed to diversify its economy; were distorting fiscal policy by creating the illusion that taxes could remain low indefinitely; and were making the province into an international environmental pariah and the oil sands a *cause célèbre* for activists.

The fact that the Progressive Conservatives held power for so long created its own gravitational pull. As the Tories controlled appointments to agencies, boards, and commissions, as well as lucrative consulting and business contracts, being a member of the winning team had tangible rewards. The same was true for ambitious politicos. For those wishing to move up the political ladder, the Tories were the only game in town, the only gateway to governmental power. Companies and individuals would donate to the party simply because failing to do so would send a potentially damaging message to those at the top.

Media coverage was also tilted toward the government. Studies show that reporters are nervous about criticizing governments that are widely popular for fear of offending their readers and viewers.[15] Both Lougheed and Klein were masters at setting the journalistic agenda and in rewarding and punishing journalists who didn't play by their rules. The tradition of

"Prairie boosterism," which made critical coverage of local institutions into a kind of sin, unabashedly right-wing newspapers such as the *Suns*, and a bevy of talk-radio hosts who served as cheerleaders for Lougheed and Klein in particular, added to the lopsided coverage. One study of the *Calgary Herald*'s coverage of the Klein government's rejection of the 1997 Kyoto Accords found that not only did the *Herald* provide positive coverage of the government's policies, but that the public's support for these policies increased dramatically as a result of the *Herald*'s reporting.[16] Another study of media coverage of the Supreme Court of Canada's decision on gay rights in *Vriend v. Alberta* (1998) revealed very different coverage on the part of the the national and Alberta press. The national press framed this as a "province-as-deviant" story because Alberta had refused to recognize gay rights and had violated the national consensus on the issue that had emerged. The provincial press, however, framed the story as a federal-provincial issue and portrayed the Klein government as a victim of federal power.[17]

While Lougheed and Klein generally benefited from favourable coverage, the media tiger would often show its teeth. Through its many difficulties, the Getty government could not avoid heavy doses of negative coverage. By Klein's fourth and last term, both the *Calgary Herald* and the *Edmonton Journal*'s coverage had also turned sour. The established press treated every misstep, scandal, and foible with often sharp and incisive coverage. Premier Alison Redford's media honeymoon was short-lived. Lacking the political skills needed to hold her government together, she was devoured by negative reporting.

Rich Vivone believes that fear also played a role in keeping the Tories in power. As Vivone put it, in so many venues, "the fear was palpable and the silence pervasive."[18] Much like Elisabeth Noelle-Neumann's well-known theory of the "spiral of silence," which argues that people tend to keep silent when they know that their opinions are not widely shared for fear of being ostracized or being laughed at, people in Alberta knew how to navigate their own entrenched political culture.[19] The danger in any one-party state is that ideas are suppressed as people come to fear a government that can operate seemingly without limits. In what writer Aritha van Herk has described as a society of "mavericks," it was sometimes difficult to avoid conformity.[20] And therein lies a paradox of politics in Alberta: as Mark Lisac has observed, the "thing about calling Albertans mavericks is it ignores a huge streak of conformism in the province, which is there often for very good reasons. Usually it's a method of meeting all sorts of outside pressures. You can see it in the way that people approach community life and politics, where there's strong pressure to all belong to the same party and vote the same way, and even sometimes believing that Albertans are mavericks—that's a method of conformism too."[21]

Apathy also played a part, as voter turnouts were stunningly low during the PC reign. From a high-water mark of 60 per cent in the close 1993 election, turnout plummeted to 54 per cent in 2012, this after dipping to below 50 per cent in 1986 and 2004. And in 2008, turnout barely topped 40 per cent—an all-time low for Canadian provincial elections. For many Albertans the logic was simple: Why go to the game if you already know the score? Majorities were so large that it seemed to make no difference if you voted or stayed home.

The Seeds of Defeat

While in chapter 2 of this volume my colleague Duane Bratt skillfully describes the failures and miscalculations that led to the Tories' defeat in the 2015 election campaign, the Progressive Conservative dynasty had been in trouble for quite some time before the election was called. While elections do make a difference—and one can certainly argue that a better campaign, with a more appealing message and a more compelling leader might have altered the Tories' fortunes—the harsh reality is that the PCs had gotten the big things wrong for many years. As mentioned previously, one prominent school of thought argues that people vote based on the state of the economy.[22] During prosperous times, governmental foibles and mistakes are easily forgiven and forgotten. During difficult economic times, there is not only little forgiveness, but politicians become targets for pent-up anger, and for every and all sins.

For much of the Tory dynasty, the party had the good fortune to govern during prosperous times. This was certainly the case through most of the Lougheed and Klein years. High energy prices, the growth brought by immigration, a talented workforce, and low taxes gave the Tory government a veneer of success. But when the music slowed with the sharp global economic downturn that began in 2008, followed by the crash in global energy prices that hit with devastating force in 2014, party fortunes began to sink. The government's much-vaunted achievements seemed to dissolve like quick sand. By the time Stelmach became premier, the government's agenda was clouded by deficits, cutbacks to government services, rising unemployment, grim lineups at emergency rooms and for operations, a massive infrastructure debt, a worrying shortage of schools, electricity rate hikes, an environmental mess, and the spectre of a monster provincial debt lurking behind what for the moment were balanced budgets. Tough times were taking the bloom off the Tory rose.

Interestingly, before the 2015 election, the only times the PCs found themselves in trouble was in 1993 when during an economic downturn the Tories came close to losing to Lawrence Decore's Liberals, and in 2012, when in the midst of the global recession Alison Redford pulled out a surprising victory in the last week of the campaign against the Wildrose Party. These near-death experiences remind us that the Tories were most likely saved from the fate of most other parties by the good fortune of having governed in mostly prosperous times.

With the energy industry cascading into disaster with the global collapse in oil prices in 2014, it became glaringly obvious that the PCs had done little to diversify the economy. Unlike governments in Norway and Alaska, which had used savings strategies to create enormous pools of capital, the Alberta Heritage Trust Fund created under Lougheed was largely abandoned by subsequent Tory governments. While policy experts had for years recommended that the government build up the fund in order to create new industries and economic strategies, the pull of immediate needs and short-term goals proved irresistible. The fund has been effectively frozen since the mid-1980s; as of 2018 its value is roughly $17.5 billion, a figure that includes so-called "deemed" assets that no longer have any real value. According to at least one estimate, had the government continued to invest in the ways that Peter Lougheed had envisioned, the fund would be worth close to $200 billion today, and possibly a lot more.[23] Norway, which funnels 100 per cent of its annual resource revenue into its Oil Fund, has watched it balloon to well over $1 trillion and it has invested in over nine thousand businesses. The Alaska Permanent Fund, which collects 25 per cent of that state's annual resource revenue annually, has a war chest of some $65 billion, from which generous dividends are handed out to individual Alaskans every year (over $1,100 per person in 2018). Unfortunately for Albertans, when the rains finally came, Alberta's famous rainy day fund offered little protection.

For years, economists and leading business executives tried to convince the PCs to bring in some form of sales tax. As Ron Kneebone and Jennifer Zwicker demonstrate in chapter 10, provincial budgets would expand and contract like an accordion due to rising and falling energy prices. Not only did this make annual planning difficult, as budgets were based on (almost always wrong) predictions about what prices for oil and gas would be, but it fed the illusion that taxes could be kept low indefinitely. Despite the fact that a sales tax might have avoided a long trail of deficits, no leader wanted to risk their political skin by instituting, or even calling for, a sales tax. The absence of a sales tax had taken on symbolic meaning. It was part of the "Alberta Advantage" the Tories had promised Albertans. Much like Kryptonite, touching it was thought to bring instant political death. Running deficits and cutting services seemed a safer idea.

The party also began to disintegrate from within. From the time that Ed Stelmach took the helm in 2006 until Alison Redford's departure in 2014, the party was effectively locked in a brutal civil war. To some degree, the race for a new leader began almost from the moment that Stelmach became premier. Dull and uninspiring the premier's popularity plummeted to the point where members began to worry that he would drive the entire party over the cliff with him. An endless barrage of threats, intrigues, attempted coups, and open displays of disloyalty and disrespect from his internal rivals ultimately pushed Stelmach from office. Redford fared no better. Elected with only minimal support from the caucus, and having tried to pull the party to the political centre even as her caucus was trying to pull the party to the right, Redford was quickly deposed. Of course, one can argue that she effectively deposed herself with her inept political style and questionable use of government funds.

While these fierce battles and the almost daily media soap opera that they created took a toll on party fortunes, perhaps the deepest self-inflicted wound came from the fact that the party's election machine had fallen into disrepair. Klein needed little in the way of organization to win elections. Stelmach's and Redford's lacklustre leadership not only divided the party but also left a dwindling membership and a rotting organization. Most critically, the party failed to renew itself by attracting star candidates. To many

Albertans, the party had become an "old boys" network—even if some of the players were women—that was increasingly out of touch with Alberta's changing social landscape. Arguably, Prentice attempted to renew the party by recruiting new people, but by then, one can argue, it was too late.

A last point to consider is that Alberta was Canada's largest emitter of greenhouse gases, and therefore its largest polluter, at a time when the international environmental movement began to make real inroads in global consciousness, and indeed in politics. The energy industry and the Alberta government seemed to be caught by surprise as the oil sands became an object of global controversy and derision. Where Alberta had once been viewed as the "last best West," images of dirty Alberta were now carried around the world. Many if not most Albertans resented this characterization, but the fact that the provincial government became a villain on the global stage did little to inspire confidence. In fact, many Albertans wondered if the Tories even had an environmental policy.

Two images can serve as bookends for the Progressive Conservatives' years in power. One, perhaps the most well-known photo in Alberta politics, was taken in 1967 and shows Peter Lougheed running arm in arm up the steps of the legislature with five other recently elected Conservative MLA's, including Don Getty, Hugh Horner, and David Russell. The photo was taken when the party was just establishing itself as a force in Alberta politics, and it portrays the unbridled vigour and determination that would carry Lougheed and his team to victory four years later, in 1971. The newly elected MLAs appear unstoppable. When the end came in 2015, another poignant moment was captured on camera. It shows the crowd at the Tory's election-night gathering at Calgary's Metropolitan Centre, and it is notable for how sparse it was. What had once been one of Canada's great political dynasties could barely muster an audience. Appearing deeply shaken, Jim Prentice announced that he was resigning from the leadership and from the seat that he had just won in the legislature. Not long after that, both the stage and the room were empty.

Notes

1   Geo Takach, *Will the Real Alberta Please Stand Up?* (Edmonton: University of Alberta Press, 2010), 89.

2   Ibid., 233–5.

3   John J. Barr, "The Impact of Oil on Alberta: Retrospect and Prospect," in *The Making of the Modern West*, ed. A. W. Rasporich (Calgary: University of Calgary Press, 1984).

4   Tamara and Howard Palmer, *Alberta: A New History* (Edmonton: Hurtig, 1990).

5   Charistopher Achen and Larry Bartels, *Democracy For Realists: Why Elections Do Not Produce Responsive Government* (Princeton, NJ: Princeton University Press, 2016).

6   Quoted in Takach, *Will the Real Alberta Please Stand Up?*, 136.

7   Ibid., 51.

8   Rich Vivone, *Ralph Could Have been a Superstar: Tales of the Klein Era* (Kingston, ON: Patricia Publishing, 2009), 190.

9   Allan Tupper, "Peter Lougheed, 1971–1985," in *Alberta Premiers of the Twentieth Century*, ed. Bradford Rennie (Regina: University of Regina Press, 2004), 223.

10   Mark Lisac, "Don Getty, 1985–1992," in Rennie, ed., *Alberta Premiers of the Twentieth Century*, 237.

11   Kevin Taft, *Oil's Deep State* (Toronto: Lorimer, 2017).

12   Ibid., 160.

13   Ibid., 164.

14   Ibid., 165.

15   Denise Savage-Hughes and David Taras, "The Mass Media and Modern Alberta Politics," in *Government and Politics in Alberta*, ed. Allan Tupper and Roger Gibbins (Edmonton: University of Alberta Press, 1992), 197–217.

16   David Danchuk, "Opinion Change in Context: Understanding Albertan Attitudes Towards the Kyoto Protocol Through the Agenda-Setting and Indexing Theory" (Master's thesis, University of Calgary, 2009).

17   Florian Sauvageau, David Schneiderman, and David Taras, *The Last Word: Media Coverage of the Supreme Court of Canada* (Vancouver: UBC Press, 2006).

18   Vivone, *Ralph Could Have been a Superstar*, ch. 5.

19   Elisabeth Noelle-Neumann, *The Spiral of Silence: Public Opinion—Our Social Skin* (Chicago: University of Chicago Press, 1984).

20   Aritha van Herk, *Mavericks: An Incorrigible History of Alberta* (Toronto: Penguin, 2001).

21   Takach, *Will the Real Alberta Please Stand Up?*, 153.

22   Lynn Vavreck, *The Message Matters: The Economy and Presidential Elections* (Princeton, NJ: Princeton University Press, 2009).

23   Max Fawcett, "Heritage Trust Fund Better Late than Never for Savings," *Albertaviews*, 1 March 2016.

Death of a Dynasty: The Tories and the 2015 Election

Duane Bratt

The 2015 provincial election was a watershed moment in Alberta and Canadian politics. In fact, the election was news around the world, for several reasons. First, the longest-serving democratic government in Canada and one of the longest-serving in the world was defeated. The governing Progressive Conservatives had been in power since 1971. (David Taras described the history of the PC dynasty in more detail in chapter 1.) Second, the party that defeated them, Alberta's New Democratic Party, had been in fourth place when the election was called. The NDP, even according to their own people, were not planning on winning the election when it started. Instead they hoped to increase their seat total from four to perhaps ten or twelve. Third, the election saw a major ideological swing on the part of the electorate, from a centre-right conservative party to a leftist social democratic party. Alberta had been governed by conservative parties since 1935: the Social Credit Party (1935–71)[1] and the PCs (1971–2015). The province's conservative tradition, along with its vast oil and gas resources, had many national and international observers calling Alberta the Texas of Canada. And now it was headed by a social democratic party that was often at odds with the oil sector's dominance of Alberta politics and the development of the oil sands.[2]

In designing this book, the editors determined that two different questions needed to be answered about the 2015 election. First, how and why did a political dynasty that had won twelve straight majority governments suddenly lose? Second, why did the NDP, rather than the Official Opposition

Wildrose, or another party, win? While Melanee Thomas addresses the second question in chapter 3, I will try to answer the first below.

My principal argument is that under the Ed Stelmach–led government, the PCs had been suffering from internal trouble since about 2008. This internal trouble spilled over into a negative public image. The PCs were seen as arrogant, entitled, and out of touch. This had almost led to the party being defeated in the 2012 election. It intensified under Premier Redford and ultimately led to her resignation. When Premier Prentice took over, the PCs were in trouble, but he added to the downfall through a series of missteps.

Methodology

This chapter adopts a narrative structure, and it is supported by my close observation of Alberta politics for well over a decade. During this time I have appeared as a TV analyst during the live broadcasts of the 2008, 2012, and 2015 elections. In addition to providing frequent analysis for the media, I have also written numerous blogs and op-eds on Alberta politics. Material from semi-structured interviews with PC candidates (successful and unsuccessful) and volunteers (both from the executive and constituency levels) from the 2015 campaign have also been incorporated. Some of the interviewees agreed to be quoted on the record, but others requested anonymity. This distinction is contained in the citations.

The Splintering of the PCs and the Rise of Wildrose

Many observers trace the PCs' slow decline to the party's 2006 leadership race. Jim Dinning, Ralph Klein's finance minister in the 1990s, was seen as the heir apparent. He had the highest name recognition, had acquired the most endorsements, and raised the most money. But he was challenged on the right by Ted Morton. Morton was a former University of Calgary political scientist who had been active in conservative politics at the federal level and was first elected as an MLA in 2004. The leadership race was conducted according to a runoff format. If no individual won a majority of the votes on the first ballot, then a second runoff ballot would be held a week later with the top three candidates. But the second ballot was a ranked ballot with voters selecting both a first and a second choice. If there was nobody with a majority on the second ballot, then this third ranked ballot would be used. With eight candidates, it was tough for anyone to win on the first ballot. Dinning won the first ballot with Morton finishing second. Ed Stelmach, who had served in a number of cabinet posts under Klein, was a distant third. The runoff ballot was seen as a battle between the centrist Dinning and the conservative Morton, but Stelmach was everybody's—including Dinning's and Morton's supporters—second choice. This allowed Stelmach to sneak up the middle on the third ballot using the ranked system. It was a surprising result. Both the heir apparent (Dinning) and the strong conservative (Morton) lost to the friendly, unassuming, steady, but not particularly distinguished Stelmach. Stelmach also benefited from a perceived PC tradition of alternating between leaders from Southern and Northern Alberta. Peter Lougheed was from Calgary, Don Getty from Edmonton, and Klein from Calgary. Both Dinning and Morton were from Calgary, but Stelmach lived in Vegreville, a farming community about an hour east of Edmonton. Thus the Southern vote was split between Dinning and Morton, and the Northern vote went to Stelmach.

As premier, Stelmach had a few stumbles in his initial years. He formed a cabinet that largely ignored Calgary, the city that had long been the party's power centre. More significantly, however, he was a poor communicator. Although he ran a lacklustre campaign, Stelmach and the PCs won an overwhelming majority in the provincial election of 2008—seventy-two of eighty-three seats, which was a larger margin of victory than even Klein had ever achieved. Stelmach should have been at the peak of his powers after an election victory as large as that, but there were storm clouds on the horizon.

The PCs had long been a big-tent party, one largely made up of fiscal conservatives and social liberals. This made them a centrist party that could tack left (as seen in some of the early policies of the Lougheed government in the early 1970s) or right (as with the Klein revolution of 1993–7). But there had always been a rump opposition of social conservatives who opposed the PCs. This constituency was strongest in rural Alberta. Although Social Credit had been defeated in 1971, it continued to win seats in rural Alberta until the early 1980s. Then there was the Western Canada Concept, a separatist party that won a seat in a 1982 by-election. In the late 1980s and early 1990s, there was a strong fear from provincial PCs that the Reform Party led by Preston Manning (formed by ex-federal Progressive Conservatives) would run provincially. However, the Reform Party decided to focus on federal politics. In 2004, Paul Hinman won a seat in rural Southern Alberta as leader of the Alberta Alliance (the name was a spinoff of the Canadian Alliance, the successor to the Reform Party). But the PCs, despite some periodic individual constituency losses, were always able to defeat its socially conservative rivals. But what would happen if fiscal conservatives left the PCs to join a new party aligned with these social conservatives? This was the threat that PCs had always feared, and in 2008–9 it started to happen under Ed Stelmach.

The erosion of the party's fiscal conservatism started to occur when, soon after becoming premier, Stelmach decided to initiate a review of oil and gas royalties in the province.[3] When the final report—called *Our Fair Share*—was released in the fall of 2007, Stelmach announced that he would be increasing royalties to acquire an additional $1.4 billion a year. This decision created quite a backlash from the oil and gas sector. This manifested itself in many ways, but at least initially it led many Tories to stay home during the March 2008 election. This did not seem too important at the time, as the PCs still won an overwhelming majority. Nevertheless, it did provide an indication that something was amiss among the PC rank and file.

More significantly, the royalty review was the trigger for the rise of the Wildrose Party as a major player on the Alberta political stage. The Wildrose Party had formed just prior to the 2008 election with the merger of two small conservative parties, the Alberta Alliance and Wildrose Parties.[4] But it was Stelmach's royalty review that gave the new entity a political shot in the arm. There were a growing number of individuals, some of them with a high profile (e.g., Rod Love, who had been Ralph Klein's chief of staff and best friend), who defected from the PCs to the Wildrose. The royalty review then set the stage for Paul Hinman's stunning victory in the Calgary-Glenmore by-election in the fall of 2009. Hinman successfully campaigned on the slogan "Send Ed a Message." The PC candidate, a local Calgary councillor, finished a poor third. Much more importantly, Wildrose started to receive some large donations from individuals and corporations within the oil and gas sector. While the big players continued to donate to the PCs, it was the junior companies who started to move their money to the Wildrose Party. In 2008, Wildrose raised $233,000. This tripled to $700, 000 in 2009, in 2010 it increased again to $1.8 million, and by 2011 it was $2.7 million.[5]

DUANE BRATT

Eventually, Stelmach began to reverse the royalty policy, almost coming full circle by the end. You can debate the merits of increasing resource royalty rates, or talk about the timing of the increase, which occurred just as natural gas prices started to fall. However, what is beyond debate is the degree of political damage that this single decision had on the Progressive Conservative brand, and indeed, the future of Alberta politics.

There were other key events in the rapid rise of the Wildrose Party. Danielle Smith, a smart, young, and telegenic former broadcaster, became leader in October 2009, thereby increasing the party's public profile. Then, in January 2010, Rob Anderson and Heather Forysthe made the stunning decision to cross the floor from the PCs to the Wildrose. Anderson was a cabinet minister from Airdrie (a Calgary suburb) and Forsythe was a former cabinet minister from Calgary. It is rare in Canada for someone to leave the governing party to join an opposition party (especially a party with only one seat), and it had never happened to the Alberta PCs before. Soon after, Guy Boutiller, another disgruntled former PC cabinet minister from Fort McMurray, crossed the floor to the Wildrose. This gave the Wildrose official party status in the legislature, which in turn allowed it more resources. The party was riding a political wave and was leading in public opinion polls.

Not only was Stelmach facing the challenge of the rise of the Wildrose, but he was beset with internal strife. Three PC MLAs had joined the Wildrose, and there were ongoing rumours of even more defections. This led to a show-down with Finance Minister Ted Morton (who led the conservative wing of the PC Party) over the 2011 budget and the size of the deficit. The result saw Stelmach announce in January 2011 that he would not seek re-election and that the PCs needed to undergo a new leadership race.

The 2012 Election

The resignation of Ed Stelmach threw the PCs into another long leadership race. The perceived frontrunner was former health minister Gary Mar. Alison Redford, a first-term MLA who had been justice minister in Stelmach's cabinet, also decided to run. Redford's campaign seemed a longshot because she lacked caucus support and had few endorsements. But Redford and her campaign manager Stephen Carter (who had helped another longshot candidate—Calgary Mayor Naheed Nenshi—get elected in

2010) devised an outsider strategy of assembling a new progressive coalition. They recruited "two-minute Tories" from groups (teachers, public-sector union members, nurses, etc.) that, historically, had never been part of the party. Redford made one substantial campaign promise—to immediately provide local school boards with an additional $107 million in funding—that crystalized her as the progressive candidate within the PC leadership race. This promise was combined with a brilliant debate performance in the immediate aftermath of her mother's death. The outsider strategy worked and Redford won a come-from-behind victory over Mar and Doug Horner on the third ballot in October 2011. It was a similar victory, using the same party leadership rules, as Stelmach's in 2006.

While Redford savoured her leadership victory, she knew that she had to go to the polls in a few months. Prior to the 2012 election, the PCs had only faced two tough campaigns: in 1971, when Peter Lougheed defeated the incumbent Social Credit Party to form his first government, and in 1993, when Ralph Klein led the "miracle on the Prairies" defeat of Laurence Decore's Liberals. Now the PCs would be facing a well-financed Opposition. The Wildrose Party's large campaign war chest allowed them to have a tour bus, professionally made advertisements, TV time, and a paid staff.

Initially, the campaign did not go well for the PCs. There were a series of financial scandals that gave the party an air of entitlement. These included a "no-meet committee" for which MLAs were paid despite never meeting; a patronage appointment to Gary Mar, which came back to haunt the party; and illegal donations from public-sector authorities.[6] The Wildrose took an immediate lead in public opinion polls—a lead that they would maintain throughout the rest of the campaign.

Eventually the PCs recovered; this was largely due to the strategy that Redford and Carter adopted, a duplication of their successful PC leadership race: run as a centrist party and attract progressive voters. For example, Redford promised to build 50 new schools and renovate another 70 schools, bring in full-day kindergarten, and create 140 family care clinics.[7] More importantly, they portrayed the Wildrose Party as right-wing extremists. This line of attack worked, as the Wildrose found itself entangled in a series of its own scandals. For example, during an online leaders' forum sponsored by the *Calgary Herald* and the *Edmonton Journal*, Wildrose leader Danielle Smith appeared to doubt the existence of climate change, saying that "we've always said the science isn't settled and we need to continue to monitor the debate."[8] While there may have been many Albertans who believed the same thing, they did not want their premier professing those sentiments. More damaging was the "lake of fire" episode.

Allan Hunsperger was a Wildrose candidate in Edmonton. He was also a Pentecostal pastor. A year before the election, Hunsperger wrote a blog post attacking Lady Gaga's pro-gay-rights song "Born this Way." In the post, Hunsperger wrote that gays and lesbians would "suffer the rest of eternity in the lake of fire, hell, a place of eternal suffering."[9] This blog post became a mainstream media and social media sensation a week before Albertans went to the ballot boxes. There were demands that Danielle Smith censure Hunsperger and remove him as a Wildrose candidate. In fact, that is what Tom Flanagan, the Wildrose's campaign manager, along with other senior Wildrose officials, also advised.[10] But Smith, a libertarian, refused, defending the freedom of speech of social conservatives. All she would say is that Hunsperger did not speak for the party.[11] The "lake of fire" episode and other "bozo eruptions" from Wildrose candidates "allowed the PCs," as Flanagan later wrote, "to run an effective campaign of fear in the final week."[12]

The result was a surprise Redford victory. The PCs would end up winning 61 seats with 44 per cent of the vote, compared with the Wildrose's 17 seats and 34.3 per cent of the vote. As Janet Brown and John Santos show in chapter 4, the polls, which turned out to be wrong, had been predicting a Wildrose majority government. Instead, progressives decided to stay with the PCs and Redford was able to attract people who normally voted Liberal. Indeed, the Liberals saw their support collapse. In 2008, the party had won 9 seats with 26.4 per cent of the vote, but in 2012 they ended up with only 5 seats and 9.89 per cent of the vote. The fear of a Wildrose government drove many Liberal supporters into the arms of Redford's PCs. Moreover, soft PC voters "who had considered switching to the Wildrose during the campaign . . . drew back at the end" because their anger at the PCs was trumped by their fear of the Wildrose.[13]

The Fall of Alison Redford

The victory in the 2012 election was the last high point for the Redford government. Gradually the premier, her government, and her party started to disintegrate. This was true both in terms of public policy and individual scandals. In the case of policy, the coalition that Redford had used to win both the 2011 leadership race and the 2012 election was purposefully and systematically dismantled. The best evidence of this was seen in Redford's very first budget, which made deep cuts to education. According to Thomas Lukaszuk, the policy reversal outlined in the budget came directly from Redford: "Three days before I left (for Vietnam for a previously scheduled charity mission), Redford appointed me advanced education minister. There was a 7 per cent cut to advanced education in the budget. I got stuck with it! The previous minister, Stephen Khan, didn't support it, the cabinet didn't support it, it came directly from the Premier's office."[14] Redford later tried to bring in draconian legislation that attacked the collective bargaining rights of public-sector unions. As Lori Williams shows in chapter 14, the contempt with which these policy reversals were met was magnified by Redford's gender. Simply put, though male politicians flip-flop all the time, the public was harder on a female premier who campaigned as a progressive and governed as a conservative.

This policy collapse was surpassed by the personal scandals in which Redford became involved. There had been periodic concerns about Redford's "culture of entitlement": her high-paid staff, large security detail, her stays in the largest suites in the most expensive hotels, her bullying of staff, and so on.[15] But there were three specific scandals that crystallized this impression in the minds of Albertans. First, there was an expense scandal over the $45,000 cost of her trip to South Africa to attend Nelson Mandela's funeral in November 2013. Then the discovery that Redford had been using the government's fleet of planes for personal purposes. The auditor general later showed that Redford had used fake passenger manifests to ensure that only the premier, her family, and her close entourage were on these flights. And finally, the issue of the "Sky Palace"—the renovation of the penthouse in a government building as a special premier's residence.

But there was a third factor in Redford's downfall. As mentioned earlier, Redford became leader with no support in caucus; her supporters had come from outside the party. This meant that from day one, Redford was leader of a caucus that never really accepted her as leader. In fact, it was members of the caucus, as well as other PC officials, that fed the media the very leaks that damaged Redford. But along with in-fighting, these leaks greatly

DUANE BRATT

damaged the party brand. As Sydney Sharpe and Don Braid wrote, "PC loyalists, caucus members, Cabinet ministers, and government confidants were all in open conflict. Ministers were routinely arrogant toward party volunteers. They wouldn't listen to the advice of campaigners and those on the ground. They shared a fundamental delusion that no matter how open and bitter their own fights became, no matter how vigorously ministers stabbed each other in the back in almost full public view, the public would still continue to accept them because the PCs were the natural governing party."[16] Redford resigned as premier on 19 March 2014, less than two years after winning a majority government in the 2012 provincial election, but the damage to her party would linger. In interviews, PC members admitted that the public was "greatly disappointed by Redford's personal behaviour," and still faced anger towards her during the 2015 election.[17]

The Rise of Jim Prentice

After Redford's downfall, the PCs were desperate for a high-profile leader, and they quickly identified Jim Prentice as their dream candidate. Prentice had many desirable qualities. He had been a highly competent former federal minister in Stephen Harper's cabinet, serving as Aboriginal affairs minister, industry minister, and deputy prime minister while representing a Calgary riding. These experiences meant that he was unusually respected in the oil sector, among environmentalists, and in Aboriginal communities. After stepping down from federal politics in 2010, Prentice became a senior vice-president at CIBC. He was also widely seen as both ideologically progressive and conservative. Prentice was also a man of personal integrity, which was important after the Redford scandals. Most importantly, he had no connection with the provincial PCs during the Redford and Stelmach years. The party brass (officials and key donors) wanted someone from the outside. The leadership race was a rout, with Prentice easily beating Ric McIver and Thomas Lukaszuk. But there were some warning sounds as the turnout was substantially lower than the previous PC leadership races in 2011, 2006, and 1992 (see Table 2.1).

Table 2.1. Number of Votes Cast in Recent PC Leadership Races

YEAR	NUMBER OF VOTES
2014	23,386
2011	78,176
2006	144,289
1992	78,251

Sources: Data compiled by the author.

When Jim Prentice took over in September 2014, the PCs were in deep trouble. They were trailing the Wildrose Party badly in the polls and were demoralized from the events that led to Redford's resignation. Prentice had an opportunity for a course correction. This was not the first time the PCs had successfully managed to change leaders at just the right moment to snatch victory from defeat. For example, Don Getty was extremely unpopular before being replaced by Ralph Klein in 1992, as was Ed Stelmach before being replaced by Alison Redford in 2011. Likewise, Prentice, with his slogan of "Under New Management," had some initial successes by reversing many of Redford's most unpopular policies. He announced that Alberta would sell its fleet of government aircraft. He also reversed the decision to get rid of the slogan "Wildrose Country" on Alberta's licence plates. (The Redford government had made this ridiculous decision because they believed that Alberta motorists were unwittingly endorsing the Wildrose Party!) Throughout these early weeks, Prentice gave off an air of high competence—something that had been lacking in the end days of the Redford regime.

Prentice did not just change the policies of the Redford government, he also undertook a number of personnel changes. His first major move in this direction was naming Mike Percy his chief of staff. This was an inspired choice because Percy was an Edmontonian while Prentice was a Calgarian. Given the enduring rivalry between the two cities, no previous government had the premier and chief of staff from these different cities. In addition, Percy had been a prominent Liberal MLA in the 1990s, so the appointment was bi-partisan. Prentice also recruited retired senior federal civil servant

Table 2.2. List of Ministers in Redford/Hancock's Cabinet, but not in Prentice's

MINISTER	REASON
Alison Redford—Premier	Retired
Dave Hancock—Premier	Retired
Doug Horner—Finance	Retired
Fred Horne—Health	Retired
Doug Griffiths—Service Alberta	Retired
Cal Dallas—International and Intergovernmental Relations	Retired
Ken Hughes—Municipal Affairs	Retired
Mary-Anne Jablonski—Seniors	Retired
Thomas Lukaszuk—Labour	Ran in 2015

Sources: Data compiled by the author.

Richard Dicerni to be the deputy minister for executive council. Prentice then formed a new cabinet that left out many of Redford's ministers (see Table 2.2). He also recruited two new ministers from outside caucus: former Edmonton mayor Stephen Mandel and former Saskatchewan MLA and Calgary Board of Education chair Gordon Dirks. This set the stage for four simultaneous, and very significant, by-elections in October 2014.

Between 1995 and 2009, Alberta held only nine by-elections. Moreover, it is rare to have even two simultaneous by-elections, let alone four. You have to go back to 9 December 1921, when there were seven simultaneous by-elections, to find more than two at once in Alberta's history. To add to the drama, these races also involved several high-profile candidates: the newly chosen leader of the Progressive Conservative Party and consequently Premier of Alberta Jim Prentice (Calgary-Foothills) and two recently appointed, but unelected, ministers, Health Minister Stephen Mandel (Edmonton-Whitemud) and Education Minister Gordon Dirks (Calgary-Elbow). Finally, two of the ridings were home to the previous two Alberta

Table 2.3. List of MLAs Who Did Not Run in 2015

Retirement	21*
Death	0
Run Federally	3
Becoming a Judge	0
Lose Party Nomination	4*
Cross Floor and Run for Another Party/Independent	12

Sources: Data compiled by the author.

Note: *There is some double-counting. For example, a person who crossed the floor and lost the party nomination (ie., Danielle Smith). In total, there were 34 MLAs (from all parties) who were elected in 2012, but did not run again in 2015.

premiers: Alison Redford (Calgary-Elbow) and Dave Hancock (Edmonton-Whitemud). The scale of the election, which included massive amounts of media coverage and unprecedented (for a by-election) television ads by the Progressive Conservative and Wildrose Parties, meant that this was more of a mini-election than an ordinary by-election. That the PCs swept all four of those by-elections represented the high-water mark for Prentice. Moreover, it demoralized the Wildrose Opposition, who failed to win even one seat despite the resources that the party had committed.

Prentice also encouraged many other existing PC MLAs to retire, which allowed him to present a new slate of candidates for the 2015 election (see Table 2.3). It is normal for there to be turnover with MLAs deciding for a variety of reasons not to run in the next election (see Figure 2.1). But the number of MLAs bowing out before the 2015 election was the second-highest since 1971. Only those elected in 1989 and declined to run in 1993 was higher. In both of those instances, there was a significant change of leadership (Klein replacing Getty and Prentice replacing Redford), which spurred the desire to bring in a fresh crop of candidates to gain a distance from the previous government (even though it was the same PC party).

Figure 2.1. Percentage of Alberta MLAs Retiring/Running with Another Party

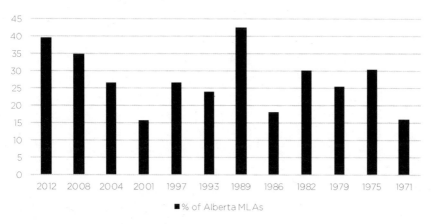

Sources: Data compiled by the author.

The Decline of Jim Prentice

As the previous section showed, Prentice enjoyed a honeymoon after becoming PC leader, but, as Janet Brown and John Santos show in chapter 4, it would soon become clear that this was to be a shorter honeymoon compared to other new Alberta leaders. This was caused by three major mistakes that Prentice made. Ironically, the first and biggest of these errors initially looked like a major victory for the PCs. In December 2014 (a week before Christmas), Prentice orchestrated an unprecedented floor-crossing. The prelude to this event came in November 2014, when two Wildrose MLAs (Kerry Towle and Ian Donovan) joined the PCs. While this was surprising—especially in the case of Towle, who was considered a close ally of Wildrose leader Danielle Smith—floor-crossing from opposition parties to the PCs were not uncommon. What was shocking was that, a month later, Smith and eight of her colleagues, after some secret high-level negotiations, also joined the PCs. Never before in Canadian history, either federally or provincially, had the leader of the Opposition joined the government. (Not even Liberal leader Wilfrid Laurier had joined Conservative prime minister

Robert Borden's "Unity Government" during the First World War!) And it was not just Smith, it was the majority of the Wildrose caucus; only five MLAs remained. Making the situation even more bizarre was the case of Rob Anderson, who had, in the immortal words of Winston Churchill, "re-ratted": Anderson had been a PC, crossed the floor to Wildrose, and then crossed back to rejoin the PCs. Smith explained that she respected Prentice (unlike Stelmach and Redford) and that all conservatives needed to unite to deal with Alberta's emerging fiscal challenges. Others suspected that Smith felt that she could never beat Prentice due to his sweep of the November 2014 by-elections and the defections of Towle and Donovan. If you can't beat them, the saying goes, join them.

Prentice, as Sydney Sharpe and Don Braid have argued, thought that "he had folded the right-wing under his wing and decimated Wildrose as a viable opposition party."[18] But he was too clever by half, because the floor-crossing generated a large feeling of betrayal. The remaining Wildrose MLAs, party officials, volunteers, donors, and supporters loudly expressed their feelings of betrayal. Four years later, there remains great anger towards the ringleaders Smith and Anderson. The PC caucus, more quietly, felt betrayed by the fact that their fiercest adversaries had been invited into their tent. And more ominously for Prentice, Albertans also felt betrayed. They found it undemocratic that the governing party would try and destroy, for partisan purposes, their political opposition. Thomas Lukaszuk, who had been Redford's deputy premier and later one of Prentice's strongest PC critics, called the floor-crossing a "hostile takeover" of the Opposition. "It was offensive to Albertans and their sense of decency, fair play, and democracy. Prentice had power but wanted absolute power."[19]

The second error was the pre-election budget released in March 2015. For months, Prentice had been signalling that he was about to deliver a transformative budget. In press conferences, speeches, and a rare televised address to the province, Prentice said that due to the precipitous drop in oil prices since August 2014, and the decades-long overreliance on resource revenue, a fundamental change to government finances was necessary. Prentice promised to present a budget that would be so transformative that he required an electoral mandate (a year ahead of the fixed-election legislation date of March–May 2016) with which to proceed. But in reality, Prentice's budget was not really transformative. Prentice had been signalling for months that the expected $7-billion hole in the budget caused by a drop in oil prices would be addressed in a relatively balanced way: a third through tax and fee increases; a third through spending cuts; and a third through a deficit. But the budget numbers were wildly different: $1.5-billion in tax and fee increases (22 per cent of the $7-billion), $323-million in spending cuts (7 per cent), and a $5-billion deficit (72 per cent) financed through the existing contingency fund.

More damaging for Prentice and the PCs was the fact that the budget upset most Albertans and satisfied few. The Wildrose set its sights on the largest deficit in Alberta history and the biggest tax increases since the late 1980s. During the subsequent leaders' debate, the Wildrose's new leader, Brian Jean, kept to a simple mantra, "we will not raise your taxes." Meanwhile, the NDP targeted cuts to health care and the introduction of a new health-care levy that Rachel Notley coined "the waiting room tax." Notley also zeroed in on the fact that while taxes and user fees went up across the board, there was no corresponding increase in corporate taxes. In fact, Prentice specifically ignored the results of a government budget survey that recommended a small increase in corporate taxes.

The third error was when Prentice decided to hold the election in May 2015 instead of in the spring of 2016. Prentice felt that, despite his leadership win and his by-election victory, he needed a complete mandate from Albertans, especially since he realized that he needed to take drastic action to deal with economic crisis in the province caused by the precipitous drop in oil prices. Prentice also believed that the economy was going to get a lot worse before it got better, and he preferred to face the electorate before the full impact of low oil prices hit the economy.

Critics argued that the early election call was illegal because it violated the fixed-election legislation that Redford had brought in soon after she became premier. But an analysis of the legislation showed that the early election call was perfectly legal in the context of the Westminster parliamentary system.[20] However, that degree of nuance was lost on most Albertans; to them, the PCs were simply violating the law—a law that they themselves had written. It was also seen as opportunistic. The Wildrose had been severely weakened by the mass floor-crossings of December 2014. Moreover, they did not have a leader at the time of the election call. Neither did the Liberals. As Richard Gotfried, a PC candidate in Calgary who ran (successfully) for the first time in 2015, said, voters on the doorstep were clearly linking the floor-crossing with the early election call. They said, "first you decimated the Opposition," then "you kicked them when they were down" with the early election call.[21] Other criticisms of the early election call included the view that Prentice needed to establish a record before he went to the voters and that the early election was a waste of money.

The 2015 Election Campaign

The three errors identified above meant that Prentice was not starting the 2015 campaign off on a good foot. In addition, the economy was spiralling downwards with the price of oil plummeting from $107 in June 2014 to just above $40 by April 2015. This meant a drop in royalty and tax revenue for the government plus increased unemployment among Albertans. Not surprisingly, as Janet Brown and John Santos show, the PCs were trailing in the polls as the campaign began. While Prentice had tried to distance himself from many of Redford's actions, in this case, he needed one of her come-from-behind wins. Unfortunately, he did not run a good campaign and the result was the defeat of the PCs and the upset victory by the NDP.

The leaders' debate was the opportunity for Prentice to shine. Unfortunately, he made the poor choice of targeting NDP leader Rachel Notley during the debate. Never before had a PC premier focused on an NDP leader during a debate. By doing so, Prentice helped to legitimize Notley as a potential premier. Not only that, but during one of their exchanges, Prentice told Notley that "math is difficult." Prentice was referring to an incident a week before, in which the NDP had made a billion-dollar error in its campaign platform. But most Albertans were unaware of this subtext. Instead, Prentice's comment showed him belittling, demeaning, and mansplaining to Notley. Voters found it sexist. As Sydney Sharpe and Don Braid wrote, "post-debate polls showed Notley was the clear winner. The premier and his advisors had grossly underestimated her."[22]

The "math is difficult" comment also brought back memories of Prentice's "look in the mirror" comment. Back in March, Prentice was being interviewed on the radio when he said, "we all want to blame somebody for the circumstance we're in. In terms of who is responsible, we all need to only look in the mirror. Basically, all of us have had the best of everything and have not had to pay for what it costs."[23] As Ron Kneebone and Jennifer Zwicker demonstrate in chapter 10, there was a lot of truth in what Prentice said. After all, for decades Albertans were able to have a high degree of government spending while enjoying low tax rate because of the province's reliance on non-renewable-resource revenue. Unfortunately for Prentice, the public interpreted this comment as blaming Albertans for the economic mess that the province was currently in. Both the "math is difficult" and the "look in the mirror" comments therefore made Prentice look arrogant and elitist.

After Prentice's poor debate performance, and with the NDP clearly gathering momentum, the PCs tried to stage a comeback in the last week of the campaign. But Prentice was put off message due to problems with some of the PCs' nomination races. Internal party nomination races are often the dirtiest of political contests. Rules are often broken through the marshalling of ineligible voters (non-Canadians, non-constituency residents, even dead voters), the improper usage of party records, and the introduction of financial irregularities, among other things. In some cases, these rule violations are ignored, but in others (minor or serious infractions) candidates are disqualified by their parties. Party leaders have also disqualified winning candidates (for a variety of reasons) and appointed candidates in other cases. In addition, no independent arbiter, such as Elections Alberta, monitors internal party elections. But in the PCs' 2015 party nominations, there was an inordinate amount of problems.[24] Taken as a whole, it appeared that the internal strife within the party that had been seen in the Stelmach and Redford years was still at play under Prentice. One contentious nomination saw Jamie Lall, who had been disqualified days before the PC nomination election in Chestermere-Rockyview, allowing Bruce McAllister, a former Wildrose MLA who crossed the floor to join the PCs in December 2014, to be acclaimed. This caused the most disruption because Lall decided to go public with his complaints, which included embarrassing text messages from senior members of the party: Executive Director Kelley Charlebois and Justice Minister Jonathan Denis. Prentice had to spend time on the campaign trail explaining why Lall had been disqualified as a candidate, but Mike Allen, a PC MLA from Fort McMurray who had been convicted of soliciting prostitutes while on government business in the United States, was not.

Making matters worse, Prentice also had to answer questions about Justice Minister Denis, who had been forced to resign his cabinet post midway through the campaign over legal issues involving his estranged wife. Denis continued to be the candidate, with the full support of Jim Prentice, for Calgary-Acadia. This legal dispute was under a publication ban, but the ban was lifted the day before the election. This resulted in front-page news containing salacious details about Denis's legal proceedings just as Albertans were preparing to vote. The back-and-forth accusations about the PCs' inner workings took them off message in the last week of a tightly contested campaign. Prentice was being asked at media events about Lall, Charlebois, and Denis—not his budget or ten-year fiscal plan.

In the waning days of the campaign, the Alberta business community launched attacks against the NDP, citing job losses, disinvestment, and threatening to move corporate head offices outside the province if the NDP was elected. For example, on the Saturday before the election, a group of five businessmen with deep ties to the PCs held a press conference in a downtown Edmonton office building at which they warned about "amateur" policies from an NDP that "do not understand how economies work."[25] This desperate attempt backfired badly.

Conclusion

Alberta's PC dynasty ended in 2015 because of a combination of factors. Clearly, Prentice made major mistakes. However, to blame the defeat solely on Prentice is unfair. As this chapter demonstrates, the PC decline began under Stelmach when the Wildrose Opposition first emerged. This decline accelerated during the Redford years. Redford had cobbled together a new electoral coalition to defeat the Wildrose, but then proceeded to alienate her new supporters. This was compounded by the series of personal scandals that drove Redford to resign, and which severely tainted the PC brand. Using the analogy of a car crash, this resulted from a combination of bad steering by the driver (Prentice), but also bad steering by previous drivers (Stelmach and Redford), compounded by backseat driving (PC caucus/officials), and the deteriorating alignment of a forty-four-year-old car.

Anthony Sayers and David Stewart discuss the future of the Alberta conservative movement in more detail in chapter 17. But some initial words need to be included here. I wrote the day after the election that we might have seen the end of the Progressive Conservative Party.[26] Historically, Alberta has been governed by successive political dynasties who ruled for a long time and then never formed government again: the Liberals (1905–21); the United Farmers of Alberta (1921–35); Social Credit (1935–71); and the PCs (1971–2015). A further complication for the PCs was that in Alberta there were two conservative parties. Even though the PCs won more votes in 2015, the Wildrose won twice as many seats. I was criticized in May 2015 for claiming that the PCs could disappear. And yet, by March 2017 (less than two years later) they were gone. So the 2015 election was not just the defeat of a government, or even the end of a political dynasty, it was the end of the Progressive Conservatives as a political entity.

Ironically, the man most responsible for killing off the demoralized, post-2015 PCs was a fellow conservative. Former federal Conservative cabinet minister Jason Kenney arrived in Calgary days before the start of the 2016 Calgary Stampede with an audacious plan to unite the right in Alberta by winning the leadership of the PCs and merging them with the Wildrose Party. The timing was not accidental, and, in fact, revealed Kenney's political acumen. It ensured that his announcement would be the political topic of conversation around the multitude of pancake breakfasts and beef-on-a-bun BBQs for the next week and a half. Other aspects of Kenney's speech—a packed hotel conference room, music, people props, his twenty-minute speech—also showed his significant political skills.

Kenney unveiled a highly unorthodox five-step plan for how he would unite Alberta's political right. Step one was to become leader of the PCs. The once-proud PCs had gone through four leaders in two years and by July 2016 held a measly nine seats in the legislature, making it the third-place party. The PCs had previously announced a leadership race commencing in October 2016 and concluding in March 2017. Step two was to open up merger talks with the Wildrose Party to create a brand new conservative party. Step three was a referendum of existing PC and Wildrose members to ratify the merger. Step four was a leadership race for the new Alberta conservative party, a race that Kenney would contest and which he expected to win. Step five was to defeat what Kenney referred to as the "accidental government" of Rachel Notley and her band of "radical ideologues" in the NDP.[27] The plan was a clear echo of the process to merge the Canadian Alliance and the

Progressive Conservative Party at the federal level in 2003–4. Kenney knew this because he had been part of that process.

As of November 2018, Jason Kenney has achieved the first four steps of his plan, and he is well on his way to step five. Step one was achieved at the March 2017 PC leadership convention, where Kenney won on the first ballot with the support of over 75 per cent of the delegates.[28] Step two, a merger agreement between the PCs and the Wildrose, occurred in May 2017. This agreement also established a new name for the party—the United Conservative Party.[29] Step three was to get the grassroots members of both the PC and Wildrose Parties to ratify the merger agreement. This was an important promise given the bad taste from the backroom deal in December 2014 that led then Wildrose leader Danielle Smith and Premier Jim Prentice to orchestrate a mass floor-crossing from the Wildrose caucus to the PC caucus. Both Kenney and Wildrose leader Brian Jean campaigned for ratification of the UCP. Again, the result was an overwhelming victory, with 95 per cent of members in both parties approving the creation of the UCP.[30] Now that the UCP had been ratified, it was time for step four, winning the new UCP leadership. As expected, Jean also ran, but so did Calgary lawyer Doug Schweitzer and former Wildrose president Jeff Callaway. Once again, Kenney won a first ballot victory with 61.1 per cent of the vote.[31] Step five will of course depend on the UCP's ability to win the 2019 election, which, according to Alberta's fixed-election law, will be held between March and May 2019.[32] It will be a stark choice between Rachel Notley and her NDP government and Jason Kenney and the new UCP.

Notes

1   Although the Social Credit Party first formed government in 1935, it wasn't until the 1944 election under its new leader Earnest Manning that the party started to adopt conservative principles.

2   Ian Austin, "Leftist Party's Win in Alberta May Affect Future of Oil Sands," *New York Times*, 6 May 2015.

3   Duane Bratt, "Stelmach's Royalty Review and the Rise of Wildrose," *Calgary Herald*, 4 April 2012.

4   The party was originally called the Wildrose Alliance Party, but then changed its name to simply the Wildrose Party.

5   Figures from Elections Alberta's financial disclosure for political parties, http://efpublic.elections.ab.ca/efParty.cfm?MID=FP_1&PID=1 (accessed 2 April 2012).

6   Tom Flanagan, *Winning Power: Canadian Campaigning in the 21st Century* (Montreal and Kingston: McGill-Queen's University Press, 2014), 170–2.

7   Licia Corbella, "Posh Promises and Bad Budgeting Lead to a Mess," *Calgary Herald*, 20 February 2013.

8   Darcy Henton, "Alta. Wildrose leader has doubts about science on climate change," *Calgary Herald*, 16 April 2012.

9   The full text of Hunsperger's blog post was reprinted in David Staples, "Wildrose candidate Allan Hunsperger on gays: 'You will suffer the rest of eternity in the lake of fire, hell,' " *Edmonton Journal*, 15 April 2012).

10   Flanagan, *Winning Power*, 182–4.

11   James Wood, "Wildrose Candidate Tells Gays in Lady Gag-Inspired Blog Post: 'You Will Suffer the Rest of Eternity in the Lake of Fire, Hell,' " *Calgary Herald*, 15 April 2012.

12   Flanagan, *Winning Power,* 177–8.

13   Ibid., 187.

14   Thomas Lukaszuk, interview with author, 26 October 2016.

15   A long-time PC volunteer claimed that Redford was "a bullying woman who demeaned staff, cabinet, caucus in public. Shouting, swearing, throwing things. It was very belittling behaviour." While Len Webber and Donna Kennedy-Glans's decision to quit caucus received the most attention, Redford's behaviour also led many PC volunteers to quit too. This would cause them damage in the 2015 election. Confidential interview with author, 4 November 2016.

16   Sydney Sharpe and Don Braid, *Notley Nation: How Alberta's Political Upheaval Swept the Country* (Toronto: Dundurn, 2015), 81.

17   Confidential interviews with author, 4 November 2016.

18   Sharpe and Braid, *Notley Nation*, 25.

19   Thomas Lukaszuk, interview with author, 26 October 2016.

20   Duane Bratt, "Alberta election may be unethical, but it's not illegal," *Globe and Mail* (Toronto), 11 April 2015.

21   Richard Gotfried, interview with author, 4 November 2016.

22   Sharpe and Braid, *Notley Nation*, 36.

23   Jim Prentice to Donna McElligot, "Alberta at Noon," *CBC Radio*, 4 March 2015.

24   Duane Bratt, "'Buddy, you are being set up' could be the PCs 'Lake of Fire' moment," *Calgary Herald*, 29 April 2015.

25   Karen Kleiss, "Tory Backers Rip 'Amateur' NDP Policies," *Edmonton Journal*, 2 May 2016.

26   Duane Bratt, "Why we may have seen the last of the Alberta PCs," *Globe and Mail* (Toronto), 6 May 2015.

27   Michael Franklin, "Tory MP Jason Kenney seeks Alberta PC leadership," *CTV News*, 6 July 2016, https://calgary.ctvnews.ca/tory-mp-jason-kenney-seeks-alberta-pc-leadership-1.2974931 (accessed 7 September 2016).

28   James Wood, "Kenney sweeps to victory at PC leadership convention," *Calgary Herald*, 19 March 2017.

29   Brian Jean and Jason Kenney, "Agreement in principle on the establishment of the United Conservative Party," 18 May 2017, https://unitedconservative.ca/Content/UnityAgreementInPrinciple.pdf (accessed 19 May 2017).

30   Michelle Bellefontaine, "Alberta's new United Conservative Party is a go. What happens next?" *CBC News*, 23 July 2017, https://www.cbc.ca/news/canada/edmonton/united-conservative-party-next-steps-1.4217922 (accessed 20 September 2017).

31   James Wood, "Kenney wins big in UCP leadership race, fires warning shot at NDP," *Calgary Herald*, 29 October 2017.

32   The relevant passage from Alberta's Election Act is as follows:

38.1(1) Nothing in this section affects the powers of the Lieutenant Governor, including the power to dissolve the Legislature, in Her Majesty's name, when the Lieutenant Governor sees fit. (2) Subject to subsection (1), a general election shall be held within the 3-month period beginning on March 1, 2012 and ending on May 31, 2012, and afterwards, general elections shall be held within the 3-month period beginning on March 1 and ending on May 31 in the 4th calendar year following polling day in the most recent general election.

Ready for Rachel: The Alberta NDP's 2015 Campaign

Melanee Thomas

Though public opinion polls predicted that the Alberta New Democratic Party would win the 2015 provincial election (see Brown and Santos, this volume), it was still a surprise to actually see it happen on 5 May 2015. Indeed, many Albertans may have doubted that the incumbent Progressive Conservatives, having held office since 1971, would ever be defeated. That their loss came at the hands of an unapologetically left-leaning alternative, rather than a more conservative party such as the Wildrose Party, was more surprising still.

Given the unusual circumstances of the PCs' loss, many would argue that the 2015 election result was an extraordinary event that had more to do with voters' anger with the PCs than their excitement with the NDP. This chapter disagrees, and instead argues that the "just an anti-PC vote" description of Alberta's 2015 election is incomplete and ignores the role of the NDP leadership, as well as strategic and effective campaign work.

In general, election results can be summarized by the answers to two questions that come to voters' minds. First, "does this government deserve to be re-elected?" Voters who answer yes may simply vote for the party in government. For those who answer no, a second question is required: "is there a credible alternative?" If voters cannot find a credible alternative to the party in government, as was arguably the case for dissatisfied voters in 2008 and 2012, then they may choose to abstain from voting or hold their nose and vote for the party in government. However, if voters decide there is a credible alternative to the incumbent party, then they may decide to vote for that alternative in large numbers. Thus, any full explanation of Alberta's 2015 election must determine why so many Albertans decided that the NDP represented a credible alternative to the status quo represented by the PCs.

This chapter outlines how the NDP, anticipating the 2015 spring election call, planned to considerably grow its position in the legislature. In so doing, this chapter places the 2015 election within the larger context of political science literature on campaigns and elections, with an emphasis on economic voting and the role of leadership in campaigns and vote choice. Further evidence is gathered from semi-structured interviews with, and public statements made by, NDP insiders.

Both groups of sources—the academic literature and NDP insiders—broadly agree: the 2015 electoral context was unique and tilted in favour of unseating the incumbent PC government. To do so, the NDP needed to have a strong campaign centred around a popular leader. Indeed, after Rachel Notley's selection as party leader in the fall of 2014, the NDP was the only party other than the PCs to claim it was running to form a government; because they were organized, the NDP had the strategic foresight to effectively respond to the economic context and the PCs' strategic errors. Though the campaign was not error-free, and while few (if any) anticipated from the outset that the party would win government outright, the NDP's 2015 election campaign was professional and persuasive. This, combined with Rachel Notley's effectiveness as a political leader, largely explains the NDP's success. Notably, the NDP did this all with a commitment to diversity unparalleled in Canadian political history, as the 2015 election produced Canada's first government caucus with near gender parity, and its first cabinet comprised of a majority of women. Taken together, these factors all support the conclusion that any explanation of the 2015 election result that does not include a considerable focus on the NDP campaign itself is incomplete.

This chapter proceeds in four parts. First, general context about Alberta in 2015 and implications derived from that context are presented. In the next two sections, key aspects of the NDP's 2015 campaign—from organization to execution—are presented. The chapter ends with a reflection on what lessons from 2015 can be applied to the 2019 election. Throughout, evidence is presented from three key sets of sources: academic research on elections and political behaviour, semi-structured interviews with staff active in the NDP's 2015 campaign, and a public panel discussion with key actors in the campaign presented at the NDP's 2016 convention.

General Context

Before examining the specifics of the NDP's campaign preparation, it is important to highlight a key part of the electoral context: the economy. Alberta experienced an oil boom in the early 2010s, but international oil prices started to decline precipitously in 2014. By the spring of 2015, most analysts suggested strongly that oil and gas prices would be suppressed for quite some time. Given the Alberta government's reliance on natural resource revenue for programs such as health care and education, the economic outlook was both grim and deeply politicized.

Research shows that voters generally integrate media reports of anticipated changes in the economy into their vote choice. [1] When the anticipated changes are positive, incumbent governments and candidates are typically rewarded; when the anticipated changes are negative, incumbent governments and candidates are punished. [2] Importantly, voters tend to react more forcefully to negative information than they do to positive information. In the context of the 2015 election, this suggests that voters would have used most, if not all, available economic information to answer the question with which this chapter was opened—does this government deserve to be re-elected?—in the negative. Other factors may have reinforced this; some are noted below, while others are discussed in greater detail in Duane Bratt's chapter about the PC campaign.

Laying the Foundation: NDP Organization before the Writ

When Rachel Notley was selected as leader of the Alberta NDP in October 2014, many party activists felt it was "the obvious time and she was the obvious choice."[3] First elected in 2008, Notley had long been identified as a potential party leader, in part because of her political pedigree, and in part because of her skill as a politician, inside and outside of the legislature. Several interviewees noted a palpable shift in public perception toward the

NDP in 2012, and a growing dissatisfaction with the PCs since 2008. This has led some to suggest that voters' increasing "awareness and openness to the party [meant] that the best thing for it would be a new, fresh face."[4] Others suggested that alternatives such as the Wildrose Party "scared more people than it inspired." Thus, with Albertans' "festering dissatisfaction" with the PCs, the NDP was seen as a newer option that people liked and identified with.[5]

For NDP campaign organizers, Rachel Notley is the foundation for their success. Every interviewee directly credited Rachel Notley with crucial parts of the NDP's successful campaign strategy and organization. Similarly, every interviewee argued that Notley was the most important factor in the NDP's 2015 campaign, due in large part to her political skills. Thus, it is both plausible and reasonable to suggest that, in anticipation of a 2015 election, Notley's selection as party leader coincided with a serious push for growth on the part of the NDP.

In addition to new leadership, the NDP employed three other identifiable pre-election strategies: candidate search and organization, discrediting the party in government (PCs), and presenting the NDP as the only credible alternative for government. Though the NDP is far from the first party to use these strategies, they proved to be particularly effective tools in the the 2015 election.

By nominating a full slate of candidates, the NDP sought to establish the narrative that the only party that should be taken seriously as a challenger to the incumbent PCs in the 2015 election campaign was the NDP, as both the NDP and the PCs were the only parties with the necessary organization to represent the whole province. The Wildrose did not field a candidate in Edmonton-Strathcona, and the Alberta Liberals and the Alberta Party both failed to nominate candidates in a considerable number of districts. Obviously, any party that wishes to credibly claim to be government must nominate a full slate of candidates. Here, part of the NDP success is predicated on the party's

> insistence that we weren't [just] campaigning in Edmonton; that the presence in Calgary was established months before E-Day. That the work in other regions was starting in a very substantial way with MLAs, candidates, and others leaving

the relative comfort of Edmonton and making sure the profile of the party, the profile of the caucus, and the profile of
the leader was established elsewhere.[6]

This strategy included the nomination of anchor candidates in four targeted ridings: Joe Ceci (Calgary Fort), Sarah Hoffman (Edmonton Glenora),
Shannon Phillips (Lethbridge West), and Marlin Schmidt (Edmonton Gold
Bar). Note the geographical distribution of these targeted seats. As expected, the NDP sought to build on its strength in Edmonton, but it also expected to build in Calgary and the south, both areas where the NDP has had
some, but not considerable, electoral support. Particularly with Ceci, a local
notable with considerable name recognition and a city-wide profile through
his past career as a Calgary city councillor, the NDP presented in 2015 as a
party determined to make gains.

In hindsight, it is fair to suggest that with these four targeted seats, a
reasonable electoral strategy for the NDP in the fall of 2014 was to try to
double the size of its caucus. Beyond this, some interviewees reported the
secondary and tertiary goals of identifying a number of other districts in
which to build over the medium term, as the party organized to form government. This supports the idea that the NDP looked to grow in 2015 and
into the future. Similarly, this narrative may bolster the argument that the
NDP wanted to frame itself for voters, the media, and the other parties as
the only credible alternative to the PCs.

The other aspect of candidate recruitment that requires examination is
the NDP's focus on equity and diversity in representation. Notably, Alberta
is the only jurisdiction in Canada in which women hold a majority of cabinet positions.[7] Just as notable—and perhaps surprising—is the fact that the
Alberta NDP nominated an equal number of women and men. The NDP
has had an equity nomination policy in its constitution since 1984.[8] Despite
this, NDP candidates have remained less diverse than the Canadian population over time. This was not the case in 2015 with the Alberta NDP, as 50
per cent of the party's nominated candidates were women. This translates to
47 per cent of the NDP's government caucus, and 31 per cent of the legislature itself (Parliament of Canada 2017).[9]

When asked why the Alberta NDP succeeded in finding and nominating diverse candidates where NDP organizers and local associations

in other jurisdictions have failed, interviewees credit Notley's leadership. In short, representational diversity was "something that was incredibly important to the leader, that candidates reflected the diversity of the province."[10] Organizers were clear: no specific instructions or quotas were given beyond the leader's preference that candidates reflect the diversity of Albertans. They report that they looked for candidates in different places than they typically might have, and they were candid that recruiting people of colour, women, and sexual minorities required more time and effort than more conventional candidates. Some quipped, "there's never a shortage of middle to older white males who are able bodied who put their hands up to run for election. There's a level of comfort there" that must instead be built among underrepresented groups.[11] What was required, then, in order to reflect the diversity of Albertans was for those in the NDP involved in candidate searches to find less common candidates and make them feel comfortable seeking a nomination. This takes considerable time and effort, but Alberta NDP organizers and local associations did this work because it was clear the leader expected them to. This mirrors Notley's own words, as she has been candid that, at least with respect to gender, space needs to be made in politics for diversity, as it will not happen organically on its own (CBC 2016).[12] This speaks to a "commitment rather than a directive" on representational diversity within the Alberta NDP,[13] and it highlights how equity in representation, at least on gendered grounds, is possible if a party and their leader genuinely want it. This is potentially an instructive case for those studying political parties in parliamentary systems well beyond Alberta or Canada.

From a political science perspective, this insight both confirms what is known from the literature about Canadian political parties, and suggests that a principal reason why other political parties do poorly on representational diversity is because of (a lack of) leadership. It is already well established that in Canada, party leaders get what they want.[14] Notley and the Alberta NDP show that if a party leader is serious about representing women, people of colour, sexual minorities, youth, and other historically under-represented groups, their parties will reflect that. This is, perhaps, similar to Stephen Harper's Conservatives, who doubled the number of women nominated as candidates between the 2006 and 2008 federal elections, presumably at the leader's request.[15] Where Notley appears to be different than other party leaders, including her NDP counterparts elsewhere in Canada, is an expectation that equity be achieved in diverse representation, rather than at a level that is merely "respectable" or "best in class."

As noted above, once candidates are nominated, every political party must then succeed in convincing voters to answer two questions in their favour. First, "does this government deserve to be re-elected?" If the answer to that question is no, the second question is, "is there a credible alternative?" For its part, the NDP had to convince Albertans of two things: that the PCs were no longer deserved to be in government, and that the NDP were, in fact, a credible alternative.

To present itself as the only credible alternative to the PCs in 2015, the NDP took advantage of freedom of information (FOIP) requests that produced information that embarrassed the PC government. A number of groups were actively engaged in FOIP research, from advocacy organizations, to organized labour, to the party itself.[16] The goal for the NDP was to take information that would hold the PCs to account and/or embarrass them, and then use the media to showcase Notley and the caucus to the media and to the public. This helped both to undermine the government and also to present Notley and the existing NDP MLAs as credible representatives. Interviewees reported that the communications staff in the NDP who had designed this strategy were happy with how it played out prior to the election call,[17] and that it helped set up a positive relationship between the NDP war room and journalists during the 2015 election campaign.[18]

The NDP did not have to do much to discredit the other parties during the election: most interviewees indicated that their challengers engaged in behaviours that the NDP could capitalize on. The PCs were seen as Machiavellian for orchestrating the Wildrose floor-crossing/takeover in December 2015. Though a fulsome investigation of the floor-crossing is beyond the scope of this chapter, it is plausible that one of the PCs' primary goals was to use this event to neutralize the Wildrose and undermine the idea that it could plausibly form government. This both alienated PC supporters who disliked the Wildrose, and also made it impossible for the PCs to credibly identify what was left of the Wildrose as their main opponent during the 2015 election campaign. This narrative arguably helped the NDP as much, if not more, than it helped (or hurt) any of the other parties.

Worse, the PCs then introduced "a budget that pleases nobody"[19] and then, according to NDP insiders, failed to defend it. One organizer observed:

> I think the PCs, if they went hard left or hard right, they would have formed government again. Specifically, if they went hard right. If they came out and said, "We are making drastic cuts across the board," I think they would have gained a lot of the Wildrose vote and formed government. Similarly, I think if they came out and said, "There will be no cuts and, in fact, we're going to invest in some of the critical public services that are needed during a recession," similarly I think they would have formed government. Instead, they did this kind of mealy-mouthed, wishy-washy half measure, and because Jim Prentice put so much political capital on a revolutionary platform, a revolutionary budget, and it came out the other end and everybody was just kind of a little disappointed. . . . [pause] People were just left underwhelmed.[20]

The idea that Albertans were "underwhelmed" may be a kind way of putting it. Other interviewees suggested that Albertans were angered by Prentice's proposed budget, because it "taxed the hell out of Martha and Henry"[21] and was tone deaf. In a televised address to Albertans, Prentice suggested that because he was new to Alberta's provincial government, Albertans themselves were to blame for the economic downturn. As such, they only needed to "look in the mirror"[22] for an explanation of how the province wound up in a financial mess.[23] Prentice seemed unaware of the irony that, though he himself might be new, his cabinet and caucus were decidedly not. It is perhaps unsurprising that voters reacted poorly to this presentation.

Here, NDP activists saw the Wildrose as helping the NDP campaign. Specifically, when the PCs refused to increase corporate taxes alongside personal taxes and fees for regular Albertans, even the Wildrose (and their supporters) appeared to be saying, "we might not want corporate taxes, but if our taxes are going up, then tax them a bit too."[24] In other words, by protecting corporations and bigger businesses from tax increases, the PCs abandoned Prairie populism, and were seen instead to advocate for corporate oil and gas, who were perceived to have done very well during the recent boom at the expense of everyday Albertans. In many respects, this rhetoric was a sharp change away from the populist "Martha and Henry" messaging of the Klein years.

Importantly, while this sentiment was shared across the Wildrose and the NDP, NDP organizers perceived it as being a net benefit for their party. Both the Wildrose and the NDP are Prairie populist parties that advocate for "the people" over powerful elites;[25] where the parties differ, according to NDP organizers, is that the Wildrose "have not been able, and still haven't been able, to counter the narrative they are primarily a rural-based party. They continue to only play to their base, and [they are] never trying to reach beyond their base. . . . They've failed to reach out to people in the city."[26]

Thus, while the PCs (perhaps unintentionally), Wildrose, and NDP were all working to discredit the PCs in government, the view inside the NDP was that only they were organized and able to take full advantage of the context leading up to the 2015 election. As one interviewee argued, "we did not create the circumstances by which the outcome of the election came to be, but we were well positioned to take advantage of those dynamics."[27] Similarly, Gerry Scott candidly stated during the 2016 NDP convention that,

> in the winter and early spring before the election was called, [Notley] and the caucus really emerged as the real opposition. I think we can all remember those days where the Wildrose and the Liberals[28] were invisible in talking about what was going on and presenting an alternative to a government that was increasingly in disarray. That meant that going into the campaign, there was real momentum around the NDP as *the* alternative. It was remarkable work, because at that point, the caucus was the fourth [largest] in the legislature, and very quickly in January emerged as the real opposition. A critical factor in my view.[29]

Scott also argued that "the campaign victory in my view wasn't in five weeks, or four weeks, or twenty-eight days. It never is in a strong campaign. The work that was done in the years and months before the campaign was absolutely critical. . . . Without the work that was done in the months after the leadership convention, we wouldn't be here today."[30]

"Leadership for What Matters": The NDP's 2015 Campaign

Though NDP insiders argue that their pre-writ work was crucial to the party's victory, the campaign itself also needed to be run well to ensure an NDP victory. As noted above, if the 2015 election were simply about anti-PC sentiment, then Alberta arguably would have changed governments in 2012. Instead, the Wildrose's 2012 campaign included notable missteps from candidates and the leader that contributed to the narrative that the Wildrose did not win that election.[31]

So, what did the NDP do during the campaign that led to their success? Interviewees all identified the leader, professionalism, the platform, key events such as the debate and the five CEOs (see below), and resources as key factors associated directly with the campaign period. Much of this comports with existing research on successful election campaigns. And, while interviewees did not directly address it by name, populism is a factor that always plays a role in election results in Alberta. Though each of these factors could be seen as distinct, they are perhaps best understood as complimentary facets that all highlighted Rachel Notley's leadership abilities for Alberta voters.

One of the first things to note about the NDP's 2015 campaign is that, with one notable exception, it was professionally run and free of gaffes. Interviewees remarked this professionalism was a conscious choice. Brian Topp and Gerry Scott, both experienced NDP campaign managers, were brought in to help run the campaign and the war room. Anne McGrath and Kathleen Monk were also brought in as the campaign progressed, and both were seen as anchors for the transition to government. The NDP was determined to run a well-financed and well-staffed campaign, long before the polls suggested that the party was going to form government. As one interviewee said, "It was probably the best-resourced campaign we've had here in Alberta. For sure. I've worked campaigns in other parts of the country; it would be on par in BC, for example, but we've never had a campaign in Alberta that was as well resourced. And that's the number of staff but also the quality of staff."[32]

Organizers and analysts alike credited Rachel Notley herself for the strength of the NDP's campaign. Academic research certainly highlights

MELANEE THOMAS

the important effects that leader evaluations have on vote choice.[33] Notably, all voters evaluate parties based, in part, on their leaders, including their assessments of a leader's competence and character. "Competence" here typically refers to whether or not voters think a leader is intelligent, arrogant, knowledgeable, or strong; "character" refers to whether a leader is viewed as honest, trustworthy, compassionate, or moral.[34] Crucial for party leaders on the political left, such as Notley, character-based assessments matter more to vote choice than do perceptions of competence; importantly, partisans across the political spectrum, including the political right, have typically evaluated left-leaning party leaders' character positively.[35]

This has implications for the NDP's 2015 campaign: in presenting itself as a credible alternative for government, the party's primary goal should have been to get voters to like Rachel. If voters found her honest and compassionate, research suggests that those voters would view Notley positively, regardless of where they sit on the ideological spectrum. Though positive leader evaluations are not typically important enough to overpower other factors such as partisanship,[36] it is plausible that in Alberta in 2015, when (PC) partisanship might have been somewhat unsettled, establishing these positive evaluations of Notley's character may have been the most important part of the campaign.

It appears as though this is precisely what the NDP campaign did. Interviewees explicitly attributed the NDP's success in 2015 to Notley's likeability. For example, as one interviewee stated,

> There's also in politics just a likeability factor; it's very difficult to describe. People like the premier, they respect and trust her, and the PC brand was severely undermined and damaged, due in no small part to the NDP and the research that was put out before [the writ], but also by the other opposition parties, to be clear. But then the choice became: if you don't trust the leader of the PC Party, do you trust Brian Jean or Rachel Notley?[37]

They went on to report that, "I think the platform was key. It was a platform that . . . [pause] and I'll put it almost entirely on the leader, Rachel Notley, something that she determined was something that we could run on, that we could perform government on."[38] Other interviewees noted that during the campaign, journalists would explicitly ask Notley why voters liked her so much. This lead one interviewee to conclude that

> the PC brand was very damaged, and there was a shift of PC voters to the NDP, and I think that the party, we've got to tip our hat a little bit to the Official Opposition, the Wildrose, because they were instrumental in undermining that brand. The PC voters, the ones that shifted, they looked at Brian Jean and that party's brand was not really rock solid either. I mean, they had the lake of fire stuff in the previous election and some climate denialism and other things. And it came down to the likeability factor: those PC voters were looking for a home . . . [pause] and they chose Rachel Notley, because she's more likeable, the platform was very well thought out, and also, I think it bears mentioning, it reflected the time that we were going into, a recession. Everyone knew it was coming. Jim Prentice let everyone know it was coming. So, the choice was "cut" or "don't cut." I think the message of investing in public services, running a deficit and weathering the storm, and this idea of "don't worry, we've got your back," that was very instrumental. It fit with Rachel Notley's personality as well; the people wanted that kind of comfort and trust.[39]

In other words, NDP insiders argue that the reason why the NDP did well was in large part because voters viewed Notley's character positively. Given the academic research on elections, the economy, and the importance of leaders, it is perhaps striking that organizers' comments so clearly comport with research. The party's focus on Notley's personality and likeability, filtered through what they determined to be a credible platform given the provincial economic context, appears to be a considerable part of the NDP's success.

Certain key events during the campaign reinforced Notley's likeability among voters. First, she "launched her campaign with unapologetic optimism about the future. . . . She stood in front of the legislature with all the candidates and she announced that she was running to be premier. She was the only candidate outside of Prentice who was willing to do that."[40] Second, Notley's brilliant performance during the leaders' debate "was a turning point for everybody." The consensus was that Notley handily won the leader's debate, and in so doing, solidified the idea that the NDP was the only real alternative to the PCs, and that Notley was both credible and legitimate. Insiders suggest that the debate was the moment at which Notley "wasn't just seen as the NDP leader, but as herself [and] as a political symbol in the province."[41]

Notley's strong debate performance arguably mitigated the campaign's one major error. A few days before the debate, the NDP was forced to issue a retraction of its promise to balance the budget by 2017, as previous cuts to health care, education, and universities were not "properly" reflected in the party's previous estimates.[42] This had the potential to be catastrophic for the NDP, as the party does not typically "own" economic issues.[43] Thus, when Jim Prentice quipped at Notley that "math is difficult" during the debate,[44] some interviewees candidly suggested that the comment was fair because of this budgeting error.

There are two reasons why the "math is hard" comment was devastating for Jim Prentice, and why the budgeting error did not stick to Notley or the NDP during the campaign. First, Sally Houser, Rachel Notley's press secretary during the 2015 election campaign, contends that the budget error was managed well by the NDP campaign: it was quickly retracted, with apology, and the party made a point of "not being arrogant or a jerk about it." This may have resulted in a softer landing on the budgeting error from the media. Second, it is clear that the debate audience did *not* view the "math is hard" comment with the NDP's budget in mind; instead they saw a man in politics try to tell a woman that she was not very good at math. Subsequently, "criticism of the PC leader exploded on Twitter."[45]

While the reasons why Prentice or the PC campaign could not legitimately mark the Wildrose as their chief rivals seem clear, what is less clear is why they did not anticipate that Notley would be a skilled political operator, given her prior tenure as an MLA (first elected in 2008). Indeed, Brian Topp had role-played being the PC leader for Notley's debate prep; he noted, "I've done a little bit of debate prep over the years, and I've never seen such a just spring-loaded, compelling counterpunch."[46] This is echoed by other NDP organizers, including one who stated that, "for anyone, this was their opportunity to see this five-foot, two-inch feisty woman just. I mean, Prentice would go after her and she just turned around and gave it back. And she proved that night that not only was she incredibly intelligent and articulate on every file that you could think of, but also that she was very clever and very funny. And she knocked it out of the park that night. . . . [pause] If we did have to pick a turning point in the campaign, that was certainly it."[47]

Interestingly, research suggests that debates typically do not have much of an effect on vote choice, so perhaps the Alberta 2015 election is the exception that proves the rule. In addition to Brown and Santos's chapter in this book, every party's support dropped after the debate except for the NDP's, and that Google searches for Rachel Notley dramatically increased after the debate as well.[48] This suggests that Notley's debate performance, and the narrative that she won the debate inspired voters to learn more about her.

The PC response to this increased interest in Rachel Notley was to run a series of advertisements admonishing voters not to vote for the NDP. One NDP organizer suggested that this may not have worked well in the PCs' favour:

> To me, that was a massive mistake on their part; they basically spent millions of dollars legitimizing the idea that we could form government. If we talked about it, that would have been met with skepticism and incredulity, but when they said it, suddenly the idea itself had legitimacy. It solidified the non-Conservative vote in Calgary behind us. If you were looking to form a government that wasn't PC, by their own admission, it was the NDP. Every time I heard that ad run, I heard it as an ad for us.[49]

Similarly, about a week after the leaders' debate, an event occurred that highlighted the momentum of the NDP's campaign; this event also highlights how populism is key to understanding election results in Alberta. On 1 May, five CEOs gathered for a press conference to argue that Albertans should re-elect the PCs. Because the NDP war room had been informed of the press conference in advance, they were able to release lists of the CEOs' donations to the PCs while the press conference was underway. This strategy was effective, as the CEOs' financial support of the PCs was integrated into most media reports of the event.[50] Cheryl Oates argued that the CEOs "went on and on about, 'why me, why should I have to contribute more, why should my business have to contribute more?' and really that was the moment that solidified a narrative for Albertans that, even despite this economic downturn, the PCs were really in it for themselves, their friends, and insiders."[51]

The CEOs' press conference sparked considerable negative reaction from the public. On social media, the hashtag #PCAAHostageCrisis was used to express discontent with the idea that the CEOs would stop donating to charitable organizations if the PCs lost the 2015 election. When interpreted through a populist lens, the CEO press conference was disastrous for the PCs, as it reinforced the idea from the PC budget that those who many Albertans perceived as benefitting most from the oil and gas boom should be shielded from the economic downturn regular Albertans could not avoid. This violated the most basic premise of Prairie populism, since it showed the PCs backing powerful elites at the expense of "the people." This key idea, that of the people versus the powerful, is deeply seeded in Alberta's political culture.[52] Notably, supporters of all of Alberta's political parties are deeply populist, as Sayers and Stewart show in chapter 17 of this book. Thus, any political party that wishes to do well in Alberta must appear to follow the principles of Prairie populism. In 2015, the NDP and Notley resonated on populism in ways that the other leaders, especially Prentice did not.

Thus, given all these factors, the 2015 election ended with the momentum clearly in the NDP's favour. Organizers reported that donations started to flood in the back half of the campaign and simply did not stop. Similarly, Scott Payne, the NDP's Calgary field organizer during the campaign, observed that

> at one point very late in the election, I plunked down in a fairly remote parking lot in southeastern Calgary with about 2,000 Rachel Notley signs, and we blasted an email out and said, "if you want a sign, come to this location." We showed up at 10 [a.m.] and were out of signs by 2 [p.m.]. Offloading that number of signs before this election was unheard of. Going out of the way, coming to you, and they're someone

you don't recognize, that tells me there's really something happening.[53]

Yet, Payne also reported that there was

no milestone that we hit that told me that we were going to a) form government or b) form a majority. It wasn't until the last twenty-four hours that I thought we would form government. And it wasn't until I was told that it was a majority. You just don't see elections like that. A once-in-a-lifetime sort of thing. . . . [pause] It's a testament to the power that the electorate has.[54]

Looking Forward to 2019

The NDP's 2015 campaign was successful, at least in part, because it was well designed by smart actors deployed at the right time with the right leader. Given the unique context of the 2015 election, what can we learn from the success of the NDP's campaign for the next provincial election in 2019? Certainly, it would be foolish to suggest that we can use the information outlined above to predict the next election's outcome; it is not unreasonable, though, to look at these factors and draw potential expectations.

Leadership will continue to be a crucial factor. The key for all parties, including the NDP, will be to get voters to like their leader and to view them through a Prairie populist lens. This will arguably be a more difficult task for Rachel Notley after a term in government than it was in 2015. She will be facing a united, socially and fiscally conservative party led by an experienced political operator, Jason Kenney, though Kenney is arguably less adept at populist appeals than Notley is. Indeed, research shows that voters evaluate leaders with new eyes during each electoral cycle, and that these evaluations are always measured against the other leaders in the campaign.[55] Thus, what made Albertans like Notley in 2015 (when she was compared to Prentice) will certainly change in 2019 (when she is compared to Kenney). What may also be important for Notley is a platform that she can credibly sell for a second term in government; again, this may be more challenging in 2019 than it was in 2015.

Similarly, the economy will be an issue, but in a very different way than it was in 2015. When Prentice announced his budget, it was clear that Alberta was at the start of a major economic downturn, with the worst of it to come after the election was finished. It appears as though the worst has now passed, and that a recovery is on its way. Research suggests that this may produce positive expectations about the future economy in Alberta; this may not necessarily help the NDP, but it certainly will not hurt it.[56] Yet, an economic recovery is not the same as an economy that is fully recovered; given that party identification colours how voters perceive information about the economy, a recovering economy may not be enough for the NDP to receive the expected incumbent boost.

It seems reasonable to expect that 2019 will be an election unlike any Alberta has seen before. Just as was the case in 2015, resources will be crucial to strong campaigns. Unlike 2015, there is a new statutory framework that will govern party and campaign finances in 2019. Despite the creation of the United Conservative Party, the NDP continues to lead all parties in financial donations, taking in over $51,000 more in the first quarter of 2018 than did the UCP. This is in keeping with financing trends between 2015 and 2017, as the NDP led both the Wildrose and the PCs in contributions prior to the UCP's formation.[57] Given this, the creation of the UCP itself, and new leadership for at least two parties in the Alberta legislature (the Alberta Party and the Alberta Liberals), 2019 may be Alberta's most interesting election to date. Yet, given the considerable importance research places on leadership, resources, and populism in Alberta elections, the insights generated from the NDP's 2015 election campaign could potentially successfully inform their future electoral strategies.

Notes

1   See Stuart Soroka, Dominic Stecula, and Christopher Wlezien, "It's (Change in) the (Future) Economy, Stupid: Economic Indicators, the Media, and Public Opinion," *American Journal of Political Science* 59, no. 2 (2015): 457–74.

2   Michael S. Lewis-Beck and Mary Stegmaier. 2007. "Economic Models of Voting," in *The Oxford Handbook of Political Behavior*, ed. Russell J. Dalton and Hans-Dieter Klingemann, 518–37 (Oxford: Oxford University Press).

3   Trevor McKenzie-Smith (pre-writ organizer), interview with author, 26 November 2016.

4   Ibid.

5   Scott Payne (pre-election Calgary organizer, Calgary field organizer), interview with author, 8 December 2016.

6   Gerry Scott, NDP campaign director, "Campaign 2019—The Path Forward" (Alberta NDP convention), Calgary, 11 June 2016.

7   Though both Justin Trudeau (federal) and Jean Charest (Quebec) have appointed parity cabinets, their cabinets remain majority male, as the chief political executive (prime minister, premier) tips the balance. As a woman, then, Notley is the first to lead a majority female cabinet in Canada.

8   See William Cross, *Political Parties* (Vancouver: UBC Press, 2004).

9   See Parliament of Canada, "Women in the Provincial and Territorial Legislatures: Current List," 2017, http://www.lop.parl.gc.ca/ParlInfo/compilations/ProvinceTerritory/ Women.aspx?Province=edad4077-a735-48ad-982e-1dcad72f51b6&Current=True (accessed 1 March 20170. Opposition parties appear to struggle to nominate women as candidates and elect them as MLAs; at the time of writing, only two women sit in the opposition benches. A third, Sandra Jansen, crossed the floor from the PCs to the NDP after allegations of gendered harassment from within her own party. See Justin Giovanetti, "Alberta Tory MLA Sandra Jansen defects to NDP, citing sexism and personal attacks," *Globe and Mail* (Toronto), 17 November 2016, http://www. theglobeandmail.com/news/alberta/former-alberta-tory-leadership-candidate-sandra-jansen-crosses-floor-to-ndp/article32902968/ (accessed 1 March 2017).

10   Payne interview.

11   Ibid.

12   "Canada's female premiers on Hillary Clinton and sexism in politics," *CBC News*, 31 August 2016, http://www.cbc.ca/news/thenational/canada-s-female-premiers-on-hillary-clinton-and-sexism-in-politics-1.3694912 (accessed 1 March 2017).

13   Payne interview.

14   See R. Kenneth Carty, "The Politics of Tecumseh Corners: Canadian Political Parties as Franchise Organizations," *Canadian Journal of Political Science* 35, no. 4 (2002): 723–45; Carty, "Parties as Franchise Systems: The Stratarchical Organizational Imperative," *Party Politics* 10, no. 1 (2004): 5–24; and Cross, *Political Parties*.

15   Melanee Thomas, "Equality of Opportunity but not Result: Women and Federal Conservatives in Canada," in *The Blueprint: Conservative Parties and Their Impact on Canadian Politics*, ed. J. P. Lewis and Joanna Everitt (Toronto: University of Toronto Press, 2017).

16   Ted (pseudonym; war room), interview with author, 6 December 2016.

17   Sally Housser (press secretary for Rachel Notley), interview with author, 4 November 2016.

18   Ted interview.

19　Houser interview.

20　Ted interview.

21　Lois (pseudonym; local campaign organizer), interview with author, 20 November 2016. Coined by former premier Ralph Klein, the catch phrase "Martha and Henry" is used to describe regular Albertans. Of course, rhetorically, who Martha and Henry are depends on the speaker's own views and goals. For example, between 2004 and 2009, feminists based in Lethbridge, organized "Martha's Monthly," sending emails on a current event related to women or women's issues to a constituency office or minister's office on the eighth day of every month.

22　This sparked the Twitter hashtag #PrenticeBlamesAlbertans, something NDP communications staff integrated into their communications strategies. See Cheryl Oates, (media relations), "Campaign 2019—The Path Forward," Calgary, 11 June 2016, and "#PrenticeBlamesAlbertans goes viral after Jim Prentice's 'look in the mirror' comment," *CBC News*, 5 March 2015, http://www.cbc.ca/news/canada/edmonton/ prenticeblamesalbertans-goes-viral-after-jim-prentice-s-look-in-the-mirror-comment-1.2982524 (accessed 1 March 2017).

23　Chris Varcoe, "Prentice says Albertans must 'look in the mirror' for the province's financial crunch," *Calgary Herald*, 5 March 2015, http://calgaryherald.com/news/ politics/prentice-says-albertans-must-look-in-the-mirror-for-the-provinces-financial-crunch (accessed 1 March 2017).

24　Houser interview.

25　See David Laycock, "Populism," *Canadian Encyclopedia*, 2015, http://www. thecanadianencyclopedia.ca/en/article/populism/ (accessed 21 March 2017), and David Stewart and Anothony Sayers, "Breaking the Peace: The Wildrose Alliance in Alberta Politics," *Canadian Political Science Review* 71, no. 1 (2013): 73–86.

26　Ted interview.

27　Payne interview.

28　The Liberal Party of Alberta could arguably have been a factor in the 2015 election campaign. However, unlike the NDP, the Liberals were poorly organized and poorly positioned to react to the context. First, many of their incumbent MLAs declined to seek re-election, either because of retirement or because they were seeking Liberal Party of Canada nominations for the upcoming federal election. Leadership was also arguably weak, as David Swann was not seen as a viable leader in the long term, and the incumbents who sought re-election did not have a cohesive message. One NDP organizer (Ted) observed:

Yeah, I think a big part of the reason why they lost out in that election campaign is because of Laurie Blakeman. Her gambit was strategic voting. Right from the beginning, "you gotta vote strategically." She was running for three parties at once, basically. There was a very clear shift in the middle of the campaign with her message, which I thought was fantastic. So, consistently saying, "vote strategically, if you want to get rid of the PCs, you gotta vote strategically," and people didn't view David Swann as a viable leader. I mean, when you go talk to voters, they put a lot of their image of the party on the leader, so the leadership definitely matters. Swann didn't really have a clear campaign message, he had some big gaffes in terms of what he had to say during televised addresses and debates, and then Laurie Blakeman didn't really help the cause because she was roaming in a different direction, and what she had to say was "vote strategically." About halfway through the campaign, I remember reading a news article with her in it saying, "DON'T vote strategically!" [laughs] So, what happened was that people said, "Yeah, we're going to vote strategically, we want to get rid of the PCs. Who's the best party to do that? Rachel Notley and the NDP!" And she clearly misread people's intentions when she was talking about strategic voting.

29   Scott, "Campaign 2019—The Path Forward."

30   Ibid.

31   See Richard Cuthbertson, "Analysis: In the last three days before the Alberta vote, the cracks in the Wildrose were showing," *National Post* (Toronto), 27 April 2012, http://news.nationalpost.com/news/canada/analysis-in-the-last-three-days-before-the-alberta-vote-the-cracks-in-the-wildrose-were-showing (accessed 1 March 2017).

32   Ted interview.

33   See Amanda Bittner, *Platform or Personality? The Role of Party Leaders in Elections* (Oxford: Oxford University Press, 2011).

34   Ibid.; see also Bittner, "Personality Matters: The Evaluation of Party Leaders in Canadian Elections," in *Voting Behaviour in Canada*, ed. Cameron D. Anderson and Laura B. Stephenson (Vancouver: UBC Press, 2010), 190.

35   Bittner, *Platform or Personality?*, especially Tables 5.3. and 5.4.

36   Bittner, "Personality Matters."

37   Ted interview.

38   Ibid.

39   Ibid.

40   Oates, "Campaign 2019—The Path Forward."

41   Payne interview.

42   "NDP's balanced budget to come a year later, due to accounting error," *CBC News*, 21 April 2015, http://www.cbc.ca/news/elections/alberta-votes/ndp-s-balanced-budget-to-come-a-year-later-due-to-accounting-error-1.3042240 (accessed 1 March 2017).

43   See Éric Bélanger, "Issue Ownership by Canadian Political Parties 1953–2001," *Canadian Journal of Political Science* 36, no. 3 (2003): 539–58.

44   Jen Gerson, "Alberta election debate 'math' remark could subtract voters for PC's Jim Prentice," *National Post* (Toronto), 24 April 2015, http://news.nationalpost.com/news/canada/canadian-politics/math-remark-during-debate-could-subtract-voters-for-alberta-pcs-jim-prentice (accessed 1 March 2017).

45   Gerson, "Alberta election debate."

46   Brian Topp, head of communications, "Campaign 2019—The Path Forward," Calgary, 11 June 2016.

47   Oates, "Campaign 2019—The Path Forward."

48   Paul Fairie, "The Election Index: How Alberta turned orange," *Globe and Mail* (Toronto), 8 May 2015, http://www.theglobeandmail.com/news/politics/the-political-index-how-alberta-turned-orange/article24352152/ (accessed 1 March 2017).

49   Payne interview.

50   See, for example, Slav Kornik and Caley Ramsay, "Edmonton business leaders support PC government; NDP dismiss them as 'PC donors,'" *Global News*, 1 May 2015, http://globalnews.ca/news/1973934/edmonton-business-leaders-support-pc-government-ndp-dismiss-them-as-pc-donors/ (accessed 1 March 2017).

51   Oates, "Campaign 2019—The Path Forward."

52   See David Stewart and Keith Archer, *Quasi-Democracy? Parties and Leadership Selection in Alberta* (Vancouver: UBC Press, 2000), and Stewart and Sayers, "Breaking the Peace."

53   Payne interview.

54   Ibid.

55   Bittner, "Personality Matters."

56   See Soroka, Stecula, and Wlezien, "It's (Change in) the (Future) Economy, Stupid."

57   See Elections Alberta, "Financial Disclosure: Parties," 2018, http://efpublic.elections.ab.ca/efParties.cfm?MID=FP (accessed 23 May 2018).

Marginally Better: Polling in the 2015 Alberta Election

Janet Brown and John B. Santos[1]

Public opinion polling is a fixture in the politics of Western democracies, particularly during the course of an election campaign. Since Gallup predicted Franklin Roosevelt would be re-elected in the 1936 American presidential election, polling has grown to become its own industry that, in addition to pollsters, now also includes polling aggregators and election forecasters. Canada is no exception to this trend, and the number of polls conducted during Canadian elections has steadily increased since the 1988 federal election.[2] This trend has since trickled down to the provincial level—in Alberta, 4 polls were published during the 2004 election campaign, 8 in 2008, 23 in 2012, and 17 in 2015.

Polls are important in that they inform the actions of parties, campaign, interest groups, the media, and voters. Moreover, polling itself is increasingly becoming the subject of media coverage over and above substantive election issues, leading to the rise of what some have called "horserace journalism."[3] Despite the importance and proliferation of polling, the polling industry in Alberta faced a credibility problem going into the 2015 Alberta election campaign. The polls were widely off the mark in the province's 2012 election, leading to such post-election headlines as " 'We were wrong': Alberta Election pollsters red faced as Tories crush Wildrose."[4] Alberta is not alone in this respect, and other notable examples of polling failures include the 2013 British Columbia, the 2014 Quebec, and the 2014 Ontario provincial elections. The 2015 Alberta election was a chance for pollsters to redeem themselves, and, at least at first blush, they did. The tone of the headlines was different this time. "Pollsters relieved at getting it right in Alberta's unlikely swing to the left," read one such headline in *Maclean's*.[5] But is that a correct assessment?

To answer that, we must first ask a different question: What are the criteria for "getting it right?" The easy answer is accuracy, but that then raises the question of what constitutes accuracy. In the 2015 Alberta election, all but one poll published after the 23 April leaders' debate was "accurate" in the sense that they showed the New Democrats ahead of all other parties, and the New Democrats eventually won the election. However, polling is about more than just predicting who will cross the finish line in first place. Polls make claims about the support of all major political parties in the race. They also include a "margin of error," which provides an upper and lower range within which actual public opinion should be—nineteen times out of twenty, of course. As such, accuracy entails more than just identifying the winner correctly. An accurate poll should also identify the correct ordering of the parties in terms of their proportion of the popular vote. As well, the difference between each party's measured level of support and their actual level of support should not exceed the size of the poll's stated margin of error.[6]

However, accuracy is difficult to assess, given that the only time we can actually verify how the public intends to vote is when they vote on election day. A pre-election poll may be different from the actual election result because it is a poorly executed poll, or because it was accurate at the time but last-minute events caused shifts in public opinion. With this in mind, pollsters, politicians, and pundits alike use qualifiers when commenting on polls, saying they are only "snapshots in time" or that "the only poll that matters is election day."[7] Yet pollsters eagerly take credit when their polls are in line with the actual election results, and—as evidenced by the previously mentioned headlines—the news media can be eager to accept pollsters' claims. In fact, at least for some polling firms, election polling is a service done free of charge as a demonstration of their capabilities and accuracy to prospective clients. As such, there is an implicit predictive value in polls.

Johnston and Pickup describe polls as "trial heats," or preliminary tests between the parties contesting elections that anticipate the eventual result.[8] While there is evidence that polls conducted closer to election day tend to more closely mirror the actual election result,[9] the pattern exhibited by the polling in the 2015 Alberta election suggests most shifts in public opinion occurred after the leaders' debate. This means that even though polls become more accurate the closer they are to election day, all of the polls conducted in Alberta after the leaders' debate should have been reasonably accurate. As this chapter will show, this was not necessarily the case. Polls did perform better in the 2015 election campaign than they did in the 2012 campaign, but they were only marginally better than other recent Canadian provincial elections that are widely regarded as polling failures. This is because most polls did not predict the correct order of the parties in 2015, and because there were systematic errors (i.e., bias) in that the polls overestimated support for political change.

Data and Methods

To facilitate this analysis, we compiled a list of all publicly available polling released during the campaign period.[10] This excludes any proprietary polling conducted for political parties, candidates, or third-party groups, the results of which would not be made available to the news media or general public. This dataset contains seventeen polls in total conducted by ten companies, using a variety of sampling sizes, sampling methods, and interview modes. These are summarized in Table 4.1. The most prolific polling firm was Mainstreet Technologies, which released five polls. Forum Research was similarly prolific, releasing four polls. The only other firm to release more than one poll was EKOS, which released two. Pantheon Research, Leger Marketing, ThinkHQ Public Affairs, Return on Insight, Ipsos-Reid, and Insights West all released one poll apiece.

The most prevalent interview mode was interactive voice response (also known as IVR, or robo-polling), whereby telephone numbers are called at random and those answering are invited by a pre-recorded voice to answer questions by pressing numbers on their phone keypad or saying their answers aloud. Mainstreet, Forum, Pantheon, and EKOS used IVR. Leger and Insights West fielded their polls through online panels, which involve sending surveys via the Internet to people who have agreed to become a member their survey panel. Only Return on Insight used the traditional method of live telephone interviews with a random sample of the population. ThinkHQ and Ipsos-Reid used a mix of live telephone interviews and interviews conducted through their online panels.

Table 4.1. Polling Summary by Firm

FIRM	# OF POLLS	SAMPLE SIZES (N)	MOE (±PP)	TYPE OF MOE	RANDOM SAMPLE?	INTERVIEW MODE
Mainstreet Tech.	5	2,013–4,295	1.5–1.9	Claimed	Yes	IVR
Forum Research	4	801–1,661	2.0–3.0	Claimed	Yes	IVR
Pantheon Research	1	4,131	1.5	Claimed	Yes	IVR
Leger Marketing	1	1,180	2.8	Equiv.	No	Online
ThinkHQ Public Affairs	1	2,114	2.1	Equiv.	No	Online/phone
Return on Insight	1	750	3.6	Claimed	Yes	Phone
EKOS	2	721–823	3.4–3.7	Claimed	Yes	IVR
Ipsos-Reid	1	761	4.1	Equiv.	No	Online/phone
Insights West	1	1,003	3.1	Equiv.	No	Online

Sources: Data from polling firm news releases, www.threehundredeight.com, and Election Almanac (www.electionalmanac.com).

Sample sizes varied from around or just under 1,000 respondents for most firms to 2,000 or greater in the case of Mainstreet, Pantheon, and ThinkHQ. Correspondingly, claimed margins of error ranged from plus or minus 4.1 percentage points, 19 times out of 20 for Ipsos-Reid's sample of 761 respondents, to plus or minus 1.5 points for Mainstreet and Pantheon's polls, with samples of more than 4,000 respondents. According to the guidelines of the Marketing Research and Intelligence Agency, the industry association of market research professionals, it is only appropriate to calculate a margin of error for random probability samples such as telephone surveys.[11] Online panel surveys are considered to be convenience rather than random samples, and as such, it is not appropriate to report a margin of error. That said, polling firms that use online panels do strive to ensure their panel sample is demographically representative of the general population, so an "equivalent margin of error" usually accompanies the results of an online panel survey; this indicates what the margin of error *would* be for a true random probability sample of the same size. Surveys that use a hybrid method involving an online panel sample and live telephone interviewing face the same limitation.

Using the dataset described above, this chapter will evaluate the accuracy of each poll based on the following criteria:[12]

1. The poll correctly anticipates the winner of the election.

2. The poll correctly anticipates the order of the parties in terms of the proportion of the popular vote won by each party.

3. The predicted vote for each party falls within the poll's stated margin of error.

4. The poll's *total absolute polling error*[13] is comparable to accurate polls in other elections.

The first three criteria compare a poll to the final election result. The fourth criterion relies on comparisons with polls conducted during other elections in Canada.

How the Horse Race Unfolded

Before analysing each poll, a simple visual examination helps set the stage for the analysis and provides some preliminary confirmation for the argument. Figure 4.1 shows all seventeen polls that comprise the dataset, plotted by the last date in field. The large symbols on 5 May indicate the actual election result. The trendlines are fitted using the LOWESS smoothing procedure[14] and illustrate the trajectory of each party's support over the course

Figure 4.1. 2015 Alberta Election Polls

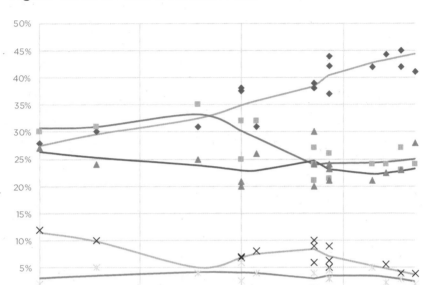

Plotted by last day in field
Final data points indicate actual election result
Lines indicate LOWESS curve; a=0.5

Sources: Data from polling firm news releases, www.threehundredeight.com, and Election Almanac (www.electionalmanac.com).

of the campaign. Two things are readily apparent in Figure 4.1. First, most polls were done in the final week of the campaign. Second, the debate serves as a turning point in the campaign as the fluctuations of party support within the pre- or post-debate periods are less than the shift in support patterns from one period to the other.

PC support does not change very much over the course of the campaign—the party went into the campaign period in an unprecedented and severely weakened state (see Bratt, this volume). The most interesting aspect of the race was the surge in support for the NDP and a decrease in support for the Wildrose, and to a lesser extent, the Liberals. The PCs did not lose the election to the NDP over the course of the campaign (see Thomas, this volume); if anything, they lost it even before the campaign began. The NDP surge was a function of anti-PC voters consolidating around Rachel Notley and the NDP after the leaders' debate.

The final thing to note in Figure 4.1 is the vertical distance between each poll's measurement of a party's level of support and the actual level of support that party receives. While the polls closer to election day are closer to the final result, PC support is consistently underestimated by all but one poll—the Leger poll that finished on 28 April. The numbers for the NDP and the Wildrose tend to be higher than the actual level of support they received, though not as marked as the PCs. The polls were accurate for the two minor parties, the Liberals and the Alberta Party.

How Accurate Were the Polls?

Table 4.2 summarizes, for each poll, the error between the poll's measured level of support for a party and the actual proportion of the vote received by that party in percentage points, the total absolute error, and which of the first three criteria the poll meets. Polls marked with an asterisk (*) denote a firm's final (or only) poll. For the column, "correct order," rows marked as "close" mean the poll incorrectly anticipated the Wildrose to be ahead of the PCs in terms of the popular vote, but that the difference between the two parties is within the poll's stated margin of error. Table 4.2 confirms the conventional wisdom that polls closer to election day tend to be more accurate.[15] However, there is still variation in the total absolute error of polls within periods that must be accounted for, especially since most of the movement in party support was between the pre- and post-debate periods, not within periods.

Almost all of the eleven polls conducted exclusively within the post-debate period correctly anticipated that the NDP would win the popular vote. The only poll that did not was the Mainstreet poll ending on 24 April, which had the Wildrose at 32 per cent and the NDP at 31 per cent—a difference within their stated margin of error. By the first criteria, the polls in 2015 were accurate.

Meeting the second criterion is more difficult. Of the same eleven post-debate polls, only three correctly anticipated that the PCs would

Table 4.2. Polling Error in the 2015 Alberta Election

Final field date	Poll	Moe (±pp)	Party support errors (±pp)					Criteria 1: correct winner	Criteria 2: correct order	Criteria 3: # of parties within moe	Criteria 4: total abs. error
			PC	Wr	NDP	Lib	AP				
7/04/	Mainstreet	1.8	-1.0	7.0	-15.0	8.0	1.0	No	No	2	32.0
9/04	Forum	2.0	-1.0	6.0	-13.0	8.0	0.0	No	No	2	28.0
13/04	Mainstreet	1.8	-4.0	7.0	-11.0	6.0	3.0	No	No	-	31.0
20/04	Mainstreet	1.8	-3.0	11.0	-10.0	0.0	2.0	No	No	1	26.0
23/04	Forum	3.0	-8.0	1.0	-3.0	3.0	4.0	Yes	No	1	19.0
23/04	Pantheon *	1.5	-7.1	8.0	-3.5	2.9	0.6	Yes	No	1	22.1
24/04	Mainstreet	1.5	-2.0	8.0	-10.0	4.0	2.0	No	No	1	26.0
28/04	Leger *	2.8	2.0	0.0	-3.0	2.0	-1.0	Yes	Yes	4	8.0
28/04	Thinkhq *	2.1	-8.0	3.0	-2.0	5.0	2.0	Yes	No	2	20.0
30/04	Roi *	3.6	-4.0	-3.0	-3.0	6.0	2.0	Yes	Yes	3	18.0
29/04	Ekos	3.7	-4.9	-2.7	1.2	2.3	2.6	Yes	Yes	4	13.7
29/04	Mainstreet *	1.9	-7.0	2.0	3.0	1.0	1.0	Yes	No	2	14.0
30/04	Ipsos *	4.1	-4.0	2.0	-4.0	5.0	1.0	Yes	Close	4	16.0
2/05	Forum	3.0	-7.0	0.0	1.0	1.0	3.0	Yes	Close	4	12.0
3/05	Ekos *	3.4	-5.5	0.0	3.3	1.6	0.2	Yes	Close	4	10.6
4/05	Forum *	3.0	-5.0	-1.0	4.0	0.0	1.0	Yes	Close	3	11.0
4/05	Insights west *	3.1	-5.0	3.0	1.0	0.0	1.0	Yes	No	4	10.0
Election result (for reference)			28%	24%	41%	4%	2%				

Sources: Data from Elections Alberta, "Provincial Results—Provincial General Election May 5, 2015," polling firm news releases, threehundredeight.com, and Election Almanac (www.electionalmanac.com).

JANET BROWN AND JOHN B. SANTOS

receive a greater proportion of the popular vote than the Wildrose (Leger, Return on Insight, and the first EKOS poll). Four polls were close, or had the gap between the PCs and Wildrose within their claimed or equivalent margin of error (Ipsos-Reid, the last two Forum polls, and the second EKOS poll). Four polls (both post-debate Mainstreet polls, ThinkHQ, and Insights West) showed the Wildrose ahead of the PCs with a gap greater than their stated margin of error. By the stricter standards set by the second criterion, the polls are less consistent in their accuracy. Note that the second criterion is only concerned with order, and not the size of the gaps, and yet the polls are already coming up short. Interestingly, the first EKOS poll actually outperforms the second EKOS poll in terms of this criterion.

When it comes to correctly anticipating the level of support for each party within the poll's stated margin of error, no poll gets it right for all five parties that won seats. Six polls had four out of five parties within their stated margin of error (Leger, both EKOS polls, Ipsos, Insights West, and the penultimate Forum poll), whereas Return on Insight and the final Forum poll had three out of five parties within their margin of error. ThinkHQ and the final Mainstreet poll got two out of five correct, and the Mainstreet poll immediately following the debate only got one party within the stated margin of error. Perhaps more concerning is that the errors have a consistent direction—namely, PC support is consistently underestimated. All but one post-debate poll (ten in total) showed the PCs at a level of support lower than what they actually received on election day, and of these ten, only one (Ipsos) was within its stated margin of error. Leger was the only firm that showed the PCs at a level of support higher than what they actually received, and Leger's poll was within the stated margin of error.

On the basis of total absolute error, the polls exhibit a wide range of total absolute errors within each time period. Among the post-debate polls, the total absolute error ranges from eight points to twenty-six points. Only when the time horizon is narrowed to polls conducted exclusively within the first four days of May does the total absolute error decrease to the low double digits. Yet, even those final four polls have total absolute errors greater than the lone Leger poll, which was finished fielding almost a week before the election and was the only poll to have a total absolute error in the single digits.

Thus, when the polls conducted during the 2015 Alberta election campaign are compared against one another on the basis of the first three criteria—correctly anticipating the winner, correctly anticipating the order, and correctly measuring each party's support within their stated margin of error—the polls become less consistent in fulfilling the criteria as the criteria become more stringent.

Not only are there clear issues with these polls when comparing them to one another, but these issues become even more clear when they are compared to polls in other elections. Using the metric of average total absolute error for the final batch of polls conducted and released in a given election, Coletto found the final polls in the 2015 Canadian federal election were very accurate and had an average total absolute error of 6.7 points, which is 10.3 points lower than the error in the 2013 British Columbia provincial election (17 points) and 16.3 points lower than the error in the 2012 Alberta provincial election (23 points).[16] Table 4.3 presents average total absolute errors for various time periods during the 2015 Alberta provincial election campaign alongside Coletto's data for comparison. The rows are the average total absolute polling errors for the respective period. The row labelled "final polls average" calculates the average based on the final—or only—poll released by each firm, which makes it an effective subset of the post-debate polls.

The 2012 Alberta election and the 2013 British Columbia election represent well-known poll failures,[17] and the total absolute error, averaged for the final election polls in those elections, was 23 points and 17 points, respectively.[18] In the case of the 2015 Alberta election, while there is a difference between the pre- and post-debate polls, there is no substantial difference between the post-debate polls and the final polls conducted by each firm; both measures have average total absolute errors of about 14.4 points. While that is an improvement over the average total absolute error of the final polls in the 2012 Alberta election, it is an improvement of less than 3 points over the average error of the polls in the 2013 British Columbia election. How can it be that the 2015 Alberta election was a vindication of the beleaguered polling industry when the polls this time around were only marginally better (2.6 points) than the "polling failure" that was the 2013 British Columbia election?

The shortcomings are even more apparent when the 2015 Alberta election polls are compared to an election in which polling was quite accurate—in this case, the 2015 Canadian federal election, in which the average total

JANET BROWN AND JOHN B. SANTOS

Table 4.3. Average Error in the 2015 Alberta Election (By Time Period)

	Time Period	Avg. Total Error
	All polls	18.7
Alberta Election	Pre-debate	26.4
	Post-debate	14.5
	Final polls average	14.4
	Election	**Avg. Total Error**
Comparators, calculated by Coletto and Breguet, 2015	Alberta 2012	23.0
	British Columbia 2013	17.0
	Canada 2015	6.7

Sources: Data from Elections Alberta, "Provincial Results—Provincial General Election May 5, 2015," polling firm news releases, www.threehundredeight.com, and Election Almanac (www.electionalmanac.com). Comparators: Data from David Coletto and Bryan Breguet, "The Accuracy of Public Polls in Provincial Elections," *Canadian Political Science Review* 9 (2015): 41–54.

absolute error was only 6.7 points across the final polls released, or less than half that of the 2015 Alberta election. Even if the sample of polls in the 2015 Alberta election were reduced to the final four polls, the average total absolute error would still be 10.9 points, which would only close half the distance (3.5 points) between the average error of the final polls in the 2015 Alberta election and the federal election of the same year. Moreover, the best-performing poll in terms of total absolute error, the lone Leger poll, had a total error of 8.0 points, which beats the average total error of the final four polls, and is much closer to the average total error from the 2015 federal election.

Discussion

These findings should give pause to the conventional wisdom that the polling companies "got it right" in 2015. While the polls were closer in 2015 than in 2012 in Alberta, they were only marginally better than the polling failure that was the 2013 British Columbia election. Moreover, the polling errors in 2015 were in a consistent direction (i.e., they were biased in a way that underestimated PC support). With the dominant narrative of the election being the David-versus-Goliath story of the NDP taking down the PCs, perhaps it was simply convenient for the commentariat to ignore the reality that, in terms of the popular vote, the PCs actually came in second. Thus, the polling companies got a pass for underestimating PC support because to look too closely at the discrepancies between polls and the actual vote would undermine the prevailing narrative. But, as has been shown with this analysis, the post-debate polls met the four criteria for accuracy either inconsistently, incompletely, or not at all.

Unlike other analyses that have used similar criteria[19] this chapter does not make a judgement about which criteria are more important in evaluating the accuracy of a poll, other than to point out that predicting the winner is too low of a bar to set for accuracy. This is especially true, given the multi-party systems that exist in Canada at both the federal and the provincial levels, and the frequency with which close electoral contests occur. Being off by five points when the claimed margin of error is two points is easier to wave away when the gap between the first- and second-place parties is over twelve points, as it was in this election. If Alberta has transitioned away from a one-party dominant system (see Sayers and Stewart, this volume), and competitive elections will become the norm, polls will have to live up to the margins of error that they claim. The uncertain prospects for the merging of the PCs and the Wildrose mean that, at least for the foreseeable future, polls will also need to worry about correctly ordering multiple parties, rather than just predicting a winner and a loser.

Finally, the bias, or systematic error, exhibited by polling in Alberta calls into question the validity of aggregating multiple polls, as several analysts and organizations do, such as ThreeHundredEight and VoxPopLabs in Canada and FiveThirtyEight in the United States. Trusting that the aggregation of multiple data points converges on the truth rests on the assumption that polling errors are normally distributed.[20] In the figures presented in this chapter, that would mean that there are as many dots above the actual result as there are below the actual result. As has been demonstrated in the 2015, anticipated levels of public support for the PCs were consistently below the proportion of the popular vote the PCs actually garnered, so the necessary conditions for effective aggregation are not met in Alberta. Therefore, aggregating polls when they are biased would just give a false sense of the actual accuracy of the data. Before we can further explore why this issue with

JANET BROWN AND JOHN B. SANTOS

Figure 4.2. 2012 Alberta Election Polls

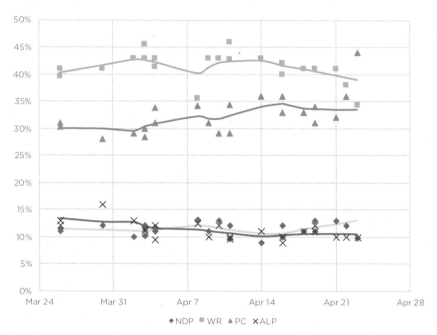

Plotted by last day in field
Final data points indicate actual election result
Lines indicate LOWESS curve; a=0.5

Sources: Data from Elections Alberta, "Provincial Results—Provincial General Election April 23, 2012," polling firm news releases, www.threehundredeight.com, and Election Almanac (www.electionalmanac.com).

accuracy occurs, it is important to note that the 2015 provincial election is just one particular instance of a larger trend of polling issues in Alberta. [21]

As alluded to earlier, the 2012 Alberta provincial election is one of the most well-known cases of polling failure in Canada. Danielle Smith's Wildrose Party was widely expected to defeat Alison Redford's PCs, and with good reason—all the polls released during the campaign said so, as seen in Figure 4.2. Throughout the course of the 2012 election campaign, not a single poll showed the PCs ahead of the Wildrose, despite the PCs eventually winning the election by a margin of 9.7 points. The PCs performed better than all but two polls anticipated, and the Wildrose performed worse than all polls anticipated. Further, the difference between each poll's estimated versus actual PC or Wildrose support was consistently above its margin of error. As stated in the previous section, average total absolute polling error was also very high. Polling in the 2012 Alberta provincial election fails to meet any of the four criteria outlined at the beginning of this chapter.

What differs between 2012 and 2015 is that the party subject to overestimation of support changes from the Wildrose to the NDP. These two parties sit at opposite ends of the political spectrum, but both were the party around which opposition to the PCs coalesced. This suggests that polling bias in Alberta has less to do with ideology and more to do with opposing the status quo. Alberta is not alone in this phenomenon, as the governing parties during the 2013 British Columbia and 2012 Quebec provincial elections also defied campaign-period polls, which tended to say that they would be defeated.

This pattern is not just limited to provincial politics in Alberta, but federal politics in Alberta as well. Figure 4.3 shows the Alberta subsamples from polls conducted during the federal election campaign. While the errors are not as stark as in provincial election data, the same pattern can be seen where the federal Conservative Party of Canada outperforms the polls. The Liberals performed at around the middle of the range anticipated by the polls, and the NDP performed at the lower end of what the polls anticipated. Using the LOWESS curve to analyse this data is particularly helpful, since it both averages and calculates trends in the data. The final data point in the LOWESS curve provide further proof of the systematic underestimation of CPC support (by 5.2 points) and overestimation of NDP support (by 7.0 points).

In 2012, the dominant narrative was was of a last-minute shift in vote intentions away from the Wildrose and towards the PCs,[22] and this is one of the shortcomings of any pre-election poll, regardless of its accuracy. The assumption in 2012 was that several pollsters reaching the same conclusion using different methodologies could not all be wrong. The final poll of that campaign, conducted by Forum Research, gives some support to this argument—it showed the closest race out of all the polls, with the Wildrose at 38 per cent and the PCs at 36 per cent. However, PC strategists maintained that their internal polling consistently showed them ahead of the Wildrose, which suggests the possibility that the Wildrose were never really as far ahead as all of the other polls suggested.[23] In the 2015 federal election campaign in Alberta, most of the movement occurred among progressive

Figure 4.3. 2015 Canadian Federal Election Polls in Alberta

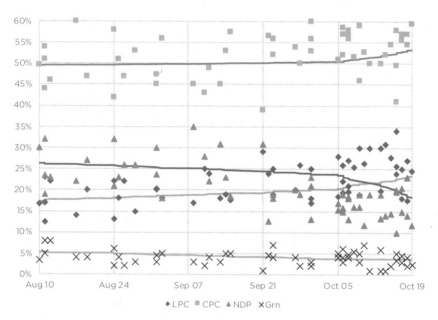

Plotted by last day in field
Final data points indicate actual election result
Lines indicate LOWESS curve; a=0.5

Sources: Data from Wikipedia, "Results of the Canadian federal election, 2015—Results by Province," polling firm news releases, www.threehundredeight.com, and Election Almanac (www.electionalmanac.com).

voters, who moved away from the NDP and to the Liberals. *On the whole*, progressive vote intentions were overestimated and conservative vote intentions were underestimated.

Despite the numerous examples of poll failures, it is important to note those elections—aside from the 2015 federal election—in which polling has been very accurate. More recently, the polls performed very well in the 2017 British Columbia provincial election, with all four polls released in the final week having total absolute errors of less than five points.[24] That the previous British Columbia election is one of the examples of poll failure demonstrates that just because a jurisdiction has a history of inaccurate polling does not mean that all future polls in that jurisdiction are condemned to the same fate. If polling methods in British Columbia can be improved between elections, there is no reason to think that the same could not happen in Alberta. However, in order for improvement to occur, pollsters will need to continue to refine their methods, and consumers of research need to demand more transparency and accountability from pollsters.

Having established that there is a trend in Alberta whereby support for political change is overestimated and support for the status quo is underestimated, the next question is why. As said previously, timing is a factor. The final Forum and EKOS polls in 2015 were among the last polls conducted during the campaign and were also among the most accurate. However, there is still variability between polls conducted around the same time, and the lone Leger poll out-performed all other polls despite being conducted almost a week prior to the final EKOS, Forum, and Insights West polls. It is possible that the Leger poll was the outlier and that all the other polls around the same time were correct, and that support patterns merely shifted in such a way that made them seem more accurate after the fact. However, most of the movement in intention occurred after the leaders' debate, and the 2015 campaign period lacked any events that could have precipitated a last-minute shift in vote intentions, which suggests that vote intentions had more or less coalesced in the final week.

Another possible explanation is methodology. When polling methodology is discussed in the media, the focus tends to be on interview mode (i.e., live-telephone, interactive voice response, or online) and sample size, to the exclusion of other aspects of methodology. In terms of interview mode, the trends are difficult to identify. Leger's was fielded through an online panel. However, other surveys that used online panels (including those that used online panels in conjunction with live telephone interviews) did not fare as well, with ThinkHQ having a total absolute error of 20.0 points and Ipsos having a total absolute error of 16.0. The most common survey mode was IVR, and those polls had a range of total absolute errors. On the higher end, Pantheon and Mainstreet's final polls had total polling errors of 22.1 and 14.0 points, respectively. On the lower end of the range, Forum's and EKOS's final polls had total absolute errors of 11.0 and 10.6 points, respectively. Live telephone interviews, considered the gold standard in polling, were only used in one poll (conducted by Return on Insight), and that poll had a total absolute error of 18.0. Thus, interview mode is not a consistent predictor of a poll's final accuracy.

One methodological aspect that does not seem to have had a bearing on accuracy is sample size. While it is true that margin of error decreases as sample size increases, this is only true *if* the sample is truly representative of the population. If the sample is biased, a larger sample size will only give the illusion of increased accuracy. Just as driving faster when one is lost will only make someone even more lost, increasing sample size when there are flaws in either the construction of the sample or in the execution of contacting that sample will only further contribute to error. In 2015, the polls with the largest sample sizes had some of the highest total polling errors. In the post-debate period, the average total absolute error for all polls with samples greater than 2,000 was 20.0 points, whereas the average total absolute error of polls with samples less than 2,000 was 12.4 points.[25] The four most accurate polls, in terms of total absolute error, all had samples that used less than 1,200 respondents (Leger, EKOS, Forum, and Insights West). Thus, the accuracy of a poll has less to do with its size and more to do with the quality of its sample. If a sample is representative, and if a polling firm takes the necessary steps to contact as many people in that sample without being too ready to replace hard-to-reach individuals, then increasing the sample beyond a certain number does not substantially decrease the margin of error, but it does substantially increase the cost of conducting that poll. This is why most public opinion polls have a sample of around 1,000 respondents—that is the "sweet spot" in terms of balancing accuracy and cost, and it is better to make sure that that sample of 1,000 is representative of the population than it would be to increase its size. The lack of a consistent effect on accuracy of either sample size or methodology in the 2015 Alberta provincial election mirrors previous findings by Coletto and Breguet.[26]

Another methodological aspect worth considering is the length of time a poll is in the field. Field length must balance the competing priorities of allowing adequate time to fully reach the targeted population sample while not taking so long that the poll is no longer a snapshot of a given moment in time. Well-executed polling, regardless of the interview mode, should make multiple attempts to contact a sampled respondent before "dropping" that respondent and re-sampling another respondent. This is because not all segments of the population are as easy to get a hold of as others. Thus, if a polling firm did not make a concerted effort to contact hard-to-reach individuals, there is a danger of introducing selection bias and only speaking to those who want to answer polls—which could be individuals who have an axe to grind against the government. Looking at the top-performing polls in terms of total absolute error, three out of four of them (Leger, EKOS, and Insights West) were fielded over periods of three to five days. The exception is Forum's poll conducted and released on 2 May. Thus, while it does not give a perfect explanation, length of time in field gives a more consistent explanation than either interview mode or sample size.

Lessons for the Future

Clearly, polling in Alberta has room to improve, and the analysis in this chapter shows that polling errors often exceed polls' stated margins of error, and are biased in a way that underestimates support for the status quo and overestimates support for change. And, while polling was better in 2015 than in 2012, it still does not come close to the accuracy of national polling in the 2015 federal election. Based on this analysis, we offer three lessons that can be learned from 2015.

The first lesson is that, while methodology is important, we must move beyond simply discussing interview mode and sample size. How well a poll's sample is constructed and the effort a firm makes to reach a wide cross-section of survey participants may be more important than how a firm interviews those respondents. Sample "stratification" and the use of sample quotas are aspects of methodology that are not often discussed. To ensure representativeness, key demographic subgroups are identified within the population. In order to create a well-constructed sample, efforts must be made to ensure that the demographic composition of the survey sample matches the actual population. This means creating a sample that, at minimum, matches the actual population in terms of age, gender, and region. Efforts should also be made to include hard-to-reach respondents. For a telephone survey, this means making multiple calls to a telephone number chosen at random, before classifying it as "unreachable." In the age of online surveys, this means sending multiple email reminders. If firms are too eager to drop a hard-to-reach respondent and simply sample another, easier-to-reach respondent, then the sample may be biased, and this bias could manifest itself in an under- or overestimation of certain opinions. Dialing 10,000 numbers to complete 1,000 interviews is different from dialing 50,000 numbers to complete 1,000 interviews. The data cannot prove or disprove that selection bias is the reason that PC support is consistently underestimated in Alberta, but the possibility exists that people who want political change are more motivated to share their political opinions, and make themselves more readily available to pollsters by joining online panels, or picking up the telephone when a polling firm calls. All that said, firms are loathe to reveal the details of their sampling and fielding methods, and these other aspects of polling are more difficult to discuss and critique in the media than the more readily understood concepts of interview mode and sample size. However, an honest discussion about which polls are methodologically rigorous cannot occur without this information.[27]

The second lesson is the problematic nature of polling aggregation in Alberta. As popularized by sites such as FiveThirtyEight in the United States and ThreeHundredEight in Canada, some analysts and commentators have taken to aggregating polls in the hopes that more information leads to more accuracy. Statistically speaking, aggregating polling data only works if the estimates of party support provided by polling data are normally distributed around actual public opinion, which, as this analysis has shown, is not the case in Alberta. In fact, in the 2015 Alberta election, a single poll out-performed the aggregation of all polls! Until the accuracy issues of polling in Alberta are resolved across the industry, it would be better to trust selected, well-executed polls than the "collective wisdom" of all polls. The 2016 US presidential election provides further evidence of this. On average, the polls were only off by a couple of points, but they systematically underestimated Donald Trump's support and overestimated Hillary Clinton's support in key battleground states with close races where the election was ultimately decided.[28]

The third point is a warning for the future. The overriding debate in Alberta in 2012 and 2015 was whether or not the PCs should be deposed. With that having happened, it is difficult to say if there is still a systematic bias in polling in Alberta, and if there is, in what way it will manifest itself. Have the NDP become the "new status quo" and will polls underestimate support for them? Or, is the NDP victory an aberration in a streak of small-c conservative governments, and will polls continue to underestimate support for one or the other or both conservative parties in Alberta? Further complicating things is the discussion of a merger between the PC and Wildrose Parties in Alberta, the outcome of which will affect the Alberta party system and the electoral dynamics in subsequent elections.

As this book goes to press, the polling industry has less than a year to resolve the general issue of accuracy and the specific issue of overestimating the desire for change. To the industry's credit, some pollsters readily acknowledge this. Frank Graves, for example, CEO of EKOS, noted the overestimation of NDP support and underestimation of PC support and the need for "better yardsticks" to gauge the effectiveness of polling.[29] It bears reiterating that, in spite of the shortcomings identified in the polling during the 2015 election campaign, there have been improvements since 2012. But there is still much room for improvement, and given the increasingly important role that polling plays in political discourse, it is vitally important that improvement continues.

NOTES

1   Janet Brown operates Janet Brown Opinion Research, a public opinion polling firm based in Calgary. John B. Santos is a project manager at Janet Brown Opinion Research, and an MA student in political science at the University of Calgary. Janet Brown Opinion Research conducts polling in Alberta, but did not release any polls during the 2015 Alberta provincial election campaign.

2   Mark Pickup and Richard Johnston, "Campaign Trail Heats as Election Forecasts: Evidence from the 2004 and 2006 Canadian Elections," *Electoral Studies* 26 (2007): 460–76. Pickup and Johnston surveyed the literature on polling in Canadian federal elections and found that 22 polls were published during the 1988 election campaign, 14 in 1993, 14 in 1997, and 23 in 2000. Their analysis focused on the 2004 and 2006 elections, in which there were, respectively, 26 and 66 polls published.

3   Elizabeth Goodyear-Grant, Antonia Maioni, and Stuart Soroka, "The Role of the Media: A Campaign Saved by a Horserace." *Policy Options* 25 (2004): 86–91; J. Scott Matthews, Mark Pickup, and Fred Cutler, "The Mediated Horserace: Campaign Polls and Poll Reporting," *Canadian Journal of Political Science* 45 (2012): 261–87.

4   National Post Wire Services, " 'We were wrong': Alberta Election pollsters red-faced as Tories crush Wildrose," *National Post* (Toronto), 24 April 2012, Accessed October 31, 2016: http://news.nationalpost.com/news/canada/we-were-wrong-alberta-election-pollsters-red-faced-as-tories-crush-wildrose (accessed 31 October 2016).

5   Bruce Cheadle, "Pollsters relieved at getting it right in Alberta's unlikely swing to the left," *Macleans*, 6 May 2015, http://www.macleans.ca/politics/pollsters-relieved-at-getting-it-right-in-albertas-unlikely-swing-to-the-left/ (accessed 31 October 2016).

6   While almost all polls report a margin of error (or an equivalent margin of error, in the case of online panels, which use non-random, or convenience, samples), polls rarely state that their reported margin of error is actually the "maximum margin of error," which applies to proportions of 50 per cent. Actual margins of error for smaller proportions are less than the maximum margin of error (see Francois Petry and Frederick Bastien, "Following the Pollsters: Inaccuracies in Media Coverage of the Horse-race during the 2008 Canadian Election," *Canadian Journal of Political Science* 46, no. 1 (2013): 1–26 for a full discussion of the reporting and misunderstanding of margins of error). To illustrate this, the maximum margin of error on a typical Alberta poll with a sample of 900 would be ±3.27 percentage points, 19 times out of 20. For a proportion of 25 per cent, the actual margin of error decreases to ±2.83 percentage points. Another difficulty for assessment arises due to polls typically excluding unlikely or undecided voters, which would increase the margin of error (due to lowering the sample size being analyzed). For ease of interpretation, this chapter uses the margin of error reported on the standard methodology "boilerplate" included with most press releases, reports, and news stories.

Pickup and Johnston, in an analysis of the 2004 and 2006 Canadian federal elections, found evidence of bias, or systematic error, in polling at the federal level (see Pickup and Johnson, "Campaign Trail Heats as Election Forecasts"). The most recent American presidential election, the most recent United Kingdom election, and the Brexit Referendum demonstrate that bias in polling may not be confined to Alberta, or even Canada in particular.

7   For example, Forum Research includes a disclaimer with their poll reports that reads, "This research is not necessarily predictive of future outcomes, but rather, captures opinion at one point in time. Election outcomes will depend on the success of the parties in getting out their vote."

8   Pickup and Johnston, "Campaign Trail Heats as Election Forecasts."

9   Elias Walsh, Sarah Dolfin, and John DiNardo, "Lies, Damn Lies, and Pre-Election Polling." *The American Economic Review* 99, no. 2 (2009): 316–22.

10   The dataset was assembled over the course of the election campaign from news releases from polling firms, stories posted on mainstream news media websites, and "poll aggregators" such as ThreeHundredEight (www.threehundredeight.com) and Election Almanac (www.electionalmanac.com). No polling firms, media outlets, or bloggers are responsible for the analysis in this chapter.

11   See MRIA's *Code of Conduct for Members*, http://mria-arim.ca/about-mria/standards/code-of-conduct-for-members (accessed 31 October 2016).

12   While these criteria make use of quantitative data (i.e., numbers), they are essentially qualitative in nature, and this chapter does not construct an "index of accuracy" using the criteria. For such an attempt, see Elizabeth A. Martin, Michael W. Traugott, and Courtney Kennedy, "A Review and Proposal For a New Measure of Poll Accuracy,"

Public Opinion Quarterly 69 (2005): 342–69, which uses similar criteria in quantitative evaluations of polling accuracy.

13   Total absolute polling error is the sum of the absolute differences between each party's level of support as measured by a poll and the actual level of support that each respective party receives at election time. See David Coletto, "Polling and the 2015 Federal Election," in *The Canadian Federal Election of 2015*, ed. Jon H. Pammett and Christopher Dornan, 305–26 (Toronto: Dundurn, 2016).

14   LOWESS stands for "locally weighted scatterplot smoothing," which is a smoothing algorithm that fits a curve through a set of data points by weighting data points closer to a point in time greater than data points further away from that point in time. This is as opposed to trendlines that use functions, or moving averages that use a moving set of data points surrounding a given point in time that are equally weighted (see Pickup and Johnston, "Campaign Trail Heats as Election Forecasts"). Pickup and Johnston use a more complex procedure that calculates the LOWESS curve based on a "poll of polls" that distributes polling data orthogonally along each date a poll was conducted. That method did not produce substantively different results than simply using the last date in field, so the latter was used to facilitate ease of interpretation.

15   Walsh, Dolfin, and DiNardo, "Lies, Damn Lies, and Pre-Election Polling."

16   Coletto, "Polling and the 2015 Election."

17   J. Scott Matthews, "Horserace Journalism under Stress?" *Canadian Election Analysis 2015: Communication, Strategy, and Democracy*, 2015, http://www.ubcpress.ca/CanadianElectionAnalysis2015 (accessed 31 October 2016).

18   Coletto, "Polling and the 2015 Election."

19   Martin, Traugott, and Kennedy, "A Review and Proposal For a New Measure of Poll Accuracy."

20   Pickup and Johnston, "Campaign Trail Heats as Election Forecasts."

21   Ibid.

22   Tu Thanh Ha, " 'Entire environment shifted': Pollsters seek answers following Alberta Election," *Globe and Mail* (Toronto), 24 April 2012, http://www.theglobeandmail.com/news/politics/entire-environment-shifted-pollsters-seek-answers-following-alberta-election/article1390916/ (accessed 31 October 2016).

23   Karen Kleiss, "Alberta Election 2012: Smith takes the reins as front-runner, poll reveals," *Edmonton Journal*, 18 April 2012, http://www.edmontonjournal.com/news/Alberta+Election+2012+Smith+takes+reins+front+runner+poll+reveals/6477884/story.html (accessed 31 October 2016). PC strategist Stephen Carter was on record saying that he was not worried about either losing the election or only winning minority government in 2012.

24   The four polls were Ipsos (conducted 4–6 May), Mainstreet Research (conducted 5–6 May), Insights West (conducted 5–8 May), and Forum Research (conducted 8 May). The total absolute errors for each poll, calculated on the basis of parties that won seats, were

1.8 (Ipsos), 4.8 (Mainstreet), 1.5 (Insights West), and 2.2 (Forum) points. See Elections British Columbia, https://catalogue.data.gov.bc.ca/dataset/44914a35-de9a-4830-ac48-870001ef8935 (accessed 8 August 2018).

25 The post-debate polls with sample sizes greater than 2,000 were the three Mainstreet polls. See Table 4.2 for the list of the relevant polls.

26 David Coletto and Bryan Breguet, "The Accuracy of Public Polls in Provincial Elections," *Canadian Political Science Review* 9 (2015): 41–54.

27 André Turcotte calls for the reporting of similar criteria. See his post-mortem on polling in the 2011 Canadian federal election, "Polls: Seeing Through the Glass Darkly," in *The Canadian Federal Election of 2011*, ed. Jon H. Pammett and Christopher Dornan, 195–218 (Toronto: Dundurn, 2012).

28 Carl Bialik and Harry Enten, "The Polls Missed Trump. We Asked Pollsters Why," *FiveThirtyEight*, 9 November 2016, https://fivethirtyeight.com/features/the-polls-missed-trump-we-asked-pollsters-why/ (accessed 31 October 2016).

29 Frank Graves, "EKOS Accurately Predicts NDP Majority Victory in Alberta . . . but should we have better polling yardsticks?" 7 May 2015, http://www.ekospolitics.com/index.php/2015/05/ekos-accurately-predicts-ndp-majority-victory-in-alberta/ (accessed 31 October 2016).

5

Alberta Politics Online: Digital Retail Politics and Grassroots Growth, 2006–16

Peter Malachy Ryan

Canadians' discussions of the potential political benefits of using online social media tools for democratic purposes have become predominantly critical after the 2016 US presidential election, with several parliamentary committees being called to deal with social media privacy and election issues in light of Canadians' concerns, specifically because of the Cambridge Analytica Facebook scandal, alongside the rise of Internet trolls, fake news, and automated software robots ("bots" for short). These relatively new and worrisome online trends demonstrate Internet users' power to shape and disrupt electoral attitudes and beliefs, and in so doing, challenge the conceptions of a dominant liberal democratic media.[1] The 2015 Alberta provincial election did not see the level of online disruption demonstrated by Hillary Clinton's private email server scandal, nor the Trump presidential campaign's use of Twitter, which as this book goes to press includes communications that are viewed by many experts as possible evidence of impeachable obstruction of justice surrounding his campaign team's alleged collusion with Russian hackers to create fake news to sway voters, and his suspected legal perils around porn star Stormy Daniels' non-disclosure agreement right before the election.

This chapter traces social media over ten years of Alberta provincial elections to show that the emergence of online trolling and the development of fake partisan news groups were prefigured at the provincial level by the viral online promotion of Alberta's "gotcha" political moments and sophisticated "trial balloon" wedge issues; in hindsight, examples of such tactics allow us to extrapolate the growing seeds of online campaign disruption into the emerging fake news era. The rise of digital politics is surely a sign of a new, tech-savvy electorate challenging and changing the "horse race" narrative propagated by the traditional media, in which political discussions occurred while sitting in front of the television or over the fence with neighbours. Political parties have to adapt to the changing demands of digitally attuned voters, which as this chapter identifies, the then governing Alberta Progressive Conservative Party did not effectively achieve in the 2015 election. This factor, along with economic uncertainty in the province, Premier Prentice's distanced, elite leadership style, and the changing electoral climate, led to the end of the PC dynasty.

Perhaps the top viral social media moment to help decide the 2015 Alberta election occurred during the televised leadership debate of 23 April. Ahead of the debate, the media had developed the narrative of a horse race between the elite, corporate-beholden Alberta Progressive Conservatives under new leader Jim Prentice, and the folksy, grassroots NDP leader Rachel Notley, who was described as being as comfortable on camera as she was knocking on doors in rural trailer parks.[2] The NDP campaigned on equity, fairness, and trust, which was highlighted by Notley's performance in the televised leadership debate when she casually parried Prentice's ill-phrased "math is difficult" quip, affixing to it the tropes of the condescending elitist versus the friendlier grassroots NDP in the eyes of many Albertans, both online and off. Twitter in particular exploded right at 7:24 p.m. with the hashtag "#mathishard" trending to mock Prentice.[3]

With this context in mind, how have Alberta's political parties used and adapted their websites and selected social media channels during provincial election campaigns over the past decade to attract voter support?

To answer this question, this chapter first identifies and summarizes the early and developing strategic party trends in online political campaigns for the 2008, 2012, and 2015 Alberta elections. The research presented here documents how a leader's mediated image is as important as her or his in-person grassroots efforts, which are also now captured in their representative digital shadows online over time. Interactive and integrated social media use thereby returns elements of what American academics in the 1990s defined as door-to-door community "retail politics," which were developed to

PETER MALACHY RYAN

counteract mass mediated broadcast leadership-centred politics. Like retail politics, social media use similarly allows for two-way discussions, mimicking face-to-face communications, and savvy online political marketing strategists can entice users to support one party over another by aligning their communications with the candidate's believed in-person authenticity.

To begin this analysis, a common content analysis study of the provincial parties' election websites provides readers with an aerial overview of the website features and social media channels selected over time by party strategists. Next, the chapter documents which social media were and were not used during the shift from the Alberta PCs' almost forty-four-year reign to the NDP's "Orange Chinook" in 2015. The analysis focuses on the developing uses of the four top social media selected by the parties, specifically Facebook (2004), YouTube (2005), Twitter (2006), and Instagram (2010), in the order of each tool's release. Those four key social media channels are examined to broadly identify how successful each party was in their use of these online tools during each election campaign.

Overall, the analysis reveals how the American retail politics strategies of the 1990s have been translated for the new century into "digital retail politics" that require the lived persona of the politician to match the expectations cast by, and framed in, their digital shadows. We have seen a similar trend over the past ten years of Alberta politics, where the parties are on a similar trajectory to that of the national Canadian parties in terms of their development of coordinated online strategies that use what contemporary social media researchers describe as "market intelligence" (i.e., analyzing publically available social media discussions and information to inform a campaign), and active "market surveillance" (i.e., creating partisan digital tools or "apps" that allow the parties to monitor and track users across online platforms, in terms of events, donations, and other metrics).[4]

The evidence revealed by the following content analysis supports a critical interpretation that in the 2015 election the NDP's grassroots efforts aligned well with Rachel Notley's brand and digital "market intelligence" strategy to attract a coalition of disgruntled PC supporters and a new generation of Albertans (see Melanee Thomas's chapter in this volume). In contrast, Prentice struggled in the 2015 election to project a successful vision for the future of Alberta, as delivered through traditional media channels like newspaper, radio, and television, and a very limited online campaign, which missed attracting younger voters. The rise of the Wildrose Party as the Official Opposition is another key social media story from 2015, as similar to the NDP it started from a grassroots effort that was then aligned with a maturing online political marketing strategy.

Trends in Provincial Politics Online: From Information Politics to Digital Retail Politics

One party's campaign disruption can obviously become a competitor's advantage. Table 5.1 below provides a quick timeline of a few key party attempts to use the Internet in an open democratic capacity, compared to some of the online disruptions in the Alberta elections from 2006 to 2016. Many of the examples in Table 5.1 may be familiar to those interested in Alberta politics, and some are taken up throughout this chapter to situate changes online during the decade in question.

It is difficult to discern if the rise of experienced online party strategists could have stopped the impact of these foibles, missteps, scandals, and "gotcha" viral social media moments in Alberta, as compared to traditional media. However, the Internet has certainly accelerated the spread of both real news and misinformation, which can put a party into crisis-communication mode with one single, ill-fated Tweet or Facebook post.

Contemporary political social media research describes how information politics has impacted election campaigning and strategies both positively and negatively. Political theorist Pippa Norris described this shift as follows:

> In the post-war era, direct communications between citizens and their representatives—which we might term "retail politics"—have been eroded by the decline of traditional mass membership party organizations. At the same time mediated communications have substantially increased in the modern campaign. . . . As a result many believe that national elections in most industrialized societies have become contests revolving around leadership-centered media campaigns.[5]

PETER MALACHY RYAN

Table 5.1. Major Party Uses of the Internet and Online Disruptions in Alberta 2006–16

TIMELINE	ONLINE EVENT OR ISSUE	CAMPAIGNS DISRUPTED
3 March 2008: Election Day		
2010	**Oil Sands Action Group:** This online social media group was created by a non-profit organization to promote facts and media frames about the oil industry. Little is known about the group's donors or sponsors, though they frequently target narratives espoused by the political left.	NDP
19 November 2010	**"Cookie exchange":** Alberta Health Services president and chief executive officer Stephen Duckett refused to respond to the media about the costly provincial health-care merger, stating he was eating a cookie. It cost him his job, Albertans $680,000 in his severance pay, and painted the PCs as a party of elites.	PC
4 April 2012	**Conscience rights:** Wildrose Party support for religious conscience rights were targeted by the Redford PCs as discriminatory, frightening, and dangerous; the story went viral online through social media.	Wildrose
16 April 2012	**"Eternity in the lake of fire":** A year-old homophobic blog post by preacher and Wildrose Party candidate Allan Hunsperger went viral online as opposition parties charged the Wildrose Party with being too extreme.	Wildrose
18 April 2012	**YouTube:** "Wildrose Momentum" YouTube video crests 100,000 views, among the most views in Canadian political history to date, and some polls have the Wildrose tied or ahead of the PCs.	PC
23 April 2012: Election Day		
13 February 2013	**Blog:** The blog called "MadamPremier: A Blog Documenting Sexism Against Premiers" highlights, identifies, and critiques Wildrose MLAs' use of sexist and misogynist language in the legislature and media over time.	Wildrose
28 October 2013	**PressProgress:** This online news and analysis group was created by the Broadbent Institute on this date; the group is modelled on the left-wing Think Progress website in the United States.	PC/Wildrose
February 2015	**The Rebel Media:** The Canadian far-right political commentary website is founded by former Sun News Network host and Albertan Ezra Levant.	PC/Liberal/NDP
5 February 2015	**Online survey:** The Prentice-led PCs use an online survey to ask Albertans how the government should deal with the 2015 budgetary deficit, then ignore parts of the results that included Albertans support for increasing corporate taxes.	PC
21 February 2014	**Economic dashboard:** The PCs release an online economic dashboard to aggregate information about the government metrics, in an effort to be open and transparent (http://economicdashboard.alberta.ca).	None: The dashboard is still in use as of this publication.
5 May 2015: Election Day		

Sources: Data compiled from online sources as indicated over the course of the 2015 Alberta Provincial Election, and summarized by the author.

Overall, the localized, pre-Internet retail politics of the early 1990s, where political candidates stumped in each neighbourhood in their riding to sell their party platform at the grassroots level, have been dramatically changed by the hyper-mediated, permanent campaigns of the twenty-first century.[6] To date, political marketing strategies in Canada have developed in concert with, and are greatly influenced by, the billion-dollar, professionalized, leadership-focused election campaigns in the United States, but they also must be contextualized within the regionalized British Westminster tradition as it is interpreted in Canada.

Provincial elections have demonstrably been a smaller-scale refinement of federal tactics rather than a test of new tools to use in the next federal election through any connected political party allegiances. This trend is mainly due to the decreased amount of financial and skilled labour resources at the provincial level, but the following analysis identifies several times that provincial tactics have led the way prior to federal elections, particularly in holding the parties to account on provincial social and policy issues (e.g., the online misogynist attacks against Premier Alison Redford in 2013, when Wildrose leader Brian Jean apologized after a 2015 viral video leak the numerous discussions of the NDP's carbon tax implementation in 2016). In this way, there is movement back and forth from the provincial to national campaigns, and from federal to provincial, in terms of strategies and use of social media, at different scales of practice.

The academic research into online provincial politics since the release of the public Web in 1992 can at this point be segmented into four distinct periods, which are outlined here to help situate the following study.

The first era, "information politics" (1992–2004), began with descriptive research studies, which used traditional content analyses or critical discourse analysis to help us better understand the early uses of the Internet.[7] In the lead-up to the 2008 Alberta provincial election, few Canadian researchers had specifically focused on online party politics. The Canadian Communication Association's first full panel on Internet politics happened in 2006, and the Canadian Political Science Association followed in 2009. Early studies mainly documented which candidates and parties could afford Web pages, or how they utilized email or early Web 2.0 tools to attract voters.[8] Generally, their theoretical responses fell within the limited dichotomies of technological determinists and cyber optimists, which would be challenged by the developing media-ecologies perspectives when social media arrived.[9]

The immediate forms of twenty-four-hour-a-day Web 2.0 social media interactions paved the way for the second era, that of the "permanent campaign" (2004–8). Researchers began creating new methods and digital tracking tools in order to reveal how politics was unfolding online when the early Web tools moved beyond simply broadcasting descriptive politician contact information, and started replacing bricks-and-mortar businesses entirely.[10] Online political communication became accelerated at this point, so researchers developed numerous ways to track online discourse, or "scrape" information, from blogs and proprietary applications such as Facebook, Twitter, and YouTube.[11] Key patterns in the research started to emerge in terms of how social media were allowing users to do more collaboratively and democratically, outside the traditional, hierarchically dominant corporate or government structures.[12]

The third era, that of political marketing and market intelligence (2008–15) saw the power of algorithmic online tracking methods become firmly established in business and political communication as market intelligence techniques were used in the 2008 election of Barack Obama. Obama's coordinated online campaign raised $403 million from 3.95 million donors at a time when mobile phones created a revolution in immediate donations at live events. In 2008, Apple launched its App Store to help iPhone users to select from over 35,000 downloadable mobile software applications within one year of its launch; these "apps" included the now ubiquitous Facebook, YouTube, and Twitter. As of 2016, there were more than 2 million apps available, with the top three earliest innovators still remaining dominant.[13] Online analytics and apps helped professional campaigns to determine and evaluate the success of their political advertising. Canadian political communication researchers started to build off American research into political marketing strategies during this period, identifying how data could be used to align a leader's image with the party's brand and online campaign.[14]

It is during the fourth and current era, that of market surveillance and digital retail politics (2015–present), that parties' marketing abilities began to mature, balancing broadcasting techniques, digital two-way communication, and local grassroots interactions. The 2015 Alberta provincial election did not reach the level of market surveillance found in the federal election of four months later, when the Trudeau Liberals were able to uniquely couple their party donor database and their Liberalist voter-management database using two new apps: first, their innovative myPlatform app, and second, their Events app.[15] Those two apps allowed for interoperability with their other systems, and allowed the party to create an ongoing means for monitoring supporter interest on key issues, alongside attendance and interests in local events, making these the first two apps made available online to Canadian voters at the federal level. These new partisan apps allowed the Liberals to have a direct, ongoing feedback of users' support of key platform issues and events, which were not previously available in a closed partisan format (previously, public Facebook groups could operate similarly, but the apps allowed the Liberals internal control of the user data to surveil which events might have enough interest for a candidate to attend, or to send out the leader, in a battleground riding).

The Liberals' data-management efforts contrasted with the Conservatives' Constituent Information Management System (CIMS, or C2G), and the NDP's Populus, which, at their most basic, provided data on traditional door-to-door, mail, and telephone campaigns, while missing further ongoing tracking of voter intentions over time through direct online interactions.[16] The updated edition of Susan Delacourt's *Shopping for Votes* (2016) describes the Console software that the federal Liberals used to amalgamate all data for their 2015 campaign. Previously, Liberalist was the main competitor to C2G, but only the latter software included GPS tracking capabilities. With the Console, the Liberals' online dominance matched the image and persona of Justin Trudeau, the "selfie king," aiding the party's efforts to get online users to hit the donation button, or become a Liberal member, while using market surveillance of user preferences on the two apps to tailor their key messaging both locally and to the masses.

Overall, these academic accounts can help contextualize how the NDP developed their grassroots efforts alongside their online political marketing to build a mature digital retail politics strategy in the 2015 campaign, as evidenced by the following content analysis.

The Case Study: A Content Analysis of Alberta Elections Online, 2006–16

As a limitation, the following analysis mainly focuses on the top three seat-winning parties in each Alberta election since 2008, though data has been collected for the other parties and is available upon request. In plain terms, the content-analysis methods employed below include counting the Web tools, social media followers, and views or uses of pertinent social media channels for each of the top parties. For those interested, more information about the research methods can be found through Ryerson University's Infoscape Research Lab website and their publications.[17]

In the following three sections, the analyses presented here explore and contextualize each of the following three Alberta elections:

1. The 3 March 2008 Alberta Election Online: Information Politics

2. The 23 April 2012 Alberta Election Online: Political Marketing to Market Intelligence

3. The 5 May 2015 Alberta Election Online: Digital Retail Politics and Grassroots Growth

The overall findings for this research reveal the growth of social media users in the political arena from the mere hundreds in 2008, to the thousands in 2012, and the tens of thousands in 2015. These trends align with the developing sophistication of the political marketing strategies described in the academic research outlined above.

The 3 March 2008 Alberta Election Online: Information Politics

Before 2006, the websites of Alberta's provincial parties focused largely on email and online profiles of candidates, with some using blogs and "RSS" feeds.[18] Proprietary social media like Facebook were just starting to be used in federal politics, but had not yet reached the provincial level. By 2008, 73 per cent of voting-age Canadians (19.2 million people) were online, up from

Figure 5.1a. Alberta NDP Website, http://www.albertandp.ca, 3 March 2008

PETER MALACHY RYAN

Figure 5.1b. Alberta Liberal Party Website, http://albertaliberal. com, 3 March 2008

Figure 5.1c. Alberta PC Party Website, http://www.albertapc.ab.ca, 3 March 2008

PETER MALACHY RYAN

Table 5.2. 3 March 2008: Alberta Partisan Election Campaign
Websites

PARTY	NDP	LIBERAL	PC
Leader	Brian Mason	Kevin Taft	Ed Stelmach
Polls Week Prior	7%	24%	55%
Final Seat Totals	2 (lost 2)	9 (lost 7)	72 (gained 12)
Splash Page	See Figure 5.1a	See Figure 5.1b	See Figure 5.1c
Source URL	http://www.albertandp.ca	http://albertaliberal.com	http://www.albertapc.ab.ca
Donation link:	Yes	Yes	Yes
Newsletter link:	Yes	Yes	Yes
Email link:	Yes	Yes	Yes
Issue summary:	Yes (on front page)	Yes (linked)	Yes (linked)
Candidate links:	Yes	Yes	Yes
*RSS link:	No	Yes	Yes
*Facebook link	No	No	Yes
*Flickr link:	No	No	Yes
*Podcasts link:	No	No	Yes
*YouTube link:	No	No	Yes
*Twitter link:	No	No	Yes

Note: *denotes a variation in use in this election. The party website information in this
table is organized from left to right on the partisan political spectrum. The social media
links are organized in order of the technology's introduction or company's founding (e.g.,
email, 1972; RSS feeds, 1995; Facebook, 2004; Flickr, 2004; podcasts, 2005; YouTube,
2005; Twitter, 2006). The poll numbers are taken from Leger Marketing on 25 February
2008, and the website images are taken from the Internet Archive. The Wildrose Alliance
Party was not included in this example as they won no seats in the election; their leader
Paul Hinman lost his seat, despite the party having 8 per cent of popular support in the
week prior to the election.

68 per cent in 2005. Globally, there were 1.5 billion Internet users and 172 million websites. Despite these high numbers, the 2008 Alberta provincial election was not a watershed moment in terms of online engagement for the nearly 3.5 million Albertans, and with a turnout rate of 40.59 per cent, it was definitely the lowest point for voter turnout in an Alberta provincial election, and significantly, in all of Canadian history.[19]

Alberta's provincial online campaigns can be placed in a historical context knowing that the publicly available Web was launched in 1992, but it was not until the 2004 Canadian federal election that the federal NDP created a professionally competitive party campaign website.[20] That 2004 website received 60,000 hits per week and 6,000 emails, which influenced the party to create its first donation page after party organizers recognized the power of the Internet to attract voter support. This timeline provides some context as to why the 2008 provincial Alberta election, as shown in Table 5.2 below, clearly lagged in terms of being an engaging online election campaign, with only the PCs having enough funding to create a full website and effectively attempt early uses of the common social media tools available at the time.

The online data captured for this election includes only a few pages still publicly saved and accessible through the Internet Archive (internetarchive. org), with many of the links to digital content unavailable even for the few pages it has archived. There is no other public backup of the party websites, and we have effectively lost parts of our provincial history as the parties commonly delete old pages so that they control the history of their brand and no past evidence can be used against them in future campaigns.

For example, a roundly criticized Flash application introduction to the 2008 PC website is no longer available in the Internet Archive, but a copy was scraped and captured by the research group at Ryerson University's Infoscape Research Lab. The Flash animation was of Ed Stelmach; it suffered from common Flash software update glitches and was rather poorly designed. For this reason, the analysis of the 2008 and 2012 elections online is based mainly on work myself and others at the Infoscape Research Lab helped to document.

The data captured in Table 5.2 was built using the content-analysis categories that political scientist Sandford Borins created in his initial analysis of each political party's website on the first day of the 2008 election. Borins argued that the Liberals had the best website at that time.[21] The PC website did not come alive until the second-last week of the campaign, countering Borins' initial critique to become the top website upon its launch. Out of all of the parties, the PCs used the most media channels to keep in touch with the electorate.

Borins would later attribute the PCs' professionally designed website to the strong funding the party had built up over the years, money that definitely paid off in terms of votes, which in turn resulted in more party funding after Ed Stelmach's landslide victory. Notably, the Liberals and NDP have kept the same domain names since 2008, whereas the PCs have rebranded their URLs for each election since, to craft particular campaign branding and messaging.

Overall, Table 5.2 shows that all party websites were using YouTube in the campaign, but the Liberals and the NDP were not using some common professional political marketing practices, including linking from their websites directly to proprietary social media such as Facebook, Flickr, Twitter, or YouTube. Only the PCs had developed their Web presence to that level. However, some unique uses of online media in the 2008 election included the NDP's list of a "top priorities" window pane, and the Liberals' posting of all of Kevin Taft's speeches. The NDP's use of a priority list was reminiscent of the federal Conservatives' innovation of a "key issues" pane during the 2006 election to sell their five-point platform to voters.

Facebook Supporters in the 2008 Alberta Provincial Election

There were 100 million Facebook users globally in 2008, four short years after the platform's initial launch in 2004. Table 5.3 provides the final results of the provincial party leaders' Facebook friend totals during the 2008 provincial election, none of which broke the 1,000-friend mark.

In other words, Facebook did not play a major role in terms of influencing many Albertans, let alone party supporters, to engage through that medium. It is a similar story for the other social media campaigns as well.

YouTube in the 2008 Alberta Provincial Election

YouTube was launched in 2005, and in 2008 over ten hours of video were uploaded each minute. The first mobile phone YouTube app was also launched in 2008, but it would not play a significant role in the 2008 provincial election.

Table 5.3. Party Leader Facebook Supporters (2008 Election—Final Results)

PARTY LEADER	SUPPORTERS ("FRIENDS")
Kevin Taft Personal Profile (Alberta Liberals)	757 friends (up by 14 from last week)
Ed Stelmach Fan Club (PCs)	465 member (up by 4 from last week)
Re-Elect Brian Mason, Edmonton Highlands-Norwood (NDP)	280 members (down by 98 from last week)
George Read (Green Party of Alberta)	233 members (up by 6 from last week)
Paul Hinman (Wildrose Alliance Party of Alberta)	128 members (down by 34 from last week)

Source: Infoscape Research Lab data scrape in 2008, available via the Internet Archive: http://web.archive.org/web/20081120212329/http://www.infoscapelab.ca/taxonomy/term/39

Similar to the party websites, the parties control their YouTube channels. The parties have removed all their previous videos from YouTube at this point; they are either lost to history or only available on some partisan's archive. Table 5.4 provides a content analysis of the top YouTube videos in the 2008 campaign. The weekly viewership was only in the hundreds of views. One week after the election, the top YouTube videos all returned to the usual coverage. In Table 5.4, the top video was Stelmach's victory speech, but after that many of the dominant issues in Alberta politics, rather than partisan posts, were being viewed. These top issues included discussions of the oil sands, conspiracy theory videos about North American possibly consolidating into one economic zone, and videos focusing on the environment and infrastructure. In other words, it was as if the election hadn't happened, and in this sense, the 2008 election did not include a major YouTube event.

PETER MALACHY RYAN

Table 5.4. Party Leader YouTube Video Views and Tone—Final Week 2008

ED STELMACH (LEADER OF THE ALBERTA PROGRESSIVE CONSERVATIVE PARTY)

Video Title	Upload Date	Views Last Week	Affiliation	Tone
1. Ed Stelmach Uncut - Chateau Louis Victory Speech Part 2	3 March 2008	613	Vlogger	Positive
2. Alberta - Fortis et liber (strong and free)	5 March 2008	598	Lobby Group: CanadaPetitions	Negative
3. Ed Stelmach says Myth - Crude Awakening Part 1 of 3	24 December 2007	594	Vlogger: Streaming CBC Media	Negative
4. Ed Stelmach says Myth - Crude Awakening Part 2 of 3	24 December 2007	585	Vlogger: Streaming CBC Media	Negative
5. Alberta PC - AGM 2007 (Part 1 of 2)	5 May 2007	576	Alberta PC Party	Positive

KEVIN TAFT (LEADER OF THE ALBERTA LIBERAL PARTY)

Video Title	Upload Date	Views Last Week	Affiliation	Tone
1. CFIB Interview with Alberta Liberal Leader Kevin Taft	29 February 2008	574	Interest Group	Positive
2. PART 2/6 : ALBERTA ELECTION ON CPAC : TAFT	28 February 2008	541	AlbertaVotes2008	Positive
3. Kevin Taft and Hugh MacDonald on the Royalty Review Report	5 February 2008	391	Alberta Liberal Caucus	Positive
4. The Heart of a Western Tiger, Part III	28 February 2008	381	Alberta Liberal Caucus	Positive
5. Meet Kevin Taft	5 February 2008	368	Alberta Liberal Party	Positive

Table 5.4. Party Leader YouTube Video Views and Tone—Final Week 2008 (con't)

BRIAN MASON (LEADER OF THE ALBERTA NDP)

Video Title	Upload Date	Views Last Week	Affiliation	Tone
1. NDP Affordable Housing Rally - Brian Mason	18 May 2007	320	Vlogger	Positive
2. National Day of Action - Brian Mason	28 November 2007	282	Vlogger	Positive
3. Deron Bilous and Brian Mason call Election '08	4 February 2008	227	NDP	Positive
4. PART 4/6 : ALBERTA ELECTION ON CPAC : BABCOCK	26 February 2008	200	AlbertaVotes2008	Neutral
5. AUPE Labour Rally - Brian Mason	28 October 2007	195	Vlogger	Positive

Sources: Infoscape Research Lab data scrape in 2008, available via the Internet Archive: http://web.archive.org/web/20081120212329/http://www.infoscapelab.ca/taxonomy/term/39.

Twitter in the 2008 Alberta Provincial Election

Twitter was founded in 2006, and it had 6 million users in 2008. Tamara Small's research tracked political leaders' uses of Twitter during this period, and Table 5.5 demonstrates how little the tool was being used at the provincial level during the 2008 election.

The 2008 Alberta election results were definitely a shock for many who predicted Ed Stelmach losing some seats to Kevin Taft's Liberals in Calgary based on a disconnect between the online media and the mainstream media. As identified above, the online media was highly dominated by the other parties' criticisms of Stelmach; many media analysts commented that the mainstream media and polls in Alberta provided a more balanced account of the campaign, with up to 30 per cent of voters undecided heading into election day. Those same 30 per cent did not show up to vote, along with

Table 5.5. Use of Twitter by MPs, MLAs, and Political Parties as of July 2009

NAME	FOLLOWERS	FOLLOWING	TOTAL TWEETS	TWEETS PER DAY
pmharper	16,802	13,410	175	0.9
premierstelmach	1,386	1,210	138	0.7
davidswann	683	1,519	105	0.5
albertaliberals	253	182	191	1.3
mypcmla	250	132	156	0.9

Sources: Tamara Small, "Canadian Politics in 140 Characters: Party Politics in the Twitterverse," *Canadian Parliamentary Review* 33, no. 3 (2010): 42.

some of their friends. Because of the voter turnout, the negative online media campaign was not emblematic of any major new political movements that were transformed into representative political power in Alberta.

In other words, Stelmach's landslide victory was not built from social media, but was instead formed on the lowest voter turnout in Canadian history. The poor voter turnout was read in many different ways in the media, including some of the following: people do not turn out to vote when they're happy with the government; people do not vote when they believe pre-election polls are going to be true; the media and the oil lobby did not sway people to vote for the Wildrose Party, and Ed Stelmach was therefore chosen as Alberta's resounding choice; or people do not vote when they do not like their options.

From this analysis, the Alberta online election of 2008 clearly falls into the "information politics" era, as the use of certain partisan digital strategies were just being developed and aimed at broadcasting party messages, not two-way communication. The campaign did not invite any major online "gotcha" moments, or sway voters' intentions. Pippa Norris's description of the leader-centric, mass-mediated election campaign are quite apt for this election, as it did not include open town halls (either online or off), or successful grassroots strategies from the PCs' competitors.

The 23 April 2012 Alberta Election Online: Political Marketing to Market Intelligence

As Duane Bratt shows in chapter 2, the oil industry's dissatisfaction with the PCs' royalty review, its rising support for the right-wing Wildrose Alliance Party (as it was branded at the time), and the increasing level of internal PC struggles, led to Premier Stelmach's resignation on 25 January 2011. Alison Redford's more liberal faction of the party supported her ascendance to the leadership on 2 October 2011, after a divided convention.

Federally, Harper's first majority government was built off of the Conservatives' social media political marketing tactics, which came to maturity during the 2011 election. Their coordinated "He's Just Visiting" online campaign against the Michael Ignatieff–led Liberals decimated the Liberal Party, and the NDP became the Official Opposition for the first time in Canadian history. Similar social media tactics affected the Alberta provincial election campaign one month earlier, as each party by then had a fully functional Web strategy, with the Wildrose in particular gaining support from the federal Conservatives' machine.[22]

In 2012, the top three provincial parties all had social media links available on their websites for this period; it was an equal playing field in terms of technology (as Table 5.6 documents). The party war rooms were also getting better at mining social media data to target possible voters, and creatively control their brand messages.

In the Alberta election of 2012, voter turnout improved to 54.37 per cent. Over 80 per cent of Canadians were online at this point, and the social media ecosystem was already being honed to focus on the common platforms of Facebook, YouTube, and Twitter; however, Flickr and podcasting were no longer being uniformly used in this election. For example, there were no direct links to podcasts on any of the party web pages, and the PCs were the only party to have a link to Flickr, though the actual account had very few pictures posted. Notably, there were no links to Instagram on the party websites for this election, despite the platform being launched in 2010.

Figure 5.2a. Alberta NDP Website, http://www.albertandp.ca, 23 April 2012

Figure 5.2b. Alberta PC Party Website, http://www.albertapc.
ab.ca, 23 April 2012

Figure 5.2c. Wildrose Party Website, http://www.wildrose.ca, 23 April 2012

Table 5.6. 23 April 2012: Alberta Partisan Election Campaign Websites

PARTY	NDP	PC	WILDROSE
Leader	Brian Mason	Alison Redford	Danielle Smith
Polls Week Prior	13%	34%	35%
Final Seat Totals	4 (gained 2)	61 (lost 5)	17 (gained 13)
Splash Page	See Figure 5.2a	See Figure 5.2b	See Figure 5.2c
Source URL	http://www.albertandp.ca	http://votepc.ca	http://www.wildrose.ca
Donation link:	Yes	Yes	Yes
Newsletter link:	Yes	Yes	Yes
Issue summary:	Yes (on front page)	Yes (on front page)	Yes (on front page)
Candidate links:	Yes	Yes	Yes
Email link:	Yes	Yes	Yes
RSS link:	Yes	Yes	Yes
Facebook link:	Yes	Yes	Yes
YouTube link:	Yes	Yes	Yes
Twitter link:	Yes	Yes	Yes
Instagram:	No	No	No

Note: The party website information in this table is organized from left to right on the partisan political spectrum. The social media links are organized in order of the technology's introduction or a company's founding. The poll numbers are taken from Leger Marketing on 10 April 2010 (with the Liberal Party having 13 per cent and the Alberta Party 3 per cent of the vote at that time), and the website images are taken from the Internet Archive. After Danielle Smith became leader of the Wildrose Alliance in 2009, the party gained four seats from the PCs from floor-crossings in 2010, to earn official party status. The Liberal Party under leader Raj Sherman lost three seats, ending up with five, while the Alberta Party led by Glen Taylor did not win any seats.

Facebook Supporters in the 2012 Alberta Provincial Election

In 2012, Danielle Smith counted nearly 30,000 supporters on Facebook as the rise of the controversial Wildrose Party in the polls threatened to end the PC dynasty (see Table 5.7). This surge gave a clearer picture of the limited Facebook numbers in the 2008 race, which was simply too early in the diffusion of innovations cycle for Facebook uptake provincially. By 2012, however, there were 1.056 billion Facebook users worldwide, which translated into a heightened scale of active users in the 2012 provincial race.

Table 5.7. Party Leader Facebook Supporters (2012 Election—Final Results)

RANK	WEEK THREE: 9 APRIL 2012		WEEK FOUR: 16 APRIL 2012		WEEK FIVE: 23 APRIL 2012	
1	**Danielle Smith** (Politician, Wildrose Party leader)	20,503 likes (+4,736 *from prior week*)	**Danielle Smith** (Politician, Wildrose Party leader)	26,252 likes (+5,746 *from prior week*) 11,591 talking about	**Danielle Smith** (Politician, Wildrose Party leader)	29,559 likes (+3,307 *from prior week*) 8,872 talking about
2	**Brian Mason** (Personal profile, NDP leader)	4,741 friends (+45)	**Brian Mason** (Personal profile, NDP leader)	4,794 friends (+53)	**Brian Mason** (Personal profile, NDP leader)	4,836 friends (+42)
3	**Brian Mason** (Places page, NDP leader) *NOTE: He is using his office address as unique page on Facebook to attract supporters.	1,819 likes (+110) 181 talking about	**Brian Mason** (Places page, NDP leader) *NOTE: He is using his office address as unique page on Facebook to attract supporters.	2,147 likes (+328) 507 talking about	**Brian Mason** (Places page, NDP leader) *NOTE: He is using his office address as unique page on Facebook to attract supporters.	2,206 likes (+59) 258 talking about
4	**Alison Redford** (Public figure, PC leader) *NOTE: Her personal page does not list the number of friends.	1,064 likes (+101) 112 talking about	**Alison Redford** (Public figure, PC leader) *NOTE: Her personal page does not list the number of friends.	1,217 likes (+153) 171 talking about	**Alison Redford** (Public figure, PC leader) *NOTE: Her personal page does not list the number of friends.	1,320 likes (+103) 124 talking about

Sources: Data compiled from Facebook pages as indicated over the course of the 2012 Alberta Provincial Election, and summarized by the author.

However, no party leader changed their rank in terms of social media supporters as compared to the previous weeks over the entire course of the election (as Table 5.7 illustrates). Danielle Smith ranked first out of all the leaders on Facebook, increasing her "likes" for her politician Facebook page from 9,955 to 29,559 over the campaign, which represented a true explosion of social media activity in Canada as compared to previous campaigns (for example, Prime Minister Stephen Harper had 2,796 "likes" for his politician Facebook page at the time). Smith's online support and the polls would not come to fruition on election day, when Alison Redford earned a majority. This would be, however, one example where provincial politics outpaced the federal level in terms of online social media campaigning numbers.

Facebook at this time had just created the new public figure page option that supporters commonly follow now, instead of "friending" a leader (which is capped at 5,000 friends), as the company was trying to simplify the multiple options of groups, place pages, and party pages for supporters (see Table 5.7). The options were quite confusing in this race (the simplification became common practice shortly after the election). Markedly, the leader pages all had far more supporters than the political party pages, which only reached around 2,000 followers at most.

YouTube in the 2012 Alberta Provincial Election

By 2012, YouTube users globally were uploading thirty-five hours of video each minute, with 2 billion views a day. Among the parties, Smith and the Wildrose used YouTube to the greatest effect in the lead-up to the election. The top video of the election was a Wildrose advertisement presenting the polls moving in favour of a possible Wildrose win, which was released one week before election day (see Table 5.8); it received more than 100,000 views. As with the 2008 videos, none of these videos are publically available online anymore, as the parties have taken them down.

Smith's social media support did not translate into the kind of support pollsters were predicting (see Janet Brown and John Santos's chapter in this volume), especially when compared to the results of the election.[23] Pundits were left pondering what forces and tactics drove Smith's large gains on social media without translating to victory on election day, with some arguing that the loss in support at the polls was based on the homophobic and climate-change-denying comments made by her Wildrose colleagues.

Table 5.8. Top YouTube Videos in the 2012 Election Campaign (Final Results)

RANK	TITLE	UPLOAD DATE	TAG	AFFILIA-TION	VIEWS TO DATE	VIEWS WEEK 3	IN-CREASE
1	Wildrose Momentum	18 April 2012	WildroseTV	Wildrose	112,569	*	112,569
2	Wildrose Balanced Budget Ad	28 March 2012	WildroseTV	Wildrose	16,054	3,970	12,084
*	Alberta Energy Dividend Ad	2 April 2012	WildroseTV	Wildrose	14,862	*	*
*	Wildrose Family Pack Ad	31 March 2012	WildroseTV	Wildrose	14,293	*	*
*	Alberta Accountabili-ty Act Ad	10 April 2012	WildroseTV	Wildrose	13,136	*	*
3	Meet Danielle Smith	5 July 2011	WildroseTV	Wildrose	7,241	3,558	3,683
4	Trailer—"It's time, Alberta!"	22 March 2012	WildroseTV	Wildrose	10,431	8,349	2,082
5	Family Care Clinics	3 April 2012	PCAlberta	PC	3,069	1,314	1,755

Sources: Data compiled from YousTube channels as indicated over the course of the 2012 Alberta Provincial Election, and summarized by the author.

To place the dominant Wildrose YouTube video in context, Canadian political watchers credit the "Culture in Danger" YouTube video launched in Quebec on 19 September 2008, four weeks before the 2008 federal election, as the first impactful social media election moment in Canadian history. The video crested 200,000 views before the election, and arguably lost Stephen Harper Quebec's support and his first possible majority government, as backlash arose after Quebec voters became aware of a controversial plan from the Conservatives to drop provincial arts funding.[24] The video was the centerpiece of a grassroots public-awareness campaign that targeted the Conservatives' policies, and it was effective particularly because it was not created by an opposition party.

Twitter in the 2012 Alberta Provincial Election

The sole common social media tool on which Smith did not surpass Redford was her Twitter base of 13,054 followers (see Table 5.9). In 2012, Twitter had 185 million users globally, which was the smallest user base of the three tools commonly promoted on the party websites. Only the Alberta Party changed their rank on Twitter during the 2012 race. In other words, social media did not have one uniform leader across all channels in the race, which reinforced the more complex market intelligence understanding of social media during this period. Researchers began to understand that the culture and context for each social media tool's "user affordances"[25] created unique social practices online that could only be described as dynamic.

Partisan practices developed beyond the use of one-way communication broadcasting techniques to include localized responses, particularly if a user base raised enough of a focalized theme for a party to build upon (e.g., criticisms were taken up by bloggers, then on Facebook and Twitter, and then by the PCs, directed at Danielle Smith's tour bus design, and her later support for conscience rights, which would allow health-care workers and other professionals to deny individual services based on religious beliefs).[26] In other words, market intelligence techniques were being used to help grow the user base of party supporters.[27] In terms of lagging technologies, the 2012 election would see the peak of blogging in Alberta, as the Infoscape Research Lab's blogometer recorded an average of about 4,500 blog posts in total, for each of the last two weeks leading up to the election. Those numbers would be the highest, as compared to the low hundreds in the 2012 election, and also higher than the 2015 election. Notably, after the election, on 13 February 2013, the blog "MadamPremier: A Blog Documenting Sexism Against Premiers" made a major critical contribution to online discourse by recording the vitriolic misogynist language that female politicians were subjected in Alberta and across Canada. This would be another example of provincial online social media leading the way in Canada; however, blogs and RSS feeds would no longer be a supported Web tool on the party websites come the 2015 election.

Table 5.9. Top Leader Twitter Accounts in the 2012 Election Campaign

RANK	WEEK THREE: 9 APRIL 2012		WEEK FOUR: 16 APRIL 2012		WEEK FIVE: 23 APRIL 2012	
1	**Progressive Conservative Association of Alberta** (@Premier_Redford)	10,928 Followers (+692)	**Progressive Conservative Association of Alberta** (@Premier_Redford)	10,928 Followers (+692)	**Progressive Conservative Association of Alberta** (@Premier_Redford)	13,054 Followers (+2,126)
		673 Tweets		673 Tweets		808 Tweets
		808 Following		808 Following		815 Following
2	**Wildrose Party of Alberta** (@ElectDanielle)	9,102 Followers (+1,208)	**Wildrose Party of Alberta** (@ElectDanielle)	9,102 Followers (+1,208)	**Wildrose Party of Alberta** (@ElectDanielle)	11,985 Followers (+2,883)
		6,199 Tweets		6,199 Tweets		6,704 Tweets
		1,733 Following		1,733 Following		1,739 Following
3	**Alberta Liberal Party** (@AlbertaLiberals)	3,764 Followers (+68)	**Alberta Liberal Party** (@AlbertaLiberals)	3,764 Followers (+68)	**The Alberta Party** (@AlbertaParty)	4,169 Followers (+405)
		3,124 Tweets		3,124 Tweets		3,808 Tweets
		2,609 Following		2,609 Following		2,203 Following
4	**The Alberta Party** (@AlbertaParty)	3,632 Followers (+112)	**The Alberta Party** (@AlbertaParty)	3,632 Followers (+112)	**Alberta Liberal Party** (@AlbertaLiberals)	4,084 Followers (+452)
		3,410 Tweets		3,410 Tweets		320 Tweets
		2,185 Following		2,185 Following		2,604 Following
5	**Alberta's NDP** (@AlbertaNDP)	2,416 Followers (+138)	**Alberta's NDP** (@AlbertaNDP)	2,416 Followers (+138)	**Alberta's NDP** (@AlbertaNDP)	2,893 Followers (+477)
		2,022 Tweets		2,022 Tweets		2,542 Tweets
		938 Following		938 Following		940 Following

Note: The shaded area identifies the only change in rank through the last three weeks of the campaign, with the Alberta Party's followers rising above the Alberta Liberal Party.

Sources: Data compiled from Twitter accounts as indicated over the course of the 2012 Alberta Provincial Election, and summarized by the author.

The 5 May 2015 Alberta Election Online: Digital Retail Politics and Grassroots Growth

It is important to mention here the mayoral campaigns of Naheed Nenshi in Calgary 2010 and 2013 and Don Iveson in Edmonton in 2013, which used social media prominently, thereby paving the way for the 2015 Alberta provincial election in several ways. Sharpe and Braid describe both mayors' Twitter strategies in *Notley Nation* (2016) as follows:

> By March 12, 2016, Iveson, (@doniveson) had 77,100 followers and had posted 15,100 tweets, while Nenshi (@nenshi) had 286,000 followers and 45,400 tweets. Both Iveson and Nenshi stress that social media are simply one facet of a campaign, and that talking with citizens face to face is far more important during the election and afterwards. The ground game is crucial in reaching out to voters, having a conversation, and laying the foundation of the campaign.[28]

The approach to social media described here balances broadcasting, localized online interactions, and in-person campaigning, which is an apt example of the trend that built towards the digital retail politics era described throughout this chapter.

The online strategies adopted by Nenshi and Iveson continued to mature during the 2015 Alberta provincial election, but they did not reach the level of "market surveillance" used by the Liberals in the lead-up to the 2015 federal election. In 2015, the provincial NDP's grassroots campaign was very strong,[29] as the party aimed to get candidates or one of its team members to knock on every door in a riding at least twice in the election, so that voters had a clear idea that the candidate was actively participating in their community. Interested potential voters would then be directed online to find more information with which to evaluate whether the party leader's online profile matched this lived impression and aligned with the voters' interests. In contrast, the other professional parties were commonly reported to limit door visits to only friendly or targeted battleground neighbourhoods based on their voter database intelligence.

It is important to emphasize, however, that we did not see the level of market surveillance in Alberta's 2015 provincial election as compared to the use of apps in the federal election.

In 2015, provincial voter turnout, at 58.25 per cent, was the highest in twenty-two years, as frustrated Albertans turned out in response to the highly contested campaign against the PC dynasty. In the 2015 campaign, like the 2012 campaign, all the parties had professionally developed websites utilizing similar social media tools (as demonstrated in Table 5.10). However, the era of listing the RSS icon on party websites was over, mainly due to the parties' attempts to attract voters using other aggregating social media feeds available through the accepted proprietary tools of Facebook, YouTube, and Twitter, with each providing more data analytics than simple RSS feeds. Notably, Instagram was not linked on the party websites, despite the fact that this relatively new tool was being used by the leaders. In this election, Instagram was still viewed as a younger generation's social media tool; it was not a mature technology as the social media numbers bear out below (see Figure 5.10 below).

Figure 5.3a. Alberta NDP Website, http://www.albertandp.ca, 5 May 2015

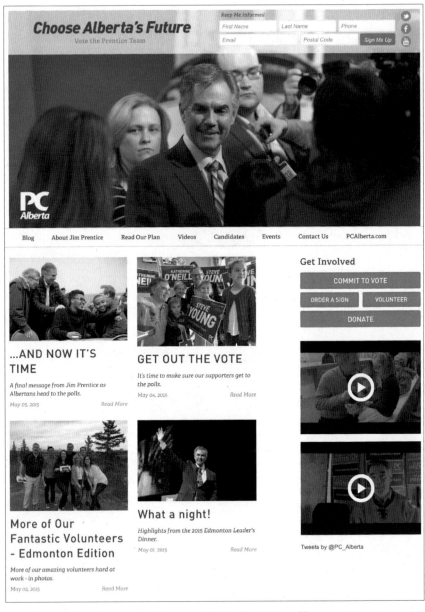

Figure 5.3b. Alberta PC Party Website, http://www.albertapc.
ab.ca, 5 May 2015

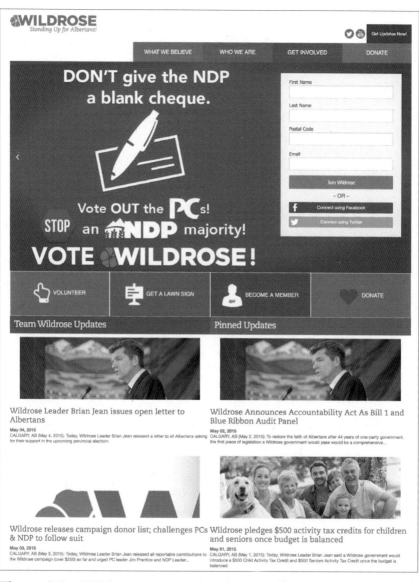

Figure 5.3c. Wildrose Party Website, http://www.wildrose.ca, 5 May 2015

Table 5.10. 5 May 2015: Alberta Partisan Election Campaign Websites

Party	NDP	PC	WR
Leader	Rachel Notley	Jim Prentice	Brian Jean
Polls Week Prior	44.5%	23.7%	25.9%
Final Seat Totals	54 (gained 50)	10 (lost 60)	21 (gained 16)
Splash Page	See Figure 5.3a	See Figure 5.3b	See Figure 5.3c
Source URL	http://www.albertandp.ca	http://www.pcalberta.ca	http://www.wildrose.ca
Donation link:	Yes	Yes	Yes
Newsletter link:	Yes	Yes	Yes
Issue summary:	Yes (on front page)	Yes (on front page)	Yes (on front page)
Candidate links:	Yes	Yes	Yes
Email link:	Yes	Yes	Yes
*RSS link:	No	No	No
Facebook link	Yes	Yes	Yes
YouTube link	Yes	Yes	Yes
Twitter link:	Yes	Yes	Yes
*Instagram Link	No	No	No

Note: * denotes a variation in use in this election. The party website information in this table is organized from left to right on the partisan political spectrum. The social media links are organized in order of the technology's introduction or a company's founding. The poll numbers are taken from ThreeHundredEight.com on 4 May 2015, and the website images are taken from the Internet Archive.

Social Media in the 2015 Election Campaign: Facebook, YouTube, Twitter, and Instagram

In 2015, the news media began using the proprietary analytics available through social media tools such as Twitter Analytics, Buffer, Hootsuite, and many other proprietary apps; their data helped to create infographics (as in Figure 5.10). The academic research methods of the early twenty-first century had now become formalized into algorithmic apps used for market intelligence and surveillance, available online to everyone. This professionalized political marketing shift has contributed to the emergence of the new era of

Figure 5.10. Party Leaders' Social Media Footprint in the early Weeks of the 2015 Provincial Election

Sources: "Alberta Election 2015: Party leaders on social media," Calgary Sun, 9 April 2015 http://www.calgarysun.com/2015/04/09/alberta-election-2015-party-leaders-on-social-media-graphic.

market surveillance, along with the changes in polling technologies, such as ThreeHundredEight.com's aggregating techniques, which Janet Brown and John B. Santos discuss in chapter 4.

In 2015, Facebook had 1.591 billion users globally, while Twitter had 305 million users. Despite the lower user base, Twitter had become the go-to social media tool for people interested in political communication and online journalism. This difference is illustrated by the fact that Jim Prentice's and Rachel Notley's Twitter followers numbered in the tens of thousands (18,652 and 12,883, respectively), but their Facebook followers only numbered in the thousands (see Figure 5.1). Tracking online media had become more complex at this point, as Facebook, Twitter, YouTube, and Instagram could all be linked together to post materials to any users' favoured accounts on their mobile phone apps, with iPhone and Galaxy users—nearly ubiquitous by this point—now downloading social media platforms to their phones to check them instantaneously and frequently.

For this reason, the limited numbers identified by the media for the YouTube subscriber information in 2015 are potentially misleading (see

Figure 1, where it is listed in the low tens), because simply following or tracking the party's officially sanctioned YouTube channels misses the wider network of back-channel groups posting and sharing videos on other social media during the election. In 2015, YouTube was receiving four hundred hours of uploaded video each minute globally, and the company recorded 3 billion users each month; users were now linking and posting videos in multiple different ways, separate from the party-sanctioned channels.

After the election, Twitter's dominance continued, with each political leaders' numbers in Alberta exploding in 2016 (see Table 5.11).

It should be noted that Prime Minister Justin Trudeau had 2.1 million Twitter followers at this time, while Stephen Harper had 1 million, Alison Redford 29,200, Danielle Smith 25,800, and Ed Stelmach 5,619. At the time of writing, new PC leadership hopeful Jason Kenney had 97,700 followers, built off the profile he built as a federal cabinet minister (it will be interesting to follow the dynamics of using such a follower base at the provincial level).

Instagram, the photo-sharing tool, was launched in 2010, and by 2012 it had 40 million users globally; by 2015, the company saw a ten-fold increase to 400 million users. As we saw in Figure 5.1, no provincial leader used Instagram effectively during the Alberta provincial election campaigns; in contrast, Justin Trudeau's 2015 federal campaign would become a model for its use. Similarly, Brian Jean, with 2,464 followers, and Rachel Notley, with 1,542, had the lead in terms of their Instagram followers in the 2015 election (see Table 5.12).

However, there were only a limited number of posts on the leaders' Instagram pages with which voters could engage.

Two other notable social media events happened after the 2015 Alberta provincial election. First, on 10 December 2015, online death threats against Premier Notley from right-wing critics came to a point where Wildrose Party leader Brian Jean was forced to denounce them publically as not representative of his party's membership. Later, on 31 August 2016, Jean apologized for a comment he had made about beating the premier, which was recorded and circulated virally on social media.

As of October 2016, the global social media ecology included Facebook's 1.71 billion users, YouTube's 3.25 billion monthly viewers, Twitter's 313 million users, and Instagram's 500 million users. The content analysis outlined broadly in this chapter situates Alberta's 2015 election as a key turning point

Table 5.11. Alberta Political Party Leader Twitter Followers in October 2016

@RachelNotley	@JimPrentice	@BrianJean
Followers: 68.9K	Followers: 16.8K	Followers: 16.4K
Following: 10.1K	Following: 300	Following: 3,145
Posts: 5,697	Posts: 1,392	Posts: 2,233

Sources: Data compiled from Twitter accounts as indicated in 2016, and summarized by the author.

Table 5.12. Party Leader Use of Instagram 2015 Election

premierrachelnotley	jimprentice_ab	brianjeanwrp
Followers: 1,542	Followers: 111	Followers: 2,464
Following: 52	Following: 15	Following: 144
Posts: 18	Posts: 21	Posts: 206

Note: The above user names were current as of time of publication; prior to the 2015 election the "premierrachelnotley" was "rachelnotley" in keeping with the NDP's campaign format.

Sources: Data compiled from Instagram accounts as indicated over the course of the 2015 Alberta Provincial Election, and summarized by the author.

in social media political marketing, shifting towards online market intelligence concerning the increasing number of active online voters in the tens of thousands in 2012, and as of 2016 into the hundreds of thousands, with new methods clearly available to track and analyze pubic users of Facebook, Twitter, and YouTube. As partisan apps were not used during this period, the shift to full mobile "market surveillance" was not reached provincially, as it was with the federal Liberals' creation of two apps in 2015, and during the American presidential election of 2016. Analytic tools used to surveil the electorate were democratized for public use in some instances in 2015, with media organizations creating new user-friendly applications like party election-promise trackers,[30] and the CBC Vote Compass app, which helps voters assess their political leanings against the party platforms.[31]

Overall, after the 2015 elections, it remains for researchers to investigate how political parties are using their voter databases and protecting the private user information obtained through apps, particularly in the areas of market surveillance, gender and identity participation online, algorithmic platform politics, research methods, and research tools for tracking and understanding online behaviour and media effects.

Conclusion: What Types of Technology Can be Used to Support the Master Party Brand?

> Social media is critical as a good broadcast tool, but not as a listening tool. . . . It's still evolving as a listening tool.
>
> —Edmonton mayor Don Iveson in 2013[32]

The above content analysis of the various Web technologies used during the 2008, 2012, and 2015 Alberta provincial elections provides strong evidence that parties have shifted away from using technologies to win a deterministic war of who has the best online broadcasting tools, to that of using social media consciously and strategically to align with their brand and leader image based on evidence-based market intelligence. In other words, social media tools are being used to listen to voters, but are also being used to monitor, influence, and shape their political intentions. By way of a concluding example, most political watchers would agree that the Trudeau campaign used the visual medium of Instagram masterfully in the 2015 federal election, while a few months prior, Alberta NDP leader Rachel Notley did not use it at all.

Similarly, little evidence was found provincially for the new political marketing trend of developing market surveillance strategies via apps to ensure messages target and reinforce the digital shadow of the leader as it aligns their face-to-face lived persona. Deviation between the two can lead to cognitive dissonance within a voter's mind concerning the abilities of a leader, or candidate, to be trustworthy and follow through on what she or he proposes to accomplish, as depicted in the representative advertising, debates, media appearances, party documents, and town halls conducted during the campaign. The authentic image and persona of the leader are, therefore, constructed in a coordinated online network, and just one part of that network can shape the electorate's views of the leader and party if it is maligned (e.g., in 2015, Danielle Smith crossing the floor, or Jim Prentice supporting a gas tax over a sales tax when most Albertans requested the latter according to the PCs' own provincial survey).

As others have similarly argued in this book, the 2015 election saw the reinforcement of the NDP's grassroots campaign by the presentation of Notley's lived persona through traditional media such as newspapers, radio, and television, and as identified in this chapter, her progressive image aligned well with the master brand also captured in her digital shadow.

The content analysis also demonstrated how the opposing parties in Alberta have professionalized their online image over time to compete with the PC dynasty, as the tools used increased in sophistication with each election since 2008. The NDP's rise coincided with an increase in the critical online discussion of provincial politics, as more Albertans chose to participate on social media, reflecting the new generation of progressive voters and thinkers described in other chapters in this book. The developing online debates have held all parties to account across the province, though more research is required to see if social media users are primarily active in the major urban centres of Calgary and Edmonton, where technologies are commonly adopted earlier, or if rural voters are similarly being changed by online social media as the province's demographics change.

Notes

I would first like to thank Duane Bratt, Keith Brownsey, Richard Sutherland, David Taras, and Chris Waddell for the opportunity to be a part of this collection; I definitely believe it is an example of a collaboration that was born simply from moving into a new office one door down from David Taras. I also have to gratefully acknowledge the work and support of the Infoscape Research Lab at Ryerson University for aiding in the development of the methods and analysis of the 2008 and 2012 Alberta provincial elections used in this chapter. In particular, Greg Elmer, Ganaele Langlois, Zachary Devereaux, Fenwick McKelvey, and Joanna Redden helped to develop the methods for scraping and tracking blogs, Facebook posts, and YouTube videos during those election cycles, which are documented in the following sources: Greg Elmer, Peter. M. Ryan, Zachary Devereaux, Ganaele Langlois, Fenwick McKelvey, and Joanna Redden, "Election Bloggers: Methods for Determining Political Influence," *First Monday* 12, no. 4 (2007), http://www.firstmonday.org/issues/issue12_4/elmer/index.html, and Greg Elmer, Ganaele Langlois, Zachary Devereaux, Peter. M. Ryan, Fenwick McKelvey, Joanna Redden, and A. Brady Curlew, " 'Blogs I Read': Partisanship and Party Loyalty in the Canadian Political Blogosphere," *Journal of Information Technology and Politics* (2009), https://www.tandfonline.com/doi/abs/10.1080/19331680902832582. Zachary Devereaux also helped with the original written analysis of the 2008 election, posted on the Infoscape website.

1   See, for example, Fenwick McKelvey, "Battling political machines: Coming to a riding near you!," *Canadian Centre for Policy Alternatives*, 19 August 2015, https://www.policyalternatives.ca/publications/monitor/battling-political-machines-coming-riding-near-you (accessed 1 July 2018).

2   See, for example, Rick Bell, "NDP boss Rachel Notley blasts Prentice and gains political traction," *Calgary Sun*, 2 April 2015, and "How 'math is difficult' (or #mathishard) blew up on social media," *Calgary Herald*, 24 April 2015, http://calgaryherald.com/news/politics/how-math-is-difficult-or-mathishard-blew-up-on-social-media (accessed 1 July 2018).

3   "How 'math is difficult' (or #mathishard) blew up on social media," *Calgary Herald*, 24 April 2015, http://calgaryherald.com/news/politics/how-math-is-difficult-or-mathishard-blew-up-on-social-media.

4   For more on political marketing intelligence and surveillance strategies see the following: Alex Marland, Thierry Giasson, and Jennifer Lees-Marshment, eds., *Political Marketing in Canada* (Vancouver: UBC Press, 2012); Alex Marland, *Brand Command: Canadian Politics and Democracy in the Age of Message Control* (Vancouver: UBC Press, 2015); Alex Marland and Thierry Giasson, eds., *Canadian Election Analysis 2015: Communication, Strategy, and Democracy* (Vancouver: UBC Press, 2015).

5   Pippa Norris, "Political Communication," *Developments in British Politics* 5 (1997): 76.

6   Greg Elmer, Ganaele Langlois, and Fenwick McKelvey, *The Permanent Campaign* (New York: Peter Lang, 2012).

7   See, for example, Richard Rogers, *Information politics on the Web* (Cambridge, MA: MIT Press, 2004).

8   See, for example, Harold Jansen, "Is the Internet politics as usual or democracy's future? Candidate campaign web sites in the 2001 Alberta and British Columbia provincial elections," *The Innovation Journal: The Public Sector Innovation Journal* 9, no. 2 (2004): 1–20; Harold Jansen and Royce Koop, "Pundits, ideologues, and the ranters: The British Columbia election online," *Canadian Journal of Communication* 30, no. 4 (2005), https://www.cjc-online.ca/index.php/journal/article/view/1483/1601 (accessed 1 July 2018).

9   See, for example, the critique of this dichotomy in Peter J. Smith and Peter J. Chen, "A Canadian E-lection 2008? Online Media and Political Competition," Paper presented at the annual meeting of Canadian Political Science Association Conference, University of Ottawa, 27 May 2009.

10   See, for example, Richard Rogers, *The End of the Virtual: Digital Methods* (Amsterdam: Amsterdam University Press, 2009), and Richard Nadeau, Neil Nevitte, Elisabeth Gidengil, and André Blais, "Election Campaigns as Information Campaigns: Who Learns What and Does it Matter?" *Political Communication* 25, no. 3 (2008): 229–48.

11   See, for example, Elmer et al., "Election Bloggers," and Elmer et al., "Blogs I read."

12   For example, see Yochai Benker's freely available *The Wealth of Networks* (New Haven, CT: Yale University Press, 2006), which describes the three top online-behaviour patterns, including the "skewed-long tail" trend that we now call "going viral."

13 All global Internet user data and social media numbers summarized throughout this chapter are freely sourced and searchable at https://www.statista.com/, and the Canadian national Internet user numbers are from the "Canadian Internet Use Survey" documents available from Statistics Canada for the following years: 2009 (http://www23.statcan.gc.ca/imdb/p2SV.pl?Function=getInstanceList&Id=130941); 2012 (http://www23.statcan.gc.ca/imdb/p2SV.pl?Function=getInstanceList&Id=130941); and 2016 (https://www.statcan.gc.ca/eng/survey/household/4432b).

14 Marland, Giasson, and Lees-Marshment, *Political Marketing in Canada*; Marland, *Brand Command*; Marland and Giasson, *Canadian Election Analysis 2015*.

15 For more on these market surveillance strategies, see Peter M. Ryan, "Mobile Platforms: The Medium and Rhetoric of the 2015 Canadian Federal Election Manifestos," Paper presented at the annual meeting of Canadian Political Science Association Conference, University of Calgary, 2 June 2016; André Turcotte, "Under New Management: Market Intelligence and the Conservative Party's Resurrection," in *Political Marketing in Canada*, ed. Marland, Giasson, and Lees-Marshment, 76–90 (Vancouver: UBC Press), 2012.

16 For more on the federal parties' use of technology in the 2015 election, see Steve Patten, "Data-Driven Microtargeting in the 2015 General Election," in *Canadian Election Analysis: Communication, Strategy, and Democracy*, ed. Thierry Giasson and Alex Marland (Vancouver: UBC Press, 2015), 14–15; Paul G. Thomas, "Political Parties, Campaigns, Data, and Privacy," in Giasson and Marland, eds., *Canadian Election Analysis*, 18–19.

17 See, for example, Elmer et al., "Election Bloggers," and Elmer et al., "Blogs I Read"; see also Infoscape Research Lab, "Publications," http://infoscapelab.ca/publications/.

18 In 2008, "RSS" stood for "Rich Site Summary," but was originally "RDF Site Summary"; it is now commonly known as "Really Simple Syndication."

19 "Low voter turnout in Alberta election being questioned," *CBC News*, 5 March 2008, http://www.cbc.ca/news/canada/edmonton/low-voter-turnout-in-alberta-election-being-questioned-1.761174 (accessed 1 July 2018).

20 Jon H. Pammett and Christopher Dornan, eds., *The Canadian General Election of 2004* (Toronto: Dundurn, 2004), 125.

21 Sandford Borins, "Alberta's election online: Off to a slow start," *IT World Canada*, 6 February 2008, http://www.itworldcanada.com/blog/albertas-election-online-off-to-a-slow-start/50054 (accessed 1 July 2018).

22 Thomas Walkom, "Wildrose, NDP defections good news for Harper, but not Mulcair," *Toronto Star*, 17 December 2014.

23 See, for example, "Wildrose, Tories neck and neck in race to lead Alberta government: poll," *National Post* (Toronto), 10 April 2012.

24 Jon H. Pammett and Christopher Dornan, eds., *The Canadian General Election of 2008* (Toronto: Dundurn, 2008).

25 "Affordances" are the tools and settings each social network such as Facebook or Twitter offers users as options they can use for interaction, such as likes, shares, emojis, 140 character limits, etc.

26 See, for example, Jen Gerson, "Alberta Election is One of the Meanest Ever," *Financial Post* (Toronto), 4 April 2012, and Mack D. Male, "Alberta Social Media Highlights," *Mastermaq's Blog*, 28 April 2012, http://blog.mastermaq.ca/2012/04/28/alberta-election-social-media-highlights/ (accessed 1 July 2018).

27 Similar market intelligence strategies were described at the federal level in Marland, Giasson, and Lees-Marshment, *Political Marketing in Canada*, 2012; Marland, *Brand Command*, 2015; Marland and Giasson, eds., *Canadian Election Analysis 2015*.

28 Sydney Sharpe and Don Braid, *Notley Nation: How Alberta's Political Upheaval Swept the Country* (Toronto: Dundurn, 2016), 114.

29 Darcy Henton, "NDP led Alberta in fundraising in days before election call," *Calgary Herald*, 21 July 2015, http://calgaryherald.com/news/politics/union-cash-helped-ndp-lead-province-in-fundraising-before-election (accessed 1 July 2018).

30 See, for example, "Alberta Election 2015: The Promise Tracker," *Calgary Sun*, 9 April 2015, http://www.calgarysun.com/2015/04/09/alberta-election-2015-the-promise-tracker (accessed 1 July 2018).

31 See "Vote Compass," https://votecompass.cbc.ca/federal/ (accessed 1 July 2018).

32 Sharpe and Braid, *Notley Nation*, 115.

PETER MALACHY RYAN

III

OIL SANDS, CARBON TAX, AND PIPELINES

Betting on Bitumen: Lougheed, Klein, and Notley

Gillian Steward

When Alberta's first NDP government swept to power in 2015, it inherited over four decades of PC energy policies. Key to these policies was development of the Alberta oil sands, which by 2015 had become the key driver of the province's economy. Two PC premiers, Peter Lougheed and Ralph Klein, had bet heavily on the oil sands, which they saw as the crown jewel of Alberta's natural resources. Yet each had an entirely different vision of the role government should play when it came to turning the extraction of this tarry bitumen into a money-making venture that would enrich both the Alberta treasury and Albertans in general. Lougheed believed that government intervention in the market was necessary if Albertans were to prosper from oil sands development. Klein believed the project should be market driven with industry leading the way.

Lougheed was so sure the oil sands were the key to Alberta's future prosperity that his government (1971–85) invested legislative heft, brain power, and hundreds of millions of dollars of government money in an effort to kick start oil sands development in northeastern Alberta. Only seven years after Lougheed left the premier's office, Ralph Klein took over. He wanted the government to get out of the oil sands business so that the petroleum industry could move into the driver's seat and steer the province to prosperity.

How did Lougheed's and Klein's energy policies get Alberta to where it is today? And how different or similar are the policies of Premier Rachel Notley when it comes to oil sands development? There have been many political, economic, and social changes since Lougheed was premier, but after two years in power, it appears that the Notley government is trying to correct the course set by the Klein government by leaning in the direction of the Lougheed model.

The Lougheed Approach to Oil Sands Development

After Peter Lougheed and the Progressive Conservatives defeated the Social Credit Party in 1971, the Alberta tar sands soon became a critical element of the government's economic policy. Lougheed saw them as a valuable resource that, with a helping hand from government, could be exploited much more than they had been to date for the benefit of all Albertans. The new premier saw an interventionist provincial government as essential if he were to strengthen "Alberta's position in Canada, shift economic power westward, build a lasting economic infrastructure, and create strong citizen attachments to Alberta and its government."[1] For Lougheed the oil sands were a reserve of riches that would extend well into the next century and thereby assure Alberta's prosperity—not that prosperity wasn't already evident in the 1970s.

Between 1973 and 1974, the price of oil quadrupled thanks to cuts in production and an embargo against Western nations, particularly the United States, by Arab members of the Organization of Oil Exporting Countries. At the time, the price for oil produced and consumed in Canada was lower than the world price due to government regulation. But between 1973 and 1978, the price of oil and natural gas in Canada rose quickly through agreements reached between the federal government and the producing provinces, although they did not reach world levels. By mid-1978, however, the gap between domestic and international prices had closed to less than $3 per barrel.[2]

In 1976, shortly after the Lougheed PCs won their second election, the government declared its first big surplus, an estimated $600 million, much of it earmarked for pay raises, mortgage subsidies, libraries, and research. With government finances solidly in the black, Premier Lougheed rose in the legislature to announce the creation of the Alberta Heritage Savings and Trust Fund, with an initial contribution of $1.5 billion and a commitment that 30 per cent of the royalties from non-renewable resources would flow into the fund.

The Lougheed government's participation in the expansion of tar sands production was achieved in a number of ways during Lougheed's fifteen years as premier. In 1973, he established the Alberta Energy Company (AEC), which was the result of a combination of government and private financing: 49 per cent of the corporation was owned by the province with the remaining equity coming from individual Albertans who were able to purchase shares at affordable prices. The AEC included investments in oil and gas, pipelines, forestry, petrochemicals, coal, and steel. The company's first share offering in 1975 attracted 60,000 buyers and was sold out in two weeks. Those shares eventually split 3-for-1 in 1980.[3]

The AEC also became a vehicle for Lougheed to promote oil sands development, particularly through Syncrude. It had been established in 1962 as a consortium of Cities Service, Imperial Oil, Royalite, and Atlantic-Richfield, with the aim of seeking approval from Alberta's Oil and Gas Conservation Board to build a second oil sands plant not far from the Great Canadian Oil Sands (which eventually became Suncor) operation north of Fort McMurray. Lougheed was so supportive of Syncrude, and oil sands development in general, that in 1974 he established the Alberta Oil Sands Technology and Research Authority (AOSTRA), a government-funded agency that aimed to accelerate the development of oil sands technology. The government pledged $100 million to AOSTRA over its first five years. Over the next eighteen years, AOSTRA spent $448 million dollars on public-private projects and institutional research, making it one of the largest research and development programs ever launched in Canada.[4] Many of the advances in oil sands extraction—including steam-assisted gravity drainage, which eventually led to dozens of in situ operations—were developed by AOSTRA.

In 1975, the proposed Syncrude project was near collapse after partner company Atlantic Richfield withdrew its support. The Alberta and Ontario provincial governments, along with the federal government, had been counting on this new mega-project to provide jobs and secure Canada's oil supply, and they were keen to see it succeed. So was the Syncrude consortium. In a series of negotiations, the remaining partners in the project—Imperial, Oil Cities Service, and Gulf Oil—used Atlantic Richfield's withdrawal to force all three governments into granting unprecedented concessions. In the end Alberta, Ontario, and Ottawa all became partners in the project—Alberta through the Alberta Energy Company. Alberta also paid infrastructure costs, including a $300-million utility plant and a $100-million pipeline from Fort McMurray to Edmonton. The province also built community schools, bridges, highways, and other services. Syncrude received world price for its oil when the oil industry in general was receiving a much lower Canadian price, and its private corporate partners received generous write-offs not only on expenses directly related to the oil sands plants but also on exploration and development projects in other parts of their operations. In the end Ottawa invested $300 million in public funds in return for 15 per cent ownership, Alberta invested $200 million for 10 per cent, and Ontario $100 million for five per cent.[5]

The scale and scope of development recommended in the government studies during the 1970s was measured. Assuming eight new projects were approved over the subsequent twenty-eight-year period, the government hoped to achieve the following benchmarks by 2000:

- An annual production rate of 1 million barrels per day

- A depletion rate of the resource at approximately 734 years

- A population of 600,000 in Fort McMurray needed to support such growth[6]

A 1972 document produced for the government of Alberta dealing with foreign ownership presents the oil sands as a unique resource capable of shifting existing trade dynamics. It notes:

> The tar sands offer a unique opportunity to change the historical trend of ever increasing foreign control of non-renewable resource development in Canada. Here is a reserve of the greatest magnitude which does not require highly speculative investment to find and prove. The world-wide demand for petroleum will be so compelling within the near future that it should be Alberta's objective to increase Canadian equity participation in the resource developments. Huge amounts of capital will be required for further development

of technology and the purchase of plants and equipment. However, to the maximum extent equity capital should be raised in Alberta and Canada recognizing that the usual past constraints of unproven reserves and uncertain markets.[7]

In a speech to Calgary's business community in 1974, Premier Lougheed warned his audience that the province had only a decade to diversify its economy. The first objective, he said, must be "to strengthen the control by Albertans over our future and to reduce the dependency for our continued quality of life on governments, institutions or corporations directed from outside the province."[8]

Another aspect of the Lougheed government's approach to oil sands development, and that would differ from the Klein government's, was its relationship with organized labour. In 1975, at the urging of the Syncrude consortium, the AEC, which was 49 per cent owned by the Alberta government, passed over the lowest bid for construction of a pipeline from the Syncrude plant, submitted by a non-union contractor, and gave the job to a unionized bidder. Syncrude had negotiated a no-strike, no-lockout agreement in return for assurances that the pipeline would be awarded to a union contractor. Lougheed recognized that if the oil sands were to be industrialized, organized labour needed to be on side.[9]

There's no question that the Lougheed government used all the power and money it had at its disposal in the 1970s to kick start oil sands development. It assumed that if the Alberta government didn't do this it would take far too long and that most of the financial benefits would flow into corporate and government coffers outside the province rather than accrue to Alberta's government and citizens. But Lougheed's interventionist approach alarmed many captains of the oil industry who would have rather seen the government play a much more hands-off role. At one point, industry leaders were so angry with his policies that they banned Lougheed from membership in the Calgary Petroleum Club. But most Albertans concurred with Lougheed and the PCs, as evidenced by the fact that they were re-elected three times between 1971 and 1982 with landslide majorities.

Even Grant Notley, the provincial NDP leader, agreed in principle with Lougheed's approach to the development of Alberta's petroleum riches. He supported the federal NDP's position on nationalizing Imperial Oil and then using the publicly-owned corporation to influence energy policy—much the same idea as Petro-Canada, which was established by the federal Liberals, and Lougheed's AEC. But Notley opposed the general nationalization of the oil industry as proposed by some New Democrats at the time. He reasoned that such a move would scare off moderate voters and hurt the party come election time. Notley also argued that complete nationalization would be prohibitively expensive, and that social democratic goals in energy policy could be achieved through regulatory means and an aggressive public presence in the industry. Lougheed and Notley both believed in government intervention in the economy, and in Alberta that meant the oil and gas industry. There were degrees of difference in their views on the government's role, but essentially they were on the same page.[10]

Enter Ralph Klein

Ralph Klein became premier seven years after Lougheed left office. But a lot had changed by then. Klein faced high unemployment rates following the recession that began in 1990 and continued until early 1992. By 1993, the national unemployment rate stood at 11.3 per cent.[11] Calgary had an unemployment rate of 10.4 per cent; Edmonton 11.2 per cent.[12] Alberta's economy had been hit by both the national recession and the low price of oil—which had fallen to an average of $16.75 a barrel in 1993.

The Alberta government was also in debt and had been running deficit budgets for several years. The provincial treasury needed much more revenue if it was to repay a debt of $32 billion accumulated over eight consecutive budget deficits, largely the legacy of the Don Getty government. But Premier Klein and his treasurer, Jim Dinning, didn't want to raise taxes or royalty rates on oil and gas. (Royalties are not a tax, but rather are considered as rent paid by producers for the use of a publicly owned resource such as oil.) They preferred to cut government spending and entice investment with low taxes. As Premier Klein reported to the provincial legislature in September 1993,

> The four-year plan identifies the problem as one of a spending problem and not a revenue problem. The four-year plan says that we will avoid the introduction of any new taxes,

GILLIAN STEWARD

including a sales tax, and we will avoid, if we possibly can, raising taxes. What we want to do is maintain as competitive a tax regime as we possibly can to attract to this province new investment and to create economic growth and prosperity.[13]

Klein's energy minister, Pat Black (she later changed her surname to Nelson), wanted to make sure that investors in the petroleum industry would not be hampered by taxes, regulations, and complicated approval processes for their project applications. In a 2012 interview, she recalled the following concerns:

> We were under three million people; we didn't really have a lot of investment coming into the province. Because, first of all, we were over taxed, we were over regulated and we didn't have a very good record as far as getting applications through on the regulatory side. So, we needed an overall fiscal structure that would be seen to be friendly to investors to come here.[14]

Lougheed had hardly been hostile to the petroleum industry, but he did see government as much more of a counterweight to its economic power. Klein, on the other hand, wanted his government to step out of the way and let the industry have an upper hand when it came to designing energy policy.

The Alberta Chamber of Resources (ACR) was eager to help in this regard. It was an industry association comprised of pipeline operators, oil-well servicing companies, and other businesses providing goods and services to the oil and gas industry; it had long been touting the oil sands as the "priority mineral resource for further development."[15]

By 1993 both the federal and Alberta governments were much more open to the ideas put forth by the ACR when it came to policy incentives to spur investment in Alberta's oil sands. Jean Chrétien's Liberals had replaced Brian Mulroney's Progressive Conservatives in Ottawa. The Western-based Reform Party was the Official Opposition; it had campaigned under the slogan, "The West Wants In." 1993 was also the year that Chrétien named Edmonton MP Anne McLellan to the cabinet as minister of natural resources.

At the time, McLellan was a lawyer with no experience of the petroleum industry. But Chrétien had other priorities in mind with her appointment, as McLellan later indicated:

> It was quite clear to me that this was the first Liberal government elected since the end of the National Energy Policy, which was of course in the first term of Prime Minister Mulroney. So I think Mr. Chrétien wanted to send a message to the Province of Alberta, and to the oil and gas industry, that things had changed. . . . I think he wanted to send a message of some reassurance to most Albertans and to the industry by appointing an Albertan.[16]

In order to formalize its position, the ACR established the National Task Force on Oil Sands Strategies. The task force's objective was to gather a "strategic group of diverse stakeholders convinced of the benefits of an action plan leading to the realization of the potential benefits of oil-sands based industrial development in this country."[17] One of the key promoters of the task force was Eric Newell, who at the time was the president of both the ACR and Syncrude Canada, the largest oil sands producer at the time.

Eventually, both the federal and Alberta governments were asked by the task force's leaders to assign representatives to its working committees so it would have the credibility of a government-sanctioned inquiry.[18] Both levels of government acceded by appointing representatives from the bureaucracy. But the vast majority of task force participants worked for private-sector corporations that were already involved in oil sands development or wanted to be. Of the 57 committee chairs and members named in the task force report, 45 came from industry ranks; 6 from the federal government; and 6 from the Alberta government. The 6 committee chairs were all industry representatives, including 2 from Syncrude.

The task force didn't hold public hearings; instead, its committees focused on researching and proposing ideas in six key areas: marketing and transportation; science and technology; environment and regulation; government and communications; fiscal and socio-economic; and materials/services and coalition-building.

Paul Precht, an economist with the Alberta Department of Energy, worked on the task force for almost two years. He recalled during an interview that the oil industry wanted to restructure the royalty and tax system so it would stimulate investment that was beneficial to the industry.[19]

After two years of study and discussion, the task force launched its sixty-two-page report at the Montreal Stock Exchange in May of 1995. Entitled *The Oil Sands: A New Energy Vision for Canada*, the report declared in its introduction that "the Task Force had identified a clear vision for growth and answered—affirmatively—the fundamental question: Should oil sands development proceed? The participants crafted an appropriate development plan, assessed the main obstacles to growth, and identified the levers of development to overcome those impediments."[20]

While many of the report's recommendations focussed on fast-tracking the development of new technologies and building collaborative networks among oil sands developers, several focused on government policy:

- The federal and Alberta governments (Finance Canada, Natural Resources Canada, Alberta treasury, and Alberta energy) should develop a generic set of harmonized tax and royalty measures based on economic profits. Such a system will provide a consistent fiscal framework for all energy projects and result in a balanced sharing of profits. These common fiscal terms are necessary for the future development of Canada's oil sands.

- Development of the oil sands should be market-driven.

- The industry will work with government agencies (the Alberta Energy and Utilities Board, Alberta Environmental Protection, Environment Canada) to develop a one-window review and decision process that harmonizes the current processes run by the Alberta and federal governments. Efforts will centre on eliminating duplication between environmental assessments and approvals done at both the federal and provincial level and between departments at the provincial level.

- Governments should continue to support pre-competitive research and development via expanded industry-led collaborative research activities under the Canadian Oil Sands Network for Research and Development (CONRAD included federal and provincial government agencies, six oil companies and two universities) and other partnerships.

- Government should maintain an attractive investment climate for science and technology efforts in the oil sands.

- Government should ensure that oil sands export restrictions are removed.[21]

According to the task force, the most important key to stimulating the necessary investment was a generic fiscal regime (taxes and royalties) for all oil sands projects rather than project-by-project agreements, which had been the case up until then. The report stated that the new fiscal regime would "divide revenues and costs fairly between investors and government, and are stable and predictable and result in a level playing field for all, including new entrants."[22]

The Alberta government didn't need a sales job. It immediately began discussions on the task force's recommendations. On 6 September 1995, four months after the release of the task force's report, the Standing Policy Committee of the Alberta government approved the generic oil sands regime. Two months later, Premier Ralph Klein announced that the new royalty regime applied to all new projects.

After decades of industry lobbying, the province implemented a generic royalty and tax regime that was devised by the industry and would apply to all oil sands projects. The province would receive a minimum royalty of 1 per cent on all production. The royalty would increase to 25 per cent on net project revenues after the project developer recovered all start-up costs, including research and development costs and a return allowance. More importantly, for project developers, all capital costs—including operation, and research and development costs—would be 100 per cent deductible in the year incurred.[23]

The generic royalty regime was designed to encourage oil sands investors by assuring them that they would pay almost no royalties until they had paid off all the costs of constructing the project. So while the project could in fact be producing oil for sale to the market at the going price, royalties would be set at only 1 per cent until the cost of construction was entirely paid off. Between 1997 and 2010, tar sands producers paid Albertans less than $20 billion in royalties and land sales for the rights to more than $205 billion worth of bitumen.[24] In other words, the industry was getting "free oil" and putting it on the market when, by 2008, US refineries were paying US$100 a barrel for Canadian crude oil.

In the end, the Klein government adopted all of the task force's recommendations that applied to government policy. It fast-tracked project-approval processes, cut back on the number of environmental reviews, introduced self-regulation—which meant oil sands operators became responsible for regulating themselves—made it more difficult for the public to express objections to projects, and funded industry research. Although the task force report did not mention unions, the Klein government took a decidedly different approach than Lougheed had. In 2006, it applied a rarely used section of the labour code so that Canadian Natural Resources Limited could have one bargaining unit for all the construction workers building its multi-billion-dollar Horizon oil sands mine and up-grader rather than separate agreements negotiated by various contractors with unionized workers. This made it much easier and cheaper for contractors to recruit foreign workers, since they didn't have to go through union hiring halls. The Christian Labour Association of Canada, an organization that is not recognized by the Canadian trade union movement, was appointed as bargaining agent. None of the workers had a vote on the matter.

Enter Rachel Notley and the NDP

When Peter Lougheed became premier in 1971 the Great Canadian Oil Sands mining operation just north of Fort McMurray was producing 30,000 barrels of oil a day. By 2014, Alberta's production of crude bitumen reached over 2.3 million barrels a day,[25] and it came from the Peace River and Cold Lake areas as well as the Fort McMurray region. Much of that growth occurred between

1996 and 2007, when oil sands production more than doubled, from approximately 540,000 barrels per day to 1.4 million barrels per day.[26]

The feverish pace of oil sands development initiated by Klein led to enormous changes in Alberta. The population increased by over 500,000 to 3.5 million as people from across the country and around the world came to Alberta to work in the oil patch and related businesses.[27] Wages in all sectors of the economy shot up as construction companies and oil sands operators competed fiercely for workers. But so did the cost of living, especially for housing, as it was in short supply compared to the demand created by newcomers. The provincial and municipal governments found themselves struggling to keep up with the demand for schools, hospitals, transportation infrastructure, and other public services. By 2006 Alberta had the highest inflation rate of all the provinces.[28] The provincial government was paying top dollar for labour and materials.

The Klein government posted hefty budget surpluses between 2000 and 2008 due to increased government revenues from the energy sector and reduced spending. But its industry-supported low oil sands royalty regime also meant that the province left billions of dollars in royalties on the table, dollars that ended up in bulging corporate coffers.[29] And Albertans could no longer count on the Heritage Savings Trust Fund to accumulate wealth for the province. It had been Lougheed's intention to deposit 30 per cent of royalty revenues annually into the fund and to use the money "to save for the future, to strengthen or diversify the economy, and to improve the quality of life for Albertans."[30]

But the royalty payments were stopped in 1987 during the Don Getty government. The Klein government changed the terms of the Heritage Fund so it could no longer be used by government for direct economic development or social investment. It became simply an investment portfolio that contributed annual earnings to the government's general revenues.[31] Even when Klein's government amassed record budget surpluses, Klein did not rebuild the Heritage Fund. In a 2009 interview, Lougheed said that "Klein wasn't interested for a variety of reasons, in sustaining The Heritage Savings Trust Fund. He set up other funds. So it never really fully met the objective of diversification."[32] By 2015 the price of oil had sunk drastically and Alberta was once again faced with the prospect of deficit budgets, soaring debt, and higher-than-usual unemployment rates. The Klein government's market-driven approach to oil sands development had not produced the long-term prosperity for the province that the industry and government had predicted.

By the time Notley came to power in 2015, the oil sands were indeed the key driver of Alberta's economy. However, just like Ralph Klein, Notley also had to contend with low oil prices and low energy revenues, along with the added strain of international requirements for lower carbon emissions and more renewable energy. Oil sands operations and their soaring greenhouse gas emissions had become a powerful symbol for climate change activists such as 350.org in the United States, and they used it relentlessly as an example of why carbon emissions must be reduced if climate change is to be blunted. Alberta also found itself in the crosshairs of international environmental organizations. In 2008, the death of 1,600 ducks on a Syncrude tailings pond brought to world-wide attention the size and scope of the oil sands extraction process and its toxic wastes. Pipeline projects designed to transport Alberta's bitumen to ports on the West Coast were denounced by people worried about tarry oil spilling from tankers and ruining the coastline. Alberta's oil sands economy was getting lots of attention beyond its borders, but for all the wrong reasons.

Notley has made it clear that while her government will continue to encourage oil sands development, like Lougheed she wants a more measured pace of development and more controls on carbon emissions and environmental consequences. This is evident in the Climate Leadership Plan, which imposes a 100 megatonne cap on oil sands greenhouse gas emissions, thereby slowing development and/or forcing oil sands operators to develop technology that significantly reduces carbon emissions.[33] The cap means that the development of oil sands operations is not an open-ended project, but must conform to government's expectations rather than market forces.

Notley's Climate Leadership Plan features a levy on the consumption of fossil fuels in the province. There was no such levy in Lougheed's day, but Notley plans to use revenue from the carbon tax to kick-start the development of renewable energy in the province much like Lougheed used government revenues to kick-start the development of oil sands technology.

Alberta's carbon-pricing scheme is linked to the plan to reduce carbon emissions put forward by Justin Trudeau's Liberal government. Trudeau needed Alberta to be an enthusiastic partner in the national plan if it was to succeed. Notley, who was elected just a few month before Trudeau, agreed in hopes that Alberta's participation would soften opposition by opponents in other provinces to proposed new oil pipelines.

The Trudeau/Notley plan hit a big bump in the road when BC NDP leader John Horgan formed a minority government with the support of three Green Party MLAs in 2017. Horgan had promised to stop the Trans Mountain pipeline expansion, which had been approved by the federal government and would triple the amount of oil shipped from Alberta to ports in British Columbia's Lower Mainland. His primary concern was the increase in oil tanker traffic and the likelihood of a spill of diluted bitumen in British Columbia's coastal waters. In early 2018, Horgan proposed legislation that would restrict shipments of bitumen through the province. Notley fought back and introduced legislation designed to restrict oil shipments from Alberta to other provinces. She also let it be known that Alberta would drop its support of Trudeau's carbon emission reduction plan if the pipeline wasn't built. By early May, US-based Kinder Morgan, the pipeline proponent, announced that it might abandon the project because the political uncertainty was costing the company's shareholders too much money. After weeks of negotiations with Kinder Morgan, the Trudeau government, with the full support of Notley, bought Kinder Morgan's old pipeline and infrastructure for $4.5 billion and vowed to restart construction of the additional capacity.

Notley's promotion of the nationalization of energy infrastructure certainly hearkened back to the 1970s, when Lougheed, with the support of Grant Notley, Rachel's father, invested heavily in such oil sands operations and infrastructure as the pipeline from Fort McMurray to Edmonton. Rachel Notley also showed the same kind of fight as Lougheed when she stood up for Alberta's interests by fiercely attacking Horgan's efforts to stop the pipeline while at the same time pushing the federal government to assert its authority on behalf of Alberta. The irony was that Notley had aligned Alberta with Justin Trudeau, whereas Lougheed had fought Justin Trudeau's father, Pierre Trudeau, over federal energy policies.

But like Lougheed, Notley has also shown a proclivity for encouraging Alberta-based energy companies to work closely with her government. Lougheed promoted his Alberta-first strategy through the AEC and his support for Syncrude. When Notley announced her Climate Leadership Plan on 22 November 2015 in Edmonton, she was joined on stage by CEOs from

Canadian Natural Resources Limited, Suncor Energy, Cenovus Energy, and Shell Canada.[34] All those companies have significant oil sands operations and, with the exception of Shell Canada, are formidable home-grown oil and gas producers.

Unlike Lougheed, however, Notley chose not to impose higher royalty rates on the petroleum industry even though a royalty review had been one of her main platform planks. Early in her mandate she struck a Royalty Review Advisory Panel to examine current royalty rates and make recommendations to government. The panel recommended a number of structural changes to the royalty system for conventional oil and gas but virtually no changes to the royalty rates over all, including the 1 per cent oil sands royalty designed by the Klein government. Notley concurred even though the NDP had pushed for higher royalty rates, particularly for the oil sands, when Premier Ed Stelmach launched a royalty review panel in 2007.

Unlike Klein or Lougheed, though, Notley has established a consultative strategy when it comes to devising energy policy. Rather than leave the development of policy to only one stakeholder—the petroleum industry—as Klein did, Notley has established several review panels and committees comprised of representatives of industry, academia, First Nations, environmental NGOs, labour, and citizens at large. These panels have been tasked with holding public hearings and/or bringing ideas and recommendations to the government. They include the Climate Change Policy Review Panel, the Royalty Review Advisory Panel, the Energy Efficiency Advisory Panel, and the Energy Diversification Advisory Committee.

Notley's government may take a more collaborative approach than those of former premiers because it doesn't have the luxury of an overwhelming majority in the legislature, as both Lougheed's and Klein's had. Since Notley's shocking win in 2015, Alberta's two conservative parties, the Alberta Progressive Conservatives and the Wild Rose Party, have united to form the United Conservative Party under the leadership of former federal cabinet minister Jason Kenney. Without the prospect of vote-splitting among conservatives, as in 2015, Notley's NDP could end up a one-term wonder. Kenney has vowed to repeal the carbon tax and is more likely to hew to Ralph Klein's way of doing things when it comes to oil sands development and energy policies in general.

Much like her father, Rachel Notley has developed her own brand of energy policies, policies that often stand in stark contrast to the policies of the federal NDP and other provincial wings such as that in British Columbia. For example, she unapologetically promotes oil pipeline proposals and works to develop new markets for Alberta's fossil fuels, which runs counter to the federal NDP's platform. Like her father, Notley seems to realize that many Albertans depend on the petroleum industry for well-paying work. Too much socialism, the elder Notley reasoned, would scare off moderate voters and hurt the party come election time. He also argued that social-democratic goals in energy policy could be achieved through regulatory means and an aggressive public presence in the industry.[35]

There's no question that both Lougheed and Klein (and her father) have influenced Notley's energy policies. But so far Notley's vision of government's role, especially when it comes to oil sands development, hearkens back to the Lougheed era. Her policies indicate that there is too much at stake for all Albertans when it comes to development of the province's energy resources to give control to one key stakeholder—the petroleum industry—as Klein did. Like Lougheed, she adheres to a vision in which government has a responsibility to consider the needs and interests of all stakeholders, particularly the owners of the natural resources—the people of Alberta.

NOTES

1   Allan Tupper, "Peter Lougheed—1971–1985," in *Alberta's premiers of the twentieth century*, ed. B. J. Rennie (Regina, SK: Canadian Plains Research Centre, 2004), 220.

2   See G. B. Doern and G. Toner, *The Politics of Energy* (Agincourt, ON: Methuen Publications, 1985).

3   See Tupper, "Peter Lougheed," and J. Richards and L. Pratt, Prairie capitalism: Power and influence in the new west (Toronto: McCelland and Stewart, 1979).

4   A Hester and L. Lawrence, *A sub-national public-private strategic alliance for innovation and export development: The case of the Canadian province of Alberta's oil sands* (Santiago, CL: UN Economic Commission for Latin America and Caribbean, 2010.

5   D. Finch, *Pumped: Everyone's guide to the oil patch* (Calgary: Fifth House, 2007); Doern and Toner, *The Politics of Energy.*

6   Government of Alberta, *Fort McMurray Athabasca tar sands development strategy,* Edmonton: Conservation and Utilization Committee, 1972.

7   Ibid., 16.

8   Quoted in Richards and Platt, *Prairie capitalism*, 233.

9   Ibid., 236.

10   See Allan Tupper, "Grant Notley and the modern state," in *Essays in honour of Grant Notley: Socialism and democracy in Alberta*, ed. L. Pratt (Edmonton: NewWest Press, 1986).

11   Statistics Canada, "National Unemployment Rates," 2015, http://www.statcan.gc.ca/pub/71-222-x/2008001/sectiona/a-unemployment-chomage-eng.htm (accessed 15 October 2016).

12   Statistics Canada, "Canada's Unemployment Mosaic in the 1990s," 1996, http://www.statcan.gc.ca/pub/75-001-x/1996001/2524-eng.pdf (accessed 15 October 2016).

13   *Alberta Hansard* (14 September 1993), P. 211 col 2, http://www.assembly.ab.ca/ISYS/LADDAR_files/docs/hansards/han/legislature_23/session_1/19930914_1330_01_han.pdf (accessed 15 October, 2016).

14   See "Interview with Pat Nelson (Transcript)," 28 June 2012, https://www.glenbow.org/collections/search/findingAids/archhtm/oilsands.cfm (accessed 15 October 2016).

15   National Task Force on Oil Sands Strategies, *The oil sands: A new energy vision for Canada. National Task Force on Oil Sands Strategies of the Alberta Chamber of Resources. Comprehensive Report* (Edmonton: Alberta Chamber of Resources, 1995), http://www.acralberta.com/Portals/0/projects/PDFs/The%20Oil%20Sands%20A%20New%20Energy%20Vision%20for%20Canada.pdf (accessed 31 October 2016).

16   See "Interview with Anne McLellan (Transcript)," 11 July 2011, https://www.glenbow.org/collections/search/findingAids/archhtm/oilsands.cfm (accessed 15 October 2016).

17   National Task Force on Oil Sands Strategies, *The oil sands*.

18   "Interview with Anne McLellan"; "Interview with Eric Newell (Transcript)," 25 May 2011, https://www.glenbow.org/collections/search/findingAids/archhtm/oilsands.cfm; "Interview with Paul Precht (Transcript)," 9 January 2013, https://www.glenbow.org/collections/search/findingAids/archhtm/oilsands.cfm (accessed 15 October 2016).

19   "Interview with Paul Precht," 10.

20   National Task Force on Oil Sands Strategies, *The oil sands*, 4.

21   See Ibid.

22   National Task Force on Oil Sands Strategies, *A recommended fiscal regime for Canada's oil sands industry. National Task Force on Oil Sands Strategies of the Alberta Chamber of Resources. Appendix C: Fiscal Report.* Edmonton: Alberta Chamber of Resources, 1995.

23   Alberta Energy "Alberta oil sands: Update on the generic royalty regime," 1998, http://www.energy.alberta.ca/OilSands/1190.asp (accessed 30 October 2016).

24   See R. Boychuk, *Misplaced generosity: Extraordinary profits in Alberta's oil and gas industry* (Edmonton: Parkland Institute, 2010), 31.

25   Alberta Energy, *Alberta at a Crossroads: Royalty Review Advisory Panel Report*, 2016, http://www.energy.alberta.ca/Org/pdfs/RoyaltyReportJan2016.pdf (accessed 15 October 2016).

26   Alberta Energy and Utilities Board, *2005 Year in Review*, 2006, http://www.assembly. ab.ca/lao/library/egovdocs/2005/aleub/67720_05.pdf (accessed 15 October 2016).

27   Alberta Treasury Board and Finance, "Economy and Statistics," 2016, http://finance. alberta.ca/aboutalberta/osi/demographics/Population-Estimates/index.html (accessed 31 October 2016).

28   Statistics Canada, "Consumer Price Index, historical summary by province or territory (2002–2006)," 2017, http://www.statcan.gc.ca/tables-tableaux/sum-som/l01/cst01/ econ150c-eng.htm. (accessed 15 June 2017).

29   See K. Taft, M. McMillan, and J. Jahangir, *Follow the Money: Where is Alberta's Wealth Going?* (Edmonton: Brush Education, 2002).

30   Alberta Treasury Board and Finance, "A History of the Heritage Fund," 2017, http:// www.finance.alberta.ca/business/ahstf/history.html (accessed 15 June 2017).

31   Ibid.

32   Canadian Press, "Lougheed upset at stagnant Alberta Heritage Fund," *CTV News*, 5 July 2009, http://www.ctvnews.ca/lougheed-upset-at-stagnant-alberta-heritage-fund-1.413840 (accessed 15 June 2017).

33   Government of Alberta, *Alberta Climate Leadership Plan*, 2015, https://www.alberta.ca/ climate-leadership-plan.aspx (accessed 15 June 2017).

34   See "Alberta's climate change strategy targets carbon, coal emissions," *CBC News*, 22 November 2015, http://www.cbc.ca/news/canada/edmonton/alberta-climate-change-newser-1.3330153 (accessed 15 June 2017).

35   Tupper, "Grant Notley and the modern state."

7

The Politics of Alberta's Carbon Tax*

Kevin Taft

The political struggle over Alberta's carbon tax is a proxy for Alberta's broader struggle to adapt to a world moving with increasing speed toward a low-carbon future. Alberta is a major producer and exporter of carbon fuels, and the province's politics are caught between forces that want to hang on to a past made prosperous by carbon, and forces trying to move the province away from carbon toward a more adaptive future. The carbon tax marks this struggle, and most indications are that the anti-tax, pro-carbon forces are prevailing. This suggests Alberta's transition to a low-carbon future is going to be more painful than it need be.

In Alberta's May 2015 general election, the NDP under leader Rachel Notley won an unexpected majority government. A carbon tax did not feature in the NDP's election platform;[1] rather, it emerged from the work of the climate change advisory panel appointed by the NDP government in the summer of 2015 and which reported in November 2015.[2] The government passed legislation establishing the carbon tax, the Climate Leadership Implementation Act[3] (known as Bill 20) in June 2016, despite heated objections from opposition parties. This act was part of a framework of legislation and regulations that included phasing out coal-fired power plants and replacing their output with electricity from renewable sources (Bill 27, the Renewable Electricity Act); capping carbon emissions from oil sands production (Bill 25, the Oil Sands Emissions Limit Act); and reducing methane

* Note to readers: This chapter was drafted in August 2017.

emissions. Phase one of the carbon tax came into effect on 1 January 2017, to be fully implemented one year later.

A carbon tax is an attempt to solve a problem of physics, using a solution from economics, applied through politics. So before we get to the politics of the matter, it's important to have a basic grasp of the physics of global warming and of the economics of a carbon tax.

To this end, this chapter starts with a brief explanation of the basic science of global warming before providing deep background on the politics of the carbon tax, which is important for understanding today's carbon tax debates. It then examines the economic principles of a carbon tax before moving on to an examination of the meaning of the carbon tax for the politics of Alberta. Finally, it considers the reaction to a carbon tax as an indicator of the province's adaptability to a world moving with increasing speed away from fossil fuels.

The Basic Science of Global Warming

A few key points provide a basic understanding of the physics of global warming. First, all objects warmer than absolute zero radiate energy, and hot objects radiate more energy than cool objects. The sun, being very hot, radiates large amounts of many kinds of energy, including ultraviolet energy, infrared energy, and visible light energy, which our eyes see as sunlight.[4] The earth absorbs a portion of all those energies from the sun, but being cooler, radiates them back out in just one form, infrared energy. Because the earth converts all these different forms of energy into infrared, it radiates a lot of infrared energy. We feel infrared energy as warmth but cannot see it (unless we're looking through an infrared camera).[5] Think of earth as an infrared heat lamp on its lowest setting, not glowing but gently warm to the touch.

Second, the infrared energy radiating down from the sun and up from the earth passes without effect through the nitrogen and oxygen in the atmosphere but is absorbed by water vapour, carbon dioxide (CO_2), methane, and other trace gases in the atmosphere, causing those gases to warm. These are called "greenhouse gases." The warmth of the CO_2 and other greenhouse gases then spreads to the rest of the atmosphere and the planet's surface. This warmth keeps the earth livable; without it, it would be a frozen planet.

Third, when fossil fuels such as coal, gasoline, and natural gas are burned, the carbon they contain, which has been locked underground for many millions of years, joins with oxygen to form CO_2, which is released into the air. The more CO_2 there is in the atmosphere, the greater the portion of the earth's infrared energy is absorbed by the atmosphere, and the warmer the surface of the earth becomes.

Fourth, since the start of the Industrial Age, humans have burned so much fossil fuel that the level of CO_2 in the atmosphere has risen 40 per cent above natural levels. The pace of this increase has accelerated in recent decades as energy consumption has increased and more countries, especially China, have industrialized. If nothing is done to slow the current rate of increase by curbing fossil fuel use, the concentration of CO_2 in the atmosphere is likely to reach 300 per cent or more of natural levels by the end of this century.[6] CO_2 stays in the atmosphere for many centuries, meaning that our accumulated emissions will affect the climate for many lifetimes.

The increasing CO_2 concentration in the atmosphere is already driving major environmental changes, including melting ice caps, rising ocean levels, droughts, and heat waves. As concentrations climb, the effects will become more severe, and to quote a presentation by American Petroleum Institute scientists to petroleum executives in 1980, they will bring "globally catastrophic effects."[7]

The Deep Roots of the Carbon Tax Debate

The politics of the carbon tax in Alberta are rooted in the debate between those who heed the legitimate research and evidence of global warming, and those who choose to ignore or deny it. The basic science of global warming has been generally understood since 1965, when the science advisory panel to the US president Lyndon Johnson delivered a paper titled, "Atmospheric Carbon Dioxide," which the president then made public.[8] The paper, written by top US scientists and based on decades of research, concluded with a warning:

> Through his worldwide industrial civilization, Man is unwittingly conducting a vast geophysical experiment. Within a

few generations he is burning fossil fuels that slowly accumulated in the earth over the past 500 million years.

The paper found that fossil fuels were emitting so much carbon dioxide that the effect "may be sufficient to produce measurable and perhaps marked changes in climate" that could be "deleterious from the point of view of human beings."[9] The repercussions included global warming, melting ice caps, and rising sea levels.

Important research into the effects of carbon emissions on global warming was conducted by governments, research agencies, and the petroleum industry in the 1970s and '80s. Scientists working for Exxon informed the company's headquarters in 1978 of a "general scientific agreement" that the global climate was warming because of fossil fuel emissions, and that while some countries would benefit, "others would have their agricultural output reduced or destroyed."[10] This memo warned that even in 1978 the clock was running fast: "Present thinking holds that man has a time window of five to ten years before the need for hard decisions regarding changes in energy strategies might become critical."[11] In the next several years, further research by Exxon and many other organizations supported and strengthened these findings.[12]

In 1980, the climate change task force of the American Petroleum Institute, the industry's main organization in the United States, reported that fossil fuel use was putting so much CO_2 into the atmosphere that big changes were coming to the climate. The timeline for the "likely impacts" of these changes was "1°C rise (2005): barely noticeable"; then "2.5°C rise (2038): major economic consequences"; followed by "5°C rise (2067): globally catastrophic effects."[13] Despite these worrying findings, in 1983 the American Petroleum Institute shut down its CO_2 and climate task force and in the late 1980s Exxon abandoned its global warming research program, though research at universities and elsewhere expanded.

By 1992, the science of global warming was so clear that more than one hundred heads of state gathered at the Earth Summit in Rio de Janeiro to launch the United Nations Framework Convention on Climate Change.[14] Even the Alberta government's Department of Energy acknowledged the danger of CO_2 emissions and prepared a plan to reduce them.[15] In the following decades the science continued to advance, and the evidence of global warming linked to the use of fossil fuels became clear and vast.

In the lead-up to the Rio Earth Summit, supporters of the fossil fuel industry began a sustained and well-financed campaign to deny and confuse public and political understanding of global warming science that continues to this day. This campaign, which has been well described and documented,[16] shapes the politics of the carbon tax in Alberta. In January 2017, for example, Wildrose MLA Don MacIntyre told a news conference that "the science isn't settled" on whether humans are the main cause of global warming.[17] MacIntyre repeated his position in subsequent weeks,[18] even while Wildrose leader Brian Jean supported mainstream science. When government MLAs challenged MacIntyre, he was backed up by members of the Wildrose caucus, including caucus whip Jason Nixon, who told reporters that NDP MLAs "should be more worried about getting rid of incompetent NDP ministers bringing in carbon taxes, making a mess of children's service and tearing up confidence in Alberta's economy."[19] MacIntyre's comments were widely reported and were endorsed by newspaper columnist Lorne Gunter.[20]

Whether or not MacIntyre, Nixon, or Gunter knew it, the message that the science of global warming "isn't settled" descends from a report done for the US Republican Party in 2002. The report, written by Frank Luntz, aimed to help Republicans improve their image on environmental issues, including global warming.[21] Luntz, who admitted in the report that the scientific debate "is closing" *against* global warming skeptics, nonetheless advised Republicans "to make the lack of scientific certainty a primary issue in the debate" on global warming. It is a wrenching and cynical piece of political advice that has been followed countless times, and as Don MacIntyre's comments show, it still echoes in the politics of Alberta's carbon tax.

In the meantime, CO2 emissions have grown to levels barely imagined a few decades ago. The increase in atmospheric CO2 predicted to cause "deleterious effects" worldwide by the US president's science council in 1965 was 25 per cent; in 2016 the increase passed 40 per cent and was rising fast.[22]

The Economic Principles of a Carbon Tax

As the science of global warming became clear, the need to reduce and then eliminate fossil fuel emissions became obvious, even to—perhaps especially to—the fossil fuel industry. An internal briefing titled, "CO2 Greenhouse Effect," and given wide circulation to Exxon management in 1982, acknowledged the science of global warming and directly stated its implications: "Mitigation of the 'greenhouse effect' would require major reductions in fossil fuel combustion."[23] Governments similarly recognized the need to reduce fossil fuel use, and unlike the industry, they pressed forward with reduction plans. These plans were formalized in a series of international agreements, including the Framework Convention on Climate Change signed at the Rio Earth Summit in 1992; the Kyoto Protocol in 1997; and the Paris Accord in 2016.

There are several ways for governments to bring down emissions. One is through regulations. Governments have passed a series of regulations to reduce greenhouse gas emissions, including higher fuel-efficiency standards for automobiles; better insulation standards for new buildings; and the mandatory phase-out of coal-fired power plants. Regulations are direct, clear, and generally enforceable, but they can also be inflexible, inefficient, and even misguided. They work best for relatively straightforward issues amenable to comparatively uniform solutions.

A second way for governments to reduce emissions is to impose a "cap and trade" system, in which a limit or "cap" is placed on all major sources of emissions, and then gradually lowered over a period of years. Emitters that exceed their caps pay penalties. At the same time, a trading system is established so that emitters that come in below their caps can earn revenue by selling their surplus allowance to those that exceed their caps. The cap forces the gradual reduction in emissions, and the trading creates incentives to reduce emissions through efficiency and innovation. Cap-and-trade systems were effective in reducing emissions causing acid rain—in which there were relatively few emitters of easily traced contaminants—but become complicated and open to abuse in the much larger world of CO2 emissions. Cap-and-trade systems are in various stages of development in Europe and a growing number of American states and Canadian provinces.

A third way for governments to reduce emissions is to increase the price of fossil fuels by adding a tax to them, a carbon tax. This uses the most fundamental principle of market economics: when the price of a product goes up, the demand for it tends to go down. By raising the cost of carbon fuels, a carbon tax will reduce their use, and therefore reduce emissions. A tax on carbon fuels, if sufficiently large, will induce consumers toward greater energy efficiency and toward alternative energy sources. A large enough tax would extinguish fossil fuel use entirely. Carbon taxes are simple and easily enforced and can be administered through existing sales tax systems. They allow consumers and markets to decide how to reduce emissions. The downside of carbon taxes is that unless they are continuously raised they lose their effectiveness because people adjust to the higher prices.

The Design of Alberta's Carbon Tax

Within months of taking office, the Notley government appointed a panel chaired by economist Andrew Leach to prepare a report to advise the government on its greenhouse gas emissions policies. The report was made public in November 2015, and it subsequently became the basis for much of the government's climate change legislation and policies, including the carbon tax. The panel recommended that a carbon tax be levied on about 90 per cent of carbon fuels on the basis that "putting a price on emissions leverages the power of markets to deploy both technologies and behavioral changes to reduce emissions over time. Carbon pricing is the most flexible and least-costly way to reduce emissions."[24] The government accepted the panel's recommendations. One of the ironies of Alberta's carbon tax debate is that the left-leaning NDP is implementing a market-based policy, which the right-wing parties are opposing.

Alberta's carbon tax applies to gasoline, diesel, coal, natural gas, and propane. The tax is calculated according to the weight of emissions released during combustion, so coal incurs more tax than natural gas, which releases less carbon to produce the same amount of energy. The tax started at $20/ton of emissions on 1 January 2017, and rose to $30.00/ton of emissions on 1 January 2018.[25] When fully implemented in 2018, the tax added ¢6.73/litre to the cost of gasoline; ¢8.03/litre to diesel; $1.517/gigajoule to natural gas; and ¢4.62/litre to propane. Various products are exempted from the tax, including farm fuels, inter-jurisdictional flights, biofuels, and fuels sold for export.

In 2018 the tax was expected to add an average of $101/year to gasoline costs for individuals and $205/year for couples with two children; and an average of $152/year to natural gas costs for individuals and $205/year for couples with two children.[26]

Alberta's situation is complicated by the Specified Gas Emitters Regulation (SGER).[27] The SGER was introduced in 2007 by the Progressive Conservative government of Ed Stelmach, and is sometimes called the first carbon tax in Canada. It is aimed at the largest industrial emitters of CO_2 and other greenhouse gases, and applies a tax per ton of emissions when a facility exceeds 100,000 tons of emissions per year. The tax applies only to those emissions above 100,000 tons, creating an incentive for industries to remain below that threshold. The tax was initially $15/ton of emissions above 100,000 ton, and rose to $20/ton in 2016 and to $30/ton in 2017. The SGER provides a complicated system through which emitters can purchase credits and offsets, reduce their emissions, or pay the tax. Revenues from the tax go into a fund that supports research and development of technologies for reducing emissions. The SGER will be replaced in 2018 by policies that integrate it with the government's other climate change plans.

The new carbon tax, when combined with the SGER and its successors, will cover up to 90 per cent of Alberta's greenhouse gas emissions.[28] The carbon tax is expected to collect a total of $6.78 billion from 2016–17 to 2020–22, and the SGER and its successor are expected to collect $2.82 billion in the same period, for a total of $9.6 billion.[29]

The use of this revenue distinguishes Alberta's plan from British Columbia's. The BC plan, though now evolving, was set up so all revenues collected by the carbon tax were used to reduce other taxes. For example, carbon tax revenues helped British Columbia maintain some of the lowest personal and corporate income tax rates in Canada.[30] The trade-off between higher fossil fuel prices and lower income taxes helped the province's government sell the carbon tax to voters.

Alberta's NDP government chose to use its revenues from the carbon tax differently, aiming a portion directly at "greening the economy." Alberta's carbon emissions are dramatically higher than British Columbia's because of emissions from petroleum production, especially from the oil sands, and because Alberta relied heavily on coal-fired power plants while British Columbia mostly used hydroelectricity. As a result, emissions per person in Alberta in 2013 were 67 tons annually, while the yearly figure in British Columbia was 14 tons.[31] By 2014, Alberta accounted for 37 per cent of Canada's emissions, the highest of all provinces, and Alberta's emissions were rising while those in Ontario, Quebec, and other provinces were falling.[32] By some measures, this imbalance was misleading, because while emissions from petroleum production, particularly the oil sands, are pinned entirely on Alberta, other provinces benefit from their use of Alberta's petroleum and from the economic activity its production creates.

Regardless, Alberta is an outlier, and with emissions per capita roughly five times higher in Alberta than Ontario, Quebec, or British Columbia, Alberta becomes an easy target for national and international criticism. As a result, Alberta's NDP government chose to direct a substantial portion of carbon tax revenues to businesses, municipalities, households, and other organizations to help them reduce emissions. Of the $9.6 billion in gross revenues collected by the carbon tax and SGER, $6.2 billion will be invested in reducing emissions. Of this, $3.4 billion will be directed to large-scale renewable energy projects, innovation, technology, and bioenergy initiatives; $2.2 billion to emission-reducing infrastructure such as public transit; and $645 million will be directed through a new organization called Energy Efficiency Alberta to improve energy efficiency in the residential, commercial, and non-profit sectors.[33] The remaining $3.4 billion will be used to help households, businesses, and communities adjust to the carbon tax. This includes $2.3 billion for consumer rebates; $865 million to reduce the small business tax rate from 3 per cent to 2 per cent effective 1 January 2017; and $195 million to help communities that are economically dependent on coal mines and coal-fired power plants to transition out of coal, and to help the transition in Indigenous communities.

Of special note are the consumer rebates, which came into effect 1 January 2017 and which were slated to increase with the rise in the carbon tax on 1 January 2018. The rebates are income dependent and will be up to $200 a year for single adults, $300 for couples, and $30 per child for up to four children per family. Two-thirds of households will receive a rebate, the large majority at the maximum, and rebates will be paid quarterly or semi-annually, depending on income.[34]

The carbon tax and the rebates are designed to work together to reduce emissions: the tax raises the cost of carbon fuels, encouraging consumers to use less of them, and the rebates enable consumers to pay for insulation, newer vehicles, and other carbon-reducing alternatives.

The Political Demographics of Alberta's Carbon Tax

Three different public opinion polls conducted in the months before the carbon tax was implemented show the broader political backdrop against which the carbon tax debate has unfolded in Alberta.[35] This backdrop held few surprises, and while it is bound to shift over time, it shows the demographic basis upon which the politics of the carbon tax are constructed. The details of each poll varied, but all three showed that a majority of Albertans opposed the carbon tax (sometimes called "levy" or "pricing" in the surveys). Opposition ranged from above 70 per cent in rural Alberta, to 66 per cent in Calgary, to 58 per cent in Edmonton. The carbon tax was supported by a majority of NDP and Liberal voters, but received very low support from PC and Wildrose voters (10 per cent and 5 per cent, respectively). Gender and income did not affect the level of support, but support was higher among university graduates than among those with less education, and it was higher among those under thirty-five than among those aged fifty-five and older. In short, public support for Alberta's carbon tax was highest in Edmonton and among well-educated and younger voters, but even in these groups a majority did not like it.

One poll compared the opinions of Albertans to residents of other provinces, and in the process exposed a deep divide.[36] Public support for carbon pricing topped 70 per cent in every province except Alberta and Saskatchewan (37 per cent and 32 per cent, respectively). This not only reflected the economic importance of fossil fuel production and coal-fired electricity in Alberta and Saskatchewan, but also portended the rise of a new chapter of fractious relations between these two provinces and the rest of the country, including the federal government. This is not a reprise of the politics of Western alienation that in the past has used the Ontario-Manitoba border to mark an East-West divide. Rather, this marks a newer divide, a "carbon divide," that could box Alberta and Saskatchewan into a smaller and politically weaker alliance against the rest of the country, especially if both provinces end up with anti-carbon-tax governments.

This same poll found that support among Albertans for carbon pricing could rocket from below 40 per cent to above 90 per cent if it led to approvals of pipelines for Alberta oil, suggesting that public opinion could move a great deal if circumstances changed. This seemed to bode well for the Alberta NDP, which had defended their carbon tax by saying it would earn the environmental credibility required to win approval of interprovincial and international pipelines.

The NDP argument made sense while Barack Obama was US president, for he had refused the Keystone XL pipeline on environmental grounds, and it was bolstered by federal and BC approvals of the Kinder Morgan Trans Mountain pipeline. But when Donald Trump assumed office in January 2017, he broke the link between US pipeline approval and the carbon tax by supporting the Keystone XL pipeline and disregarding global warming. The NDP argument still held for pipelines within Canada, but not for those heading south of the border. (At the time of writing, no polling was available to assess the impact of the approvals of the Trans Mountain and Keystone XL pipelines on public support for carbon pricing.)

Factors in the Carbon Tax Debate from Outside Alberta

Alberta politics are part of a hyper-connected world, one that is softening the elements that have traditionally defined Alberta's identity. The lines that solidly delineate Alberta on a map are remarkably porous in the real world, allowing the passage every year of tens of billions of dollars in trade, tens of thousands of migrants, more than twenty million air passengers, and countless digital connections.[37] Alberta is tied into highly integrated national and international systems of finance, trade, recreation, communication, education, and culture, all of which influence its politics. Overlaying these is the physical reality of global warming, which becomes more pressing every year, and the need for sufficient global action to address it. Alberta's carbon tax was not implemented in a vacuum.

The Price of Oil and the Economy

What may be the single largest factor shaping the politics of the carbon tax is out of the hands of any Alberta politician: the international price of oil. Low oil prices brought Alberta's economy to its knees the year before the carbon tax was introduced, and the carbon tax soon became a magnet for the fear and anger of people who were hurt by the economic slowdown, and for the politicians who wanted to stir them up. The price impact of the tax on a litre of gas was less than the price swings that precede many long weekends, and in a stronger economy it may have barely been an issue. But in a depressed economy, the carbon tax became a flash point. If the economy recovers, the carbon tax may weaken as a political issue.

The Federal Government

The federal government set a mandatory price on carbon emissions of $10/ton in 2018 that will increase $10 a year to $50/ton in 2022.[38] If a province does not put a system in place to achieve these prices, then the federal government will impose one. This almost makes opposition to a carbon tax in Alberta pointless, except as an opportunity to score political points. An Alberta government that cancels the carbon tax will be signalling its desire to confront Ottawa and return Alberta politics to chronic feuding with the federal government.

Other Provinces

In addition to the federal government, the other provincial governments affect Alberta's carbon tax debate. When she headed the Liberal government in British Columbia, Premier Christy Clark was able to face down intense opposition to the expansion of pipelines from Alberta to the West Coast by citing Alberta's carbon tax: "I think Alberta following British Columbia on that really helps us make the case that Canadians do care about climate change. We do care about protecting our environment."[39] Clark's support was important for Kinder Morgan's Trans Mountain pipeline, and not having a carbon tax would have made her support less likely. However, the Clark government was narrowly defeated in May 2017, replaced by a minority NDP government with the Green Party holding the balance of power. The Greens, led by climate change scientist Andrew Weaver, compelled the NDP government to oppose the Trans Mountain pipeline, regardless of Alberta's carbon tax. This set the BC government against both the Alberta and federal governments, and at the time of writing the issue had not been settled. In October 2017, the Federal Court of Appeal was scheduled to hear an appeal of the National Energy Board's approval of the Trans Mountain project launched by a large coalition of First Nations and environmental groups. The BC government applied for intervener status in the case. If the appeal is lost there is a risk that other actions—including civil disobedience—will be staged in an effort to halt the pipeline. The way forward for this project will not be easy; cancelling the carbon tax would seem certain to inflame its opponents.

The Alberta government's support for a carbon tax will not be lost on pipeline projects in other provinces. Landlocked Alberta needs co-operation from other jurisdictions, and when it comes to the carbon tax, the national political climate exerts a forceful blowback in Alberta. A repeal of the carbon tax would likely injure Alberta's reputation and reduce the likelihood of pipeline support in other provinces.

International Politics

The federal government operates in an international setting in which pressure to reduce emissions is steadily intensifying, notwithstanding the election of Donald Trump. In the long run (and the starting pistol for the long run was fired in 1992 at the Rio Earth Summit), ignoring global warming is not an option. The 174 countries that signed the 2015 Paris Agreement on Climate Change—including all European countries, China, Japan, and Canada—recognize this.

The election of Donald Trump has slowed but not stopped American action on global warming. Major US corporations (e.g., Google, GM), leading states (California, New York), municipalities, and individuals, will continue the transition toward lower emissions in America, and the transition will eventually accelerate as the cost of not acting becomes ever more apparent.

Internal Pressures Influencing the Carbon Tax Debate in Alberta

Large Oil Sands Producers

In November 2015, when Premier Rachel Notley announced her government's Climate Leadership Plan—including the framework of the carbon tax—she was joined on stage by executives of four of the province's largest oil companies, Suncor, Shell, Cenovus, and Canadian Natural Resources Ltd., who spoke in favour of the plan. These major oil sands companies each produced more than 250,000 barrels per day, and they believed that stronger environmental policies would help obtain pipeline approvals to get their oil and bitumen to markets.[40] Their support for the Climate Leadership Plan, including the carbon tax, was crucial for the government. If these companies had openly opposed the carbon tax it is possible the tax would never have been launched.

Alberta's petroleum industry dominates both its economy and its politics, and on carbon tax and climate change policies the industry is divided between the giants of the oil sands and almost everyone else. Each of the companies that supported the premier during her launch of the carbon tax produce enough oil and bitumen from the oil sands to fill a major pipeline on its own, and they send most of their product out of the province and out of the country. Steering an oil sands plant through feasibility, approvals, design, financing, and construction can take a decade, and production can continue for forty years or more. Suspending production when oil prices are low is neither financially nor operationally feasible, so once the flow starts it does not stop. For all these reasons, oil sands companies have unusually long-term global perspectives. They have deep pockets and work with local, provincial, state, and national governments of many political stripes in Canada and the United States. Operating on the scale they do, Alberta's carbon tax is just one more detail.

Further, these companies had been operating under a form of carbon tax since 2007, when the Specified Gas Emitters Regulation was introduced for all facilities producing more than 100,000 tons of CO_2 annually. For these companies, the added cost of the carbon tax was small, and the potential benefit in terms of easier pipeline approvals was large. As a TD Economics report on the impact of the carbon tax on oil sands producers stated,

> The bottom line is that the oil sands need to reduce their carbon footprint, and Alberta's climate change plan is a step in the right direction. . . . The cost [of the carbon tax] to the oil sands sector is unlikely to be excessive enough to reject a project that would otherwise go ahead. . . . In fact, oil prices, efficiencies and market access will remain the largest determinants of investment in the sector.[41]

Small and Intermediate Oil and Gas Companies

In contrast, small and intermediate companies in Alberta's oil and gas sector often spoke out forcefully against the carbon tax and in so doing became a driving force behind those opposing it. These companies most often worked in conventional oil and gas as explorers, drillers, service providers, and producers (less than 10,000 barrels of oil equivalent per day for small firms, and 10,000–200,000 for intermediate firms).[42] Their budgets were small compared to oil sands companies and their timelines much shorter. A conventional well could be drilled in a few days and peak production could begin to decline in two years. These companies were tuned to the finer, short-term details of costs and markets. The carbon tax was an added cost they did not want. It was also a symbol of unwanted government intervention and a harbinger of more threats to the fossil fuel industry.

Companies working with conventional oil and gas were geographically spread throughout Alberta and were often locally owned and operated, so they could have an impressive political reach by talking to their many local MLAs and sharing their views with employees and community organizations. Among the outspoken opponents of the carbon tax were the Explorers and Producers Association of Canada,[43] many individual company owners,[44] and commentators such as David Yager, who was a petroleum industry investor and a key organizer, as well as a one-time president of the Wildrose Party.[45] Among the largest of the intermediate companies opposing a carbon tax was Crescent Point Energy, whose CEO Scott Saxberg was outspoken on the issue.[46] These voices were heard repeatedly throughout the province, were used to organize protests and petitions, and were plugged directly into the political process, where they found many allies. In general, it appeared that the small and intermediate companies were much more active in seeking political change than the large oil sands producers.

Opposition to the Carbon Tax among Political Parties

On 7 June 2016, when the the legislation to implement the carbon tax was voted on in the Alberta legislature, all opposition parties voted against it. Even the Alberta Liberal Party and the Alberta Party, each with only one seat and each claiming to support the concept of a carbon tax, found reasons to vote against Bill 20.[47]

The Wildrose and PC Parties led the political charge against the carbon tax. Wildrose leader Brian Jean called on the government to "scrap the carbon tax,"[48] while his party launched a petition called "Stop the tax on everything."[49] During the debate on Bill 20 in the legislature, Jean was clear: "I can't see me ever supporting a carbon tax."[50] His three largest objections were that it would cost families; hurt the economy by adding costs to oil, gas, and coal producers; and hurt non-profit groups and charities.

In the legislature, the PCs took a similar approach, opposing Bill 20 for a long list of reasons, including that it was bad for the economy, would hurt the tourism industry, and channeled money to green energy projects that were not feasible. On the final day of debate on Bill 20, veteran PC MLA David Rodney skated around a solid commitment to the science of global warming: "Progressive Conservatives understand that climate change is real and that human activity has impacted how the effects have been felt globally. Some say that the difference on this side of the House is that some here might consider it real and some might consider it just a problem."[51] Jason Kenney, running for the PC leadership, promised to abolish "the job-killing carbon tax" if he became premier.[52] In an unusual move, Michelle Rempel, a federal Conservative MP from Calgary, rose in the House of Commons in Ottawa to criticize large oil sands companies for supporting the carbon tax: "the few rich CEOs of Canada's big energy firms probably support [the carbon tax] because it may force junior firms out of the market, enabling them to make a play for assets."[53] Her comments were a pointed indication of the sharp divide between several large oil sands producers and the rest of the industry when it came to the carbon tax.

Alberta Liberal leader David Swann, on the other hand, applauded Bill 20 but voted against it because it had enough small weaknesses to risk being ineffective. It lacked "performance targets" and a "cost-benefit analysis," and "perhaps most importantly, the bill is not revenue neutral such as the B.C. model."[54] Alberta Party leader Greg Clark took a similar approach, telling the legislature, "I support a carbon tax, but I cannot support this carbon tax. This carbon tax should be revenue neutral."[55] Whatever their reasons, no other parties voted with the NDP government.

The day before the tax came into effect on 1 January 2017, some Wildrose and PC politicians posted photos of themselves filling up their vehicles at gas stations, though the province-wide average price of gasoline fell the following month from $1.09/litre to 98¢/litre.[56]

Other Voices on the Carbon Tax

Many other people and groups spoke out on the carbon tax in the lead-up to its implementation. Calgary mayor Naheed Nenshi did not like it,[57] and neither did the right-wing Canadian Taxpayers Federation.[58] But the carbon tax had supporters too. Edmonton mayor Don Iveson regarded the tax as "a wellspring for innovation and investment"[59] because it encouraged businesses and governments to begin adapting to a lower-carbon economy. University of Calgary economist Trevor Toombe repeatedly spoke to support the carbon tax,[60] as did the Pembina Institute[61] and Greenpeace.[62]

The NDP Government

Despite the loud opposition, the NDP government implemented the carbon tax. It spent $9 million dollars promoting and advertising its Climate Leadership Plan, including the carbon tax,[63] and more importantly, it was buoyed by approvals from the federal and BC governments for the Kinder Morgan Trans Mountain pipeline in late 2016 and early 2017. Prime Minister Trudeau and Premier Clark praised the Alberta climate plan and carbon tax for easing the approvals.

The NDP government, for its part, was prepared to let time pass for people to adjust to the tax and for the benefits of its revenues to be felt. No doubt it was hoping the rebate cheques sent to a majority of Alberta households might convert opponents into supporters.

What Does This Mean for Alberta Politics?

The NDP government of Rachel Notley is standing firm on its carbon tax. Meanwhile, the conservative political movement in Alberta has been transformed. The Progressive Conservative Party under the leadership of former federal Conservative cabinet minister Jason Kenney, and the Wildrose Party under the leadership of former Conservative MP Brian Jean, voted to merge into the new United Conservative Party. Kenney and Jean, the two front-runners for the leadership of the new party, both opposed the carbon tax. After winning the October 2017 leadership race, Kenney committed his new party to ending the carbon tax and the array of other measures the New Democrats put in place to deal with greenhouse gas emissions.

Both the Alberta Liberals and the Alberta Party seem likely to remain on the sidelines of Alberta politics with marginal levels of support, though some disaffected PCs may consider backing the Alberta Party to raise it to higher prominence. As many elections demonstrate, the unexpected happens in politics, and no one is to be counted out.

In many ways this turmoil is only detail. It seems certain that the carbon tax will be fought as one issue in a broader campaign. The conservative messages in that campaign may pivot on slogans of job-killing taxes, bloated public services, unsustainable public debt, competitive disadvantages, or the need for pragmatism over ideology, but no matter what the messages, the dominant purpose will be to defeat the NDP and protect the interests of small and intermediate oil producers. Ironically, if the United Conservative Party wins the election and goes on to dismantle the carbon tax, it may well damage Alberta's oil industry by losing legitimacy in other provinces and even foreign markets. Until the physical reality of carbon emissions and global warming is fully accepted by Alberta's political and economic leaders, the province's future will see unnecessary turbulence and even self-harm. Alberta must travel with the rest of the world to a post-carbon future, or be left by the wayside.

The carbon tax serves as a marker for a larger package of issues and a symbol of people's individual politics. It pits people and interests who are global warming skeptics, anti-tax, older, less educated, and more rural, against those who accept the science of global warming, regard taxes as the price of civilization, and are younger, more urban, and more highly educated.

It is quite possible that in the 2019 election, the NDP will hang on to the voters who until 2015 traditionally supported the Alberta Liberals, especially if Justin Trudeau and Rachel Notley continue to work well together. If the weakness continues with the Alberta Liberal Party and the Alberta Party, then the NDP may be the only viable choice for the 30 to 35 per cent of Albertans who steadfastly vote progressive. This will be especially true if their main opponent, the United Conservative Party, assumes positions that are socially conservative and fiscally harsh. Progressive voters who have historically supported other parties may be drawn to the NDP, as was shown by the floor-crossing to the NDP of one-time PC leadership candidate Sandra Jansen. If the NDP win in 2019, Alberta will continue with its own carbon tax; if the party loses, Alberta will get Ottawa's carbon tax. Either way, Alberta will have a carbon tax.

If the United Conservative Party wins the 2019 election, the party's unwinding of the carbon tax will be a messy affair. The process won't be as simple as cancelling health-care premiums or changing income tax rates. Cancelling the carbon tax will mean ending regular cheques to more than half of Alberta's families; losing credibility on environmental issues in jurisdictions where environmental credibility is important (especially in British Columbia and Ottawa); and cancelling the billions of dollars' worth of projects that the tax will be funding. It is also likely to entail a confrontation with the federal government, which will impose a price on carbon from afar if one is not imposed by Alberta itself, returning the province to a politics of resentment and confrontation vis-à-vis the rest of Canada. To be sure, the politics of resentment may suit some supporters of the United Conservative Party. And if Alberta's economy continues to stagnate into the 2020s, which is certainly possible, it will be easy to fuel such resentment. But resentment will not change the underlying weaknesses in the province's economy, nor will it alter the physics of global warming.

Global warming is going to disrupt a great deal more than our natural environment; it is going to disrupt our politics and economics too—more so in Alberta than most other places, because of our large fossil fuel resources. The carbon tax is just a precursor to much bigger disruptions in the future that will melt industries and political parties as surely as it melts the glaciers of the Alberta Rockies. Global warming is driving a much larger matter than the carbon tax onto the political agenda of Alberta: the operating of the provincial government without a gushing flow of royalties from oil and natural gas. Balancing Alberta's budget looms on the near horizon as the much tougher, bigger, and uglier political sibling of the carbon tax, and whoever wins the next election will be staring that project in the face.

The carbon tax is a transition issue, a policy intended to start Alberta on a path toward a post-carbon future that is coming whether the province wants it or not. It is only a beginning in what will be a wrenching, decades-long process of replacing Alberta's economic, social, and political foundations. The carbon tax will be overshadowed by other issues that each form a part of the same process: downward pressure on oil prices; slackening world demand for oil and bitumen; unemployment and recession; burgeoning provincial debts driven by gutted royalties; cuts in public services; increases in other provincial taxes, and so on.

The politics of the carbon tax are a small part of this larger struggle. How they play out will indicate whether Albertans are ready to face the reality of global warming and move forward, or simply want to hang on to a fossil-fuelled past that is melting away.

NOTES

1   Alberta NDP, "Leadership for What Matters: Election Platform 2015," April 2015, https://d3n8a8pro7vhmx.cloudfront.net/themes/5538f80701925b5033000001/ attachments/original/1431112969/Alberta_NDP_Platform_2015.pdf?1431112969 (accessed 18 January 2018).

2   Andrew Leach, "Climate Leadership: Report to Minister," Government of Alberta, 20 November 2015.

3   A copy of Bill 20 may be obtained on line at http://www.assembly.ab.ca/ISYS/ LADDAR_files/docs/bills/bill/legislature_29/session_2/20160308_bill-020.pdf.

4   See "The Radiation Balance," *Calspace*, http://earthguide.ucsd.edu/virtualmuseum/ climatechange1/02_3.shtml (accessed 18 January 2018).

5   See Janet Fang, "Snake infrared detection unravelled," *Nature*, 14 March 2010, http:// www.nature.com/news/2010/100314/full/news.2010.122.html (accessed 18 January 2018).

6   R. K. Pachauri and L. A. Meyer, eds., *Climate Change 2014: Synthesis Report. Contribution of Working Groups I, II and III to the Fifth Assessment Report of the Intergovernmental Panel on Climate Change* (Geneva: United Nations Intergovernmental Panel on Climate Change, 2014), 151.

7   "Minutes of Meeting, CO2 and Climate Task Force, American Petroleum Institute, February 29, 1980," made public by *Inside Climate News*, http://insideclimatenews.org/ sites/default/files/documents/AQ-9%20Task%20Force%20Meeting%20%281980%29.pdf (accessed 25 January 2017).

8   Roger Revelle, Wallace Broeker, Harmon Craig, C. D. Keeling, and J. Smagorinsky, "Atmospheric Carbon Dioxide," *Report of the Environmental Pollution Panel, President's Science Advisory Committee* (Washington, DC: The White House, 1965), appendix Y4.

9   Ibid., 126–7.

10   Neela Banerjee, Lisa Song, and David Hasemyer, "Exxon: The Road Not Taken," *Inside Climate News*, 16 September 2015, http://insideclimatenews.org/news/15092015/ Exxons-own-research-confirmed-fossil-fuels-role-in-global-warming (accessed 25 January 2017).

11   Ibid.

12   See, for example, the untitled memo from Roger W. Cohen, Director of Theoretical and Mathematical Sciences Laboratory, Exxon Research and Engineering Company, to A. M. Natkin, Office of Science and Technology, Exxon Corporation, 2 September 1982, made public by *Inside Climate News*, http://insideclimatenews.org/sites/default/files/ documents/%2522Consensus%2522%20on%20CO2%20Impacts%20%281982%29.pdf (accessed 25 January 2017).

13   "Minutes of Meeting, CO2 and Climate Task Force, American Petroleum Institute, February 29, 1980."

14   United Nations, "UN Conference on Environment and Development (1992)," 23 May 1997, http://www.un.org/geninfo/bp/enviro.html (accessed 31 January 2017).

15   Energy Efficiency Branch, Alberta Department of Energy, *A Discussion Paper on the Potential for Reducing CO2 Emissions in Alberta, 1988–2005, Executive Summary*, September 1990, Alberta Legislature Library Sessional Paper 547/2002.

16   For examples, see the following: Jane Mayer, *Dark Money: The Hidden History of the Billionaires Behind the Rise of the Radical Right* (New York: Anchor Books, 2017); Michael Mann, *The Hockey Stick and the Climate Wars: Dispatches From the Front Lines* (New York: Columbia University Press, 2012); Chris Turner, *The War on Science: Muzzled Scientists and Wilful Blindness in Stephen Harper's Canada* (Vancouver: Greystone Books, 2013); and Banerjee, Song, and Hasemyer, "Exxon: The Road Not Taken."

17   " 'Science isn't settled' shows Wildrose attitude to climate change, minister says," *CBC News*, 3 January 2017, http://www.cbc.ca/news/canada/edmonton/science-isn-t-settled-comment-wildrose-attitude-climate-change-environment-minister-1.3919777 (accessed 1 February 2017).

18   Todd Vaughan, "Q&A with Don MacIntyre: Innisfail-Sylvan Lake MLA talks carbon tax and climate change," *Sylvan Lake News*, 12 January 2017, http://www. sylvanlakenews.com/news/410553005.html?mobile=true (accessed 1 February 2017).

19   Emma Graney, "NDP demands removal of Wildrose critic over climate change row," *Edmonton Sun*, 3 January 2017, http://www.edmontonsun.com/2017/01/03/ndp-demands-removal-of-wildrose-critic-over-climate-change-row (accessed 1 February 2017).

20   Lorne Gunter. "Don't let climate alarmists muzzle your skepticism," *Toronto Sun*, 7 January 2017, http://www.torontosun.com/2017/01/07/dont-let-climate-alarmists-muzzle-your-skepticism (accessed 1 February 2017).

21   Images of parts of the report are available at various websites, including the following: https://www.motherjones.com/files/LuntzResearch_environment.pdf. For further analysis on this issue see Anthony Leiserowitz, Geoff Feinberg, Seth Rosenthal, Nicholas Smith, Ashley Anderson, Connie Roser-Renouf, and Edward Maibach, "What's in a Name? Global Warming versus Climate Change," *Yale Project on Climate Change Communication* (New Haven, CT: Yale Center for Environmental Communication, 2014).

22   "The Keeling Curve," Scripps Institute of Oceanography, University of California at San Diego, https://scripps.ucsd.edu/programs/keelingcurve/ (accessed 31 January 2017).

23   Exxon Research and Engineering Company, "CO2 Greenhouse Effect," 12 November 1982, made public by *Inside Climate News*, http://insideclimatenews.org/sites/default/files/documents/1982%20Exxon%20Primer%20on%20CO2%20Greenhouse%20Effect.pdf (accessed 25 January 2017).

24   Andrew Leach, "Climate Leadership," 5.

25   See Government of Alberta, "Carbon Levy and Rebates," 2016, https://www.alberta.ca/climate-carbon-pricing.aspx (accessed 18 January 2017), and "Fiscal Plan," 2016, http://finance.alberta.ca/publications/budget/budget2016/fiscal-plan-complete.pdf, 5–6 and 93–8 (accessed 18 January 2017).

26   Government of Alberta, "Fiscal Plan," 96.

27   Leach, "Climate Leadership"; Government of Alberta, "Industrial Emissions Management," 9 August 2016, http://aep.alberta.ca/climate-change/programs-and-services/industrial-emissions-management.aspx (accessed 23 January 2017); Alison M. Sears, "Changes to the regulation of greenhouse gas emissions in Alberta: The Government of Alberta announces first step in new climate change strategy," *Canadian Energy Law*, 26 June 2015, http://www.canadianenergylaw.com/2015/06/articles/climate-change/changes-to-the-regulation-of-greenhouse-gas-emissions-in-alberta-the-government-of-alberta-announces-first-step-in-new-climate-change-strategy/ (accessed 23 January 2017).

28   Government of Alberta, "Fiscal Plan," 94.

29   Ibid., 6.

30   Government of British Columbia, "B.C.'s Revenue-Neutral Carbon Tax," 2016, http://www2.gov.bc.ca/gov/content/environment/climate-change/policy-legislation-programs/carbon-tax (accessed 18 January 2018).

31   Calculated from information in Paul Boothe and Felix-A. Boudreault, *By the Numbers: Canadian GHG Emissions* (London, ON: Lawrence National Centre for Policy and Management, Ivey Business School, University of Western Ontario, 2016).

32   Environment and Climate Change Canada, "Greenhouse Gas Emissions by Province and Territory," 14 April 2016, https://www.ec.gc.ca/indicateurs-indicators/default. asp?lang=en&n=18F3BB9C-1 (accessed 23 January 2017).

33   Government of Alberta, "Energy Efficiency Alberta," https://www.alberta.ca/energy-efficiency-alberta.aspx (accessed 23 January 2017).

34   Government of Alberta, "Fiscal Plan," 5.

35   Mark Henry, "Albertans's Views on Climate Leadership Plan," *ThinkHQ*, 29 September 2016, http://thinkhq.ca/albertans-views-on-climate-leadership-plan/ (accessed 24 January 2017); Faron Ellis. "Alberta Provincial Politics Carbon Tax and Coal-fired Electricity Generation," October 2016, Lethbridge College Citizen Society Research Lab, http://www.lethbridgecollege.ca/sites/default/files/imce/about-us/applied-research/ csrl/csrl_lethbridge_college_-_fall_2016_alberta_study_-_carbon_tax_and_coal.pdf (accessed 24 January 2017); Bruce Anderson and David Coletto, "Climate, Carbon, and Pipelines: A Path to Consensus?" *Abacus Data*, 18 October 2016, http://abacusdata.ca/ climate-carbon-and-pipelines-a-path-to-consensus/ (accessed 24 January 2017).

36   Anderson and Coletto. "Climate, Carbon, and Pipelines."

37   Government of Alberta, "Economic Dashboard," 2016, http://economicdashboard. alberta.ca (accessed 26 January 2017).

38   Government of Canada, "Pricing carbon for clean growth," 13 November 2016, http:// www.climatechange.gc.ca/default.asp?Lang=En&n=32BC8D0A-1 (accessed 26 January 2017).

39   Tom Fletcher, "Clark applauds Alberta carbon tax plan," *Terrace Standard*, 24 November 2015, http://www.terracestandard.com/news/353186211.html (accessed 26 January 2017).

40   Government of Alberta, "Climate Leadership Plan will protect Albertans' health, environment and economy," 22 November 2015, https://www.alberta.ca/release. cfm?xID=38885E74F7B63-A62D-D1D2-E7BCF6A98D616C09 (accessed 26 January 2017); Claudia Cattaneo, "Secret deal on Alberta's oil sands emissions limits divides patch," *Financial Post* (Toronto), http://business.financialpost.com/news/energy/secret-deal-on-albertas-oilsands-emission-limits-divides-patch (accessed 27 January 2017).

41   Dina Ignjatovic, "What does the carbon tax mean for the Canadian oil sands?" *TD Economics Special Report*, 22 November 2016, https://www.td.com/document/PDF/ economics/special/Canadian_Oil_Sands.pdf (accessed 22 January 2017).

42   "Canadian Intermediate Oil and Gas Listing," http://iq.iradesso.ca/index. php?page=intermediates_listing (accessed 15 August 2017).

43   Gary Leach, "Welcome news on pipelines, but Trump's agenda signals tough competition," *Calgary Herald*, 1 December 2016, http://calgaryherald.com/opinion/ columnists/leach-welcome-news-on-pipelines-but-trumps-agenda-signals-tough-competition (accessed 27 January 2017.

44 Reid Southwick, "Smaller oil patch producers fear carbon tax fallout will restrict competition," *Calgary Herald*, 5 October 2016, http://calgaryherald.com/business/energy/smaller-oilpatch-producers-fear-carbon-tax-fallout-will-restrict-competition (accessed 27 January 2017).

45 David Yager, "The problem with carbon taxes and why Alberta's timing on $3 billion in new carbon taxes is terrible," *EnergyNow*, 2 November 2016, http://energynow.ca/problem-carbon-taxes-albertas-timing-3-billion-new-carbon-taxes-terrible-david-yager-yager-management/ (accessed 27 January 2017).

46 Geoffrey Morgan, "Companies leave CAPP as divide over carbon tax policies widens," *Financial Post* (Toronto), 21 June 2017, http://www.calgarysun.com/2017/06/21/companies-leave-capp-as-divide-over-carbon-tax-policies-widen (accessed 15 August 2017).

47 *Alberta Hansard*, 7 June 2016, 1545–57, Legislative Assembly of Alberta, 29th Legislature, Second Session, http://www.assembly.ab.ca/ISYS/LADDAR_files/docs/hansards/han/legislature_29/session_2/20160607_0900_01_han.pdf#page=5 (accessed 30 January 2017).

48 James Wood, "Wildrose Leader Brian Jean vows to scrap Alberta carbon tax, battle federal carbon tax," *Calgary Sun*, 5 October 2016, http://www.calgarysun.com/2016/10/05/wildrose-leader-brian-jean-vows-to-scrap-alberta-carbon-tax-battle-federal-carbon-price (accessed 31 January 2017).

49 Wildrose Party of Alberta, "Stop the tax on everything," http://www.taxoneverything.ca (accessed 31 January 2017).

50 Brian Jean, quoted in *Alberta Hansard*, 7 June 2016, 1552, Legislative Assembly of Alberta, 29th Legislature, Second Session, http://www.assembly.ab.ca/ISYS/LADDAR_files/docs/hansards/han/legislature_29/session_2/20160607_0900_01_han.pdf#page=5 (accessed 30 January 2017).

51 David Rodney, quoted in Ibid., 1546–8.

52 Unite Alberta: Kenney, "How high will NDP carbon tax go?" 5 December 2016, http://www.jasonkenney.ca/how_high_will_ndp_carbon_tax_go (accessed 31 January 2017).

53 James Wood, "Rempel slams big oilpatch players for carbon tax support," *Calgary Herald*, 5 October 2016, http://calgaryherald.com/news/politics/rempel-slams-big-oilpatch-players-for-carbon-tax-support (accessed 31 January 2017).

54 David Swann, quoted in *Alberta Hansard*, 7 June 2016, 1549, Legislative Assembly of Alberta, 29th Legislature, Second Session, http://www.assembly.ab.ca/ISYS/LADDAR_files/docs/hansards/han/legislature_29/session_2/20160607_0900_01_han.pdf#page=5 (accessed 30 January 2017).

55 Greg Clark, quoted in Ibid., 1552.

56 "Gas prices in Calgary," *CBC News* (n.d.), http://www.cbc.ca/calgary/features/gasprices/ (accessed 31 January 2017).

57 Helen Pike, "Nenshi says carbon tax puts unfair strain on municipalities," *Metro News*, 14 April 2016, http://www.metronews.ca/news/calgary/2016/04/14/naheed-nenshi-alberta-budget-carbon-tax-municipalities.html (accessed 31 January 2017).

58　Paige MacPherson, "Alberta's crippling carbon tax," *Financial Post* (Toronto), 3 December 2015, http://business.financialpost.com/fp-comment/albertas-crippling-carbon-tax (accessed 27 January 2017).

59　Nola Keeler, "Carbon tax will lead to more Edmonton jobs, says mayor," *CBC News,* 20 December 2016, http://www.cbc.ca/news/canada/edmonton/carbon-tax-will-lead-to-more-edmonton-jobs-says-mayor-1.3904305 (accessed 31 January 2017).

60　Trevor Toombe, "What carbon pricing means for Canadian households," C.D. Howe Institute, 19 October 2016, https://www.cdhowe.org/intelligence-memos/trevor-tombe-what-carbon-pricing-means-canadian-households (accessed 31 January 2017).

61　Sara Hastings-Simon, "FAQ: Carbon pricing," Pembina Institute, 19 May 2016, https://www.pembina.org/blog/faq-carbon-pricing (accessed 31 January 2017).

62　Emilia Kennedy, "Ambitious, effective and achievable? Assessing Alberta's new climate change strategy," Greenpeace, http://www.greenpeace.org/canada/en/blog/Blogentry/ambitious-effective-and-achievable-assessing-/blog/54868/ (accessed 31 January 2017).

63　"$9M in ads to sell Alberta's climate plan angers Wildrose, Tories," *CBC News,* 7 December 2016, http://www.cbc.ca/news/canada/edmonton/climate-change-advertising-blitz-1.3886612 (accessed 31 January 2017).

Notley: The Accidental Pipeline Advocate

Deborah Yedlin

The oil and natural gas pipelines that keep societies moving and economies growing around the world are the midwives of the energy sector, the bridge between the site of production and the end-user, whether commercial enterprises or individuals.

Pipeline infrastructure has been an important component of Canada's economic engine, supporting the development of the country's oil and natural gas bounty. More than 825,000 kilometres of pipelines criss-cross this country, their regulation overseen by the National Energy Board since 1959; if one laid all the pipe in North America end to end, it would circle the globe twenty times.

So why is it that pipelines are under siege today, when their development more than fifty years ago went largely unnoticed and uncontested?

One could say it's a question Canada's oil patch has been wrestling with ever since 1977, when the Berger Inquiry into the Mackenzie Valley pipeline—which was to carry natural gas and, later, oil from the Artic south into Alberta—declared a ten-year moratorium on the project, effectively killing the project. While that pipeline was ultimately revived in 2006, the economics behind it changed dramatically due to the steep and sustained drop in natural gas prices, and it remains a symbol of failure in the context of pipeline approvals in Canada.

Since 1977, there have been dramatic changes in the North American energy landscape stemming from the development and implementation of new technologies. This has transformed the United States from the most important customer for Canadian oil and gas production, to a competitor for both commodities. This means Canada must aggressively seek new markets overseas in order to realize the full value of what is produced and ensure that its natural resource endowment, symbolized by the 170 billion barrels of oil contained in the oil sands of Northern Alberta, are developed, not left stranded.

The changes in the economics of energy development have coincided with a rise in environmental activism, opposition from First Nations peoples, and increased fragmentation of the media, which has enabled many perspectives on the issue to gain exposure—even as the information put forward is inaccurate. Layer on the need to gain political capital at both the provincial and federal levels, and the pipeline quagmire at times appears intractable.

The pipeline infrastructure of old was meant to serve all Canadians, bringing oil into Canada from the US Northeast or natural gas into urban centres in Alberta. The true catalyst for Canada's pipeline network was the discovery of the Leduc #1 well by Imperial Oil in 1947. By 1950, the Interprovincial Pipeline, or IPL, had built a line running from Edmonton to Superior, Wisconsin, which later expanded to Sarnia, Ontario. By 1953, the system was shipping oil from Edmonton to Vancouver. Back then, the building of a pipeline was a straightforward exercise, as was its purpose: it delivered a needed product to end-users.

Prior to the establishment of Canada's National Energy Board—constituted in 1959 as a quasi-judicial body with a mandate to regulate provincial and interprovincial pipelines in an attempt to take the politics out of pipeline regulation—the responsibility for each pipeline fell to the respective provinces. If the project crossed provincial boundaries, the Federal Transport Commission was involved alongside the provinces in question. This is essentially how the initial leg of the Trans Mountain pipeline was built in 1953. It's worth noting that before Trans Mountain was built, British Columbia received most of its oil via tanker from California. Trans Mountain was deemed to be in the public interest and, ironically, the fears over the project centred on the prospect of oil being exported to the United States instead of being used to supply the Vancouver-based refineries for the benefit of British Columbians.

The best example of the differing views on the need for pipeline infrastructure and the establishment of depoliticized regulatory oversight was the fight to approve TransCanada's mainline project, which required a debate in Parliament in 1956 spearheaded by the trade and commerce minister at the time, C. D. Howe.

Howe's position—and that of the ruling Liberal government—was that it was in the best interests of the country that the pipeline be built entirely in Canada, where it would carry natural gas from the West to the East. The debate lasted almost a month, and the resulting bill—which also included the approval of a loan for a portion of the construction—was passed in June 1956. The pipeline was in service by 1958.

Canada's pipeline infrastructure continued to grow through the decades, providing important support for continued investment in the oil and gas resource bounty of Alberta, Saskatchewan, and British Columbia. Whether it was the TransCanada, IPL (now Enbridge), Trans Mountain (now Kinder Morgan), Pembina pipelines, and other, smaller carriers, there were few impediments to the building of pipelines until the demise of the Mackenzie Valley initiative in 1977.

Many in the oil patch view the failure of that project as an example of what happens when a regulatory process is not well defined. Especially telling were the opening words of Justice Berger's report: "We are now at our last frontier. It is a frontier that all of us have read about, but few of us have seen. Profound issues, touching our deepest concerns as a nation, await us there." Berger recommended the project be put on ice for ten years, during which long-standing First Nations land claims issues would be addressed and conservation areas that would protect sensitive areas would be established. But Berger's recommendations also included that no pipeline ever be built across the northern Yukon. If anything, then, Mackenzie Valley has come to be seen as the beginning of First Nations finding their collective voice through opposition to resource or infrastructure development.

The National Energy Board reopened hearings into the project in 2006, and in 2009 a joint review panel recommended the project proceed, upon the fulfillment of 176 conditions; it was then sent back to the National Energy Board, which in December 2010 granted its approval pending the consortium meeting a total of 264 conditions. Though the pipeline received federal approval in 2011, it remains on hold indefinitely. In this way, the project symbolizes a lost opportunity for Canada and its energy sector as low natural gas prices and a surfeit of supply in the United States have rendered the project unfeasible.

The energy sector's poor track record in terms of gaining approvals for projects over the last forty years stems from the inescapable fact decisions are made in office towers far removed from the actual sites of operation. This has created a natural tension between those who own the rights to develop the resource and those who live on the lands and are impacted by such development, in both positive and negative terms.

Yet even with these challenges, and in spite of the eventual disappointment with respect to the Mackenzie Valley project, pipelines transporting oil, natural gas, and diluent have been built in recent decades. Many have managed to fly under the radar, so to speak, not capturing much attention or opposition. Examples of this include the Express and Alliance pipelines and Kinder Morgan's Anchor Loop Extension, which runs through Jasper National Park—a UNESCO World Heritage Site. Anchor Loop was completed in 2008 without a whiff of the opposition faced by the expansion of Trans Mountain.

So what has so fundamentally changed to alter the landscape for pipeline approval? Arguably, one has to go back to the start of opposition to oil sands development and the rise of the "off oil" environmental movement, which has since translated into pushback on pipeline development as environmental groups have realized they are unlikely to stop oil sands production.

Specifically, there are three important inflection points to examine. The first was the 2006 decision by the Alberta government—then headed by then premier Ralph Klein—to make its case regarding Canada's importance as a secure supplier of oil to the United States by displaying trucks used in the oil sands mining process on the Mall in Washington, DC. Needless to say, the plan backfired. While it might have been motivated by the best of intentions, the event turned the oil sands into the focal point for the off oil movement. The resulting visuals were easy to parlay into a narrative that stirred up sentiment against the oil industry. Indeed, it was not long after that a photo essay of oil sands mining operations appeared in *National Geographic*.

But things got worse in April 2008, when 1,600 ducks died after landing on a tailings pond at the Syncrude site near Fort McMurray. According to Jim Ellis, the deputy environment minister in the Alberta government at the time, this was a pivotal moment for the province; overnight the oil sands became a global issue—a target—for environmental groups.

The pace at which this negative publicity gained momentum caught the oil sands companies—and its industry association, the Canadian Association of Petroleum Producers—flat-footed. To them, the way to counter the increasingly negative light in which the industry was being viewed was to come back with a myriad of facts about the oil sands. The reasoning was that if people understood how crucial energy was to their daily lives, they would stop protesting. But it was too late: pipelines had become an emotional issue—and fighting back with facts and equations was not the way to win the battle.

And none of this was helped by the approach taken by the federal government under Stephen Harper.

While notionally from Calgary—he was elected in the riding of Calgary Glenmore in 2006—it seemed to many Harper went out of his way to ensure no one could accuse him of favouring the energy sector. Initially, his election was seen as positive for the sector, despite the fact he had no connections whatsoever to the C-suite of Canada's oil patch. That said, Harper did realize the centrality of oil and gas development to Canada's economy—the industry comprises 20 per cent of the GDP—and he was committed to growing that segment of the country's economy, stating during his first overseas speech as prime minister in July 2006 that Canada was an emerging energy superpower.

Getting there, however, was going to prove more complicated than Harper and his government ever expected.

Harper's decade in office coincided with a number of important developments in the global energy sector. By the time he took office, the "peak oil" narrative was well underway, which translated into the largest surge in investment in Canada's oil sands. Between 2006 and 2014, the amount invested in oil sands development totalled $365 billion. This was also the period when oil prices marched towards their record high of US$147.27 per barrel (reached in July 2008). Alongside all this was the rise of the elusive concept of social licence (an unfortunate term coined by a former mining executive); a rising tide of environmental activism funded by a number of American non-governmental organizations; and growing opposition to oil sands development by Canada's Indigenous peoples.

Making things more challenging was the fact that more than 90 per cent of Canada's oil production was going to one customer—the United States—which would unlock its own resource bounty through the use of technology by the time Harper's third term was underway.

Indeed, if opposition to oil sands development caught Canada's oil patch by surprise, so too did the increase in US oil and natural gas development that has taken place over the last decade. The US Energy Information Agency recently estimated US oil production will reach 10 million barrels a day in 2018, surpassing the old record of 9.6 million barrels a day set in 1970. This will represent a doubling of production from 2008. The same story has played out with natural gas, with production reaching record highs between 2011 and 2015, increasing 52 per cent since 2005.

These facts made projects such as the Keystone XL pipeline, proposed by TransCanada in 2008 to facilitate the transport of crude from the oil sands to its refining complex on the Gulf Coast, and Enbridge's Northern Gateway pipeline, which would take oil sands production to the West Coast and open up new markets for Canada's oil production in developing countries, extremely important. And gaining access to markets off the coast of British Columbia wasn't the only option.

In 2013, TransCanada released a plan to convert much of its existing natural gas mainline to ship 1.1 million barrels of oil a day to an existing deep water port in Saint John, New Brunswick. Dubbed Energy East, this $15.7 billion project would decrease the need for refineries in Eastern Canada to import 730,000 barrels of oil from other oil producing jurisdictions; it would also allow for the export of oil to countries such as India, which has a huge refining complex and an increasing demand for hydrocarbons.

As oil prices averaged US$93.17 per barrel in 2013, the Canadian Chamber of Commerce calculated the Canadian economy was losing $50 million (Canadian) per day because the oil produced in Western Canada was hostage to one market and not receiving the world—or Brent—price. Capturing that lost revenue, which would go a long way toward funding government budgets, was, and is, very important.

To avoid the failures of the Mackenzie Valley project, the Harper government introduced legislation in 2012 that placed a limit on the amount of time allotted for pipeline hearings. Among the criticisms that had been voiced by the oil patch was the seemingly open-ended time frame associated with project approval, which made committing capital to projects very difficult.

Working with industry, the federal government settled on an eighteen-month time frame, with the possibility of a six month extension. In addition, the National Energy Board would submit its recommendation to the federal cabinet, which would then have six months to make a final decision. The Harper government managed to streamline the process while at the same politicizing it. By the time Canadians went to the polls in October 2015, the National Energy Board's credibility had become an election issue.

But streamlining and setting time limits—while well intentioned—weren't going to be enough to get Northern Gateway off the drawing board and into the ground. And yet, unlike previous prime ministers, Harper held a very high disdain for First Ministers' conferences. While some might dismiss these events as political grandstanding, there is nonetheless some value to the prime minister convening meetings with the provincial and territorial leaders to work through challenging issues. Instead, Harper preferred individual meetings with the premiers, which if anything, pitted one province against another. The result was a lack of constructive dialogue with respect to potentially challenging issues like pipelines. For example, the conditions put forward in 2012 by BC premier Christy Clark outlining what her province required to allow the construction of a pipeline to the West Coast was distressingly outside the spirit of what it means to be part of this confederation called Canada, and a prime example of the consequences of Harper's hands-off approach.

Clark said her province would require the successful completion of the environmental review process; world-leading marine and land oil-spill prevention and response systems; the resolution of Aboriginal treaty rights and the opportunity for First Nations participation; and that BC receive its fair share of the economic and fiscal benefits of any subsequent project.

Characteristically, Harper stayed out of this fight, leaving it to then Alberta premier Alison Redford to take on Clark. It might have been more constructive for Harper to step up and say that what British Columbia had asked for fell largely under the purview of the federal government, and that a solution would therefore come through the involvement of the federal government, alongside British Columbia and Alberta. A similar scenario played out when Ontario and Quebec joined forces to jointly issue seven conditions that would have to be met for Energy East to go move forward.

In 2015, with the country stuck in a war of words, two game-changing events happened. In May of that year Albertans elected an NDP government led by Rachel Notley, turfing the ruling Progressive Conservative party after more than forty years in office. The change in government was soon followed by the establishment of a Climate Leadership Panel, which was charged with making recommendations to the government with respect to implementing a new carbon pricing regime. Alberta had been the first jurisdiction in North America to establish a carbon price under Premier Redford (the Specified Gas Emitters Regulation, or SGER), but it was not high enough for the province to get any credit for it, much less to change consumer or corporate behaviour, or to provide support for proposed pipelines.

The end game for Notley was to put in place a substantive, broad-based carbon pricing scheme that could help the province gain approval for pipeline projects in both Canada and the United States.

The Climate Leadership Panel was tabled prior to the Paris Climate Change Conference (held in November 2015), and it recommended setting a carbon tax at an initial rate of $20 per ton, with an escalation feature. In addition, it called for the establishment of an emissions cap in the oil sands, which was seen as another way for Alberta to demonstrate its environmental stewardship and in so doing bolster support for—and gain approval of—proposed pipeline projects.

The second game-changing event was the election of a Liberal federal government under Justin Trudeau in October 2015. Trudeau was on the record supporting Kinder Morgan's Trans Mountain expansion project and TransCanada's Keystone XL project, but he solidly opposed Enbridge's Northern Gateway project.

Like Notley, the new prime minister didn't waste any time laying out a platform illustrating the fact that energy development and environmental stewardship need not be seen as mutually exclusive. To that end, his government set about putting in place a $1.5 billion marine spill response plan, setting a price on carbon to be adopted by provinces lacking a carbon pricing scheme, and carrying on with the Harper government's commitment to phase out coal-fired power by 2030.

With these chess pieces in place, in late November 2016 Trudeau announced his government's approval of Kinder Morgan's Trans Mountain expansion, as well as the replacement and expansion of Enbridge's Line 3 pipeline running from Hardisty, Alberta, to Superior, Wisconsin, but Northern Gateway was officially denied approval. The end of that project had already been telegraphed in June 2016, when the Federal Court of Appeal overturned the Harper government's approval of Northern Gateway on the grounds that the government did not carry out its duty to consult.

The fact that an NDP government in Alberta and a Liberal government in Ottawa were able to move the pipeline agenda forward when former Conservative governments in both jurisdictions did not make any meaningful progress speaks to the importance and efficacy of the collaborative approach undertaken by Trudeau.

In his book *Triple Crown: Winning Canada's Energy Future* (published posthumously in early 2017), former Alberta premier and federal cabinet minister Jim Prentice argued provincial rivalries hold the country back, and that it was important not to let such rivalries compromise the important infrastructure that ties this country together—pipelines included.

In December 2016, when Prime Minister Trudeau's cabinet approved Kinder Morgan's Trans Mountain pipeline expansion, Clark's conditions appeared to have been met—but not until Kinder Morgan also agreed to pay the government $1 billion over twenty years. That money will be put toward a new BC Clean Communities Program, which will fund small local environmental projects, the creation of recycling programs, and the establishment of new parks. But there is another way of looking at this $1 billion windfall: as a paid ransom.

If Harper's lack of constructive involvement—Prentice called it "clumsy support"—can be said to have been one of the barriers to progress on the pipeline file, another of the key developments that affected the pace of pipeline development during the decade of federal Conservative rule was the rise of coordinated opposition to energy development by environmental groups and First Nations. One could argue each was using the other to further their own agenda, but there was no denying that this resulted in the pipelines being stuck in the middle.

There was also some evidence, primarily surfaced by Vancouver-based journalist Vivian Krause, that some of the pipeline opposition was being funded by US organizations such as the San Francisco-based Tides Foundation, which Krause alleges has paid out US$35 million to more than a hundred anti-pipeline groups, and which also created the Tar Sands Campaign with money from the Rockefeller Brothers Fund.

Two companies in particular—Enbridge and TransCanada—have taken it on the chin in terms of fending off opposition to proposed developments. By 2010, TransCanada had successfully built what it called "base Keystone," which extended from Hardisty, Alberta, to Steele City, Nebraska, and in 2008 it sanctioned the development of an additional leg that would seamlessly connect crude from Alberta—and the North Dakota Bakken—to its Gulf Coast refining complex. The fact base Keystone had not encountered any opposition was reason enough to believe the XL portion would be given similar treatment.

The sanctioning of the project coincided with the election of US president Barack Obama, who, in his inauguration speech, was very clear that his was going to be an administration that was committed to the environment.

In his book *Dysfunction: Canada after Keystone XL*, retired Trans-Canada executive Dennis McConaghy makes the point that the project became the target of the environmental movement when it realized that stopping oil sands production was unrealistic. But he also points to the Harper government's failure to move in the direction of instituting a carbon price, despite the failure of the Waxman-Markey legislation, which would have resulted in carbon pricing south of the border and likely resulted in Keystone XL being approved.

Canada's—and TransCanada's—case was not helped by Harper's comment in New York in 2011 that approving Keystone XL was a "no brainer." And so, on 6 November 2015, Obama officially turned down the project, despite the fact his own State Department had issued several reports stating that the pipeline would not exacerbate greenhouse gas emissions nor cause more of the oil sands to be developed. Instead, Obama acquiesced to the hyperbolic protests of the environmental movement and the exhortations from Hollywood and other celebrity types—none of which had shown themselves to be encumbered by the facts, much less to display a willingness to decrease the size of their respective carbon footprints.

The disconnect became laughable when Leonardo de Caprio—who had filmed part of *The Revenant* in the Alberta foothills—said he had witnessed climate change firsthand, referring to the dramatic change in temperatures brought on by the Chinook winds. What de Caprio didn't share with his followers was that he had rented a house outside of Calgary from an oil patch executive and he was flying on a private jet between Calgary and Los Angeles every weekend.

While Keystone XL has since been revived under the current US administration, Northern Gateway is no longer an option.

The challenge of gaining approval for new projects has meant both TransCanada and Enbridge chose to make game-changing acquisitions in the United States, with TransCanada buying Columbia Pipelines and Enbridge buying Spectra Energy. Buying pipe that's already in the ground is far less complicated than trying to build something new.

If Keystone was an example of the politicization of a project based on fuzzy objectives for how the United States intended to manage its greenhouse gas emissions, Northern Gateway was an illustration of the consequences of the well-intentioned but ill-defined requirement of government's—both provincial and federal—duty to consult. This stems from section 35 of the Constitution Act, 1982, which outlines the Crown's duty to consult with, and accommodate, Aboriginal groups in situations where projects authorized by government regulators may infringe on their Aboriginal or treaty rights.

But while this is laid out in the Constitution, what has transpired over the years is much different. The oil and gas industry sees itself as having "carried the bag for the Crown" on the duty-to-consult file. In real terms, this has translated into dollars exchanged in return for approval and access to Aboriginal lands, either for resource development or laying down a pipe. This was made clear in a ruling handed down by the Federal Court of Appeal in June 2016, which overturned the permit granted by the previous Conservative government and gave Enbridge the green light to proceed with its Northern Gateway project—pending the company meeting the 209 conditions stipulated by the National Energy Board.

The Court of Appeal's decision was a damning indictment of the Harper government's virtual abdication of its duty to consult with Aboriginal and First Nations groups with respect to the Northern Gateway project. In the words of the decision, "Canada offered only a brief, hurried and inadequate opportunity . . . to exchange and discuss information and to dialogue. . . . It would have taken Canada little time and little organizational effort to engage in meaningful dialogue on these and other subjects of prime importance to Aboriginal Peoples. But this did not happen."

As pointed out in Prentice's book, if Canada is to gain access to offshore markets, an alignment of interests that includes Indigenous peoples, project proponents, and politicians is required: "Everyone's capital, whether financial or political, must be brought to the investment," wrote Prentice.

A new generation is taking the reins of leadership in many First Nations communities—in BC and elsewhere. This generation recognizes the important economic opportunities that come with responsible resource development. Their true involvement as partners, which goes beyond the more traditional impact benefit agreements, is the direction that needs to be taken. But in addition to being economic partners, as Prentice wrote in his book, it's equally important that companies and governments alike recognize that British Columbia's First Nations are self-governing and exist within the overall context of the Canadian confederation and their attachment to the environment on the Pacific coast; compromising that environment is not something they are prepared to do.

But while that may be true, it is also a reality that consensus for projects does not mean 100 per cent approval; the pareto principal in economics, which states that 80 per cent of the work is sufficient, also applies in this context. There are some First Nations communities that will never approve a project, regardless of what is offered.

The revisions to the National Energy Board announced in July 2017 seek to modernize the organization's governance structure, which will look very similar to that of the Alberta Energy Regulator. But the one thing this new structure will not do is depoliticize the approval process because the final say still rests with the federal cabinet of the day, despite what the National Energy Board determines.

While regulation, legislation, and so-called social licence continue to be important factors in the pipeline approval process, there is one more aspect that continues to impact the narrative on both energy and pipeline development. There is an adage in the oil patch that goes like this: ask an engineer a question and they will answer it with an equation.

Ever since opposition to oil sands and pipeline development gathered steam in the earlier part of this century, the tendency has been to answer opposition with facts: that energy is vital to economic growth and everyday living, that we all rely on it and that it has been an important factor in lifting billions of people around the world out of poverty. But even messages about the need to eliminate energy poverty around the world—including among First Nations communities in this country—don't resonate, not even across Canada.

In 2012, the University of Calgary's School of Public Policy completed an excellent three-part study of the state of energy literacy across the country. The conclusions of the report were simply, and distressingly, that many Canadians who ought to know how energy is produced, transported, and regulated, don't know much about the subject. In fact, many haven't a clue what happens when they flick a light switch.

This knowledge gap is exacerbated by the increasing fragmentation of the media. There was a time when everyone in the country started their discussions using information gleaned from sources such as national or local newspapers and local television or radio. In other words, we all started—more or less—from the same place. But the rise of social media, which has effectively dissolved the traditional media infrastructure, has meant that anyone looking to justify an idea or opinion—including those not based on fact—can do just that. Even worse, social media allows for comments to be continuously circulated.

More than a century ago Mark Twain said a lie gets halfway around the world before the truth can get its pants on. And that was long before the instant flow of information that characterizes our daily living became a reality.

The development, use, and transportation of energy has become an issue driven by emotion, not fact. It is nothing short of appalling that the children of Calgary energy executives attending post-secondary schools outside the province, and most especially in British Columbia, are not comfortable telling their friends what their parents do for a living. And yet, the comfort of all their lives is made possible through continuous consumption of energy, 24 hours of every day, 365 days a year.

And the challenges are not over. At the time of writing, legislation is pending that will replace the National Energy Board. More important are developments that took place in April and May 2018 regarding the Trans Mountain expansion and Kinder Morgan. Frustrated by the lack of progress, along with continued obfuscation and obstruction by the minority NDP government in British Columbia that was elected in May 2017 (and which remains propped up by the Green Party), Kinder Morgan delivered an ultimatum saying the provincial and federal governments had until 31 May to provide assurances the project would be allowed to proceed unimpeded, or it was going to walk.

There's an adage that says nothing focuses the attention like the prospect of a hanging in the morning. The Trans Mountain expansion was about to join the ranks of Mackenzie Valley, Northern Gateway, and Energy East without strong government action.

And indeed, the federal government, alongside the Alberta government, has sprung into action with the announcement on 29 May 2018 that the federal government would be buying the Canadian pipeline assets, including the Trans Mountain expansion, from Kinder Morgan for $4.5 billion. The Alberta government is coming to the table with $2 billion that will be used to cover the "eligible costs" associated with the construction of the expansion. The assets will sit in a Crown corporation, allowing the government to expeditiously deal with jurisdictional issues.

The end game entails the government selling the assets to the private sector—likely to a group of buyers that could include pension funds, private equity players, or other pipeline operators. Predictably, this decision has brought about an outcry from many sides: Why couldn't the Trans Mountain expansion be built even as it had received the requisite approvals? When is a permit not a permit? What kind of message does this send to the international investment community?

Ultimately, the federal government made its decision based on two major factors. One was the need for the project to open new markets, heightened by the ongoing challenges of renegotiating the North American Free Trade Agreement that served to underscore the need to expand to new markets. The other was the fact that if the project was to be pulled, the message sent to international investors would be worse than that sent by temporary government ownership. Extraordinary circumstances call for extraordinary measures. This was one of them.

That said, it wasn't to be clear sailing.

Despite 17 legal cases decided in favour of Trans Mountain, the 18th sided with the proponents.

On August 30th, the same day Kinder Morgan shareholders approved the sale of the pipeline to the federal government, the Federal Court of Appeal quashed the federal government's approval of the project on the grounds that the Crown had failed to carry out its duty to consult. It also said the National Energy Board had fallen short of its obligations in not considering the impact on marine mammal life from increased tanker traffic.

If this sounds familiar, it should. It is the same ruling—by the same court—that killed Northern Gateway. The only thing that is different is that the Liberals hold office, rather than the Conservatives. But the implications are enormous, beyond the immediate impact on energy investment and the jobs that are bound to be lost. It doesn't send a positive message that Canada is open for business when it comes to attracting investment.

The issue of consultation—and what it really means—remains undefined. No company will be willing to risk meaningful capital until this is clarified. When the Supreme Court ruled in 2004 that the government must accommodate "the collective aboriginal right in question," it left that open to interpretation.

In the case of Northern Gateway, the Federal Court of Appeal criticized the Crown for not appropriately carrying out its duty to consult. It made the same argument in the most recent case involving Trans Mountain—even as the government had extended the consultation period, with the Federal Court of Appeal stating there was a lack of meaningful dialogue in the final consultation phase.

This also means the federal climate plan—because Alberta stated its intention to withdraw as result of the ruling—is in peril. One of Prime Minister Trudeau's key messages, as he defended both the approval of Trans Mountain and the criticism of the climate plan that includes a carbon tax levied in provinces that have not set a price on carbon, is that Alberta is integral to the success of that plan. Here's why: Alberta has to be on board for Canada to meet its emissions targets. It doesn't get more complicated than that.

As University of Alberta professor Andrew Leach stated in an article published in *Maclean's* in February 2018, those targets cannot be achieved without Alberta. "This is a symbiotic relationship: federal climate policy backstops put a stronger foundation under the Alberta plan and, with the Alberta plan in place, there is a credible although still very challenging path for Canada to meet its 2030 target. Without Alberta's plan, that credible path disappears," wrote Leach.

The federal government will either appeal the ruling, or move to address the gaps highlighted in the judgement. As the owners of the Trans Mountain pipeline, Canadians will not be kind to a government that forked out $4.5 billion for an asset whose value is in question. Either way, it means another delay at a time when all three existing major pipelines are at or near capacity and the number of barrels being shipped by rail is at record highs.

Notley was unequivocal in her criticism of the federal government following the release of the judgement, saying the province had "done everything right" and despite that, had been let down.

What remains truly remarkable in all this—particularly from an Albertan's perspective—is the fact that Rachel Notley, elected as an NDP premier, has become the unlikely advocate for Alberta's energy development on the national stage. One could easily make the argument Alberta hasn't been as strongly represented since the days of former premier Peter Lougheed. As Lougheed knew, and Notley understands, Canada's energy future—and Alberta's economic prosperity—lies in its ability to access new markets beyond North America. The old infrastructure was developed during a time when the concern was one of energy scarcity, not energy abundance, on the continent.

It is Asia—which continues to develop, industrialize, and urbanize—that will dominate energy consumption over the next fifty years, at least. The continent a long way to self-sufficiency, when current production is about 8 million barrels a day and consumption is at 30 million barrels a day and growing.

The energy-hungry countries in the developing world are getting frustrated with Canada's inability to get out of its own way when it comes to developing pipelines to the West Coast to export oil production. They will—and they are—seeking other sources of supply. That means that Canada's window of opportunity—especially as OPEC members continue to expand their market share in Asia—is not going to stay open indefinitely. For the developing world, scarcity of supply is a daily issue, and those countries will source their barrels wherever they can.

Simply put: Canada's inability to move forward with the development infrastructure risks the country's economic future.

DEBORAH YEDLIN

IV
THE NDP IN POWER

After Forty-Four Years: The Alberta New Democrats and the Transition to Government

Keith Brownsey

In the 5 May 2015 Alberta general election, the New Democratic Party under the leadership of Rachel Notley, won 54 of the provincial legislature's 87 seats. The New Democrats' majority ended the forty-four-year reign of the Progressive Conservative Party. In office since 1971, the Progressive Conservatives faced a sudden and unexpected defeat. Many in the media and business community expected a chaotic transition to a new government. After all, the Progressive Conservatives were the government party: they understood what needed to be done and how to do it. Any other party coming into government, it was thought, would create havoc and misery for the province. What happened, however, proved the critics of the new government wrong. New Democrats were sworn in by Alberta's lieutenant-governor as the fifth political party in the province's history to hold government.

The transition from the embedded Progressive Conservatives to the New Democrats—a move from a right-of-centre to a left-of-centre government—was much less traumatic than pundits, journalists, and many academics had expected. In fact, it has been argued that the new government brought stability to the province's parliamentary government for the first time in a decade. After a tumultuous ten-year period that saw 5 PC premiers, 8 ministers of finance, 7 ministers of energy, and over 100 assorted cabinet ministers, the Notley government set about enacting its agenda and bringing stability to a political system that had been battered by factional rivalry within the Progressive Conservative government and party. What took place in the days before the 5 May election and until the New Democrats brought in the March 2016 budget may be defined as the party's transition to government.

Several factors explain how the transition occurred and why the province did not descend into anarchy. One is that the Alberta public service was prepared for the new government. Having seen five premiers and various cabinet changes over the previous nine years, the senior ranks of the public service had undergone three transitions, the last one as recently as September 2014. They understood the process of transition. And, as soon as it was apparent that there could be a change of party, the public service refocused its efforts to incorporate different party platforms into its planning. Second, the New Democratic leadership began to plan for the transition ten days before the election. With the real possibility of forming government, Rachel Notley and her campaign team did not want to be caught unprepared. It was at this point that individuals in other jurisdictions who had experience in government and, most importantly, in a transition, were contacted and enlisted in the transition process. A third factor in the transition was the post-election disarray of the opposition parties, especially the PCs. Reduced to nine MLAs, the PCs were not able to mount an effective opposition to the new government. The Wildrose Party—returned as the Official Opposition—could not manage a coherent response to the New Democrats, other than to declare that they had failed even before they were sworn into office.

But a common theme explains the actions of all the actors in the transition process. This is the institutional context of the parliamentary system. The parliamentary system creates a framework within which both the public service and the political parties operate. When the election was called the PCs became caretakers. By convention they were unable to access information or support from the public service. On the other hand, after it became clear that the Conservatives would not form a majority government, the public service began to closely examine the platforms of the Wildrose Party, the New Democrats, and the Alberta Party. The senior ranks of the public service modelled a series of different scenarios, involving various party configurations, from minority to majority government. In the last week of the election the public service took a much closer look at the New Democratic policy proposals. While the actors in both the public service and the NDP made preparations, they did so in isolation from one another and with little contact between them until the election results were known on the evening of 5 May. The people involved on both the political and administrative sides were guided by the conventions and practices of the transition process found within the Westminster parliamentary system.

Types of Transitions

In liberal-democratic systems, transitions from one government to another often go unnoticed. However, transitions entail the transfer of power from one set of leaders to another. It is a time when a complex series of processes are set in motion to ensure the continuity of the state.[1] This can occur when the governing party selects a new leader, when a party is returned to office, or when the government is replaced by a different party through an election or some other device. The transition is complete when the new government takes full control over the apparatus of the state.[2] Governments assume office with what appears to be little effort before implementing the policy proposals outlined during the recent election campaign or leadership race. But the transitions of government in democratic systems are complex processes that involve both politicians and bureaucrats in an institutional and personnel change from one set of leaders to another.

Transitions are often defined in temporal terms, such as the time from the election or leadership victory to the formal assumption of power. This definition includes the naming of a cabinet and the appointment of senior officials in the political and administrative executive. But the act of taking power is a much more complex phenomenon. It does not account for the ability to control the institutions of the state. For example, after winning office in 1971 it took almost three years for Peter Lougheed and the PCs to put into place the processes and personnel needed to implement the government's program. This institutional definition of a transition encompasses the broad scope of government activity.

There are several different categories of transitions within the Canadian parliamentary system.[3] The first is a change in the leadership of the governing party. In this situation, the party chooses a new leader, who then becomes premier. Between 2006 and 2014, Alberta had four examples of internal-party-leadership transitions. They included the leadership contest of 2006, which was precipitated by the resignation of the premier and PC leader Ralph Klein; in 2011, when Ed Stelmach, Klein's replacement quit; and 2014, when Allison Redford stepped down and was replaced for five months by long-time cabinet minister David Hancock. Hancock made way for Jim Prentice, who was selected by a vote of party members in September 2014.

The second category of transition occurs when a government is re-elected. Although the same party is in place, there are inevitably changes in the cabinet and administrative processes. Since forming a government after the 1971 provincial election, the PCs were re-elected twelve times. A recent example of a party winning re-election under a new leader occurred in 2008, when the PCs were returned to office under Ed Stelmach. After taking over from outgoing premier Ralph Klein in December 2006, Stelmach won a majority government in the March 2008 provincial election. Under the direction of the deputy minister to Executive Council, transition material was prepared for the incoming Stelmach government in both December 2006 and again after the March 2008 election. Although the premier selected a new cabinet, most of the transition planning was conducted by the public service.

There is a third category of transition in the Westminster parliamentary system. This is when a different party wins the election. In most provinces this happens on a regular basis. Governments are defeated and replaced. The civil service as well as the winning party has experience with transitions and has prepared for a change in government. But there is a subcategory of the typical government transition model. This is when a long-serving government is defeated and replaced in office. A recent example of this is the May 2015 Alberta provincial election, in which the New Democrats defeated the PC government led by Jim Prentice. This may be the most difficult type of transition. The incoming government will be inexperienced. After the defeated party's decades-long tenure there will be few, if any, members of the new government with experience in office. The public service may be weary of the incoming party, while the new government may associate the civil service with the policies of the defeated government. Many government members will be unaware of the role of the public service. They will not understand the relationship between the political and the administrative functions found in a parliamentary system. In such a situation, inexperience, suspicion, and ignorance can derail a new government, causing it political harm.

The situation in Alberta, however, was different. The public service had expected a change of government after Alison Redford's March 2014 resignation. Throughout the spring and summer of that year, committees were struck in each department and in the Executive Council Office to prepare for a new PC leader and premier. The May 2015 election would initiate the fourth transition in eight years and the public service would be well prepared for a new government. Approximately ten days before the election, senior New Democratic staff realized their party had a very good chance of forming government. They also understood that replacing a forty-four-year-old government would be a very difficult task. These officials along with the leader began to meet on a daily basis to plan the transition. On election night the administrative and the political elements of the parliamentary system came together to initiate the first change of party government in the province of Alberta in more than four decades.

Conservative Transitions: Practice Makes Perfect

Beginning with Peter Lougheed in 1971, there have been eight premiers and thirteen transitions of government. Seven of these transitions occurred when the PCs were returned to office under a new leader. The PC transitions began with the party's victory under Peter Lougheed in 1971. The PCs defeated the thirty-six-year-old Social Credit government led by Harry Strom. When Lougheed walked into the Premier's Office in September 1971, he found the shelves bare. The only papers left behind by the outgoing Strom were the results of pre-election polling in a desk drawer. Refusing to read the material, Lougheed immediately gave the papers to an aid, Jim Seymour, who returned them to Strom. There were, moreover, no formal or informal meetings between the outgoing government and the new premier and his staff.[4] Even William Macdonald, the secretary to cabinet and clerk of the legislature refused to return to Edmonton, choosing instead to remain in Medicine Hat.[5] The lack of continuity between the outgoing and incoming governments illustrated the pre-institutionalized structure of Alberta governance.

When Lougheed retired in 1985 he was replaced by Don Getty, a former cabinet minister and oil company executive. Getty made few changes to the government other than replacing several cabinet members. When

Getty retired in 1992, his replacement as leader and premier was Ralph Klein. Klein took a very different approach to the transition process than his predecessor. With his advisor Rod Love, Klein made fundamental changes to the decision-making process. After winning the PC leadership race in early December 1992, Klein began his transition process by installing Love in the Premier's Office as executive director. With an understanding of the provincial government's administrative structure, Love was critical of what he perceived to be its cumbersome decision-making apparatus, and he did not consult with officials from the Getty government. As Love said in a later interview, "we didn't need any meetings, we knew what we wanted to do."[6] With a limited agenda of reducing the provincial debt and eliminating the deficit, Love set about reorganizing government. He eliminated cabinet committees, installed communications officials in every ministerial office, and set up a series of caucus committees to engage backbench MLAs. Within a few months, the decision-making process was fundamentally altered without the advice of either the party or the public service.

When Klein left office in late 2006, the incoming premier, Ed Stelmach, a long-time cabinet member, kept the caucus committees and the much-reduced cabinet committee system. Nevertheless, transition binders were prepared by the civil service for the new premier and his cabinet ministers outlining how the various departments were organized and what issues faced the government in the immediate, medium and long term. The Stelmach government had control of the levers of power within a few weeks.

Stelmach resigned as premier and party leader in early October 2011. His successor, Allison Redford, came to office with little support from the government caucus, and her transition was less than fulsome. Redford's team, which consisted of friends and supporters, was unfamiliar with the provincial government and somewhat suspicious of the public service. While transition material had been prepared for the incoming government, Redford's group spent just two weeks putting staff in place and making adjustments to the cabinet committee system. As well, the transition group recommended the end of the standing policy committees. On the advice of her team, Redford replaced the deputy minister to Executive Council[7] and dismissed ten deputy ministers.[8] The transition team considered the process complete after the government was sworn into office. The Premier and her staff, however, never seemed to get control of caucus, cabinet, or the

KEITH BROWNSEY

legislature. After two and a half years Redford resigned from office in March 2014. David Hancock, a long-time PC cabinet minister, was appointed interim premier by the government caucus until the party could select a new leader. Because of Redford's surprise resignation, both the public service and the party had little time to prepare for a transition. In fact, the existing cabinet remained in place except for those members who resigned to seek the party leadership.

In September 2014, Jim Prentice, a former federal MP and cabinet minister, was selected by the party membership as the new leader and premier. Peter Watson, the deputy minister to Executive Council, and other senior public servants began to prepare for a new government immediately after Redford's resignation in March. On 13 June 2014, Watson was appointed to head the National Energy Board. He was replaced as deputy to the Executive Council by Stephen MacDonald. When Prentice was sworn into office in September 2014, he and the rest of the government received briefing binders describing the roles and responsibilities of the various departments as well as the issues the government would face in the next thirty, sixty, and ninety days. One of Prentice's first acts was to appoint Richard Dicerni as deputy minister to Executive Council, replacing MacDonald.[9] With experience under a variety of different party governments, at both the provincial and federal levels, Dicerni was tasked with revitalizing the civil service after more than a decade of constant change. But Dicerni's efforts to rebuild the Alberta public service would be curtailed when Prentice called an election in late March 2015 for 5 May.

The civil service is supposed to treat any new government, regardless of party, the same. In Alberta, for example, the public service has prepared briefing binders containing departmental organization charts, the names of key personnel, and other administrative information for an incoming government. As well, there is usually a summary of issues facing the department. These issues are commonly broken down into three categories. The first are the thirty-day issues. These are problems that need immediate attention from the minister. The second category consists of those problems needing attention in the medium term; these are often called sixty-day issues. And third, there are the long-term, or ninety-day issues. Although the questions may vary according to the policy agenda of each new government, they are identified and categorized by the senior levels of the public service.

The 2015 Transition

Approximately ten days before the 5 May 2017 election, Brain Topp, the NDP campaign chair, and Gerry Scott, the party's campaign manager, recommended to Notley that she authorize a transition planning committee. Topp had seen the crowds for Notley's campaign tour and believed there was the possibility of an NDP victory. Moreover, signs and other campaign material had run out, and "$1 million went through the door."[10] This indicated to the campaign team that the New Democrats would do very well on election day. There was a sense that something was changing in their favour.

And yet there was some hesitation on the part of the campaign leadership to establish a transition team, who believed that transition planning might waste time and resources that would be better spent on bringing voters to their cause. As well, some senior campaign officials were concerned that if the public knew of the transition planning they would think the party was taking victory for granted. Moreover, several senior officials were superstitious: they did not want to derail the campaign through some misconceived action that could possibly anger voters. Despite these reservations, when Notley and her senior campaign staff read the party's polling data they began meeting to plan a transition to government.

The resulting transition team was chaired by Topp and it consisted of those involved at the top levels of the campaign. But within a few days, NDP organizers from other provinces were brought in to provide assistance. One of the transition group's first acts was to schedule a daily meeting. These meetings were held, for the most part, by telephone. They lasted approximately one hour. But as the election outcome became clear the calls increased in length and intensity. On the advice of party officials in other provinces and Ottawa, the transition team quickly decided to construct a timeline. The timeline was important to the extent that it put the various pieces of the transition into place. Another early decision was to meet the legislature at an early date. This would accomplish two things. First, it would demonstrate to the public that the new government was capable of presenting a legislative agenda. Second, the leader and her advisors did not want to run the province on lieutenant-governor warrants. It was decided to present the legislature with a supply bill until a budget could be introduced sometime later in the year.[11]

As mentioned above, the transition team was led by Brian Topp, Notley's campaign strategist and a federal NDP leadership candidate in 2011–12. Both Adrienne King and Brian Stokes were part of the group as well. King, the campaign's "wagon master," was responsible for campaign events and media briefings. Before the election she had been Notley's chief of staff and she was familiar with the three incumbent caucus members, the local and provincial party organization, and the eighty-three other candidates running across the province (although it would be an exaggeration to claim that anyone in the campaign had a familiarity with all those running).

Stokes, the party secretary for the Alberta NDP, also knew the party organization, the candidates, and their backgrounds. He was able to provide the premier-designate with advice on potential cabinet picks. Several other individuals also belonged to the transition group, including Cheryl Oates, the campaign press secretary, and Kathleen Monk from caucus communications. Notley also relied on Jim Gurnett, the executive director of caucus, who was set to retire after the May election.

Of the out-of-province party functionaries brought in to help with the transition, the first was John Heaney. Originally from Edmonton, Heaney was chief of staff to BC NDP leader John Horgan when he was asked to come to Alberta. Heaney was familiar to the Alberta New Democrats and had transition experience in British Columbia in 1991, 1996, and again in 2001. Jim Rutkowski, also an advisor to Horgan, worked with the public relations firm Hill and Knowlton in Victoria. He was brought in to help with the transition in the last days of the campaign. Originally from Edmonton, Rutkowski had transition experience in British Columbia. Ann McGrath was another central figure with the transition. McGrath worked for the national party in Ottawa under both Jack Layton and Tom Mulcair. She had been in Ottawa when Jack Layton and the federal party went from 43 seats to 103 in the 2011 federal election, and she was involved with transitioning the federal New Democrats from third-party status to Official Opposition.

Notley's transition group discussed various scenarios, such as what the constitution required in the case of a tie in seats and what the opposition parties would do in this situation. Preliminary discussions around cabinet selection also occurred. Most importantly, however, they asked colleagues in British Columbia, Saskatchewan, Manitoba, and Ottawa for help. With their assistance, the Notley transition team put together a list of items thought to be essential for a transition in a Westminster system.

The proposed governing model was based on the T. C. "Tommy" Douglas government in Saskatchewan. Topp had been deputy chief of staff to Premier Roy Romanow in the 1990s, and was therefore familiar with the history of the New Democrats there. Notley and Topp were supporters of cabinet government and were determined to restore it after years of what they believed had been Conservatives neglect. They thought the Alberta NDP should govern rather than "fiddle with government."[12] They were committed to the existing institutional structure and were determined to enact their agenda.

On the other side of the political-administrative divide was the Alberta public service. The deputy minister to Executive Council, Richard Dicerni, had directed the various departments to prepare transition binders for the new government. The media's expectation was that the PCs would be returned for a thirteenth time. The transition started when Prentice sent a note to all ministers that the government was in a caretaker situation. At the same time Mike Percy, the premier's chief of staff, contacted all ministerial chiefs of staff with the same message. As a result of the caretaker situation, ministers were not able to access the tools of state during the election. With the experience of the September 2014 transition behind them, the civil service began preparations for a new government.

Several weeks before the election, Dicerni tasked a group of deputy ministers with doing "a deep dive on the policy platforms of all parties." With opinion polls showing a possibility of a minority government, Dicerni needed "to understand where the policies of all the parties converged and diverged."[13] But about ten days from the election the political outcome seemed to change. Dicerni asked the deputies to spend the weekend of 2–3 May reviewing all party platforms as they pertained to their departments. He wanted a notional agenda for the incoming government, regardless of partisan persuasion, but was aware that the New Democrats had a very good chance of forming the government. The public service was aware that there was a difference between an "internal transition and a new party" in office. The key question concerned the nature of the new government's first three months in office. The 26 March 2015 budget had not been passed and supply ran out at the end of June. The government would have to pass a budget, continue the supply measures, or operate on warrants issued by the lieutenant-governor. There was even a review of the province's fiscal situation as the "economic assumptions had changed by April."[14] As well, a number of senior appointments were needed to fill vacancies in an array of provincial agencies, boards, and commissions. Any incoming government would need to fill these vacancies. The public service now looked to support NDP policies such as a royalty review on oil and natural gas, raising the minimum wage, and measures to reduce greenhouse gas emissions.

On election night Topp telephoned Dicerni and passed the telephone to the premier-designate. Notley and Dicerni met the following day. Dicerni provided Notley with three iPads containing information on the structure of the government and other machinery-of-government issues. As well, members of the transition team were given offices in the Legislative Annex. Dicerni and other officials from the Executive Council Office came with binders. While useful, some of the briefings contained phrases such as: "Alberta is a huge province that produces oil and gas."[15] It was apparent that some in the public service were unfamiliar with both Rachel Notley and the New Democrats.

All members of the newly elected NDP caucus were contacted on election night or the next morning by Brian Stokes or another party official. Stokes asked the incoming MLAs if they needed anything and then told them to be in Edmonton on Friday 8 May for meetings at Government House. At the meetings the caucus was introduced to the realities of political life. They were given some media training by political staff and briefed on the issues facing the new government. A briefing by Treasury Board and Finance Department staff indicated that the province's financial situation had changed since late January and early February, when the economic assumptions for the March budget had been locked in place. Finance officials presented the most recent data, which indicated that the province's financial situation had deteriorated.[16] No decisions had been taken in cabinet, but the MLAs were told how to dress and act in public—there should be no track pants worn in the supermarket.[17]

Notley, along with Topp and others in her transition group, decided on a particularly small cabinet of twelve ministers plus the premier. Topp had been involved in the 1991 transitions in Saskatchewan, when the New Democrats under Roy Romanow defeated the PC government of Grant

Devine. He believed that a small cabinet could function as a coherent group. Moreover, it reduced the hiring of senior staff and the risk of mistakes. It also gave the backbench MLAs a chance to show what they could do. Another consequence of a smaller cabinet was that fewer cabinet committees would be required, as decisions could be taken in full cabinet. It was decided that ministers would have two or more portfolios. For example, veteran NDP MLA Brian Mason was given Transport and Infrastructure. Transport was considered a difficult assignment, while Infrastructure was less demanding. These dual portfolios were designed to give the premier and her staff time to judge the abilities of the other, newly elected members of the New Democratic caucus. Several new positions were also added to the Premier's Office. Topp established the position of director of issues management as well as the director of house business. These positions were borrowed from the Manitoba New Democrats.

Notley asked Topp to stay in Alberta as her chief of staff while Cheryl Oates was appointed communications director. Other positions in the Premier's Office were filled by campaign staff as well as party officials from other jurisdictions. NDP operatives and political staff were recruited to fill a number of positions across the government left vacant by the departing Conservatives. This is a common practice, not just with the New Democrats, but other parties as well when they take office. The provincial transition team sought advice from their fellow partisans in other jurisdictions such as British Columbia, Manitoba, and Saskatchewan, as well as the national party in Ottawa. Many of these individuals were from Alberta or had worked for New Democrats in other jurisdictions. For example, John Heaney joined the Executive Council Office in August as deputy of policy.[18]

Several members of the transition team were concerned about a public service that had worked for a PC government for forty-four years. But the civil service was excited about working for a new government. Many individuals in the public sector felt that the Conservatives were no longer governing. Moreover, Dicerni and the senior ranks of the public service had prepared for a change of government and had worked to calm any fears of the NDP among their colleagues. For her part, Notley moved quickly to reassure the public service. She made calls to individual deputy ministers and met them as a group at their August Deputies Council. Dicerni was able to establish a relationship of trust between the political and administrative sides of the provincial executive. His experience in the public service, and especially with governmental transitions, allowed him to help the New Democrats to begin governing.

Dicerni had a checklist for the incoming premier and her cabinet. He discussed the premier-designate's intentions concerning the size of the cabinet, finalized changes to the cabinet committee structure, and confirmed times of meetings. These structural issues were supplemented by briefing binders requiring immediate attention; they covered such issues as the question of bills of supply and/or warrants from the lieutenant-governor to keep the province solvent. Dicerni also went through the list of deputies with the Notley transition team. Unlike the Redford transition, Notley decided to keep all the deputies. Although some adjustments needed to be made because of vacancies and approaching retirements, a decision was taken "not to fiddle with government, but to govern."[19] The premier-designate was aware of the need for continuity in the civil service and wanted to put an end to the churn in the public sector.

Notley met the week after the election with the outgoing premier, Jim Prentice. Although this was a formality, it was an important symbol, one that signalled the continuity of the provincial government. Meanwhile, reports circulated that PC staff were shredding documents. Although she had no authority to do so, Notley issued instructions that the destruction should stop.

One of the first tasks of the new government was to choose a cabinet. With only four members of the new caucus with legislative experience—and who were therefore assured a place at the table—it was a difficult job to pick ministers from the remaining caucus. Brian Topp, the incoming chief of staff, Cheryl Oates, Notley's press secretary, Adrienne King, as well as the three members of the previous caucus, Darron Bilous, David Eggan, and Brian Mason, all provided input for the premier-designate. The next significant decisions concerned the timing of the swearing-in ceremony, when to recall the legislature, and what issues the New Democrats could expect when they took office. It was decided to hold the swearing-in on 24 May, nineteen days after the election. The cabinet was announced as the assembled government MLAs proceeded to the ceremony.[20]

The new government had twelve cabinet ministers plus the premier. Four cabinet committees were named: treasury board, legislative review, economic development policy, environment and climate change, and social policy.[21] The caucus was divided into committees that mirrored the cabinet committees. One other major change was the creation of a Ministry of Status of Women.

The hiring of staff began almost immediately. The new ministers needed executive assistants and other staff. Thousands of applications flooded the office of the premier-designate as well as the party offices and the offices of the elected MLAs. Many PC staff made a case that they should be retained; some did not understand that they were there by political appointment. They argued that they knew the government and could be of assistance. The hiring process was tedious. It involved interviewing "many, many people."[22] Some ministerial executive assistants were pulled out of the public service, while others were taken from the private sector and even recruited from outside the province.

On 15 June 2015, forty days after the election, the Notley government met the legislature. The government's agenda seemed to be in place. The Throne Speech was described as "unusually short, remarkably focused and historically significant." The first piece of legislation introduced—Bill 1— aimed to reform campaign finance laws in an effort to eliminate corporate and union donations.[23] As well, a supply bill was passed to allow the province to continue operating until the government could introduce a budget during the fall sitting of the legislature.

Over the summer and early fall the New Democrats continued hiring staff for ministers and MLAs. They also began a review of the appointments, processes, and pay of the province's 301 agencies, boards, and commissions. A commission to assess the royalty rates paid by oil and natural gas companies was established. It released its report on 16 January 2016. As part of its climate initiative, the NDP government promised to eliminate coal-generated electricity by 2030 and implement a carbon tax on the use of fossil fuels.

But while the new government had initiated a variety of new policies, they still had not fully articulated their legislative program. It was not until the 14 April 2016 provincial budget that many in the Premier's Office and the party believed they had finally gained control of the machinery of government. The NDP leadership had learned the processes and procedures of government in a Westminster system. The operational requirements of forming a government had been met by the April 2016 budget. The New Democrats presented a budget that was their own and not simply a rewrite of what the previous Conservative government had put forward in March 2015.

Conclusions

It was not until ten days before the provincial election that the senior ranks of the Alberta public service and the NDP campaign staff realized there was a possibility of a change in government. By election day, both the administrative and political actors had made preparations for the transition of government. The criteria by which a transition of government in Alberta could be judged successful were procedural. In this sense, the handover went smoothly. There were no major mistakes. What is missing from this account, however, is the months it took the new government to understand and adjust the machinery of government to their policies. Still, within a matter of weeks the New Democrats had been sworn into office, had presented a short "but remarkably focused" Throne Speech, and were setting about implementing their campaign manifesto.

None of this would have been possible without the co-operation of three sets of actors—the public service and the incoming and outgoing governments. Indeed, the defeated PC government of Premier Jim Prentice was in disarray. They could not act as an effective opposition to the inexperienced New Democrats. This was the result of Prentice's resignation as party leader and MLA on election night and the loss of all but eleven seats. Almost immediately their focus turned to rebuilding their party. They needed to choose an interim leader, assess the consequences of the election defeat, and plan for the future. Although Prentice met with Notley the week after the election, this was viewed as merely a formality. The shredding of documents can be understood as the actions of ignorant political staff upset with their party's defeat. Simply put, the outgoing PCs did not place obstacles in the way of the new government, if for no other reason than they were in disarray. This was much to the benefit of the incoming government.

The Wildrose Party, the newly re-elected Official Opposition, however, was much more aggressive in their approach to the transition. One of their spokespersons declared five days after the election that the incoming government had failed and should resign.[24] While the Wildrose was unalterably opposed to the social-democratic NDP, they could do little more than make absurd statements about the incoming government having failed. The reasons for this are both institutional and personal. As an opposition party, their contacts with the bureaucracy had been limited, and they did not appear to understand how the transition process worked. As well, many in their caucus had little or no experience in provincial politics. For these reasons, they were unable to pose much of an opposition to the New Democrats.

The civil service was prepared for the transition. Peter Watson, his interim successor Steve MacDonald, and Richard Dicerni, who was appointed deputy minister to Executive Council on 15 September 2014, all had considerable experience with transitions. Dicerni, for example, had worked in both the Ontario and the federal public service and had been involved in several transitions. When Alison Redford resigned as PC leader and premier in March 2014, Watson initiated preparations for the ensuing transition. MacDonald continued this process when he was appointed deputy to Executive Council in June 2014 in preparation for a new Conservative premier.

With material from the 2011 and 2014 transitions to guide them, the public service prepared for a new government in 2015, but not for a change of party, as it was widely expected that the PCs would be returned to office. As the election campaign progressed and the results became less certain, Dicerni asked his deputy ministers to read the major parties'—the PCs, Wildrose, Liberals, and the New Democrats—election platforms and prepare for a change of party. This work was crucial for a transition from the Progressive Conservatives to the New Democrats.

The New Democrats were of course a key part of the transition. Unlike the Prentice, Redford, and Stelmach, governments,only three members if Notley's new caucus had experience in the legislature, and none had been in government. This lack of familiarity with the processes and conventions of government were part of the rationale for a small twelve member caucus. As well, Notley decided not to make any significant changes to the public service. This allowed for some continuity with previous governments and permitted the new administration, as well as the backbench members of caucus, to learn how government operates in the Westminster system. Notley also appointed the three members of her caucus with legislative experience to portfolios with which they had some experience as critics. This allowed them to move into cabinet with some familiarity of the issues facing the government.

The NDP campaign team represented another crucial set of actors in the transition process. Campaign chair Brian Topp had experience with transitions in Saskatchewan, while John Heaney and Jim Rutkowski had been through transitions in British Columbia. Ann McGrath had wide experience working with the federal party and was able to contribute to the 2015 transition process in Alberta. Moreover, the campaigning team/transition team asked New Democrats in other jurisdictions for advice and help. They contacted party officials across the country to construct a checklist of items and a timeline for a transition. Although the campaign team did not begin preparations for taking office until ten days before the election, the intensity of the transition meetings increased dramatically until election. The choice of a twelve-person cabinet minimized the risk that the new government would make serious mistakes. Calming fears in the public service of mass dismissals and in the caucus about a public service that had worked for the previous forty-four years under a series of PC governments, contributed to the ease with which the New Democrats took office. And finally, it should be recognized that after the election, there was no break for the campaign staff. It was as if nothing had changed; they were still working long days to understand and prepare for their new role as government.

It was the confluence of these various elements of the transition process that permitted the new government to meet the legislature less than a month after taking office and obtain effective control of the machinery of government within the ten months, or from May 2015 until March 2016. If the outgoing PCs, for example, had been better organized, or the civil service less familiar with the transition process, or if the campaign team had decided not to engage in transition planning, it is unlikely that the New Democrats would have been able to move as quickly and efficiently as they did on taking the levers of power.

NOTES

1   See David Zussman, *Off and Running: The Prospects and Pitfalls of Government Transitions in Canada* (Toronto: University of Toronto Press and the Institute of Public Administration of Canada, 2013).

2   This definition is borrowed from Carl M. Brauer, *Presidential Transitions: Eisenhower through Reagan* (New York: Oxford University Press, 1986), xxx–xiv.

3   Zussman, *Off and Running*, 14–17.

4   Peter Lougheed, interview with author, Calgary, 9 August 2007. This story is related in a slightly different fashion in David Woods, *The Lougheed Legacy* (Toronto: Key Porter Books, 1985).

5   Ted Mills, interview with author, Calgary, 27 October 2009.

6   Rod Love, interview with author, Calgary, 21 November 2007.

7   Robert Hawkes, interview with author, Calgary, 12 June 2013.

8   Richard Dicerni, telephone interview with author, Calgary, 25 October 2016.

9   "New deputy minister line-up unveiled. Alberta Premier Jim Prentice has appointed Richard Dicerni as the new Deputy Minister of Executive Council," press release, Government of Alberta, 15 September 2014.

10 Brian Topp, telephone interview with author, Calgary, 17 January 2017.

11 It should be noted that a budget had been presented in the provincial legislature by the Progressive Conservative government led by Jim Prentice. The budget, however, had not been passed. By the time the New Democrats came to office, the government was running out of funds and needed to pass a supply bill.

12 Topp interview.

13 Dicerni, correspondence with author, 31 July 2017.

14 Topp interview.

15 Ibid.

16 Ibid.

17 Michael Connolly, interview with author, Calgary, 17 October 2016.

18 For a case study of the recruitment of political staff, see Anna Lennox Esselment, "Birds of a feather? The role of partisanship in the 2003 Ontario government transition," *Canadian Public Administration* 54, no. 4 (December 2011): 465–86.

19 Topp interview.

20 Connolly interview.

21 Dicerni, correspondence with author.

22 Anne McGrath, interview with author, Calgary, 17 January 2017.

23 Graham Thompson, "NDP government's first throne speech promises a seismic shift," *Edmonton Journal*, 16 June 2016.

24 Justin Giovanatti, conversation with author, Calgary, 9 May 2015.

Fiscal Constraints on the Orange Chinook

Ron Kneebone and Jennifer Zwicker

The ambitions of any government are constrained by the fiscal conditions in which they must operate during their term of office. Winning office during a period of economic expansion yields a great many more policy options than doing so during a period of contraction. The severity of the restraints on policy choices depends as well on the extent to which previous governments have "left the cupboards bare," and to what extent they may have made spending and tax obligations that tie the hands of the incoming government.

The purpose of this chapter is to provide some context, using historical budget data, to understand the political, social, and other choices with which the newly elected NDP government was confronted. We begin with a brief historical overview of the government of Alberta's fiscal decisions from 1905 to 2016. In so doing, we highlight decisions made by previous governments with the hope of better informing the discussions carried out in other chapters about how future choices by the current government might be constrained and what choices might be considered.

To this end, we highlight several key issues, including the growth in health-care spending and its implications for taxes and the other spending programs, and the implications for social programs of an overreliance on borrowing (deficits) and energy revenues. The NDP government faces serious financial constraints, and while for the most part, these constraints are not of the government's making, they must nonetheless deal with them, and this will constrain, at least to some extent, their policy options.

A Short Budgetary History, 1905–2016

The defining characteristic of the government of Alberta's finances is its heavy reliance on the revenue it receives from the production and sale of non-renewable resources, in particular oil, natural gas, and coal. Although the provincial government has received revenue from non-renewable resources nearly from the start of its entry into Confederation in 1905, it was only with the discovery of a major pool of oil near Leduc in 1947 that these revenues began to make a noticeable contribution to the provincial treasury.

Figure 10.1 presents data on key elements of the provincial budget spanning the period 1915 to 2016. The data is presented in real per capita terms, which is to say that they have been adjusted for both population growth and inflation.

The dashed line shows values of total provincial government spending per person measured in 2016 dollars. This includes spending on programs (health, education, and social services) and the spending required to pay interest on the government's outstanding debt. The light grey line shows values of taxes (personal and corporate income tax) paid to the government by Albertans, as well as investment income earned on savings and the value of federal government transfers. The solid black line shows the real per capita value of non-renewable resource revenues received by the government. Subtracting the height of the dashed line (total expenditures) from the vertical sum of the light grey and black lines (which identify the sum of taxes, investment income, federal transfers, and non-renewable resource revenues available to the government) defines the government's surplus. This amount is represented by the height of the grey bars. Positive values of the grey bars identify a budget surplus while negative values identify a budget deficit.

Pre-Leduc, 1905–47

In the years prior to 1947, the provincial government maintained more or less balanced budgets. That is to say, total expenditures were closely matched by total revenues, resulting in very small budget imbalances—both positive (surpluses) and negative (deficits). This pattern reflects a policy preference during this period for matching requests or needs for new spending with new taxation.

RON KNEEBONE AND JENNIFER ZWICKER

Figure 10.1. Key Components of the Alberta Budget, 1915–2016

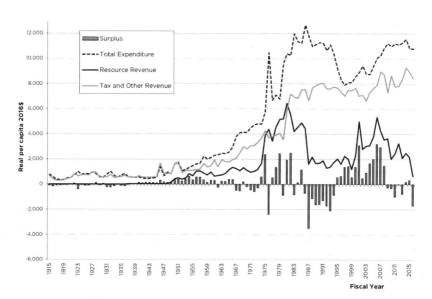

Sources: Data on Alberta government finances spanning the period 1905 to 1990 are from Paul Boothe (1995). Data since 1990 are from Government of Alberta Public Accounts (various years). Nominal values are deflated using estimates of the Canadian Consumer Price Index (1914-78) and the CPI for Alberta (1979-2015). These data are from CANSIM database, series v41693271 and v41694625, respectively. Population data is from Boothe (1914-1970) and from CANSIM series v469503 (1970-2015).

Leduc to OPEC, 1947–72

For twenty-five years after the discovery of oil near Leduc, the provincial government enjoyed the advantage of receiving an average of $800 per person in non-renewable resource revenue. This enabled the government to expand spending from less than $700 per person in 1947 to $4,700 per person in 1972. It was during this period that spending lost what had been its previously close connection to tax revenue. By 1972, tax revenue was $3,100 per person, leaving a $1,600-per-person gap between what taxpayers received by way of government spending and what they paid for in taxes. For most of this period, the gap between spending and taxes was more than filled by resource revenue, which allowed the government to report budget surpluses.

The Oil Price Shocks of the 1970s

OPEC's attempt to raise world oil prices proved successful beginning in 1973, with a second large price increase coming in 1979, and the government of Alberta benefitted enormously. Resource revenues increased dramatically, reaching a peak of $7,200 per person in 1982.[1] This dramatic increase in revenue prompted a similarly dramatic increase in spending and a widening in the gap between spending and the taxes Albertans were required to pay. The dependence on resource revenues to pay for spending was therefore growing. By the late 1970s, resource revenues were capable of financing two-thirds of provincial government programs. Revenues were so strong during this period that the government introduced the Alberta Heritage and Savings Trust Fund in 1976, with an initial endowment of $1.5 billion (the equivalent of $6 billion in 2016 dollars) and a commitment to directly divert 30 per cent of resource revenues to that fund and away from the treasury. As the decade came to an end, the provincial treasurer, noting satisfaction with low levels of taxation, high levels of government services, and successive budget surpluses, could afford to raise the possibility of increasing the share of resource revenue committed to the AHSTF.[2]

The End of the First Boom

The early 1980s saw Alberta confront two events that severely impacted the province and the provincial government's finances. The first was a policy-induced change that dramatically impacted the energy sector: the National Energy Program, introduced in October 1980 by the federal government. The second was a deep recession that struck the Canadian economy in 1981. The NEP slowed the growth in resource revenues to the province and prompted the government to increase spending in the form of support to the energy industry.[3] To mitigate the effect on the budget of this new spending and the loss of revenue, the government reduced the flow of funds into the AHSTF from 30 to 15 per cent of resource revenues, and it diverted all investment income earned on the fund to the treasury. These two fiscal adjustments, the impact of which can be observed in Figure 10.1 by the large upward adjustment in the "tax and other revenue" line in 1982, were envisioned at the time to be temporary measures lasting only for two fiscal years. These measures, plus a gradual increase in Canadian oil prices,[4] enabled the provincial government to remain in budgetary surplus for most of the period to 1985.

A Second Shock

A sudden fall in oil prices in 1986 saw the government lose 40 per cent of its resource revenues and a third of its total revenue. In response, the government completely abandoned contributions to the AHSTF and directed all energy revenues to the treasury. Despite this, and despite efforts to curtail spending that saw real capita spending fall from over $12,500 per person in 1986 to $11,000 per person in 1993, the failure of oil prices to recover meant the government realized very large deficits from 1987 to 1993. During this period the government saw its net asset position dissolve into a significant net debt.[5]

The Klein Revolution

The 1993 provincial election was fought over how to respond to the rapid accumulation of debt that had occurred since 1986. All three major political parties—Liberal, Progressive Conservative, and New Democrat—supported taking strong steps to eliminate the deficit, and both the Liberal and Progressive Conservative Parties advocated deep cuts to government spending in order to achieve this. The PCs, led by new leader Ralph Klein, were elected to a majority government in June 1993 on a platform that included a 20 per cent cut to spending.

As can be seen in Figure 10.1, Klein was true to his word and real per capita spending was reduced from $11,000 in 1993 to just under $8,000 by 1997. The gap between spending and tax and other revenue was at a level not seen since the early 1960s. The gap was now small enough that even with low energy prices the government was able to maintain large budget surpluses beginning in 1996.

Back on the Royalty Rollercoaster

Unfortunately, the government returned to its dependence on energy royalties after 1997. This was followed by a sharp increase in energy prices in 2001. For the next seven years, resource revenues were twice what they were in the preceding decade. Unfortunately, spending increased faster than energy revenues, and so the dependence on royalties returned. By 2009, the gap between spending and tax revenue was nearly $4,000 per person, and with the fall in energy prices in 2010 deficits returned as well.

As shown in Figure 10.1, when the New Democrats won the 2015 election they inherited a budget with near record spending and tax revenues and low resource revenues. Then it got worse. In 2016, real per capita resource revenues collapsed to a level not seen since the 1950s, and the deficit increased to a level last seen before the election of Ralph Klein.

The Current Fiscal Situation

To understand the current fiscal situation, and to appreciate what fiscal options are available to respond to that situation, it is helpful to take a closer look at recent spending and revenue choices.

Spending Choices

The provincial government's three largest expenditures are, typically, those in support of health care, education, and social services, and so we focus on those categories. Because of the role it has played in the fiscal decisions made by previous governments, we also look at the amount the government has spent servicing its outstanding debt. Figure 10.2 presents data on these four expenditure categories since the 1980–81 fiscal year. As in Figure 10.1, the data are measured in inflation-adjusted dollars per capita.

The rapid increase in debt following the oil price shock of 1986 saw a rapid rise in debt-servicing costs. By 1994–5, the servicing of the outstanding debt bypassed spending on social services as the third largest spending category. Analysts of that period highlighted the fact that the need to pay debt holders was threatening to crowd out spending on services to Albertans as a reason why drastic budgetary action was required. Premier Klein and those who voted for his platform chose to respond with spending cuts. In the three years following Klein's election, real per capita spending on health by the province fell by 20 per cent. Over the same period, spending on education and social services fell by 13 per cent and 29 per cent, respectively.[6] The cuts left Alberta's real per capita spending on health care 12 per cent below that of other provinces.[7] After 1995, the provincial government began compensating for its earlier restraint on health spending. Between 2000

Figure 10.2. Key Spending Categories, 1980–81 to 2015–16

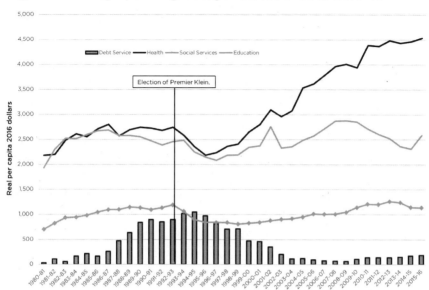

Sources: Government expenditure data are from Government of Alberta Public Accounts (various years). Nominal values are deflated using the CPI for Alberta (CANSIM series v41694625). Population data is from CANSIM series v469503.

and 2008, Alberta's real per capita expenditure on health doubled, with the result that in 2008 spending was 15 per cent higher than in other provinces.[8] Over the entire period since 1995, real per capita health spending has increased 114 per cent (from $2,100 in 1995–6 to $4,500 in 2015–16). Notably, Alberta in 2015 had the highest level of expenditure per adjusted capita ($4805), with expenditure on physicians and hospitals as cost drivers.

Alberta's per capita provincial health spending in 2016 was the second highest in the country after Newfoundland and Labrador. Family physicians in Alberta paid under the fee-for-service model earned 35 per cent more than the national average, and in 2014–15 they were the highest paid in Canada.[9] Alberta's specialists under fee-for-service were also among the highest paid in Canada in 2014–15, earning 24 per cent more than the national average.[10] Spending on health care, then, has been a long-standing priority, with the result that by 2015–16 it was consuming 45 per cent of total revenue, up from 18 per cent in 1980–81.

The ratio of social to health spending is a potential avenue through which the government can impact population health outcomes. The literature suggests that additional spending on health does not necessarily impact population health outcomes,[11] yet in all provinces, health spending increased rapidly after a drop in the mid-1990s while social spending remained relatively flat. As shown in Figure 10.2, spending on education and social services in Alberta has not increased at nearly the rate of health spending. This is despite recent work by Elizabeth Bradley and colleagues suggesting that an exclusive focus on health-care expenditures in the health-care reform discussion is misleading.[12] Their argument, backed by comparative data from thirty industrialized countries, is that health outcomes are influenced by the total amount spent on both health *and* social programs.

Sources of Revenue

Real per capita revenue in Alberta has trended upward since 1980–81 (as seen in Figure 10.1). Major provincial revenue categories include corporate and personal income tax, natural resource revenue, federal transfers for health and social programs, and other revenue.

Over time, the composition of total tax revenue (which is mainly in the form of the personal and corporate income tax) has grown, slowly, as a percentage of total revenue. Notably, these tax revenue sources combined contribute to total revenue more than twice what they did in 1980–81. In contrast to the steady upward trend in the share of total revenue provided by taxes, resource revenues have been volatile. By 2015–16, resource revenue contributed the smallest percentage of total revenue since 1980, which is in stark contrast to the early 1980s, when resource revenue contributed over half of total revenue.

Another source of revenue volatility, and one that is not often recognized, is federal transfers. Federal transfers fell as a percentage of total revenue in the mid-1990s. This was the result of the federal government trying to get its own fiscal house in order by cutting spending in the form of transfers to the provinces. Since that time federal transfers have stabilized, but the earlier experience of the federal government solving its fiscal issues on the back of provincial finances should serve as a cautionary tale.

RON KNEEBONE AND JENNIFER ZWICKER

Figure 10.3. Federal Government Transfers to the Government of Alberta

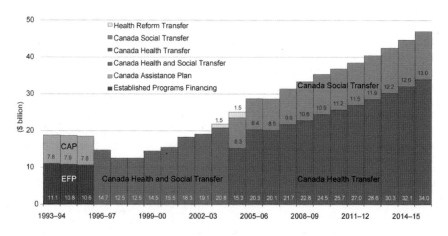

Source: https://www.fin.gc.ca/fedprov/his-eng.asp

The recession of the 1990s saw significant fiscal restraint at both the federal and provincial/territorial levels, as well as a gradual shift away from cost-sharing arrangements towards provincial block grants for health and social services (see Figure 10.3). Federal-provincial fiscal arrangements impacted the politics of health care and social services when federal transfers were shifted from Established Program Financing and the Canada Assistance Plan to the Canada Health and Social Transfer (CHST). The shift to the CHST marked a reduction of transfers of $2.5 billion in 1996–7 and $4.5 billion in 1997–8.[13] This combined funding, allocated on an equal per capita basis, was intended for the provision of health care, post-secondary education, social assistance, and social services. With economic growth on the upswing at the end of the decade and concerns about access and wait times for health care growing, provincial governments mainly used transfers to reinvest in the provision of health care. As is clear from Figure 10.2, provincial spending on education and social services has been noticeably less sensitive to the growth in federal transfers.

The focus on health in the growth in federal transfers is the result of the federal government using its spending power to increase its involvement in this area of provincial jurisdiction. By 2002, both the Kirby Report and the Romanow Commission advocated for increased federal spending accompanied with greater accountability from provinces and health care providers.[14] In response, the 2003 First Ministers' Accord on Health Care Renewal restructured the CHST, with 62 per cent going to the Canada Health Transfer (CHT) and 38 per cent to the Canada Social Transfer (CST) to be spent on post-secondary education, programs for children, and other social programs.[15] The CHT are block grants provided by the federal government to fund health care under terms governed by the Canada Health Act. This transfer is provided on a "no-strings-attached" basis, and there are no cost-sharing provisions (i.e., a provision intended to discourage provinces from freely spending "50 cent dollars"). An additional $16 billion over five years was provided through a new Health Reform Transfer targeting primary health care, home care, and catastrophic drug coverage.[16]

In 2004, a ten-year, $41-billion health accord was signed that promised to be the "fix for a generation."[17] The goal was to strengthen health care by improving access to care and diagnostic services, reducing wait times for surgical interventions, roll out electronic health records, alleviate health human resource shortages, reform primary health care, investments in home care, and implementation of a national pharmaceutical strategy.[18] This additional funding commitment to provinces and territories for health included increases to the CHT through a base adjustment and an annual 6 per cent escalator. The health-reform transfer was consolidated into the CHT in 2005. Alberta recently experienced a large growth in federal transfers due to a change in the formula used to calculate CHT payments that occurred in 2014–15, when the program became a pure per capita transfer (Di Matteo, 2012).[19] Transfers to Alberta subsequently increased by 33 per cent from the previous year's level, due to the policy change and rapid population growth.

More recently, federal transfers have been in the spotlight again as a result of the 2016–17 health accord negotiations. The "no-strings-attached" policy with a 6 per cent escalator was extended by Prime Minister Stephen Harper until 2017. Unless another deal was negotiated, the CHT would grow in line with a three-year moving average of nominal GDP growth, with funding guaranteed to increase by at least 3 per cent per year. Discussions around a pan-Canadian agreement fell apart at the end of 2016. Health Minister Jane Philpott then negotiated separate transfer agreements with each province. At the time of our writing this chapter, twelve provinces and territories have accepted the $11-billion deal on top of $37 billion in annual funding through the CHT. The negotiated CHT in 2017–18 ranged per province from a 3.5 per cent escalator for Alberta to a 2 per cent escalator for New Brunswick. Alberta negotiated new targeted funding over ten years for investments in home care and mental health care.[20]

Changes in Net Debt

The crash in energy prices in 1986 defined the beginning of a volatile period in Alberta's net financial position. The 1986 crash, combined with the disinclination on the part of the government to respond to the resulting loss of revenue, resulted in a very rapid accumulation of net debt. Between 1984–5 and 1993–4, each Albertan took on nearly $15,000 in new debt. It was in part due to this rapid accumulation of debt that Albertans elected Premier Klein on a platform of spending cuts. The combination of spending cuts (initially) and revenue growth (later) enabled the government to run budget surpluses in every year from 1994–5 to 2007–8. The result was a rapid reduction in net debt. By 2004–5, Albertans had shed all of the net debt accumulated since 1984–5. The province's asset position continued to improve until 2007–8, after which net debt slowly increased as the government dealt with first the worldwide financial crisis of 2008–9 and then the collapse of energy prices beginning in 2015.

Fiscal Issues for the New Government

The impact of the Alberta government's dependence on resource revenue on the provincial budget is not a new concern. In the past, when resource revenues have fallen and remained low for prolonged periods, the government has had to choose between tough spending choices and considering new revenue sources. Those choices have historically tended to favour cuts to spending in order to protect the so-called Alberta Advantage of low tax rates and no provincial sales tax. The current government is faced with similar options for dealing with the loss of resource revenues, but it is not, of course, obligated to make the same choices. Maintaining or abandoning the Alberta Advantage approach, like all policy choices, has pros and cons. Choices, though, need to be made.

Here we highlight some key expenditure and revenue issues that need to be addressed. On the revenue side, uncertain economic growth, reduced resource revenue, and likely reductions in federal health transfers suggest that policy shifts towards more sustainable revenue sources need to be made. While health-care costs continue to grow, income support caseloads are also increasing, as are debt-servicing costs, providing further illustration of the need to curb health spending in the face of increasing need.

Uncertainty Regarding Resource Revenue

Volatility in the resource revenues received by the government has been an enduring feature of provincial finances in Alberta. Booms and busts are a common feature of resource-based economies, and economists are unanimous in recommending to governments that they keep that volatility of the private sector from negatively effecting its fiscal position.[21] The way to implement this recommendation is simple: save all or most of the revenue earned on the sale of non-renewable resources.

Unfortunately, governments in Alberta have tended not to heed this advice.[22] The result has been wide swings in the government's net asset position and occasional deep cuts to spending (see Figure 10.2). The former response creates uncertainty with respect to future tax rates and so discourages private-sector investments, while the latter represents a direct harm to Albertans hoping to enjoy the benefits of securely funded health care, education, and social assistance programs. These are difficult choices involving trade-offs between conflicting goals.

To avoid these problems, the current government ran on a platform aimed at getting off what has been dubbed the "royalty rollercoaster." This is hard, of course. It involves reducing spending and/or increasing tax rates to levels that establish a tolerable budget balance even when energy prices are low. As noted earlier, this feat was accomplished in the mid-1990s under Premier Klein, mainly via the use of spending cuts. The choice of spending cuts is not inevitable, of course. Other options include raising tax rates and introducing new sources of tax revenue. Among these options is the choice to introduce a sales tax harmonized with the federal GST—a policy long advocated by economists. Like spending cuts, tax increases carry costs, both

RON KNEEBONE AND JENNIFER ZWICKER

political and economic. But if it is serious about weaning itself off its dependence on energy revenues, the NDP government, like all governments, must make hard decisions involving spending cuts and/or revenue increases.

Uncertainty Regarding Long-Term Economic Growth

The NDP won what might be considered a pyrrhic victory by winning an election just as energy prices collapsed, thereby throwing the economy into recession and the provincial budget into a deep deficit. Normally, governments console themselves by emphasizing that the economic situation is temporary—that a recession will be short-lived and that, when it ends, the province's return to prosperity will mean a return to balanced budgets and strong job growth.

Alberta's economic prosperity is closely tied to a robust energy industry, which in turn depends on high energy prices. Unfortunately, the current government cannot assume that the economic situation it finds itself in is a temporary one. There is little in the way of consensus among energy analysts that energy prices will return to the levels that fostered the high rates of growth and employment creation seen during the late 1990s and 2000s.[23] The risk faced by the current government is that rather than inheriting an economy in temporary recession, they have inherited an economy settling in to a "new normal" of lower economic growth. The implications of possibly permanent lower revenues and stubbornly persistent high deficits is a potential reality with which the government must come to grips.

Debt-Servicing Costs

With revenue sources being uncertain, the government's budgetary response to the loss of revenue suffered because of the fall in energy prices has been limited to running very large budget deficits. The most recent budget suggests that the government plans to moderate spending increases but in the main to "hold the course." It is adamant in refusing to consider spending cuts as it endeavours to protect so-called front-line workers from layoffs. It is also hesitant to raise taxes during a period of high unemployment. The fiscal plan, then, would appear to be to continue to run large deficits—and so accumulating significant new debt—while hoping for a return of high energy prices that will balance the budget.

One consequence of this approach is that the government can expect a steady increase in the cost of servicing its growing debt. The government needs to be concerned that this may cause debt-servicing costs to begin to crowd out other spending. Figure 10.2 reminds us of this danger. As noted earlier, the rapid accumulation of debt in the late 1980s and early 1990s— when the government similarly ran large annual deficits hoping for a return to higher energy prices—resulted in very fast growth in debt-servicing costs that quickly bypassed spending on social services to become the third largest spending category. From Figure 10.2 we see a slow but steady increase in debt-servicing costs. If deficits remain large, this increase will accelerate under the current government.[24] If the current low interest rate environment changes, it will accelerate still faster.

Uncertainty Regarding Federal Transfers and the Implications for Health Spending

The negotiations between the provinces and the federal government in 2016–17 have highlighted what one writer calls the "sick politics of healthcare."[25] The federal government's offer to the provinces was that the CHT would drop from a 6 per cent annual escalator to 3.5 per cent, with an additional $11.5 billion over five years for home care and mental health. Intent on a higher escalator, the provinces rejected the deal at the end of 2016. By August 2017, a precedent was set for province-by-province (and territorial) negotiations. Individual agreements with the federal government for different growth rates and dedicated funding to home care and mental health were reached, with growth in CHT ranging from a high of 3.5 per cent in Alberta to a low of 2 per cent in New Brunswick.[26] From 2017 to 2027, the federal government will provide Alberta with an additional $1.3 billion, which will include funding for home care and mental health initiatives.

The signing of the new federal transfer agreements will provide some degree of certainty to the provincial budget. However, the growth in the federal transfer will be slower than the growth in health spending, resulting in several difficult choices for the provincial government: to raise taxes, to cut spending in other areas, or to re-evaluate how it spends on health care. If additional revenue is not raised, then as health spending grows, expenditures on social services and education are likely to decline. This is despite international research highlighting the importance of both social

RON KNEEBONE AND JENNIFER ZWICKER

and health spending when trying to improve health outcomes. The NDP government will need to make spending choices in the face of the ever-increasing chronic care demands present in the system.

Rising Health-Care Costs and Rising Income Support Caseloads

Where to spend the marginal dollar in health care, and who decides, are two of the most important and pressing questions in health policy. As noted in a recent OECD report, "Healthcare costs are rising so fast in advanced economies that they will become unaffordable by mid-century without reforms."[27] As seen in the expenditure data shown in Figure 10.2, Alberta is no exception to this. But while some studies suggest that additional health-care spending does not correlate with health outcomes, social policy is becoming a legitimate consideration for major health stakeholders.[28] Health outcomes respond to the socio-economic factors termed "the social determinants of health," which include income, education, employment, and social support networks, among other factors. Our recent Canadian analysis suggests that health care is not the highest-return ministry to spend on to improve population health outcomes. Using provincial expenditure data in Canada, we found that more spending on social services per dollar spent on health-care services is associated with better health outcomes.[29] In other words, if a government had $600 million dollars to spend (approximately the increase in health spending in Alberta this year), it might do more for population health to spend that money on social services than health care. This is because population health is measured in terms of outcomes like life expectancy and potentially avoidable mortality, and social services can mitigate the factors that lead to these poor health outcomes. By international standards, Canada spends the least on social programs as a percent of GDP compared to ten other high-income countries.[30] The CHT are not tied to health expenditures and there is potential to reallocate provincial spending. Despite our understanding of historical budget allocations, we lack evidence that supports the idea that additional spending on health care is the most efficient way to improve health outcomes.

Thinking carefully about how to spend health dollars is perhaps particularly appropriate when we consider that social assistance caseloads have ratcheted upward over the past fifteen years. From an average of about 25,000 caseloads per year in the early 2000s, the average jumped to 35,000 in the 2010s, and since 2015 has averaged over 50,000.[31] While income support caseloads are sensitive to the state of the economy, the observation that they are not returning to pre-recession levels is cause to be concerned.

This social policy issue has health implications. Social policy in Canada can impact health in two complementary ways: by both reducing poverty (from welfare payments to old age security) and reducing social inequalities with measures and programs that encourage social mobility (e.g., subsidized university tuition), labour force participation (e.g., subsidized daycare), or good physical health (e.g., free and accessible medical care).

An interesting implication of these findings is that reigning in health spending may be possible without a negative impact on health outcomes— and without straining an already stretched budget—by reallocating program spending from health to social policy initiatives. This possibility presents interesting policy choices for social democratic governments, which traditionally favour social policy initiatives.

Conclusion

Historically, Alberta governments, with the support of voters, have employed a high-risk strategy wherein Alberta's economic success depends on high energy prices. This dependence on a source of revenue that is inherently volatile to fund public services such as health, social services, and education means that tough choices have to be made when energy prices are low. The budget deficit is available to act as a "buffer" to insulate program spending and tax rates from the effects of revenue fluctuations. However, as we saw in the mid-1990s, on occasion energy prices have remained low for so long that accumulated deficits—and the debt-servicing payments they require—have grown large enough to force difficult choices to eventually be made between tax increases or cuts to programs. As we have discussed, when they have been faced with this choice, Conservative governments have eventually responded with drastic cuts to spending in order to protect the Alberta Advantage of low taxes. Unfortunately, this choice involves cutting health and social programs even while the health and social problems that they are designed to alleviate persist.

The new NDP government can make different fiscal choices, in terms of both revenue generation and expenditures, than those made in the past. In

RON KNEEBONE AND JENNIFER ZWICKER

particular, they could respond more quickly to the fall in energy prices than previous Conservative governments. Were they to do so, they could ease the budgetary adjustment to a new low-price environment without the need for the draconian cuts to spending that former governments eventually introduced after years of delay. That gradual adjustment to a low-energy-price environment could take the form of slowing the rate of spending growth, or a gradual increase in taxation. Or the adjustment could be more dramatic, for example by taking the advice of economists and introducing a sales tax harmonized to the federal GST, which would provide the government with a way to wean itself off its dependence on energy revenues. Different allocation decisions around expenditures to improve population health outcomes could also see an allocation of health budgets to social services and education, which can impact health outcomes through their influence on the social determinants of health.

However, the NDP government is following a similar path to that of previous governments: it is choosing to avoid dramatic changes to spending or revenue in the hope that high energy prices will return. As it waits, the deficit remains large and both the level of debt and the cost of servicing that debt climb. If, as suggested by many analysts and as evidenced by low prices in energy futures markets,[32] high energy prices do not return, the new government will eventually need to make some hard fiscal choices. If this comes to pass, the price for delaying budget adjustments will be larger than if the government reacted more quickly, and the need among vulnerable populations will continue to grow. If, on the other hand, higher prices do return, a sigh of relief will be in order as the government once again has the time to consider whether it might be best to get off the energy rollercoaster once and for all.

NOTES

1   The treasury also benefited from the effort of the new premier, Peter Lougheed, to negotiate a new royalty-sharing agreement with the industry. Bruce Doern and Greg Toner, *The Politics of Energy: The Development and Implementation of the NEP* (London: Methuen Publications, 1985), 89–90.

2   1978 Alberta budget cited in Paul Boothe, "The Growth of Government Spending in Alberta," in *Canadian Tax Paper No. 100* (Toronto: Canadian Tax Foundation), supra note 9, at p. 43.

3   Provincial support for the industry included a $5.4 billion program, introduced in 1982, consisting of royalty reductions and grants designed to increase the flow of revenue to the industry. See Doern and Toner, *The Politics of Energy*, 114.

4   Following its introduction in October 1980, the NEP controlled oil prices in Canada. Through a series of negotiated settlements between the province of Alberta and the federal government, the prices for "old oil" (discovered prior to 1980) were set as a percentage of the world price. The price of "new oil" was allowed to rise to the world price in an agreement signed in 1983.

5   All governments hold both financial assets and financial liabilities. If the value of assets exceed liabilities, the government is said to be in a financial net asset position. If the opposite is true, the government is described as being in a net debt position.

6   Part of the fall in spending on social services was due to the economy recovering from the 1990–91 recession, which resulted in fewer people receiving social assistance. However, policy changes were the major reason for the fall in spending. The social assistance payment to a single person fell by 16 per cent from $5,832 in 1992 to $4,927 in 1994. These are nominal dollar values kindly provided by Sherri Tjorman, Anne Tweddle, and Ken Battle, and they are reported in real dollar terms in Tweddle, Battle, and Tjorman, *Welfare in Canada, 2016* (Ottawa: The Caledon Institute of Social Policy, 2017).

7   Greg P. Marchildon and Livio Di Matteo, *Bending the Cost Curve in Health Care: Canada's Provinces in International Perspective* (Toronto: University of Toronto Press, 2014).

8   Ibid. With a younger population relative to other provinces, age and gender standardization only causes expenditures relative to other provinces to be more pronounced.

9   See Canadian Institute for Health Information, *Physicians in Canada, 2016: Summary Report* (Ottawa: CIHI, 2017), https://secure.cihi.ca/free_products/ Physicians_in_Canada_2016.pdf and Alberta Health, "Physician payment and service comparisons," 2016, http://www.health.alberta.ca/health-info/health-economics- dashboard4.html (accessed 31 January 2017).

10 Ibid.

11 R. Evans and G. Stoddart, "Consuming Health Care, Producing Health," *Social Science and Medicine* 331, no. 12 (1990): 489–500.

12 See E. Bradley and L. Taylor, *The American health care paradox: Why spending more is getting us less* (New York: PublicAffairs, 2013); E. H. Bradley, M. Canavan, E. Rogan, K.

Talbert-Slagle, C. Ndumele, L. Taylor, and L. A. Curry, "Variation in Health Outcomes: The Role Of Spending On Social Services, Public Health, And Health Care, 2000–09," *Health Affairs* 35, no. 5 (2016): 760–8; and E. H. Bradley, B. R. Elkins, J. Herrin, and B. Elbel, "Health and social services expenditures: Associations with health outcomes," *BMJ Qual Saf* 20, no. 10 (2011): 826–31.

13 Gerard W. Boychuk, *The changing political and economic environment of health care in Canada* (Ottawa: Commission on the Future of Health Care in Canada, 2002).

14 See M. J. Kirby and M. LeBreton, *The health of Canadians—the federal role.* Report of the Standing Senate Committee on Social Affairs, Science and Technology, 37th Parliament, 2nd Session, 8th report (Ottawa: Queen's Printer for Canada, 2002), and R. Romanow, *Building on Values: Report of the Commission on the Future of Health Care in Canada* (Ottawa: Privy Council Office, Government of Canada, 2002).

15 Department of Finance, "History of Health and Social Transfers," (2014), https://www.fin.gc.ca/fedprov/his-eng.asp (accessed 31 January 2017).

16 Ibid.

17 See Government of Canada, "A 10-year plan to strengthen health care," 16 September 2004, https://www.canada.ca/en/health-canada/services/health-care-system/health-care-system-delivery/federal-provincial-territorial-collaboration/first-ministers-meeting-year-plan-2004/10-year-plan-strengthen-health-care.html (accessed 28 January 2017).

18 Ibid.; D. Naylor, N. Fraser, F. Girard, T. Jenkins, J. Mintz, and C. Power, *Unleashing innovation: Excellent healthcare for Canada. Report of the Advisory Panel on Healthcare Innovation* (Ottawa: Health Canada, 2015).

19 L. Di Matteo, "Canada Health Transfer Changes: The Devil Is in the Details," *Evidence Network*, 2012, https://evidencenetwork.ca/changes-to-the-canada-health-transfer-mean-a-large-windfall-for-some-provinces-shortchange-for-others/ (accessed 20 January 2017).

20 Health Canada, "Canada Reaches Health Funding Agreement with Alberta" (news release), 10 March 2017, https://www.canada.ca/en/health-canada/news/2017/03/canada_reaches_healthfundingagreementwithalberta.html (accessed 28 August 2018).

21 In an article well known to economists ("Intergenerational Equity and the Investing of Rents from Exhaustible Resources," *American Economic Review* 67, no. 5 [1977]: 972–4), John Hartwick showed that the long-term success of an economy dependent upon the extraction of non-renewable resources is dependent on the government transforming the declining resource stock into a new, productive capital stock that will produce a perpetual stream of pay-offs to future generations. Application of the so-called Hartwick Rule has been recognized as requiring that governments save resource revenues and spend only the income generated by that saving. This advice, closely followed by the government of Norway, prevents resource revenues from entering the government's budget and so prevents their volatility from forcing periodic cuts to essential programs and/or rapid accumulations of debt.

22 For a review of the on again, off again efforts made by governments in Alberta to commit to saving resource revenues, see Ronald Kneebone, "From Famine to Feast:

The Evolution of Budgeting Rules in Alberta," *Canadian Tax Journal* 54, no. 3 (2006): 657–73.

23 For an interesting review and comparison of the recent and past oil price shocks, see Robert Skinner "A Comparative Anatomy of Oil Price Routs: A Review of Four Oil Price Routs Between 1985 and 2014," *SPP Research Papers* 8, no. 39 (November 2015): 1–33.

24 In the 2017 budget, the government reports that debt-servicing costs are expected to reach $2.3 billion by 2020. This compares to $0.8 billion in 2016 and $0.2 billion in 2009.

25 E. Solomon, "The sick politics of a national health accord," *Macleans*, 22 December 2016.

26 See R. Collier, "Health accord side deals bad for Canada, say doctors," *CMAJ News*, 30 January 2017, http://cmajnews.com/2017/01/05/health-accord-side-deals-bad-for-canada-say-doctors-cmaj-109-5381/ (accessed 13 February 2017).

27 OECD, *Fiscal Sustainability of Health Systems* (Paris: OECD Publishing, 2015).

28 See J. S. House, *Beyond Obamacare: Life, death, and social policy* (New York: Russell Sage Foundation, 2015).

29 D. J. Dutton, P. -G. Forest, R. D. Kneebone, and J. D. Zwicker, "Effect of provincial spending on social services and health care on health outcomes in Canada: An observational longitudinal study," *Canadian Medical Association Journal* 190, no. 3 (2018): E66–E71.

30 See I. Papanicolas, L. R. Woskie, and A. K. Jha, "Health care spending in the united states and other high-income countries," *Jama* 319, no. 10 (2018): 1024–39.

31 See "Income Support Caseloads in Alberta," *Social Policy Trends, School of Public Policy* (2017), https://www.policyschool.ca/wp-content/uploads/2016/02/Social-Trends-Income-Support-for-April-Issue.pdf (accessed 28 August 2018). These are caseloads for individuals defined as "expected to work" by the provincial social assistance program. The data does not include caseloads of those on the Assured Income for the Severely Handicapped program.

32 Investors make bets on the future direction of commodity prices in what are called "futures markets." Observing these bets are a useful way of determining what experts in energy markets believe will be the price of energy in the future. At the writing of this chapter, futures markets are very pessimistic about the price of oil rising above the level that is currently causing the government to suffer historically high budget deficits.

RON KNEEBONE AND JENNIFER ZWICKER

Beyond the "Lovey-Dovey Talk": The Orange Chinook and Indigenous Activism

Brad Clark

> Until we have "walked in the Indian's moccasins" we have little chance of gaining his confidence or influencing him in any way. It seems to me that the integration of the Indian into the social and economic life of Saskatchewan is the desirable goal and this will become more acceptable to him if we can put across our socialist idea of "sharing" and "production for use"...
>
> —John Sturdy, special assistant to Tommy Douglas, Co-operative Commonwealth Federation premier of Saskatchewan, in a 1960 election document[1]

The socially progressive New Democratic Party, through the policy pronouncements of its forebear, the Co-operative Commonwealth Federation (CCF), has had a sympathetic eye on Indigenous peoples for more than half a century. Federally, CCF MP Frank Howard introduced a private member's bill to grant the franchise to "Indians" in 1957, three years before the Diefenbaker Progressive Conservatives would make the necessary amendments to the Canada Elections Act.[2] The patronizing sentiment expressed by John Sturdy (quoted above) captures colonial governments' failure to understand and reform what Tommy Douglas's provincial administration referred to as the "Indian problem" and the struggle to find a socially just, well-meaning argument for assimilation. At the same time it belies the pragmatism political parties embrace to appeal to different segments of the electorate. Sturdy's nod to the sizeable Indigenous population in Saskatchewan came at a time when Indians in that province were about to vote in a provincial election for the first time, and it expressed a desire to win their support, if not a concern that they might cast their ballots for other parties.

Fifty-five years later, in the territories of Treaty 6, 7, and 8 First Nations, as well as the Métis Nations of Alberta and Métis settlements, Rachel Notley's New Democrats won the Alberta legislature on a typically progressive platform of "major changes to tax and social policy; an aggressive climate-change plan . . . gender balance in politics and society; a higher minimum wage; [and] *a new and more respectful relationship with First Nations*" (emphasis added).[3] This chapter explores this "relationship" between Indigenous peoples in Alberta and the Notley NDP almost exclusively from the perspective of First Nations, Métis, and Inuit voters and leaders. It examines how the New Democrats' policies and decisions are perceived in Indigenous media from the day the writ was dropped by Jim Prentice and the Progressive Conservatives through the NDP's first nineteen months in office.

The analysis demonstrates the diversity of perspectives brought to bear by Indigenous people in Alberta on a range of issues, but it also underscores a growing sense of empowerment, activism, and influence in effecting political change in this province and beyond. While highlighting the actions and concerns of their communities, Indigenous media have consistently framed the Notley administration as agents of change, protectors of the environment, and more respectful of Aboriginal viewpoints than their Progressive Conservative predecessors.

These themes are also captured in this chapter by a detailed examination of voting data captured by Elections Alberta. That analysis suggests that higher rates of participation among Indigenous peoples had an impact on the 2015 election's outcome, and it indicates much wider support for the New Democrats among voters in First Nations and Métis communities than in the general population. In fact, votes from Indigenous communities appear to have propelled NDP candidates to victory in at least two ridings.

For Indigenous leaders across Canada, the Alberta provincial election was a sign that real political change is possible, and that First Peoples can work to bring such change about. Moreover, the role that Aboriginal communities played in the Orange Chinook set the stage for Indigenous voter mobilization in the federal election six months later. Calls for change reverberated through the federal campaign, with the result that another long-standing Conservative regime tumbled.

Election Night Delight and Indigenous Support

The unprecedented demise of a forty-four-year political dynasty will always warrant considerable interrogation and analysis in the mainstream media, which might explain why the *Calgary Herald* took several days before finding space to comment on the connection between Alberta's Indigenous communities and the rise to power of the New Democrats. An article that ran on page A21 noted the incoming New Democrats had made "sweeping promises to aboriginals during the campaign" and that Premier-Elect Rachel Notley had specifically referenced Alberta's First Nations and Métis in her victory speech.[4] Amid the pumping of orange placards and chants from ecstatic supporters, Notley pledged the following: "To Alberta's Indigenous peoples: the trust we have been given tonight is a call to be better neighbours and partners. I'm looking forward to consulting with you and learning from you."[5] Even the *Herald* noted that, though this brief reference took only about a minute to deliver, it was a minute more than PC premier Alison Redford devoted to Indigenous issues in her acceptance speech just over three years earlier.[6] The *Herald* story went on to quote a few First Nation leaders who expressed optimism about both the election results and Notley's speech. While this might have been a revelation for the mainstream consumers of Post Media's Calgary publication, Indigenous news organizations had already devoted considerable coverage to the NDP's unexpected rise to power and its commitment to First Peoples. A number of First Nations chiefs and commentators issued statements or told reporters of their belief that they could work with the New Democrats in ways they had not with previous Progressive Conservative governments. Despite a premier with a substantial history in Indigenous issues (Jim Prentice), and Alberta's longest-serving Indigenous MLA (Pearl Calahasen), it was the NDP rather than the PCs who garnered the support of many Métis and First Nations voters.

It is important to note that there is no uniform "Indigenous vote," and that the First Peoples of Alberta are made up of distinct linguistic and cultural groups, with different economic interests and governance structures. The "Aboriginal Identity Population" in Alberta, according to Statistics Canada, numbers more than 220,000 and represents 6 per cent of the provincial population, consisting of "116,670 First Nations people, 96,870 Métis, and 1,985 Inuit, with the rest reporting other Aboriginal identities (3,300) or more than one Aboriginal identity (1,875)."[7] The same report notes the significant urban Indigenous population, with 28 per cent living in Edmonton and 15 per cent in Calgary; moreover, 40 per cent of First Nations people in Alberta (46,600) make their homes on reserves. There are 140 reserves in the province and 45 First Nations in the three Treaty areas; the most commonly spoken Indigenous languages are Blackfoot, Cree, Chipewyan, Dene Sarcee, and Stoney (Nakoda Sioux).[8] Alberta is the only province in Canada to recognize Métis land rights, having signed the Alberta-Métis Settlements Accord in 1989, which granted local autonomy to eight settlements and about 5,000 residents in the "east-central and northern areas of the province."[9]

However, as the NDP took office, the challenge of following through on its election promises were significant. Government data show that Indigenous people, especially those living on reserve, trail non-Indigenous Albertans in virtually every measure of well-being. Life expectancy for First Nations individuals is 72.5 years, 10 years less than for non-natives and comparable to rates in "Guatemala, Paraguay and Cambodia."[10] Compared to non-Indigenous Albertans, First Nations people experience double the rate of infant mortality, triple the suicide rate, twice the prevalence of diabetes, and five times the rate of narcotic- and opioid-related trips to the emergency room.[11] Health studies of Métis show better outcomes generally than among First Nations, "but [they] tend to experience slightly worse health results in many areas compared to the non-Aboriginal population of the province," including "elevated levels" of the same diseases affecting First Nations, such as diabetes and circulatory ailments.[12] As in other parts of the country, the colonial legacy of racism, the Indian Act, the reserve system, and the legacy of residential schools have taken a terrible toll. Against this backdrop, many First Nation and Métis people looked to the 2015 Alberta election for change.

Heading into the campaign PC leader Jim Prentice had a long track record on Indigenous issues, having worked as a commissioner for the Indian Land Claims Commission, serving as the Minister of Indian Affairs and Northern Development in the Harper cabinet, and taking on the Aboriginal relations portfolio as premier in 2014. Nonetheless, the PC government took certain actions that rankled many in the Indigenous communities across the province. Prentice opposed calls for an inquiry into Missing and Murdered Indigenous Women (MMIW); there was ongoing frustration over persistent Métis and First Nation calls for resource revenue sharing; and controversial Bill 22, the Aboriginal Consultation Levy Act, had drawn heavy criticism, to the point where it was boycotted by many First Nations.[13] That legislation "allowed the province to regulate consultation with industry over development on Aboriginal land," but Indigenous leaders said they were never consulted before it was introduced.[14] Simmering disdain for federal Conservatives might also have extended to the Prentice Tories, particularly over the demise of the Kelowna Accord and the refusal to implement the United Nations Declaration on the Rights of Indigenous Peoples (UNDRIP). Moreover, the provincial PCs focused very little of their election platform on Aboriginal issues, beyond plans to "improve the First Nations Engagement Strategy to strengthen relationships with Aboriginal leaders and communities," according to an analysis by the Parkland Institute.[15]

In sharp contrast, the NDP targeted several issues of concern brought on by the policies of two levels of conservative government. In fact, the New Democrats offered a comprehensive "Aboriginal Platform" that sought to do the following:

- We will implement the 2007 United Nations
  Declaration on the Rights of Indigenous Peoples,
  and build it into provincial law.

- We will support a National Inquiry into Missing and
  Murdered Indigenous Women, which will have at
  its centre Indigenous women and the families of the
  missing and murdered women.

- We will work with Alberta Indigenous Peoples to build a
  relationship of trust and ensure respectful consultation.

- We will work with the federal government to ensure Indigenous communities have reliable access to clean and safe drinking water.

- We will improve the representation of Indigenous culture and history in Alberta's school curriculum in consultation with Indigenous leaders and Elders, and improve availability of First Nations language programs.

- We will repeal Bill 22, which was passed without consulting First Nation groups and imposes requirements on First Nations Bands not required of other business arrangements.[16]

At 57 per cent, voter turnout on election day was the highest it had been in twenty-two years, since former big city mayors Ralph Klein (Calgary) and Laurence Decore (Edmonton) led the Progressive Conservatives and Liberals, respectively, on platforms of "massive cuts" versus "brutal cuts" to provincial spending.[17] At least three media outlets (*First Nations Drum, Alberta Native News,* and The Aboriginal Peoples Television Network [APTN] News) reported Indigenous peoples lined up at the polls in record numbers; as *Alberta Native News* put it, "perhaps for the first time ever, [these voters] helped to sway the numbers in favour of the NDP."[18] APTN attributed the higher turnout among Aboriginal voters to social media, where election and campaign information was distributed widely according to Lowa Beebe, a Calgary-based social media blogger and First Nations activist: "This is now a tool in our history. Our communities always worked together and were stronger together, well on social media we are now together.... It's us talking and having discussions on this new medium that's here to stay."[19] Foreshadowing a social media phenomenon of the 2015 federal election campaign, the hashtag #RockTheIndigenousVote—a rallying call for voter participation—was shared in the context of an election campaign for the first time.[20]

Based on Elections Alberta data,[21] the Indigenous vote very much "rocked" in favour of the New Democrats. Using provincial electoral maps,

Figure 11.1. Percentage of vote in First Nation and Métis communities and in the general population.

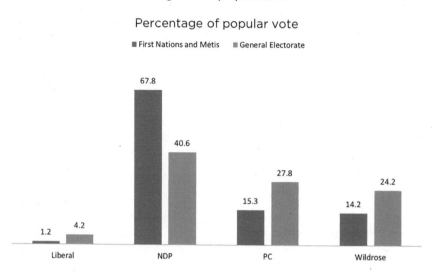

Percentage of popular vote

■ First Nations and Métis   ■ General Electorate

Sources: "Election Results," Elections Alberta, 5 May 2015, http://officialresults.elections. ab.ca/orResultsPGE.cfm?EventId=31 (accessed 8 January 2017). Statistics on Indigenous and Métis voters compiled by author from that website.

Table 11.1. Provincial ridings where First Nations and Métis votes had a significant impact on the outcome.

RIDING	NDP MARGIN OF VICTORY	TOTAL FIRST NATIONS AND MÉTIS VOTES
Lesser Slave Lake	717	1,434
Peace River	292	751
Wetaskiwin-Camrose	1,580	840

Sources: Data compiled by author from "Election Results," Elections Alberta, 5 May 2015, http://officialresults.elections.ab.ca/orResultsPGE.cfm?EventId=31 (accessed 8 January 2017).

eighty poll locations were identified on or near First Nation reserves and communities and Métis settlements. A spreadsheet was then used to collate the voting data by party. As Figure 11.1 shows, the New Democrats captured a high proportion of these votes, almost 68 per cent, which amounts to more than four times the total for the nearest major party, the Progressive Conservatives.

It is important to point out that in the eighty polls included in this analysis non-Indigenous voters would have contributed to the results as well. Similarly, Indigenous voters living in urban ridings would fall outside the data set. Nonetheless, votes from First Nations/Métis communities contributed to NDP victories in eight ridings, and in two of those—Lesser Slave Lake and Peace River—Indigenous voters more than accounted for the margin of victory (see Table 11.1). The New Democrats captured sixty-five of the eighty polls in this analysis. In no riding did the First Nations and Métis ballots contribute in any significant way to an electoral victory by any of the other major parties.

Given these results, it seems appropriate that amid the orange T-shirts, placards, balloons, and bursts of applause at NDP campaign headquarters in Edmonton on election night, Rachel Notley would devote at least a minute of her victory speech to Indigenous peoples in Alberta. Over the next few days congratulations would stream in from Métis and First Nation communities and leaders from across the province, even though no Aboriginal candidates were elected for the New Democrats (or any other party). Some Aboriginal people took to social media to express joy—"So #happy #notleycrue #Yay #WayToGoVoters #Change #ThankYouCreator #FirstNation #NDP"—while others remained skeptical—"Will the NDP keep the racist white card? Respect our treaty rights, a status card should be good enough #ABVotes #FNPoli #Treaty8."[22] Amid such high expectations, a legacy of often troubled relations between the provincial government and First Peoples, and conflicting interests among many factions of New Democrat support, the Notley team took office, gingerly finding its feet and slowly advancing its platform. The next section of this chapter examines the NDP's governing tenure from the day after the election through to the end of 2016 and interprets the policy decisions and actions taken by the New Democrats through the lens of Indigenous media.

Indigenous Media and the NDP

The voter data analysis outlined above sought to separate broad voting trends among Indigenous peoples from non-Indigenous Albertans to arrive at authentic findings. This section seeks to do much the same, examining news media perspectives through a purely Aboriginal media filter. The approach here is informed by post-colonial theory, which distinguishes mainstream media coverage of marginalized groups from the decolonized perspectives of minority or alternative news organizations. Indigenous media typically challenge the dominant, often stereotypic representations of First Nations, Métis, and Inuit found in mass media. Production is controlled by Indigenous managers and journalists, allowing the news to be gathered and framed through self-representation.[23] APTN has been identified as a good example of this view, covering issues important to Indigenous people from an Indigenous perspective and communicating to all viewers that "Aboriginal cultures do have rich cultural knowledge that is worth becoming familiar with, which counters the general assumptions of many Canadians."[24] Some research suggests that Indigenous media not only offer more context on First Nations, Métis, and Inuit issues, but more overall balance as well.[25]

Digital news stories from Indigenous news organizations were collected between 6 May 2015 and 31 December 2016. The stories come from *Alberta Native News*, APTN, *First Nations Drum*, and three media organizations under the Aboriginal Multi-Media Society umbrella, *Alberta Sweetgrass*, *Windspeaker*, and CFWE-FM Radio. Over that time period, articles were chosen for analysis that in some way considered NDP governance and policy in Alberta. (Media accounts of the fires that swept through communities in and around Fort McMurray in the spring of 2016 were excluded.) A total of seventy-one stories met these criteria. Those articles were then broken down by their tone towards the provincial New Democrats—positive, neutral, negative—and by themes (news frames analysis).

Countless pundits, scholars, and media critics have observed an overwhelmingly negative tone in political news coverage. A recent study of US president Donald Trump's first hundred days in office concluded that 80 per cent of news stories were negative, and in some weeks this reached 90 per cent.[26] One analysis of European and US political coverage found that

Figure 11.2. Positive and negative tone towards the Alberta NDP in news stories by Indigenous media.

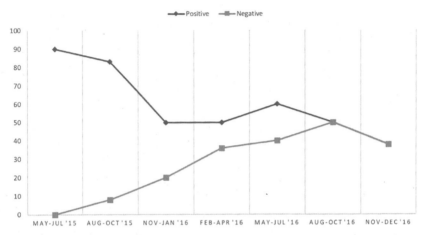

PERCENTAGE OF +/-STORIES
IN EACH TIME PERIOD

Sources: Data compiled by the author.

"good news" amounted to about 6 to 15 per cent of the total output, and another concludes that "the existing body of evidence hints to predominant, increasing, and overarching negativity towards individual political protagonists and parties."[27] Rachel Notley's approach to media relations bears few of the stylistics of Donald Trump's; however, the positive coverage her party has garnered from Indigenous news organizations nonetheless represents quite an anomaly compared to the typical media discourse. This is particularly true of the NDP's first six months in office, during which it was able to advance some of the more straightforward commitments to First Nations and Métis made in its election platform. Over time the coverage remained fairly positive or balanced, as demonstrated in Figure 11.2, and even in the final two time periods shown below, remains balanced.

A closer look at the individual stories behind the tonal analysis above allows us to see a range of views on New Democrat policy among Indigenous leaders, commentators, and activists in context. These can be broken down into specific events and issues that emerged during the NDP's first nineteen months as a government, and which dominated Indigenous news media coverage, as discussed below.

Election Reaction, Comment, and Analysis

Given the decisive electoral action taken by Métis and First Nations voters detailed earlier in this chapter, perhaps it is not surprising to see such strikingly positive coverage of the New Democrats' victory in the Aboriginal media. In addition to documenting higher voter turnout, there was acknowledgement of the party's Indigenous platform, captured in this editorial that appeared in *Alberta Native News*:

> The NDP has also set a new precedent by presenting something that the PCs failed to do, both here in Alberta and in Ottawa. They presented an Aboriginal Platform, something that neither Alberta's Conservative Party or Stephen Harper's "new" Conservative government has ever done.[28]

Indigenous news stories also featured congratulatory messages from chiefs across all three of the province's Treaty areas, as well as the president of the Métis Nation of Alberta, Audrey Poitras, who described the NDP win "as nothing short of a political game-changer."[29] In some cases those well-wishes were tinged with hints of skepticism. The assessment of Athabasca Chipewyan First Nation chief Allan Adams, commenting on Notley's reference to First Nations in her victory speech, is a good example: "Finally, we are going to go somewhere, if she means what she says."[30] Others recognized the opportunity for change. The then regional chief of the Assembly of First Nations (AFN) Alberta, Cameron Alexis, said it was "time for a new government to be given a chance," and that "the Progressive Conservatives have had 43 years to get it right and I still haven't seen it."[31] However, amid the expressions of optimism were a few notes of caution as well, including this from Treaty 8 Grand Chief Steve Courtoreille, who warned that the NDP's electoral victory would "push everything back and it's not what we need, almost starting over again. . . . I sensed a willingness on the part of the (Prentice government) wanting to work with us."[32]

First Months in Office

In the weeks following the NDP's election night celebrations, several actions were taken by the newly formed government—each varying in political significance—that caught the attention of the Indigenous press and drew generally positive comments from these sources. When Notley's cabinet was sworn in news stories took note of a blessing provided by a Métis Elder, as well as an honour song performed by a member of the Enoch Cree Nation. When Notley attended Treaty 6 Recognition Day, in Edmonton, *Alberta Sweetgrass* pointed out that it was the first time a premier had been in attendance in several years.

However, the two biggest stories on the Indigenous news agenda were an apology on behalf of the province to residential school survivors, and the implementation of UNDRIP. The latter was one of the NDP's key election promises, but the residential school apology was somewhat unexpected. In the Legislative Assembly, and with survivors in the gallery, Notley acknowledged the damage done by the residential school system, stating that "members of this chamber did not take a stand against it," and she reached out to Indigenous Albertans: "In the journey of reconciliation you no longer have to walk alone. Your truth has woken our conscience and our sense of justice."[33] Twenty-five of the 139 residential schools in Canada were in Alberta, where there are an estimated 12,000 survivors, according to the Truth and Reconciliation Commission.[34]

In *Alberta Native News*, Chief Randy Ermineskin of the Ermineskin Cree Nation said he was impressed: "a lot of governments haven't quite listened to us the way they should. This new government is really proving something to others—that we need to include everybody."[35] Treaty 6 Grand Chief Bernice Martial was on hand for the apology; she told APTN, "It was overwhelming for me. I thought, 'Wow!' finally coming from a premier."[36] In the same address, Notley also committed her government to working with other governments on an inquiry into MMIW, though at this stage the Harper government was opposed to that process. The support for an MMIW inquiry was part of the NDP's Aboriginal election platform, as was the implementation of UNDRIP. In early July 2015, Notley instructed her cabinet ministers to review their departments' "policies, programs and legislation" in an effort to accommodate the changes required to meet the principles of the UN declaration.[37] The move caught the attention of AFN Chief Perry Bellegarde, who described the NDP government as "a human rights leader in Canada . . . [since Notely] highlighted that Indigenous peoples must benefit both from the development of natural resources in the province and conservation of the environment."[38]

Resource Development and the Environment

One of the themes that comes up most consistently in the Indigenous news coverage of the Alberta government is the concept of resource revenue sharing as part of a more equitable arrangement between the province and its Indigenous population. It is an issue supported in the UN declaration—a fulfillment of treaty terms—that First Nations leaders repeatedly mention as a reason for optimism vis-à-vis the new provincial government. They maintain that they never signed away their rights to benefit from resources and have been actively pursuing a formal agreement at the provincial level for many years. Back in 2013, a group of chiefs produced a study that supported their position. According to APTN, that report showed that "if First Nations received only 5 per cent of provincial resource revenues they would be more than capable of financial independence."[39] And yet, when Alberta chiefs met with the Tory Aboriginal relations minister at the time to discuss revenue sharing they were reportedly told that "we're not going to take a share of our resource revenues and give it to First Nations."[40]

When Craig Mackinaw stepped in to the role of AFN Alberta regional chief just weeks after the NDP's election win, he promised to press this issue but remained hopeful, saying, "I'm waiting to see. I guess we will see within the next year how they stand and how they're going to work with us."[41] However, Mackinaw's position on the NDP government became much clearer in just half that time. After the release of the royalty review by a government-appointed committee in early 2016, Mackinaw questioned the New Democrats' commitment to their election promises and criticized the process for a lack of Aboriginal input: "The only notice I got was having a town hall-type meeting and that's not really discussing the issues to the specifics."[42] Also noted in the coverage was support for resource revenue sharing from industry, including such key oil sands players as Shell, Syncrude, and Suncor.[43]

In a similar vein, the provincial NDP's more aggressive approach to climate change and the environment was also very much on the agenda of Aboriginal leaders, as portrayed in the Indigenous press. As with resource revenue sharing, the news accounts detail Indigenous leaders' efforts to work with the Alberta and federal governments on green initiatives, but also frustration and an eagerness to move beyond just talk. At one of those joint Edmonton-Ottawa environmental meetings, then Treaty 6 Grand Chief Randy Ermineskin explained his participation this way:

> Our peoples are waking up . . . it will be our Indigenous peoples who will save our Mother Earth. This is why we have come together to discuss what we need to do to protect and heal our lands, water and air. So we will listen to Canada's plan and Alberta's plan. . . . We owe it to our children and grandchildren to do all we can.[44]

While the New Democrats' plans to phase out coal-fired electrical generation, impose a carbon tax, and cap greenhouse gas emissions in the oil sands was generally well received, the Notley administration ran into trouble in its attempts to balance development in a deep recession against territorial concerns. Almost a year after taking office, the NDP government found itself on the end of a lawsuit filed by the Fort McKay First Nation over a proposed oil sands lease near Moose Lake, in the band's traditional territory. The Fort McKay First Nation states on its web site that "we believe the practice and preservation of our traditional ways of life can occur simultaneously alongside continuous and responsible oil sands development,"[45] but the project, which was spearheaded by Prosper Energy Ltd., would come within two kilometres of an area described as "irreplaceable" in a news release. At the end of April 2016, Chief Jim Boucher explained how existing policy and the Alberta Energy Regulator worked against each other, pointing out that "one department of government is barreling ahead with development while Minister [Shannon] Phillips [Environment and Parks and responsible for the Climate Change Office] and other government officials are working with us to protect the same area from development."[46]

When first ministers from across Canada met to discuss climate change in Vancouver a week later, Premier Notley and the other leaders drew heavy criticism for the limited scope of the talks. Athabasca Chipewyan Chief Allan Adams left the meeting in total frustration, decrying the lack of discussion around the need to "take care of mother earth" and vowing to challenge the government. "We're not going to stand around and wait for these guys to do what they've got to do," he said after the meeting. "Alberta wants to develop more, well, we will be there to stand in the way. We will not sell out to corporations nor will we ever be silenced ever."[47]

Pipelines

During the election campaign, and then in government, the NDP have tried to marry a progressive climate change agenda with its reliance on Alberta's main economic engine, the energy industry. News coverage in the Indigenous media has captured this dynamic in the context of Métis and First Nations interests, often providing more balance than is typically found in mainstream reporting. This was especially evident in news stories about pipelines. For example, when US president Barack Obama rejected the Keystone XL project in late 2015, *Windspeaker* noted that this would force more bitumen to be transported by rail, and referenced work by the conservative Fraser Institute, "which found that rail is over 4.5 times more likely to experience an incident when compared to pipelines in Canada."[48]

Other news accounts mentioned support for pipelines among groups such as the Federation of Saskatchewan Indian Nations. At the same time Indigenous media referenced the need for the provincial government and Ottawa to better consult with Aboriginal peoples, and documented widespread community opposition, both in Alberta and across the country. When Obama labelled oil sands crude as "dirty oil" there was approval among some First Nations in Northern Alberta, including Melina Laboucan-Massimo, a *Greenpeace* activist and a member of the Lubicon Cree, who said, "I was happy to see his strong words."[49]

A year later, Premier Notley was guardedly celebrating federal approval of Kinder Morgan's Trans Mountain pipeline expansion, suggesting her government's climate change policies paved the way for approval. In a statement she praised the Trudeau government without even mentioning that Enbridge's Northern Gateway proposal had just been rejected. Aboriginal media coverage included extensive reaction from Notley and Prime

Minister Justin Trudeau. There was reference to the 157 conditions that the National Energy Board said must be met before Trans Mountain operations begin, and to the support of 39 Indigenous communities for the project, but as APTN noted, "Moments after Trudeau announced the approval of the Trans Mountain project, calls went out on social media to begin organizing opposition to the project."[50] At the time, Twitter, Facebook, and Instagram were filled with posts in support of those protesting the Dakota Access Pipeline near the Standing Rock Sioux Tribe reservation in North Dakota, galvanizing an "anti-pipeline movement [that] has electrified a continent-wide movement against new oil pipelines."[51]

However, an editorial in *Alberta Native News* underscored the challenge for the NDP government on the pipeline file, and for Indigenous communities. The piece tracks the emergence of an anti-pipeline coalition of First Nations and environmental groups, the Treaty Alliance Against Tar Sand Expansion, which followed within weeks by the rise of a rival, pro-pipeline group. Against that backdrop, the editorial describes the struggle to find common ground between these groups' respective positions. Stephen Buffalo, the head of the Indian Resource Council explained:

> We've always been consumers of goods and services, not producers of goods and services. We need to fit into that chain somewhere. That's wealth creation, that's job creation. We will make sure that things are done right to protect Mother Earth, but we need a revenue stream too.[52]

The editorial concludes, that "it is time to quit the bickering," and for Indigenous communities to sit down and find approaches "that ensure a healthy environment while at the same time creating growth and allowing all Nations to benefit through economic development opportunities."[53]

The positive-negative tonal arc traversed by Indigenous media over the sample period shifts from a largely positive to a more critical but balanced perspective. Early New Democrat policy decisions—adopting UNDRIP, apologizing for residential schools—were likely to be supported by Indigenous peoples and not seen as controversial. However, over time the challenges of managing the range of disparate interests across the province invariably results in the kind of political compromises that draw opposition from some quarters. Support for the MMIW inquiry came swiftly and with considerable ease compared to the ongoing complexity of navigating a pipeline policy that works for a range of First Nations and industry. At the same time it is worth pointing out that even in the final months of the sample period, Indigenous media coverage of the New Democrats reflects a degree of balance between positive and negative tones that would be the envy of most parties in power.

Alberta and Indigenous Political Activism

The "Orange Chinook" that brought the NDP to power in Alberta was driven in part by growing political activism among Indigenous peoples. Several Aboriginal media organizations reported high participation rates among First Nations and Métis voters. At the same time those media accounts referenced a tremendous sharing of information related to political platforms, events, and polling hours and locations. Coupled with festering dissatisfaction after forty-four years of Progressive Conservative rule, a detailed platform with genuine Aboriginal initiatives appears to have provided ample motivation for the Indigenous electorate.

Yale Belanger identifies "key barriers" to First Nations participation in elections, including "a lack of effective communication," the perception that Aboriginal people do not make up a significant proportion of the vote to "wield actual influence" in most electoral districts, and "feelings of exclusion" from the rest of the electorate.[54] In the case of the 2015 Alberta election, these barriers seem to have been overcome. The Twitter hashtag #RockThe IndigenousVote, discussed earlier in this chapter, is just one example of how social media were able to support effective communication among Aboriginal peoples. Resignation about the limited impact of individual votes seems to have been overridden by a motivation to bring about change. Moreover, the power of First Nations voter blocks *did* have an impact in some ridings, as indicated by the election data analysis above. And perhaps feelings of exclusion on the part of some Aboriginal voters were addressed by the fact that the NDP's election platform featured more than mere token references to Indigenous concerns.

The lessons from Alberta were picked up by Indigenous groups across Canada. If voters could unleash such dramatic change in Alberta, why not in

Ottawa? The parallels between the provincial campaign in the spring of 2015 and the federal race held that fall are manifold: a multi-term Conservative regime that did not seem to be listening to its constituents anymore, that refused to back an MMIW inquiry, that would not adopt UNDRIP, and that failed to address chronic housing and drinking water issues on First Nations. The difference in the federal campaign was that the NDP victory in Alberta had already set a precedent; it provided a template of political action and hope. Even First Nations singer-songwriter Buffy Sainte-Marie weighed in on the Notley victory, telling the *Huffington Post*, "The Alberta election, that's a change, that's inspiring to a lot of people. Sometimes people get to feeling so dis-empowered when it appears that things are going wrong. We can pick up on momentum like the Alberta election or like Idle No More."[55]

And the momentum from Alberta did carry through. Manitoba Grand Chief Derek Nepinak told the *Toronto Star* that the drive to remove Stephen Harper from office "awoke the sleeping giant in our people."[56] Indigenous leaders across Canada mobilized their communities. AFN National Chief Perry Bellegarde said the level of excitement was "huge. I know certain chiefs shut down their communities and bused their people to the stations. Some chiefs went door to door, knocking on their reserves, to make sure people were educated and aware that it is voting day."[57] On social media "the hashtags #RocktheVote and #RocktheIndigenousVote were used on election day as people posted selfies of their trip to the ballot box."[58] As in Alberta, Indigenous voters went to the polls in record numbers in October 2015, and there were reports of as many as six communities running out of ballots.[59] More importantly, if the goal, as Nepinak suggested, was to bring in a government more sympathetic to Indigenous issues, electoral activism paid off.

However, once regime change has been accomplished, the work of holding new governments to account begins anew. For some, skepticism toward a new government is well earned. Not long after the New Democrats were elected in Alberta, an editorial in the *Windspeaker* captured this sentiment well:

> It's the long-term progress of all this new-found lovey-dovey talk that we'll be judging. . . . It wouldn't be the first time that First Nations have been used as handy props to woo votes. The proof will be in the pudding going forward, is all we're saying. We've become a little nauseated by the promises to

　　　　　　　　　　　　　　　　　　　　　　　BRAD CLARK

First Nations by provincial governments. There's a big photo op and then the bubble bursts on the way home in the car.[60]

Buffy Sainte-Marie suggests that casting a ballot is just the beginning of change. "You don't vote and go home and give them the keys to the car, he'll drive you right off a cliff. You have to help people to stay honest."[61]

At the time of this writing, the Alberta New Democrats have continued to demonstrate a level of commitment to Indigenous issues with their apology to survivors of the "Sixties Scoop," a practice in the 1960s of taking children from Indigenous families and placing them with non-Indigenous foster or adoptive parents. The United Conservative Party (UCP), riding a substantial lead in opinion polls, has just come off its first policy convention. Media reports suggest there was not much discussion of Aboriginal issues at the gathering, though as Don Braid pointed out in the *Calgary Herald*, "one delegate fumed about how fed up she is with First Nations people who 'take and take.'"[62] That comment was apparently met with some boos. However, just 3 out of 114 policy resolutions to emerge from the UCP convention were related to First Peoples. Under the heading "Indigenous," one calls for the strengthening of "economic opportunities and entrepreneurship," while the other two appear to present dog-whistle tropes of First Nations and Métis people as privileged and corrupt (one recognizes all Albertans "as equal under the law," the other calls for "accountability and transparency into all provincially funded indigenous programs").[63]

There has been no real "lovey-dovey talk" directed at Indigenous voters on the part of UCP leader Jason Kenney, and very little coverage of the party in the Indigenous news media considered in this chapter. One story that did appear in *Windspeaker* detailed "disbelief and anger" in the face of comments made by Dave Schneider, the UCP MLA for Little Bow, in Sothern Alberta. Early in 2018, Schneider lamented to a local news reporter that the redrawing of electoral boundaries meant his new riding includes "the biggest reserve in Canada. . . . Not that that's bad, but these people don't traditionally vote, and how is the population going to get engaged in this political system in the province."[64] Schneider later apologized on Twitter to "any offended by my choice of words."[65] The *Windspeaker* story also included this pointed observation: "Rachel Notley's NDP government was swept into power, on part [*sic*] thanks to a strong Indigenous platform, which included adopting the United Nations Declaration on the Rights of Indigenous Peoples."[66]

The writer might have additionally noted that the progressive NDP platform resonated with many Indigenous voters and boosted turnout at the polls, according to Indigenous media and the data analysis here. In fact, the findings described in this chapter provide a stark contrast to Schneider's comments. Political parties that fail to take these facts into account do so at their peril.

NOTES

1   F. Laurie Barron, *Walking in Indian Moccasins: The Native Policies of Tommy Douglas and the CCF* (Vancouver: UBC Press, 1997), xviii.

2   Ibid., 134.

3   Sydney Sharpe and Don Braid, *Notley Nation: How Alberta's Political Upheaval Swept the Country* (Toronto: Dundurn, 2016), 121.

4   Reid Southwick, "NDP overture encourages aboriginals; Notley promises to be 'better neighbours and better partners,' " *Calgary Herald*, 9 May 2015, A21.

5   Alberta's NDP, "Rachel Notley thanks Albertans for electing her Premier," 5 May 2015, http://www.albertandp.ca/rachel_notley_thanks_albertans_for_electing_her_premier (accessed 20 April 2017).

6   "Alison Redford Victory Speech," YouTube video, posted by *Calgary Herald*, 24 April 2012, https://www.youtube.com/watch?v=2mnsNrLlIJk (accessed 20 April 2017).

7   "Aboriginal Peoples: Fact Sheet for Alberta," Statistics Canada, 14 March 2016, http://www.statcan.gc.ca/pub/89-656-x/89-656-x2016010-eng.htm. (accessed 1 May 2017).

8   "First Nations in Alberta," Indigenous and Northern Affairs Canada, 15 September 2010, https://www.aadnc-aandc.gc.ca/DAM/DAM-INTER-AB/STAGING/texte-text/fnamarch11_1315587933961_eng.pdf (accessed 10 January 2010).

9   "Metis Settlements," Alberta Indigenous Relations, 2017, http://indigenous.alberta.ca/Metis-Settlements.cfm (accessed 31 January 2017).

10 "Resources: First Nations Health Trends-Alberta "One-Pagers," Alberta First Nations Information Governance Centre, 12 January 2016, http://www.afnigc.ca/main/includes/media/pdf/fnhta/HTAFN-2016-01-12-FNLifeExp.pdf (accessed 3 May 2017).

11 Ibid.

12 Jason R. Randall, Andrew Harris, Larry Svenson, Don Voaklnader, and Sara Hassen Parker, *Health Status of the Metis Population of Alberta* (Edmonton: Metis Nation of Alberta Association and the University of Alberta, 2012), 101.

13   Brandi Morin, " 'We're getting things done': Alberta Aboriginal Affairs minister taking action to implement UNDRIP mandate," *APTN News*, 15 July 2015, http://aptnnews. ca/2015/07/15/were-getting-things-done-alberta-aboriginal-affairs-minister-taking-action-implement-undrip-mandate/ (accessed 29 January 2017).

14   Ibid.

15   Ian Hussey, "Planks in the platforms: Comparing 11 key policy issues," *parklandinstitute.ca*, 30 April 2015, http://www.parklandinstitute.ca/planks_in_the_platforms_comparing_11_key_policy_issues (accessed 3 February 2017).

16   John Copley, "Alberta First Nations welcome NDP government and Premier Rachel Notley," *Alberta Native News*, 16 May 2015, http://www.albertanativenews.com/alberta-first-nations-welcome-ndp-government-and-premier-rachel-notley/ (accessed 28 January 2017).

17   Duane Bratt, "Analysis: Playing the politics of Alberta's multibillion-dollar debt," *CBC News*, 18 March 2017, http://www.cbc.ca/news/canada/calgary/alberta-budget-debt-deficit-analysis-1.4030544 (accessed 22 May 2017).

18   John Copley, "Alberta First Nations welcome NDP government and Premier Rachel Notley," *Alberta Native News*, 16 May 2015, http://www.albertanativenews.com/alberta-first-nations-welcome-ndp-government-and-premier-rachel-notley/ (accessed 28 January 2017).

19   Brandi Morin, "New Premier tells Alberta's Indigenous peoples: 'I am looking forward to consulting with you and learning from you,' " *APTN News*, 7 May 2015, http://aptnnews.ca/2015/05/07/46350/ (accessed 29 January 2017).

20   "#rocktheindigenousvote since:2015-04-07 until:2015-05-06," *twitter.com*, 22 May 2017, https://twitter.com/search?l=&q=%23rocktheindigenousvote%20since%3A2015-04-07%20until%3A2015-05-06&src=typd&lang=en (accessed 22 May 2017).

21   "Election Results," Elections Alberta, 5 May 2015, http://officialresults.elections.ab.ca/orResultsPGE.cfm?EventId=31 (accessed 8 January 2017).

22   "NDP #ABNDP OR #and OR #firstnation OR #blackfoot OR #treaty7 OR #metis OR #treaty6 OR #treaty8," *twitter.com*, 23 May 2017, https://twitter.com/search?l=&q=NDP%20%23ABNDP%20OR%20%23and%20OR%20%23firstnation%20OR%20%23blackfoot%20OR%20%23treaty7%20OR%20%23metis%20OR%20%23treaty6%20OR%20%23treaty8%20since%3A2015-05-05%20until%3A2015-05-06&src=typd (accessed 23 May 2017).

23   Faye Ginsburg, "Embedded aesthetics: Creating a discursive space for Indigenous media," *Cultural Anthropology* 9, no. 3 (1994): 378.

24   Kerten Knopf, " 'Sharing our stories with all Canadians': Decolonizing Aboriginal media and Aboriginal media politics in Canada," *American Indian Culture and Research Journal* 34, no. 1 (2010): 89–120.

25   Brad Clark, "Framing Canada's Aboriginal Peoples: A Comparative Analysis of Indigenous and Mainstream Television News," *The Canadian Journal of Native Studies* 34, no. 2 (2014): 42.

26 Thomas E. Patterson, "News Coverage of Donald Trump's First 100 Days," *Shorenstein Center on Media, Politics and Public Policy* (2017): 8.

27 Gunther Lengauer, Frank Esser, and Rosa Berganza, "Negativity in Political News: A review of concepts, operationalizations and key findings, *Journalism* 13, no. 2 (2011): 189.

28 Copley, "Alberta First Nations welcome NDP government."

29 Shari Narine, "Alberta First Nations optimistic with NDP at the helm," *Windspeaker,* 15 May 2015, http://www.ammsa.com/publications/windspeaker/first-nations-optimistic-ndp-helm (accessed 2 February 2017).

30 Brandi Morin, "New Premier tells Alberta's Indigenous peoples: 'I am looking forward to consulting with you and learning from you,' " *APTN News*, 7 May 2015, http://aptnnews.ca/2015/05/07/46350/ (accessed 29 January 2017).

31 Narine, "Premier-elect Notley pledges to consult with Aboriginal people," *Alberta Sweetgrass* 22, no. 6 (2015), http://www.ammsa.com/publications/alberta-sweetgrass/premier-elect-notley-pledges-consult-aboriginal-people (accessed 29 January 2017).

32 Ibid.

33 John Copley, "Alberta Premier Rachel Notley's apology is an important step to reconciliation," *Alberta Native News*, 28 July 2015, http://www.albertanativenews.com/alberta-premier-rachel-notleys-apology-is-an-important-step-to-reconciliation/ (accessed 26 January 2017).

34 Ibid.

35 Ibid.

36 Brandi Morin, "Alberta becomes second province to apologize to residential school survivors, then calls for action on MMIW," *APTN News*, 23 June 2015, http://aptnnews.ca/2015/06/23/alberta-becomes-first-province-apologize-residential-schools-calls-action-mmiw/ (accessed 2 February 2017).

37 Shari Narine, "Notley applauded for move to implement UNDRIP," *Alberta Sweetgrass*, 9 July 2015, http://www.ammsa.com/publications/alberta-sweetgrass/notley-applauded-move-implement-undrip (accessed 31 January 2017).

38 Ibid.

39 Brandi Morin, "New Alberta AFN regional chief says treaties guaranteed resource revenue sharing," *APTN News*, 29 June 2015, http://aptnnews.ca/2015/06/29/new-alberta-afn-regional-chief-says-treaties-guaranteed-resource-revenue-sharing/ (accessed 3 February 2017).

40 Ibid.

41 Ibid.

42 Shari Narine, "Royalty review excludes Aboriginal resource revenue sharing," *Alberta Sweetgrass*, 1 February 2016, http://www.ammsa.com/publications/alberta-sweetgrass/royalty-review-excludes-aboriginal-resource-revenue-sharing (accessed 2 January 2017).

43 Ibid.

44   "Alberta Chiefs call for meaningful engagement on climate change," *Alberta Native News*, 30 November 2016, http://www.albertanativenews.com/alberta-chiefs-call-for-meaningful-engagement-on-climate-change/ (accessed 7 May 2017).

45   Fort McKay First Nation, "We Believe," 31 January 2017, http://fortmckay.com (accessed 2 February 2017).

46   "Fort McKay First Nation begins legal action to protect culturally sacred Moose Lake area," *Alberta Native News*, 27 April 2016, http://www.albertanativenews.com/fort-mckay-first-nation-begins-legal-action-to-protect-culturally-sacred-moose-lake-area/ (accessed 2 January 2017).

47   Ibid.

48   Shari Narine, "Indigenous action played key role in Keystone rejection," *Windspeaker*, 7 November 2015, http://www.ammsa.com/publications/alberta-sweetgrass/indigenous-action-played-key-role-keystone-rejection (accessed 2 February 2017).

49   Ibid.

50   "Tsleil-Waututh Nation vows to stop Trans Mountain pipeline despite Trudeau government approval," *APTN News*, 30 November 2016, http://aptnnews.ca/2016/11/30/tsleil-waututh-nation-vows-to-stop-trans-mountain-pipeline-despite-trudeau-government-approval/ (accessed 3 February 2017).

51   Ibid.

52   John Copley, "Speaking Out: Consensus comes from sincere discussions and meaningful negotiations," *Alberta Native News*, 24 November 2016, http://www.albertanativenews.com/speaking-out-consensus-comes-from-sincere-discussions-and-meaningful-negotiations/ (accessed 7 May 2017).

53   Ibid.

54   Yale D. Belanger, " 'You have to be involved . . . to play a part in it': Assessing Kainai attitudes about voting in Canadian elections," *Great Plains Quarterly* 29, no. 1(2009): 31.

55   Joshua Ostroff, "Buffy Sainte-Marie On Idle No More, Stephen Harper And Residential Schools," *Huffington Post Canada*, 3 June 2015, http://www.huffingtonpost.ca/2015/06/03/buffy-sainte-marie-idle-no-more-harper_n_7424654.html (accessed 3 May 2017).

56   Tanya Talaga, "Behind the scenes on the push to rock the indigenous vote," *Toronto Star*, 23 October 2015, https://www.thestar.com/news/canada/2015/10/23/behind-the-scenes-on-the-push-to-rock-the-indigenous-vote.html (accessed 17 May 2017).

57   Ibid.

58   Ibid.

59   Ibid.

60   "Has the corner been turned," *Windspeaker*, 20 August 2015, http://www.ammsa.com/publications/windspeaker/has-corner-been-turned-editorial (accessed 25 May 2018).

61   Ostroff, "Buffy Sainte-Marie on Idle No More and Stephen Harper."

62   Don Braid, "UCP meeting tilted hard right on social policy," *Calgary Herald*, 12 May 2018, http://calgaryherald.com/news/politics/braid-ucp-meeting-tilted-hard-right-on-social-policy (accessed 25 May 2018).

63   United Conservative Party, "Policy Declaration" https://www.unitedconservative.ca/Content/UCP%20Policy%20Declaration.pdf, p. 10 (accessed 25 May 2018).

64   "Uninformed, offensive, disrespectful: Alberta MLA's attitude on First Nations—'these people,' " *Windspeaker*, 17 January 2018, http://www.windspeaker.com/news/windspeaker-news/uninformed-offensive-disrespectful-alberta-mlas-attitude-on-first-nations-these-people/ (accessed 25 May 2018).

65   Ibid.

66   Ibid.

Alberta's Cities under the NDP

James Wilt

The Alberta NDP is a party of the cities.

It's a popular notion. After all, Edmonton has served as the NDP's fortress since the party's Ray Martin–led surge in 1986, with urban issues such as public housing, mass transit, and other major infrastructure projects typically anchoring its list of policy priorities. And the May 2015 election appeared to validate this reputation. The NDP swept Edmonton, Red Deer, Lethbridge, and, surprisingly, claimed over half the seats in Calgary. Its election platform explicitly pledged to "provide stable, predictable funding to both large and smaller municipalities and ensure they have resources they need to fulfill infrastructure priorities, such as transit."[1] One would think it safe to assume that the new government would prioritize issues facing cities in 2015 and beyond.

After all, it had a perfect opportunity. Under section 92 of Canada's Constitution, cities exist as "creatures" of the provinces. That means that almost all municipal powers are granted by the province, and that no inherent powers reside outside of that framework. Alberta's Municipal Government Act (MGA)—the massive piece of legislation that grants existence and powers to all 344 of the province's municipalities—had been under formal review since 2012, providing the new NDP government a once-in-a-generation chance to powerfully redefine how cities raise revenue, plan growth, and interact with other governments. There were very high expectations to finally fix what Grande Prairie mayor Bill Given dubbed a "local government system that's rooted in the Alberta of a hundred years ago."[2] So in order to assess whether the Alberta NDP lived up to such hopes—and its broader reputation as an urban-oriented party—almost two-dozen phone interviews were conducted with subject experts between August and November 2016.

The former minister of municipal affairs Danielle Larivee emphasized that all 344 municipalities have different needs and relationships with neighbouring governments.[3] While this is true, there are many easily identifiable commonalities between them. As a result, the Alberta NDP could have taken a number of fairly obvious and innovative steps to rectify some of the outstanding problems identified by many mayors throughout the province. The near-consensus is that it failed to do so. Instead, it appears the new government capitulated to strong pressures from counties and business lobby groups to avoid adjusting assessment calculations or mandating regional revenue sharing. The NDP refused to expand own-source taxation powers for cities, keeping them trapped within the unpopular political boundaries of property taxes, user fees, and underwhelming grants from higher levels of government. And it effectively accepted the free-for-all voluntary planning model introduced by former premier Ralph Klein. As a result, the NDP selected to preserve the province's anachronistic and paternalistic relationship with its cities, as outlined in the MGA. This arguably betrays any alleged commitment the NDP has to urban municipalities, likely in order to protect future political viability.

Five Key Points of Context

The most obvious way of assessing the validity of these fairly significant claims is by exploring the nuances of Bill 21, the Modernized Municipal Government Act. The city charters for Edmonton and Calgary also offer a frame through which to view these issues, and an assessment of what the charters will mean for the big cities is therefore included near the end of this chapter. But first, it's important to establish some context. Alberta's municipalities face some of the same challenges as municipalities across the country, but there are key distinctions. What follows are five important historic factors that help inform the evaluation of the Alberta government's current relationship with its cities and help explain its arguably underwhelming decisions with regards to the MGA.

Municipal Dependence on Property Taxes

Alberta's municipalities don't have a lot of financial wiggle room: they're not allowed to run deficits, are restricted by debt and debt-serving limits, and don't tend to borrow as much as they can; in 2015, Calgary was at 45 per cent of its debt limit, while Edmonton was at 54 per cent.

This model has proven sufficient for covering operating costs, which are largely covered by own-source revenues. But as Calgary mayor Naheed Nenshi put it, this reality "makes it very, very hard to plan for very big-ticket budget items."[4] Even if municipalities can hypothetically borrow more, they remain unable to pay back the loans.

This is because Canadian cities rely heavily on property taxes, which account for almost half of their total revenues. There are indeed upsides to this funding mechanism. Property taxes are extremely visible, easy to administer, and provide cities with a very stable source of revenue. As Minister Larivee pointed out: "Property tax really doesn't have substantial limits. It's up to [municipal governments] to find the results with the residents."[5] This is technically true. But there's a reason that Alberta's municipal property taxes are around the same as they were in 1988 in percentage of personal income (2.5 per cent).[6]

Enid Slack, director of the Institute on Municipal Finance and Governance at the University of Toronto's Munk School of Global Affairs, noted that homeowners are *annually* reminded of the amount they're being taxed.[7] Property taxes are distinct in this regard from income tax—which, unless you're self-employed, is withheld at source—and the sales tax: both usually just rise with the rate of inflation or consumption, whereas there are no autonomic adjustments with property tax. This can create an annual groundswell of opposition to property tax hikes, despite cities' arguably desperate need for additional revenue to build and maintain infrastructure and social services. It likely doesn't help that the province requires municipalities to raise 32 per cent of its education budget via municipal property taxes, a set-up that Edmonton mayor Don Iveson has previously described as "extremely irritating."[8]

Mayors will often argue that the property tax doesn't represent people's capacity to pay, especially when it comes to retirees living in gentrifying areas who may be asset rich but income poor. While that is a potential issue,

Table 12.1. Breakdown of Twelve Common Municipal Revenue Sources for all Albertan Municipalities in 2011

MUNICIPALITY REVENUE SOURCE	2011 REVENUE TOTALS FROM ALL MUNICIPALITIES	PERCENTAGE OF 2011 REVENUES
Property Tax	$4,808,356,295	42.85%
Business Tax	$212,484,611	1.89%
Special Taxes	$9,264,899	0.08%
Business Revitalization Zone Taxes	$3,665,315	0.03%
Local Improvement Taxes	$37,977,813	0.34%
Well Drilling Equipment Taxes	$26,346,455	0.23%
Developer Agreements + Levies	$172,949,456	1.54%
Sales and User Charges	$2,918,315,262	26.02%
Franchise and Concession Contracts	$375,057,714	3.34%
Fines/Penalties	$193,192,205	1.72%
Provincial Grants	$2,193,118,342	19.54%
Federal Grants	$271,761,973	2.42%
Total Revenue	**$11,222,490,340**	100%

Sources: MGA Review Discussion Paper, December 2013.

credit and grant systems do exist for people in such situations, and these could feasibly be expanded. The main issue with the property tax is that it's very visible and thus deeply unpopular.

Currently, Alberta's municipalities don't have the power to levy other forms of own-source revenues, such as local sales, income, or land-transfer taxes. Mayors argue that this has locked them into a structural deficit of sorts, preventing them from expanding capital expenditure for much-needed infrastructure and social services. It's a political predicament that informs the remainder of the discussion in this chapter.

Withdrawing of Federal Involvement from Cities

This is only a particularly acute problem because higher levels of government have gradually withdrawn financial involvement in municipalities. Borrowing is generally cheapest for the federal government. Yet public capital stock ownership has effectively flipped in the last half-century, with the federal government's 44 per cent share in 1955 dropping to 13 per cent in 2011, and the amount owned by municipalities increasing from 22 per cent to 52 per cent in the same window.

Overall, public infrastructure spending as a share of GDP plummeted from over 3.7 per cent after the Second World War to below 2 per cent in 2000.[9] Municipalities, constrained by an absence of politically viable tax options and in some cases a lack of taxable population base, haven't picked up the tab.

This has contributed to a national infrastructure deficit that has now risen as high as $570 billion; merely maintaining existing infrastructure would require a return to infrastructure spending as a share of GDP of 2.9 per cent.[10] In March 2016, Nenshi told the *Globe and Mail* that Calgary had $25 billion in unfunded projects.[11] Mayor Given of Grande Prairie said his city requires around $100 million in investments to get its infrastructure up to snuff: "A lot of the needs are very basic infrastructure: roads, sewer, storm sewer."[12]

Ottawa has indeed made some substantial reinvestments in cities via the Gas Tax Fund and Building Canada Fund. But such value is expected to erode with inflation and new demands unless increased.[13] In addition, there hasn't been any sustained investment from the federal government in areas like social housing since the 1980s; and what funding there is only available for emergency and transitional facilities. It's not like cities have picked up the tab. Many units just haven't been built. "In many ways, the cities have been starved for their infrastructure," said Jan Reimer, former mayor of Edmonton. "And not just physical infrastructure but social infrastructure as well."[14]

These realities have helped nudge municipalities into private-public partnership (or "P3") arrangements, which can allow cities to keep obligations off the books in the short-term but often end up costing significantly more in the long-term; many private projects borrow at a higher rate than governments, and also expect a higher rate of return; Canadian investors are on the look for "stable, predictable returns in the seven to nine per cent range."[15] A 2014 report by the auditor general of Ontario concluded that seventy-four P3 projects, mostly in the health-care sector, had cost citizens almost $8 billion more over nine years than if they had been contracted out and managed by the public sector; the auditor general also found "no empirical data" for the claim that P3s cut the risk of cost and time overruns by over four times.[16]

Yet the very same year, a "P3 screen" was introduced for any federally funded infrastructure project over $100 million. At the time, Nenshi responded to the criteria by arguing that "P3 Canada's processes are onerous and they are expensive."[17] Toby Sanger, senior economist with the Canadian Union of Public Employees, argued that the federal government was "essentially forcing municipalities to engage in P3s in that way," and that "municipalities that wanted some federal money just didn't have any choice in that area."[18] Both of Alberta's recent ring road projects—Edmonton's Anthony Henday Drive and Calgary's Stoney Trail—used P3 approaches, as did Kananaskis Country's Evan-Thomas Water Treatment and Wastewater Treatment Facility project.

The federal government's new infrastructure plan will also rely on "leveraging" private capital via a $35-billion public fund, an approach that some fear will lead to higher long-term costs and user fees (it's estimated by Sanger that such an approach could double the cost of infrastructure over thirty years).[19] The federal Liberals have committed $186 billion to infrastructure funding over a dozen years, but it's unclear at the time of writing how much of that is expected to be "leveraged" from the private sector.

Politicization and Backtracking of Provincial Grants

The province has also played a significant role in perpetuating the chronic underfunding of municipalities. The most obvious example of this is the cuts in transfers that hit cities during the Klein Revolution of the 1990s, which Reimer described as a "succession of ongoing punitive cuts with no thought."[20] It also manifested more recently—and subtly—with the failure of the Municipal Sustainability Initiative (MSI), which was introduced in 2007 as a planned, decade-long burst of funding to Alberta's municipalities: aside from the first two years, provincial funding didn't meet the pledged amounts; from 2010 to 2013, Calgary was promised $407 million per year, but only received an annual allotment of between $254 and $256 million.[21]

Nenshi noted that his predecessor, Dave Bronconnier, committed most of the city's total MSI allotment on the West Line of the LRT.[22] Since cash flows haven't matched what was promised by the province, the city has racked up "nine-figure interest payments on the debt" after borrowing

JAMES WILT

against future funds.[23] "For provincial governments, it's very, very easy to cut future cash flows," Nenshi said. "But what they've forgotten about is in the big cities, that money has already been spent."[24] While the NDP did commit an additional $4.5 billion over five years to infrastructure, it was explicitly advertised as stimulus spending as opposed to long-term investments.[25] Al Duerr, former mayor of Calgary, noted that "revenue streams are largely at the whim of the provincial government," and that "many people think [these funds] are gifts from senior governments, not . . . a redistribution of wealth to source."[26] This echoes calculations made by the Federation of Canadian Municipalities, which found that municipalities only receive eight cents of every tax dollar collected.[27] "Every time a provincial government screws up, who gets hurt?" Duerr asked. "The municipalities. But the municipal needs don't change. It's that another order of government has screwed up."[28]

In April 2016, the Alberta NDP cut an extra $50 million in MSI funding that it had promised.[29] Only four months later, the government announced it would be cutting future infrastructure funding from one-third of infrastructure project costs to only 25 per cent following the announcement of increased funding by the federal government; mayors across the country are currently pushing for a 50-33-17 split between the federal, provincial, and municipal governments for infrastructure costs that better reflects their capacity to pay.[30] This arrangement also allows the province to commit funding to extremely visible infrastructure. UC Berkeley College of Environmental Design's Gregory Morrow (previously at the University of Calgary) said there's "absolutely" a bias towards funding certain types of projects, which itself shapes urban form and growth patterns. "That has impacts," Morrow said. "Once you put in Stoney Trail, it incentivizes a certain pattern of growth around it."[31]

Stephen Carter, who served as chief of staff for former premier Alison Redford and campaign strategist for Calgary mayor Nenshi, said that such a system of funding has led to Calgary and Edmonton only receiving funding for ring road infrastructure at the expense of light rail transit investments. He argued that "the provincial government now gets to allocate money based on vote-getting as opposed to allocating money based on revenues to be received in a rational fashion. I'm not saying the ring road isn't the right thing. The city of Calgary may have wanted a ring road. But we didn't get a choice because it was dictated by the province of Alberta."[32]

Carter said that this has resulted in a disproportionate power arrangement whereby MLAs have more power than a mayor, and he added that there's been a "real bias" in funding rural programs over urban ones.[33] The NDP even acknowledged this in its pre-election survey when the party claimed that "We believe we must remove partisan choices from capital allocation decisions."[34] But while it committed to establishing an "Infrastructure Sunshine List" to prevent the politicization of capital spending, it instead opted to only release three full pages of unfunded projects listed on the province's website, including schools, hospitals, courthouses, and roads; opposition parties were pushing for a ranked list that would help prevent spending based on immediate political needs.[35]

The construction of major new sports venues in Calgary and Edmonton have become a significant public policy issue in recent years. In 2013, Edmonton City Council considered using increased MSI funding to help pay for the new Rogers Place arena and Winter Garden, but it later decided to negotiate a "community revitalization levy" (CRL) with the province— the same mechanism being used in Calgary's East Village development. This meant that all municipal and provincial property taxes for that part of the city that exceed the baseline over the next twenty years will help pay for the project. The proposed CalgaryNEXT sports complex also included the use of a CRL. However, in June 2016, the Alberta NDP announced that it was no longer accepting applications for CRLs due to the ongoing review of the MGA. Since then, the province hasn't made any public statements about its willingness to help fund sporting facilities.

This fiscal framework also presents a unique problem for mid-sized cities. For example, Lethbridge mayor Chris Spearman noted that there are funding opportunities for cities whose population is under 45,000 people, and for large cities such as Calgary and Edmonton, but little in between.[36] Red Deer mayor Tara Veer expressed concern that such funding disparities might widen with the introduction of city charters; she cited a recently announced transit pilot for low-income users launched in Edmonton and Calgary, making explicit reference to the fact that both are "charter cities."[37] In addition, Veer noted that the granting of new tax powers to larger cities could exacerbate the competitive disadvantage that smaller cities face in

JAMES WILT

attracting investments and expansion, as property taxes could ostensibly be reduced in tandem.

Across the board, there was an extremely palpable desire from mayors for stable, predictable, and long-term funding from the province. Some, like Carter, went even further, suggesting that "we shouldn't have MSI grants in a society where cities should be able to get the revenues that they need from the populations that exist."[38] But at the time of the MGA review, the cities were very clearly still creatures of the province.

The Ongoing Absence of Regional Planning

The opposite is true in the sphere of planning, with the province adopting an extremely hands-off approach since the mid-1990s. It's had equally as disastrous an effect. The University of Alberta's Sandeep Agrawal said that from the 1950s to the 1980s, Alberta boasted a fairly mature set of policies and guidelines governing the growth of its cities.[39] During this period the province played a key role in development patterns and regional planning, encouraging annexing and authoritative planning bodies. Then came Premier Ralph Klein, who repealed the Planning Act of 1977, and all regional and metro planning commissions. This occurred when many other cities were heading in the direction of the "unicity" model. Duerr described the move as "one of the shortest-sighted, purely ideological things that the province did," and he claimed it has led to a ring of "ultra -low-density residentials surrounding Calgary that have all kinds of servicing issues."[40] Reimer said the move made collaboration with the surrounding municipalities extremely difficult, as everyone was attempting to protect their tax base.[41] Agrawal said: "Essentially, since 1995 until about 2008, there was a total policy vacuum vis-à-vis regional planning in Alberta. That had its own consequences that we are still trying to grapple with."[42]

Area structure plans (ASPs) and area redevelopment plans (ARPs) are the only statutory policy documents that municipalities can use to leverage types of development. Calgary and Edmonton have deployed "community revitalization levies," in which assessments are frozen for a gentrifying region and future tax revenue gets directly reinvested in the area. But those are, by nature, extremely ad hoc and localized. For the vast remainder of municipal planning, an overall lack of big-picture regional planning throughout the province has resulted in hyper-local competition and infighting. That has, in turn, made it extremely difficult to coordinate transportation systems and land-use planning regimes to maximize much-needed economies of scale. "There's no point in every municipality having their own fire, their own police, their own transit," Agrawal said. "This could all be done in a much more centralized, rather [than] regional, way, which would benefit a much larger area and population, and perhaps integrate different economies that exist in those places."[43]

In 2008, the Capital Region Board—which effectively forced Edmonton and twenty-three surrounding municipalities, including Strathcona County, St. Albert, and Spruce Grove, to work together on sustainable growth—was formed, and the Alberta Land Stewardship Act (ALSA) was introduced, providing a regional land-use framework. While the ALSA was proclaimed in 2009, four of the seven regional plans still do not exist as of early 2017. Tensions are still extremely pronounced between many neighbouring municipalities. The decade-long rivalry between Rocky View County and Calgary over residential density requirements and the potential increased burden on roads, water, and sewage infrastructure serves as an obvious example. The Calgary Metropolitan Plan, ratified by the voluntary regional partnership, still hasn't been implemented due to such tensions.[44]

Political blogger David Climenhaga noted that there has also been "a lot of tension and dislike and bad feeling and disputes" between Sturgeon County and St. Albert, the latter being the second-largest city in the Edmonton Capital Region.[45] "Almost anywhere there's a major urban area next to a county, there are some tensions and problems of these kinds," Climenhaga said. "Some of the fallout's not necessarily obvious."[46] And while many argue that competition between jurisdictions is fine, even desirable, it would be preferable if such competition was more regional in nature. Much of the problem returns to the dual issues of service usage and revenue sharing. In 2016, the city of Grande Prairie calculated that linear properties—oil and gas wells, transmission lines, pipelines—generate $845 million per year in tax revenues, but that cities only receive 7.7 per cent of these funds, with municipal districts (MDs) and counties receiving 77.6 per cent.[47] In other words, there's a significant disparity in per-capita assessment between urban and rural communities.

And yet urban municipalities end up providing many of the services that rural residents use: recreation centres, libraries, police stations, roads.

This also means that counties and MDs can afford to have a lower property tax rate than nearby municipalities, attracting investments such as malls and shopping centres. The situation has reached its most extreme form in Cold Lake, where the mayor and council have long pushed for the chance to dissolve and merge with surrounding rural districts in order to stay financially viable.[48] Medicine Hat mayor Ted Clugston said: "It has been frustrating for us providing all the services, the leisure, the libraries, the event centres, everything, and not having an agreement with our partners. Basically paying for everything and they use it."[49] This is the inevitable outcome of a free-for-all planning regime in which hundreds of municipalities are battling for their own interests with next to no intervention from the province.

Government-assigned arbitrators and mediators attempt to resolve these disputes, often at great cost to municipalities. But some tensions just can't be resolved in the current planning regime. That would require significantly more intervention by the province. "The only way you solve the problem of regional governance is for the province to be willing to be involved," said Jack Lucas, a political scientist at the University of Calgary.[50] Agrawal agreed: "It's only some other provincial entity that could do this job."[51]

Future Demands

The situation facing Alberta municipalities is fairly dire already, with a significant lack of money for infrastructure projects and a dearth of planning direction from the province. That's not even considering the increased burdens that will be placed on cities in coming years. The seniors population in Alberta will double by 2031 according to Alberta Health.[52] This will put increased burdens on cities in regards to mobility, affordable housing, and emergency services. The province's population is also expected to increase by almost 2 million people by 2041, with 46 per cent of the anticipated growth from international migration.[53] And while the homeless count in Calgary—which accounts for 54 per cent of the province's homeless population, compared to 34 per cent in Edmonton—has stabilized in recent years at around 3,200 people, it's still nowhere near the goal of zero that was articulated in the city's ten-year Plan to End Homelessness by 2018.[54] In other words, municipalities are already struggling with building and maintaining infrastructure and services for their current populations.

Then there's the looming crises related to climate change. Sara Hastings-Simon, director of the Pembina Institute's Alberta-focused Clean Economy Program, said it's critical that governments begin to invest in mitigation and adaptation now, as it's much cheaper to do so ahead of time.[55] The National Round Table on the Environment and the Economy has estimated that climate change will cost Canada about $5 billion per year by 2020, and at least $21 billion a year by 2050.[56]

Climate-resilient infrastructure will require addressing stormwater infrastructure, flood retention, distributed grids, installing permeable surfaces, and planting more trees for shade.[57] "A lot of municipalities have old infrastructure that's not able to handle this higher volume of rainfall," said Grande Prairie mayor Bill Given. "Things that would be a 1-in-100-year event are happening more and more often. We're going to see basic infrastructure like storm sewer upgrades and storm retention plans that need to be made."[58]

Some of this will be addressed with regulatory overhauls aimed at allowing for more efficient permitting processes, with government procuring investments from the private sector. But much of it will simply require more upfront investments and interventions from various levels of government. Interestingly, Mayor Nenshi has publicly opposed the application of carbon pricing to municipalities; in an interview, he noted that Calgary has long had a mandated LEED Gold Standard for new buildings and retrofits, and it has used 100 per cent renewable electricity for things like the C-Train.[59] As a result, he has petitioned the province for the municipalities to receive rebates. Hastings-Simon said she was "very surprised" at Nenshi's position on carbon pricing, which she claims represents "short-term thinking and framing around the costs." "Of course, the carbon levy comes with costs," she said. "But that's meant to drive behaviour. There's reason for it. It's not a punitive approach."[60] In contrast, Edmonton mayor Don Iveson expressed support for the mechanism, stating in a 2016 interview with the CBC that it made the city's plan to purchase electric buses considerably more viable than before.[61]

Comparing Expectations to Realities

So let's see how Bill 21—which was tabled on 31 May 2016, and received royal assent on 9 December 2016—looks within the context of the aforementioned factors.

A growth-management board was made mandatory for the Calgary region, an implicit recognition of the failure of the previously attempted voluntary regime. In addition, all municipalities in Alberta—all the way down to tiny summer villages—are now required to develop municipal development plans (MDPs) and intermunicipal collaboration frameworks (ICFs). Deron Bilous, the NDP's first municipal affairs minister, stated in September 2015 that "funding is a great way to help incent that behaviour," referencing the hoped-for collaboration between municipalities.[62] Rebecca Graff-McRae, research manager at the Parkland Institute, said that the minister's comments were widely interpreted as a potential for "big carrot . . . [encouraging] municipalities to put together revenue-sharing plans."[63] And yet, as she pointed out, "instead, it seemed that they went the opposite direction . . . [by] making that collaboration issue mandatory—you have to have a regional collaborative plan—but the revenue-sharing stipulations are all voluntary and very vague." However, Graff-McRae noted that even the concept of mandatory collaboration may simply result in neighbouring municipalities "mandatorily agreeing that they have nothing to work on."[64] Cold Lake mayor Craig Copeland suggested that mandatory ICFs will only increase friction between urban and rural governments: "I believe people lobbied very, very hard to keep the revenue in rural Alberta," he said.[65]

Significantly, the new MGA will also expand the scope of off-site levies and tax exemptions for brownfield development, widen the duties of the provincial ombudsman, allocate to the province the assessment of industrial properties, and allow for inclusionary zoning. Affordable housing expert Alina Turner stressed that municipalities already had the authority to use inclusionary zoning in land-use bylaws but haven't historically exercised it due to fears of exposing themselves to litigation from developers.[66] In late November, the president of the Canadian Mortgage and Housing Corporation echoed this sentiment, suggesting that municipalities should address "rezoning restrictions, density limits, development fees, and the time it takes for approval of new supply" before asking for more funding.[67]

In addition, the revamped MGA will allow municipalities to split non-residential property tax rates into more subcategories than just "vacant" and "improved." It will also mandate a maximum property tax ratio of 5:1 for non-residential and residential properties, meaning the tax rate on offices, retail, and industrial properties will only be allowed to be *five times* higher than the tax rate on residential properties. In 2017, property tax ratios were as follows: 3.5:1 in Calgary; 2.8:1 in Edmonton; 2.4:1 in Lethbridge; and 2.3:1 in Medicine Hat. Grande Prairie's mayor noted that "you wouldn't necessarily think that these are traditional NDP priority areas, or voices that would have influence with the NDP."[68]

Many of the changes were welcomed by mayors. But they were fairly minor in scope, representing tweaks to the legislation that any party could have conceivably backed. Part of that may be explained by the fact that the MGA has been under formal review since 2012, and debated since 2008. Larivee, who previously worked as a registered nurse for Alberta Health Services, was the province's sixth municipal affairs minister since December 2013. In the past decade, department ministers have included Ray Danyluk, Hector Goudreau, Doug Griffiths, Ken Hughes, Diana McQueen, and Deron Bilous. Larivee herself was replaced in January 2017 by Shaye Anderson. Graff-McRae acknowledged that the NDP "almost ended up with the worst of both worlds," with "half of it done but having to engage in another round of consultations and town halls."[69] Mayors and reeves were getting sick of it too. Nolan Crouse, former mayor of St. Albert and chair of the Capital Region Board, said: "I think the review's a gross misuse of resources. I think it's a gross misuse of commitments and time. People are almost tired of it. Give me a break on this one."[70]

But Graff-McRae also suggested that the blowback on the controversial Bill 6—which expanded Workers' Compensation Board coverage and Occupational Health and Safety standards to farm workers—may have exhausted the NDP's willingness to anger rural residents and governments.[71] Some mayors also pinned the blame on the inexperience of the new crop of NDP MLAs, the party's lack of knowledge about urban-rural tensions, and the reduction in the size of cabinet from twenty ministers under the PCs to twelve under the NDP. "So not only is it centrally controlled but fewer ministers means they don't have enough time in the day," said Crouse.[72] Both Given and Clugston indicated that they wished the NDP had approached municipal issues as aggressively and decisively as they had the climate change file.[73] "That's the kind of thing that could have resulted in them really solidifying their position in the cities," Climenhaga said. "I think it's a real failure of nerve to say 'they're going to hate us in the rural regions if we do this, so we better not.' Well I've got news for the NDP: they're going to be hated in the rural regions anyway."[74]

An Additional Note on City Charters

City charters have long been pointed to as a potential solution for Calgary and Edmonton's fiscal woes. Jack Lucas of the University of Calgary said there are two key dimensions to the concept: first, a symbolic acknowledgement that such cities are different entities from smaller municipalities; and second, a desire to make new fiscal tools available. Toronto received "charter status" in 2007, allowing it to introduce a land-transfer tax and vehicle registration tax (the latter of which Rob Ford famously eliminated in 2010, during his first full council session as mayor). Other major Canadian cities, including Vancouver, Winnipeg, and Montreal, have city charters in place with their respective provinces, each featuring different powers and approaches.

While city charters can increase local powers and efficiencies around bylaws, administrative processes, and other significant areas, they haven't historically changed the relationship between cities and provinces in any fundamental sense. The same looks to be the case in Alberta.

In response to renewed discussions about the possibility of city charters following the NDP's 2015 win, the coalition See Charter, Think Tax was launched in 2015 by such right-wing organizations as the Canadian Taxpayers Federation and Canadian Federation of Independent Business. However, the new city charter regulations—under review since October 2014—won't allow for any new taxation powers for Calgary and Edmonton. Instead, the cities will receive fairly small allowances, including the ability to run multi-year operating deficits accompanied by expenditures to cover the deficit over three years, to use electronic means to administer tax notices and other assessment notices, to issue loans for affordable housing, and delegating responsibilities on issues including secondary suite applications.[75]

A new infrastructure program was also announced, tying municipal funding for capital grants directly to provincial revenues, which tend to be wildly unpredictable from year to year. Despite that, Edmonton mayor Don Iveson told the CBC that it moves the city "in the direction of sustainable, predictable, guaranteed revenue sharing to support infrastructure."[76] The actual funding formula hasn't been made public yet, nor is there any indication that the province will see dramatically increased revenue in future years that would result in improved infrastructure funding for cities.

What the NDP Could Have Done

This brings us to the million-, or multi-billion-, dollar question: What should the NDP have done differently with the MGA and city charters if it really wanted to be the party of cities? Once again, the answer to this question varies based on municipality. But there were common items among most interviewees.

First, give municipalities the ability to gather more own-source revenues, including local sales, income, and land-transfer taxes. Better yet, allow for the levying and redistribution of such taxes on a regional basis to prevent mid-sized cities such as Grande Prairie and Medicine Hat from losing investments to the counties. If done correctly, this could free cities from the politically binding option of only increasing property taxes and user fees, resulting in more own-source revenue for both operating and capital plans. It's no panacea, but it would be a start.

Second, update assessment calculations for farmland, and machinery and equipment. Minister Larivee said that farmers "would likely not necessarily see it as a good thing."[77] That is true. The same goes for owners of refineries, upgraders, chemical plants, agri-food facilities, and paper plants. But the continued suppression of assessments for such industries means that other sources—namely residential and business properties—effectively subsidize them. Foregoing such revenue is a specific policy decision that could, and arguably should, be addressed.

Third, mandate revenue sharing between cities and rural areas, especially in the case of adjacent counties with high revenues from linear properties. Counties receive a vast majority of the tax revenue from linear properties and displacing service fulfillment onto the cities, meaning they can also afford to keep property tax rates lower than in the cities. Revenue sharing would mean that rural municipalities have to pay at least a share of what their residents use.

Fourth, in some situations—especially in Northern Alberta—consider encouraging and allowing for the merging of urban and rural municipalities. Minister Larivee stressed that the province was "in no way . . . going to do mandatory amalgamations," which indicates that the government wants municipalities to make such decisions on their own.[78] But given the aforementioned disparity in revenue, it's rather unlikely that rural governments will ever be interested in that. Mayor Copeland pointed out that there are already three examples of how amalgamation can work in the form of specialized municipalities such as Lac La Biche, Strathcona, and Wood Buffalo. It would require some political will from both mayors and the province. Redrawing the province's electoral boundaries to create mixed urban-rural ridings could assist with this. Amalgamations would not be as urgent a need if the previous concept of revenue sharing was pursued.

Fifth, address regional planning. Morrow noted that there are many examples of what this could look like, including deploying both "carrots" and "sticks" to incentivize collaborative, cost-efficient, and sustainable growth.[79] Regional bodies created by the province would allow for far better coordination and long-term planning, which would help achieve more sustainable growth patterns. Simply put, the province must become more involved.

Sixth, ensure that funding promises to cities are fulfilled, legislated, and indexed for inflation. As Clugston emphasized, "you'll hear this from every municipality: all they want to know is some consistency. Tell us what it's going to be and tell us it's going to be three, four, five years and you're not going to change it"[80] It's an extremely simple but crucial step.

Seventh, petition the federal government for even more stable, predictable, and long-term funding for cities. Carter noted that Mayor Nenshi of Calgary should use the "bully pulpit" to acquire more funds from the province for the Green Line, like former Edmonton mayor Stephen Mandel did for his city's downtown arena.[81] It's a fair point. But given present economic conditions, the NDP has arguably run out of political capital—not to mention financial capital—for the near future. The alternative is calling for upfront infrastructure investments from the federal government in "unprofitable" projects such as social housing, transit to low-income and underserved communities, and climate adaptations. That alone would cost billions, and can't currently be shouldered by the province.

Conclusion

The Alberta NDP failed to take advantage of a massive opportunity to permanently reform the way that cities raise revenue, plan for growth, and interact with other levels of government. It's clear that this was the result of a series of political calculations: revenue sharing, increased taxes, and more provincial involvement in planning may not exactly be a winning combo in the rural ridings, despite the obvious need. Perhaps the approach will prove successful for the 2019 election, winning the party an extra few seats in the rurals. Eventually, Calgary and Edmonton may end up with a few additional powers, although Premier Rachel Notley has suggested those won't include new own-source revenue tools.[82] But the rest of Alberta's cities will effectively be left in the same condition they have been in for the past few decades: cash-strapped, dilapidated, and forced to shoulder an increasing share of service provision as demands compound with climate change and an aging, and increasing, population. The consequences won't immediately manifest. As a result, this issue may win or lose an election, or even appear on a list of major policy items. But it's arguably one of the most important subjects facing the province, regardless of which party wins in 2019. The Alberta NDP may consider itself to be a party of the cities. It certainly hasn't shown itself to be that in practice.

Notes

1   Alberta NDP, "Leadership For What Matters," 10 April 2015, http://d3n8a8pro7vhmx. cloudfront.net/themes/5532a70aebad640927000001/attachments/original/1429634829/ Alberta_NDP_Platform_2015.pdf?1429634829 (accessed 24 June 2017).

2   Bill Given, interview with author, 24 August 2016.

3   Danielle Larivee, interview with author, 19 October 2016.

4   Naheed Nenshi, interview with author, 11 October 2016.

5   Larivee interview.

6   Bev Dahlby and Melville McMillan, "Do Local Governments Need Alternative Sources of Tax Revenue? An Assessment of the Options for Alberta Cities," *School of Public Policy Research Papers* 7, no. 26 (2014): 6.

7   Enid Slack, interview with author, 25 October 2016.

8   Elise Stolte, "'Extremely Irritating' 8.7-per-cent Education Tax Increase Hits Edmonton Homeowners," *Edmonton Journal*, 19 April 2016, https://edmontonjournal.com/news/local-news/extremely-irritating-8-7-per-cent-education-tax-hits-edmonton-homeowners (accessed 24 June 2017).

9   Philip Bazel and Jack Mintz, "The Free Ride is Over: Why Cities, and Citizens, Must Start Paying for Much-Needed Infrastructure," *School of Public Policy Research Papers* 7, no. 14 (2014): 10.

10   Canadian Chamber of Commerce, "The Foundations of a Competitive Canada: The Need for Strategic Infrastructure Investment," 18 December 2013, http://www.chamber.ca/media/blog/131218-The-Foundations-of-a-Competitive-Canada/ (accessed 24 June 2017).

11   Bill Curry, "Where Will $125-billion in Infrastructure Spending Go?" *Globe and Mail* (Toronto), 12 March 2016, https://www.theglobeandmail.com/news/where-will-125-billion-in-infrastructure-spendinggo/article28228477/ (accessed 24 June 2017).

12   Given interview.

13   Federation of Canadian Municipalities, "The State of Canada's Cities and Communities 2012," 2012, https://www.fcm.ca/Documents/reports/The_State_of_Canadas_Cities_and_Communities_2012_EN.pdf (accessed 24 June 2017).

14   Jan Reimer, interview with author, 14 September 2016.

15   Michael Sabia, "Getting to Growth," speech to the Toronto Region Board of Trade, Toronto, ON, 3 March 2016, http://www.actuarialsolutionsinc.com/wp-content/uploads/2017/03/March-3-2016-Michael-Sabia-Getting-to-Growth.pdf (accessed 24 June 2017).

16   Adrian Morrow, "Government-managed Projects Could Save Ontario Money: Auditor-General," *Globe and Mail* (Toronto), 9 December 2014, https://www.theglobeandmail.com/news/politics/private-partnerships-cost-ontario-taxpayers-8-billion-auditor-general/article22012009/ (accessed 24 June 2017).

17   Nenshi quoted in Robson Fletcher, "Building Canada Fund Has 'Major Problems': Calgary Mayor Naheed Nenshi," *Metro* (Calgary), 13 February 2014, http://www.metronews.ca/news/calgary/2014/02/13/building-canada-fund-has-major-problems-calgary-mayor-naheed-nenshi.html (accessed 24 June 2017).

18   Toby Sanger, interview with author, 5 October 2016.

19   See Toby Sanger, "Banking on Privatization?" *Progressive Economics*, 31 October 2016, http://www.progressive-economics.ca/2016/10/31/banking-on-privatization/ (accessed 24 June 2017), and Andrew Jackson, "Private Infrastructure Bank Not In The Public Interest," *Broadbent Institute*, 29 October 2016, http://www.broadbentinstitute.ca/

andrew_ajackson/private_infrastructure_bank_not_in_the_public_interest (accessed 24 June 2017).

20   Reimer interview.

21   Jason Markusoff, "Calgary, Other Cities Face Municipal Grant Shortfalls," *Calgary Herald*, 8 March 2013, http://www.calgaryherald.com/news/alberta/calgary+other+cities+face+municipal+grant+shortfalls/8063331/story.html (accessed 24 June 2017).

22   Nenshi interview.

23   Ibid.

24   Ibid.

25   Justin Giovannetti, "NDP Budget Signals Shift in Alberta's Economic Direction," *Globe and Mail* (Toronto), 27 October 2015, https://www.theglobeandmail.com/news/alberta/alberta-budget/article27003816/ (accessed 24 June 2017).

26   Al Duerr, interview with author, 24 August 2016.

27   Federation of Canadian Municipalities, "The State of Canada's Cities and Communities."

28   Duerr interview.

29   Lisa Osman, "Provincial Infrastructure Cuts Could Affect Property Taxes, AUMA Says," *CBC News*, 15 April 2016, http://www.cbc.ca/news/canada/edmonton/provincial-infrastructure-cuts-could-affect-property-taxes-auma-says-1.3536798 (accessed 24 June 2017).

30   Bill Curry and Justin Giovannetti, "Edmonton Mayor 'Side-Swiped' By Alberta's Infrastructure-funding Decision," *Globe and Mail* (Toronto), 24 August 2016, https://www.theglobeandmail.com/news/alberta/edmonton-mayor-side-swiped-by-albertas-infrastructure-funding-decision/article31547884/ (accessed 24 June 2017).

31   Gregory Morrow, interview with author, 25 August 2016.

32   Stephen Carter, interview with author, 4 October 2016.

33   Ibid.

34   City of Calgary, "Cities Matter: Alberta NDP 2015," 2015, http://www.citiesmatter.ca/search/label/Alberta%20NDP%202015 (accessed 24 June 2017).

35   Otiena Ellwand, "Infrastructure Sunshine List Doesn't Live Up to Expectations in Alberta Budget," *Calgary Sun*, 15 April 2016, http://www.edmontonsun.com/2016/04/15/infrastructure-sunshine-list-doesnt-live-up-to-expectations-in-alberta-budget (accessed 24 June 2017).

36   Chris Spearman, interview with author, 14 September 2016.

37   Tara Veer, interview with author, 4 October 2016.

38   Carter interview.

39   Sandeep Agrawal, interview with author, 29 September 2016.

40 Duerr interview.

41 Reimer interview.

42 Agrawal interview.

43 Ibid.

44 Dave Dormer, "Calgary Metropolitan Plan Lurches Forward Following Mediation," *Calgary Sun*, 28 March 2014, http://www.torontosun.com/2014/03/28/calgary-metropolitan-plan-lurches-forward-following-mediation (accessed 24 June 2017); Calgary Regional Partnership, "Moving Forward with the Calgary Metropolitan Plan," 19 February 2015, http://www.calgaryregionfocus.com/moving-forward-with-the-calgary-metropolitan-plan/ (accessed 24 June 2017).

45 David Climenhaga, interview with author, 26 August 2016.

46 Ibid.

47 Erica Fisher, "City Wants Changes to Linear Property Assessment Shares," *My Grande Prairie Now*, 30 March 2016, http://www.mygrandeprairienow.com/17065/17065/ (accessed 24 June 2017).

48 City of Cold Lake, "Cold Lake Looks for Assurances Regarding its Sustainability," 15 December 2016, http://www.coldlake.com/content/cold-lake-looks-assurances-regarding-its-sustainability (accessed 24 June 2016).

49 Ted Clugston, interview with author, 7 September 2016.

50 Jack Lucas, interview with author, 9 November 2016.

51 Agrawal interview.

52 Erika Stark, "Aging Alberta Population to Reach 6.2 million by 2041," *Calgary Herald*, 11 August 2015, http://calgaryherald.com/news/local-news/aging-alberta-population-to-reach-6-2m-by-2041 (accessed 24 June 2014).

53 Finance Alberta, "Population Project: Alberta and Census Divisons, 2016–2041." 21 June 2016, https://open.alberta.ca/dataset/90a09f08-c52c-43bd-b48a-fda5187273b9/resource/509cc23c-e135-4004-b4dc-4845a12d273c/download/2016-2041-alberta-population-projections-census.pdf (accessed 24 June 2017).

54 Bryan Passifiume, "Calgary Homeless Population Remains Tops in Alberta, Says New Count," *Calgary Sun*, 8 February 2015, http://www.calgarysun.com/2015/02/08/calgary-homeless-population-remains-tops-in-alberta-says-new-count (accessed 24 June 2017).

55 Sara Hastings-Simon, interview with author, 16 September 2016.

56 Angela Mulholland, "Climate Change Will Cost Canada Billions: Report," *CTV News*, 29 September 2011, http://www.ctvnews.ca/climate-change-will-cost-canada-billions-report-1.704453 (accessed 24 June 2017).

57 Hastings-Simon interview.

58 Given interview.

59 Nenshi interview.

60 Hastings-Simon interview.

61   Nola Keeler, "Carbon tax will lead to more Edmonton jobs, says mayor," *CBC News*, 20 December 2016, https://www.cbc.ca/news/canada/edmonton/carbon-tax-will-lead-to-more-edmonton-jobs-says-mayor-1.3904305 (accessed 24 June 2017).

62   Lucas Myer, "NDP Govt Announces New Municipal Government Act," *660 News*, 25 September 2015, http://www.660news.com/2015/09/25/ndp-govt-announces-new-municipal-government-act/ (accessed 24 June 2017).

63   Rebecca Graff-McRae, interview with author, 2 September 2016.

64   Ibid.

65   Craig Copeland, interview with author, 13 October 2016.

66   Alina Turner, interview with author, 15 September 2016.

67   Quoted in Matt Robinson, "City of Vancouver Looks to Reduce Building Permit Waits as Citizens Suffer," *Vancouver Sun*, 2 December 2016, http://vancouversun.com/news/local-news/city-of-vancouver-looks-to-reduce-building-permit-waits-as-citizens-suffer (accessed 24 June 2017).

68   Given interview.

69   Graff-McRae interview.

70   Nolan Crouse, interview with author, 2 September 2016.

71   Graff-McRae interview.

72   Crouse interview.

73   Given interview; Clugston interview.

74   Climenhaga interview.

75   John Himpe, "No New Tax Powers In New City Charters For Calgary, Edmonton," *Global News*, 10 August 2017, http://globalnews.ca/news/3661271/no-new-tax-powers-in-new-city-charters-for-calgary-edmonton/ (accessed 24 June 2017).

76   Alexandra Zabjek, "From Bar Closing Times to Infrastructure Grants: City Charter Takes Another Step Forward," *CBC News*, 10 August 2017, http://www.cbc.ca/news/canada/edmonton/city-charter-takes-another-step-forward-1.4242184 (accessed 24 June 2017).

77   Larivee interview.

78   Ibid.

79   Morrow interview.

80   Clugston interview.

81   Carter interview.

82   James Wood, "Notley Says New City Charters Not a Priority," *Calgary Herald*, 16 December 2016, http://www.calgarysun.com/2016/12/16/notley-says-new-city-charters-not-a-priority (accessed 24 June 2017).

The End of Exceptionalism: Post-rural Politics in Alberta

Roger Epp

By the political standards of a province jolted in one election from what had seemed like two long generations of single-party somnolence, the events of late 2015 stand as extraordinary. Farmers drove trucks and tractors in highway convoys. Protestors hoisted posters on pitchforks at mass rallies at the legislature and in cities throughout the province. Thousands signed petitions, one of which ("Save Alberta Farms") was circulated by an online "Rebel" broadcaster with a sharp ideological agenda. On social media platforms, anonymous thugs threatened all manner of violence, angry prophets warned of jackbooted safety inspectors about to smash through the barn door, and a well-known country singer, in more conciliatory tones, asked the new premier for respect, time, and honest conversation with farmers and ranchers, who "feel like you are trying to tell them how they have to live."[1]

Premier Notley—just returned from a very different stage, the United Nations Climate Change Conference in Paris, where she had other balances to strike in defence of the province's flagship energy industry—responded in early December with an open letter to Albertans. It, too, was posted on social media platforms. The premier was unapologetic about the intent of her government's contentious Bill 6, the Enhanced Protection for Farm and Ranch Workers Act, which would extend the workplace injury and occupational safety provisions in existing provincial labour standards to agriculture. She could not accept that farm fatalities and injuries were "simply a fact of life." Family farms were "thriving" and farmworkers were safer in other provinces, where similar provisions were already in place;

such legislation, the premier argued, was overdue in Alberta. But Notley also apologized and accepted responsibility for the mistake of introducing a bare-bones bill without being clear that it would apply only to paid farmworkers—not to neighbours helping out, not to farm children working with their parents, doing chores, or participating in 4-H activities. In keeping with the coded language of those who had protested against the bill, she affirmed that farming in Alberta was "a way of life," and promised a "common sense framework" of regulation that "protects paid farmworkers while allowing for the day-to-day realities of life on a family farm."[2] Before the end of the year, an amended version of Bill 6 was passed into law.

Journalistic interpretations of the controversy tended to view it through the lens of the next election: on one hand, an inexperienced New Democratic Party government, acting on a long-standing policy commitment, and possibly learning a lesson about communication and consultation in the process; on the other, an opportunistic opposition finding an issue on which to portray the government as ideologically driven, out of touch with Alberta values, and not to be trusted with a second term in office. In subsequent months, the government appointed stakeholder working groups, chaired by experienced mediators and populated by farm, labour, and professional members, to work out technical details. Over the course of 2016, injury compensation claims from farmworkers more than doubled—a measure of expanded eligibility under the new legislation. One mainstream farm leader declared that the mandatory coverage was "far better" than the private liability insurance most employers had carried before.[3]

Meanwhile, the wildfire of outrage fanned by talk radio and social media moved onto bigger issues like the carbon tax introduced into an economy hit hard by a prolonged oil price slump. In style and sometimes in content, the protests echoed the politics that helped elect Donald Trump as US president in 2016; but they were also reminiscent of the home-grown pockets of public anger seen in the early 1980s in the wake of the National Energy Program, when the separatist Western Canada Concept held raucous rallies in places like Edmonton's Jubilee Auditorium, and elected an MLA in a by-election in Olds-Didsbury.[4] Alberta is a province, as a long-time observer has noted, that is "wracked by crankiness and fear"[5]—despite, and sometimes because of, its boom-and-bust prosperity.

The Bill 6 episode, however, did expose something old and something new. What was old was a rural-urban divide. Culturally, that divide had opened earlier in fall 2015, when three sisters aged eleven and thirteen were killed in a farm accident near Rocky Mountain House after being buried in canola seed in the box of a truck while it was filled from a hopper. The accident—and one that followed involving the death of a ten-year-old Hutterite boy driving a forklift that overturned[6]—helped to shape urban political support for the government's farm safety legislation on the assumption that it would also restrict child labour, which seemed indefensibly dangerous. The labour minister said nothing at the time to dispel this impression. The father of the girls, as if to anticipate the larger political issue, posted a family photograph on his Facebook page in which he is wearing a T-shirt with the message "Born to farm"; the image is accompanied by a caption that reads, "This is our life. It is not sterile like city life."[7]

The political side of that rural-urban divide had required skillful political management in recent decades, while the population of Alberta's cities grew rapidly—a trajectory that was only belatedly reflected in the provincial electoral map—and especially whenever volatile energy revenues did not allow governments the freedom to spend visibly on public infrastructure in all parts of the province. In some ways, the divide had become increasingly evident by the end of the Klein era (1992–2006), when a deeply entrenched patron-client exchange of government generosity for political support in the countryside was eroded gradually by spending cuts.[8] Rural people lived increasingly on the defensive. They experienced the consolidation of schools, hospitals, and other services, the loss of population, especially young people, as well as the negative impacts of intense resource development; and they had begun to imagine that the benefits of the so-called Alberta Advantage were concentrated in the Highway 2 corridor, between Calgary and Edmonton. Indeed, an internal government study in 2003 confirmed significant regional disparities—not just in age, but also in measures having to do with wealth, education, and health.[9]

Ed Stelmach became Ralph Klein's surprise successor late in 2006, thanks to a final-ballot groundswell of rural voters under the Conservative Party's one-member, one-vote leadership-selection rules. When the new premier appointed a cabinet that seemed top-heavy with rural lieutenants— many of them, like him, former municipal politicians—the response from

Calgary in particular was visceral. Much of it came from within the governing party. One columnist observed that the new premier had "reawakened" a "slumbering contempt" informed by "cartoon images of rural hicks."[10] Another, more sympathetic to the critics, wrote: "The political, economic, social and cultural core of power will remain outside Alberta's two major cities"—and in the hands of "a lot of farmers"—"as long as Team Stelmach remains in power."[11] Stelmach's government may have quietly reinvested in rural Alberta, but it also consolidated regional health divisions into a single provincial authority. Most of all, it provoked a property-rights backlash in the countryside by its centralized approach to the approval of new electricity corridors, ostensibly to meet increasing demand for power in the cities.

When Stelmach resigned after one election and was replaced by his justice minister, Alison Redford—a Calgary lawyer, female, urbane, at home in international circles—the party barely survived the 2012 election. It was dislodged from rural seats in the southern half of the province by its conservative rivals, the Wildrose—the first time in living memory that so many rural voters were represented on the Opposition side of the legislature, though the party made no such inroads in the cities. The Wildrose leader, Danielle Smith, would later concede the challenge of building a successful party in a province where "Calgary and Edmonton are far more progressive on social issues than the rural areas."[12] How much of that is true and how much is a matter of self-justification is not the point here; rural Alberta is a much less monolithic place than any of its caricatures would have us believe, and it was, after all, candidates in Calgary and Edmonton whose comments with respect to race and homosexuality caused the party the most political harm in 2012. Still, the lingering political recognition and reproduction of a rural-urban fault line is worth noting.

What was exposed for the first time in the Bill 6 episode—and what this chapter proposes to explore—goes beyond that fault line: it is the prospect of a post-rural politics. By that I mean something different than the historic balancing of rural and urban in a governing coalition or in public policy, and different again from the kind of raw resentments sometimes expressed across that divide. Post-rural does not mean anti-rural. Instead it describes something closer to a politics where rural, whether as a *coherent idea*, a *policy lens*, a *standing exception*, a *"heartland,"* or *rhetorical touchstone*, no longer figures prominently—not in the way the government imagines and speaks to Albertans, not in the kind of economy it proposes to build, nor in the way it approaches its own re-election. Tellingly, the NDP government assigned Bill 6 to the minister of labour, not the minister of agriculture. In the first instance, this was a bill about workers and workplaces; it removed a farm *exception*. The post-rural shift in language and orientation may or may not be detrimental for rural people, especially those for whom the older political scripts were too confining or condescending or else turned them into "salt-of-the-earth cover" for someone else's agenda.[13] But a post-rural government comes without old-style champions or self-styled protectors; even in good times, the shift would take some adjustment. In Alberta's chastened economic circumstances, it has invited a backlash. But as I will argue, appeals to the rural in this context signify not so much a precise geography or a farm-based economy as a sense of grievance or outsider status that is readily mobilized in a politics of resentment.

The Eclipse of Rural Alberta, in Stages

One of the myths shattered by the NDP election victory was that rural voters have an unfair and unbreakable stranglehold on political power in Alberta. The 2012 election had already strained that logic. And while the NDP in 2015 won some rural seats in northwestern and mountain regions, and in communities around Edmonton, it did so without a dedicated rural campaign or a serious policy platform. The post-election government caucus of fifty-four MLAs contained only one person with an active farm background,[14] and not a single former county reeve.

Two days after Bill 6 was tabled in the legislature, Rachel Notley gave her first speech as premier to the annual fall convention of the Alberta Association of Municipal Districts and Counties (AAMDC). This event has a venerable place in the calendars of cabinet ministers and in the stories told about how power worked in the old Alberta of single-party dominance. It was where loyalty was cemented, influence exercised, and the right measure of intimidation applied as needed. Notley recalled her own roots in the northern community of Fairview—"Heart of the Peace"—and she assured her audience that "communities like yours are extremely well-represented in our government."[15] Though Bill 6 had come up in an earlier open session with government ministers, she did not mention it in her speech. Instead, she focused on the climate change and budget files. She asked for delegates' support as community leaders for her government's made-in-Alberta approach to environmental protection and climate change, which was intended to provide the province's energy industry with the social licence to answer its critics. She promised that communities directly affected by the controversial phase-out of coal-generated power would not be abandoned. She spoke reassuringly about provincial budget plans. She said that her government was committed in difficult times to maintain public services, planned capital projects like rural hospitals, and infrastructure grants in support of roads, bridges, and water treatment. Most notably, she promised that the pending review of the Municipal Government Act would "not compromise the ability of rural municipalities to serve their residents" by redistributing revenues from the taxes they collect on linear assessment (pipelines, power lines, oil and gas installations)—a continuing sore point for cities, as James Wilt's chapter in this volume points out, and a curious no-go file for the NDP in power.

Successful or not, Notley's speech demonstrated her willingness to speak in the idiom of rural politicians and communities. It stands as possibly the most rural speech she has given as premier. By comparison, the government's first two Throne Speeches were more circumspect. The first, in June 2015, struck an inclusive note for a new government. It described Alberta as a "province of indigenous peoples" and a "province built by wave after wave of pioneers and settlers, farmers and oil workers, researchers and students, job seekers and job creators." There are still rural builders, even farmers, in the first Throne Speech, but they do not get first or exclusive billing. When the speech addressed the goal of a "sustainable, diversified and prosperous economy," it moved from education ("the single best investment our province can make"), to energy and the environment, a new relationship with Indigenous peoples and fair pay for workers, and, then, to the "need to ensure this province's rural and resource communities have the tools they need to keep contributing to the prosperity of Alberta."[16] Not lead it, just keep contributing. The 2016 Throne Speech, by comparison, made no reference to the rural at all.

Previous Conservative governments were seldom so circumspect. While Throne Speeches may not be good measures of public policy initiatives actually delivered, and while they are likely to be read by only a

ROGER EPP

fraction of voters, they are nonetheless carefully crafted political communications. They imagine the province at a particular moment in time; they reflect choices about what to say and not to say; and invariably they will be cited by government MLAs as proof of a commitment to act on a set of priorities.

In 2003, the Klein government's Throne Speech began with its own panorama of Albertans, in a different order: "farmers, public servants, homemakers, oil field workers, doctors, students, volunteers." When it came around to the economy, it began with agricultural producers and rural communities—"the *backbone* of this province's economy"—who would not be abandoned by the government while they struggled with the effect of drought and spiralling farm input costs.[17] A year later the Klein government promised a "new rural development strategy to help ensure that the people and businesses in rural Alberta enjoy every opportunity to reach their full potential."[18] The 2005 and 2006 Throne Speeches returned to that same priority of rural prosperity, noting specific new support in areas like housing, highways, health, education, apprenticeships, and water systems: "Vibrant rural communities are vital to this province."[19]

The Klein government had not always offered this kind of rhetorical recognition and reassurance. Nor had it always defined the government's role in such positive, activist terms. The ground shifted noticeably after a 2002 by-election in a bedrock rural constituency, Battle River-Wainwright, where turnout was so low that the Conservative candidate won with the support of about one in seven eligible voters. The new MLA was quickly appointed co-chair of a task force whose 2004 report, *Rural Alberta: Land of Opportunity*,[20] introduced the language of "vibrant" communities and led to a fuller rural development strategy, *A Place to Grow* (2005), which began with the declaration that the government "officially recognizes the importance of rural Alberta and its contributions to the Alberta Advantage."[21] The strategy conceded that government cuts had hurt rural communities, and it recommended reinvestment in public services, adaptation of programs to fit rural circumstances, and support for rural innovation. In effect, the strategy announced a retreat from the textbook neo-liberal policies that, for the previous decade, sought to attract global capital by positioning the province and its resources as a low-tax, low-regulation environment. By the end of the Klein era, the government had accepted in successive Throne Speeches that it was the government's job to "sustain and strengthen the rural economy" (2005) and to "help rural communities become more prosperous" (2006). The latter hinted at stable, long-term funding to support rural development—what was announced in that spring's budget as a $100-million fund to support model community and regional projects.[22]

The Stelmach government picked up this mission with enthusiasm. It asked ministries to incorporate elements of the rural development strategy into their planning processes and struck an inter-departmental committee at the level of assistant deputy ministers to coordinate rural initiatives. It issued progress reports, one of which, in 2009, gave a thirteen-page, small-print inventory of government actions: $1.87 million in funding for rural artists and arts organizations; $268 million in loans to rural businesses; 89 affordable housing units for seniors; $2.3 million to support rural rotations for medicine students; 465 new post-secondary spaces, and so on.[23] In advance of the 2008 election, the Stelmach government's Throne Speech declared agriculture in particular to be an economic and cultural "cornerstone"; after the election, it inaugurated the new legislative session with a pledge: "While Alberta towns and cities continue to grow and flourish, this government will never take for granted the cultural and economic importance of vibrant rural communities and competitive agriculture, food, and forestry sectors."[24]

The rhetorical reassurances—rural as backbone, as cornerstone— masked the difficulties of rural development that have confronted provincial and state governments across North America. In some ways, *A Place to Grow* did at least challenge traditional thinking. For example, it defined rural Alberta broadly enough to include Indigenous communities; and it put altogether more emphasis on arts and culture, public services, municipal infrastructure, and education than it did on agriculture when it came to ensuring future vibrancy and prosperity. In 2011, and not for the last time, a Throne Speech mentioned the government's commitment to achieving last-mile broadband internet access in homes across the province, an increasingly significant point of urban-rural disparity. But rural remained very much a political concept; for that reason, its borders were flexible. The MLA Task Force report, *Rural Alberta: Land of Opportunity*, had conjured a common-sense "picture" of rural as "farms and small towns and villages," to which it added the qualifier that rural municipalities had a population below 10,000 and were located "beyond the commuting zones of larger urban centres."[25] In 2006, by contrast, the Conservative government introduced an incentive bursary for rural students of $1,000 for each of the first two years of a post-secondary program. The bursary was meant to improve the chronically low rural participation rates in post-secondary education by offsetting the financial costs for those who needed to leave home to do it—a real structural inequality. The program, however, defined rural as "any community outside of Edmonton, Calgary, Sherwood Park and St. Albert,"[26] which essentially meant everywhere beyond a metropolitan transit route to a full set of post-secondary options. A more restrictive definition would have had a rougher ride in the government caucus.

What is clear is that a preferential option for the rural was politically difficult to sustain beyond the Stelmach era; moreover, the case for its practical success was difficult to make. The annual progress reports on the rural development strategy were apparently discontinued before Stelmach's departure. A subsequent report by the Conference Board of Canada, commissioned by the government, concluded that in the 2006–11 period, economic growth in rural Alberta "decelerated noticeably." The rural share of the population continued to decline. Though rural Alberta grew in absolute numbers—here again, definitions of rural matter—that growth did not keep pace with the province as a whole and was not evenly distributed; some communities and regions experienced a decline. Per-capita income levels remained "well below" those in urban centres.[27]

While the Redford government prepared for its first election in 2012 with a Throne Speech that contained some of the standard reassurances about the importance of rural communities and the values left by the "settlers and farmers who founded this province,"[28] its post-election Throne Speech to a new legislature, three months later, was silent on rural Alberta, where it had lost seats. Instead, it promised to "treat all Albertans with fairness and respect *no matter where they live*," and, "most importantly . . . [to] get out of Albertans' way so they can unleash their creative potential and build a prosperous province."[29] Indicatively, in post-secondary education, the government softened the previous emphasis on accessibility and transferability, so that more students could complete at least part of their programs close to home, in favour of reducing program duplication in the name of system efficiency.

The Conservatives under Redford's leadership had proven the political possibility of winning an election without winning the countryside, but as a party they were not ready to relinquish their hold on rural seats permanently. After Redford's surprise resignation in 2014, followed by the selection of a replacement, former federal cabinet minister Jim Prentice, and then the spectacular floor-crossing of the Opposition leader and half of her remaining Wildrose caucus, the government set about repairing its relationship to rural Alberta.

The Prentice government's only Throne Speech, in November 2014, began by striking some general notes about sound fiscal management in difficult economic times, an end to entitlements, and the restoration of public trust—distancing itself, in other words, from its predecessor. It described a prosaic assortment of new commitments to rural Alberta: a Rural Business Centre, highway and bridge maintenance, and health. But it also contained a more important political signal, Bill 1, introduced that same day, which aimed to put to rest lingering rural discontent over property rights: "Private ownership of land is a fundamental and essential principle of our democracy and our economy. This government respects the property rights of Albertans. . . . Bill 1 signals the beginning of government's commitment to rebuild relationships with property owners in Alberta."[30] At the same time, the government released a new Rural Economic Development Action Plan—the work of another task force of government MLAs.[31]

Against this history, the Notley government's post-rural orientation stands in sharp relief. Rural is no longer a backbone or cornerstone. In a challenging economy, it is a heritage on which to draw—hard work, ingenuity, and perseverance—but it is not the only one.[32] Certainly rural is not the engine of the current or future economy. The premier's state-of-the-province speeches in spring and fall of 2016 canvassed a long list of themes: families, resilience, job creation, competitiveness, infrastructure, public services, fiscal restraint, new markets and value-added production for energy, climate leadership, diversification, and the knowledge economy.[33] The 2016 budget stressed the same themes.[34] Both documents avoided rural-urban spatial differentiations; they referred instead to families, workers, communities, and sectors of the economy. They contained none of the traditional rural pieties, only brief references to renewable resources and agri-food innovation in the context of diversification.

ROGER EPP

The government's defence of energy *as a sector*, including the oil sands, new petrochemical plants in the Heartland industrial region northeast of Edmonton, and planned pipelines to take bitumen to international refiners, is instructive in this context. That defence is not mere posturing. Given the importance of energy to the provincial economy, employment, and the government's own fiscal capacity, it might not be a surprise. But it still has come at the cost of open conflict with environmental activists, Indigenous communities, and New Democrats, both nationally and in British Columbia. In the case of the Alberta NDP, what is seldom remembered is that the party's origins were in organized labour—not in the older agrarian socialism of the Cooperative Commonwealth Federation—and, in particular, in the Oil, Chemical and Atomic Workers (OCAW). Neil Reimer, the party's first leader, had come to Edmonton in 1951 as the union's Canadian director to organize workers in the new refineries and petrochemical plants; Reg Basken, also out of the OCAW, was party treasurer in the 1960s. Confronted with politically protected company unions, their organizing efforts had met with only partial success in Alberta, mostly in the petrochemical industry and the heavy-oil plant at Lloydminster; but over time a significant union presence developed in the oil sands, construction, and refining sectors of the energy industry. In the early 1960s, Reimer indeed had encouraged development of the Athabasca oil sands, albeit under public ownership.[35] The fact that the NDP won its first seats in rural constituencies of Pincher Creek (1966) and Spirit River-Fairview (1971) was an anomaly, as was the fact that Grant Notley, Reimer's successor, was a farm boy from Didsbury who "firmly believed that Neil did not understand rural Alberta" and disagreed with his strategic focus on urban ridings.[36] When the party became the Official Opposition after the 1986 election, all but two of its seats came from metropolitan Edmonton and Calgary; but at the time there were still enough members of that caucus with connections to the countryside to generate a substantial task force report on "the family farm and the future of rural Alberta."[37]

A generation later, however, that rural sensibility is much harder to locate in the government caucus—which, in part, may simply reflect the reality of an increasingly urban province. The lack of a rural instinct and or informal rural network was apparent, for example, when the government rolled out details of its carbon tax in late 2016 without any adaptation to places like Foremost or Tulliby Lake, places where driving and distances and long school-bus rides are daily realities. In particular, the tax tied carbon rebates to income, not location. It did, though, make an exemption for farm fuels in its initial announcement, and later committed energy efficiency grants specifically to livestock and greenhouse operators. Days before the tax took effect, the government hinted that further offsets might be coming for agricultural producers.[38] But those measures seemed an afterthought. A re-elected Conservative government might well have been forced to introduce its own carbon tax out of a similar instrumental concern to secure social licence and protect energy markets, but safe to say it would have done so differently; from the start it would have wrapped any such measures in the language of protecting and exempting rural Albertans.

Redrawing the Electoral Map

The most significant and immediate next step towards a post-rural politics in Alberta involved the redrawing of the electoral map. This exercise has been a point of contention given the province's dramatic demographic shifts in recent decades, especially since 1989, when the Supreme Court set legal limits around the maximum deviation from the average constituency population, and 1994, when the provincial appeals court ruled unambiguously that the electoral map could not be drawn again, as it had been, by a committee consisting solely of government MLAs, "if Alberta wishes to call itself a democracy."[39] Since then, there have been four electoral boundaries commissions, reporting in 1996, 2003, 2010, and 2017—typically after two elections. The appointment of the most recent commission required a legislative amendment to allow for a review earlier than the mandatory eight years, since the Prentice government had called an election ahead of the fixed calendar range, so that redistribution could occur in time for the next scheduled election in 2019.

The outcome of the previous reviews has been a modest redistribution in favour of cities, but each time the process has brought to the surface deep rural anxieties about declining political representation and influence. Alberta's allowable variance in riding population—25 per cent—is as large as any in Canada, and much larger than most provinces (in Saskatchewan, for example, it is only 5 per cent). In addition, the Electoral Boundaries

Commission Act allows for as many as four designated low-population constituencies on the perimeter of the province with a variance of as much as 50 per cent. In advance of the previous review, the Stelmach government introduced legislation to add four constituencies—increasing the provincial total from 83 to 87—so as to diminish the possibility that rural seats would actually be taken away. The 2010 commission, however, recommended that the legislature would in future have to think differently about the representation of large rural and northern ridings before the next review. Its final report included the dissenting position of one member who essentially said that difficult decisions should not have been deferred, that the commission had heard many concerns over the differential value of rural and urban votes, and that "the preservation of representation in sparsely-populated rural constituencies when urban constituencies are ballooning continues to be controversial."[40] According to the minority position, the practice of thinking about the electoral map in terms of three blocks—Edmonton, Calgary, and rural—was increasingly problematic. Not only did it mask population decline in some regions, since the "rest of Alberta" category included several fast-growing, mid-sized cities; it also neglected the increasing dissatisfaction in those cities with the practice of being fragmented into hybrid rural-urban ridings—a means of containing their size—as if they constituted communities of interest.

The 2016–17 boundaries review was established amid expectations and rural fears of a more dramatic redistribution of seats in favour of cities and, presumably, the NDP's political interests. Curiously, that speculation overlooked the fact that after the 2015 election the NDP held five of the seven ridings identified in the 2010 review as having the greatest negative deviation from the average constituency population, including the two large, northern "special consideration" ridings (Dunvegan-Central Peace and Lesser Slave Lake), as well as the next smallest (West Yellowhead). The party, in other words, did not have an unqualified interest in more urban seats.

The question of rural representation did preoccupy the commission, which was headed by an Edmonton judge and contained four other members, two each nominated by the NDP and Wildrose Opposition. Rural municipalities immediately began making their public case about the need to maintain reasonably scaled rural seats and a rural political voice in what looked like a zero-sum redistribution.[41] In the end, the commission's recommended changes were relatively incremental and measured: new seats in Edmonton, Calgary, and Airdrie-Cochrane, at the expense of southeast, west-central, and northeastern rural regions. But its justification was blunt: "Alberta is no longer entirely or primarily rural in nature." Accordingly, the "disproportionate preservation of the rural voice" was not a justifiable consideration under legislation; to treat it as such would "defeat the principle of representation by population."[42] The commission made parity of voting power its first principle and began, by way of methodology, with the cities—though, as it also noted, even under its recommendations a vote in the most populous Calgary riding would carry about one-third the weight of a vote in the special-consideration northern ridings. Nonetheless, one of the Wildrose-appointed commission members chose to submit a minority report that echoed the language of rural exceptionalism: "If Alberta continues to grow at such a rate, a critical part of our history, culture, and primary economic voice will be lost."[43] The idea that a boundaries commission would somehow have the mandate to restore rural Alberta's mythic unity and influence suggests that exceptionalism dies hard. But the reality is that in the next election, a smaller number of seats outside the cities will matter less to all parties.

Rural Identity and Grievance in a Post-rural Alberta

Those who study politics are well advised never to make bold claims about inevitable trajectories, tidy historical divisions, and the certainty of a post-*anything* era. That caution certainly holds for a chapter about the prospect of a post-rural politics in Alberta—one in which "rural," whether as a coherent idea, a policy lens, a standing exception, a heartland, or rhetorical touchstone, is less-and-less central to the full spectrum of politics from elections to government policy.

The most obvious objection to the claim advanced here is that it reads too much into the NDP's 2015 electoral victory: a post-rural government is not evidence of a post-rural politics, especially if that government's prospects of re-election are uncertain. That the NDP has a post-rural orientation is clear enough. The government thinks and speaks most comfortably in terms of families, workers, communities, and economic sectors—even entrepreneurs and educators. It does not start from the assumption that "rural

ROGER EPP

Alberta" is a singular place, substantially different from "urban Alberta," and that it therefore requires special consideration in public policy or deference in political speech. When Premier Notley got past the opening pleasantries in her second appearance at the AAMDC ("a great advocate," "our partner"), she presented her government's priorities in terms that would have fit a downtown Calgary audience without much alteration: fiscal restraint, stable public services for communities, infrastructure investment, climate leadership, and new markets for key sectors of the economy beyond energy alone. She noted that agriculture as a sector meant $10 billion in annual exports and 89,000 *jobs*. That's not the way that farmers regard themselves, but it was an implicit reminder that the sector itself is bigger than farmers, and not only rural in its location.[44]

The post-rural shift did not start with the NDP. In some ways it was prefigured by the Redford Conservatives, who might be dismissed as being another aberration, not a "real" Alberta government, except that such so-called political anomalies also reflect and add up to real change. They point to demographic, economic, and electoral dynamics at work over a generation. The idea of a homogeneous rural Alberta, set within a simple rural-urban binary, strains increasingly against the realities in which people live and make a living. The idea may have a certain coherence in the realm of municipal politics, so that the AAMDC can represent a shared set of rural interests, say, in taxation, infrastructure (from roads to digital connectivity), and public services (from schools to hospitals). But the organization's members find common ground mostly in a defensive posture—that is, in securing the status quo against the threat of consolidation or redeployment to other government priorities (or cities).

Beyond that, member municipalities are increasingly differentiated by demographic trajectories and economic futures, which are determined by factors like proximity to larger population centres or major resource developments. When rural is defined more generously, as it sometimes has been in policy, to mean everything outside of metropolitan Calgary and Edmonton, that sense of coherence is further diminished. The emergence of a caucus of twenty-two mid-sized cities representing close to a million people complicates the political math that once divided the province neatly into thirds: the two big cities plus rural Alberta, each entitled to its share. The best evidence for the success of previous governments' rural development initiatives, if credit is due, might be found in the flourishing of regional centres, with their own big-box retailers, new hospitals, and post-secondary campuses that can hold their own against the lure of Calgary and Edmonton. The irony is that they have done so in part by drawing shoppers, young people, medical professionals, and especially retirees out of smaller communities within their catchment areas. Increasingly, it is difficult to say where is rural and where is not.

In one important sense, though, the word "rural" is not about to disappear from the political lexicon. What it lacks in conceptual coherence it retains in its power to define an outsider identity and a set of grievances. Katherine Cramer has explored what she describes as "rural consciousness" in her book *The Politics of Resentment*, which focuses on Wisconsin, and in her response to the election of Donald Trump. Cramer's book is the result of extended conversations with rural people—often, she acknowledges, the older white men who are the ones who tend to gather in public—in communities across the state. She is not wholly unsympathetic to her subjects. By consciousness, Cramer means "a strong sense of identity as a rural person combined with a strong sense that rural areas are the victims of injustice: the sense that rural areas do not get their fair share of power, respect, or resources and that rural folks prefer lifestyles that differ fundamentally from those of city people."[45]

Such rural consciousness is inherently oppositional. It is rooted in a sharp sense of dichotomy, but it affords plenty of room for people to define rural and urban for themselves. It distinguishes between the deserving and undeserving—the latter defined as "others," not like them, who are "eating their share of the pie."[46] They might be public servants and university professors in Madison with good jobs or the urban poor in Milwaukee who are supported by government welfare. In a politics where issues and direct economic interests become secondary to identity, Cramer argues, a rural consciousness is ripe for mobilization by politicians who can present themselves as either "like us" or at least likely to "understand us."

There are recognizable echoes of Cramer's Wisconsin in Alberta, particularly in the angry Bill 6 rallies and the Main Street truck parades against a carbon tax, and indeed in an undercurrent of Alberta politics with a much longer history. If it is increasingly difficult to draw definitive lines around what is rural, it is possible to map remarkable disparities across the province

ROGER EPP

on measures like income, age, education, and access to government services. Rural resentment has simmered for at least as long as people figured out that the Alberta Advantage was mostly for those living inside the Highway 2 corridor.

What has changed fundamentally with an NDP government is that people are less afraid to express that resentment in public; they no longer need to be polite about it. They imagine that the government is "alien" to them, and that those Albertans who supported Bill 6, to quote another country singer, "likely haven't had to go out after a full day of work and help a mama cow safely deliver her calf in a cold, snowy night."[47] In the same unrestrained spirit, municipal councillors at the AAMDC's 2016 fall convention booed the deputy premier for her comments on the carbon tax and the phase-out of coal power.[48] Not long ago, such an open show of defiance would have been unthinkable. But the sense that the government's climate plan will singularly disadvantage rural Alberta is a powerful one, whether it is expressed in convention halls or coffee shops.

The NDP government may not win a second term, but if that is the result the reason will be that it failed to hold seats in Calgary. By itself, that does not refute the idea of a post-rural shift. At the same time, the sense of rural grievance will be available for political mobilization even if the number of rural ridings has shrunk. It will serve as evidence with some audiences that the NDP is too incompetent, ideological, or just plain un-Albertan to be trusted with the levers of government. And if such a mobilization helps to produce a change in government, more rural voters will find themselves represented on the government side of the legislature; they will feel like insiders once again. Bill 6 will be repealed, good policy or not, as the leader of the United Conservative Party has pledged. But such a result would scarcely amount to either a restoration of political power or a reversal of the underlying trends. It would not change the fact, for example, that more than four in five Albertans live in what Statistics Canada calls urban population centres—more by far than in every province except Ontario and British Columbia.[49] It would not be enough to allay anxieties around the viability of rural communities and land-based livelihoods. It would not overcome the real political limits that have confronted the case for rural exceptionalism, valid or not, on a range of policy fronts for the past quarter-century. For that matter, it would not make rural Alberta a single place with a single voice and a single, distinctive set of political interests—as if it ever was.

The Orange Chinook, in other words, has been the occasion but not the cause for the rise in political temperatures in the countryside. The NDP government's handling of files like farm safety might have been less awkward, its rural instincts might have been stronger, and it might then not have made such a ready target for outrage, manufactured or real, so early in its term. But the geographic centre of gravity in Alberta politics shifted some time ago. That reality presents choices, and risks, both for the government and for people living in the *outer* Alberta.

The latter can pursue a politics of grievance and hope that it is rewarded. Such a politics is curiously fixated on what happens in Edmonton and on the need for a strong champion, a patron, who can protect against perceived threats, ensure that the rural gets its share, and otherwise keep government out of people's lives. There is a recognizable path dependency in such a politics. But a politics of grievance can easily make rural people the kindling in someone else's fire. Not only that, it can overwhelm the alternative forms of political action that have been generated in recent times in the countryside. Those forms are invariably more local and regional in scope. They are often conservative in their own way. They might be about protecting a foothills ecology against the prospect of intensive resource exploitation, or monitoring downwind air quality, or saving a short-line railway that corporate interests would have sold for scrap.[50] They might be about building something new: a theatre, a co-operative, a municipal solar installation, a relationship with a neighbouring First Nations community. Invariably they take time, energy, effective leadership, and practices of citizenship. Though they may require provincial funding or favourable legislation, they do not rely wholly on what a provincial government in Edmonton decides to do.

For the NDP government, political realism alone might dictate that the votes are too scarce to spend much time in rural Alberta before the next election. A post-rural politics can readily become disengagement; it can mean never having to *go there*. In hard times, and in the face of imagined hostility, it justifies a preference for large-scale solutions applied from the centre. But a post-rural politics can also represent a different form of engagement with its own points of connection. There is room within the NDP's focus on communities to work creatively with local authorities to tackle problems such as those having to do with housing and homelessness, affordable child care, small schools, transportation, and digital connectivity. Those problems may manifest differently than they do in the core neighbourhoods of Edmonton and Calgary, but they are no less corrosive in rural and remote communities. Likewise the focus on jobs and innovation. There is good reason to pay attention to the community-level initiatives through which people in places like Westlock and Flagstaff County continue to learn about enterprise, resilience, and their own surprising civic power. The reason is not that they are rural; it's that they might be able to help imagine the next Alberta.

The promise of the Orange Chinook is still that it might blow a fresh, warm wind across old spatial-cultural divides, power relationships, and economic disparities. The risk is that it will blow through quickly, only to be replaced by the kind of cold air mass that settles in for a long time and freezes everything it touches in place—including, in this case, a politics of grievance, a strange reliance on government, and an industrial countryside whose resources are extracted without restraint for as long as markets can be found for them.

NOTES

1   Some of the most thorough and balanced news coverage of the Bill 6 controversy can be found in the *Western Producer* (Saskatoon). See, for example, Mary MacArthur, "Bill 6 passes: Anger 'out of all proportion,' " 17 December 2015, http://www.producer.com/2015/12/bill-6-passes-anger-all-out-of-proportion/ (accessed 21 January 2017). See, for comparison, Sheila Gunn Reid, "Sign the petition: Stop Bill 6 and save Alberta farms," *Rebel Media*, n.d., http://www.therebel.media/savealbertafarms (accessed 21 January 2017). Singer Paul Brandt's "An Open Letter to Premier Notley," posted on 4 December 2015, is at https://www.facebook.com/331522040635/posts/10153162177670636/ (accessed 21 January 2017).

2   Rachel Notley, "An Open Letter to Alberta," posted 6 December 2015, at https://www.facebook.com/notes/rachel-notley/an-open-letter-to-albertans/10153682598741427 (accessed 21 January 2017).

3   James Wood, "WCB claims soar under farm safety bill," *Edmonton Journal*, 6 December 2016, A2. For background, see Shirley McDonald and Bob Barnetson, eds., *Farm Workers in Western Canada* (Edmonton: University of Alberta Press, 2016).

4   I was present as a journalist at the Jubilee Auditorium in Edmonton on the night in 1980 when the crowd chanted "Free the West, Free the West!" People wore hats that read "Republic of Western Canada." One chanted "Sieg Heil." At least one spat on an Edmonton city councillor who stood outside the auditorium holding a Canadian

flag. See my description, "Christie feeds eager flock of separatist converts," *Lethbridge Herald*, 21 November 1980.

5   Mark Lisac, *Alberta Politics Uncovered* (Edmonton: NeWest Press, 2004), 2.

6   Canadian Press, "Farm death of boy shocks members of Alberta Hutterite colony," *CBC News*, 23 November 2015, http://www.cbc.ca/news/canada/edmonton/farm-death-of-boy-shocks-members-of-alberta-hutterite-colony-1.3331336 (accessed 21 January 2017).

7   "Three sisters dead after farm accident in central Alberta," *Edmonton Journal*, 15 October 2015, http://edmontonjournal.com/news/local-news/two-children-dead-one-in-critical-condition-after-farming-accident-in-central-alberta (accessed 21 January 2017). Though farming is increasingly practised with large, expensive machinery and farm knowledge is increasingly held by technology, agriculture, in its defence, is still a rare form of livelihood in which children work with their parents and learning is intergenerational and experiential. In this, it has few remaining cognates; the closest might be traditional land-based practices in Indigenous communities.

8   I have explored this relationship in "The Political Deskilling of Rural Communities," in *Writing Off the Rural West: Globalization, Governments, and the Transformation of Rural Communities*, ed. Roger Epp and Dave Whitson, 301–24 (Edmonton: University of Alberta Press, 2001), and *We Are All Treaty People: Prairie Essays* (Edmonton: University of Alberta Press, 2008), ch. 9: "Two Albertas: Rural and Urban Trajectories."

9   Government of Alberta, Economic Development, Business Information and Research, "Regional Disparities in Alberta: Resource Package," 4 March 2002. This document was retrieved at the time by a journalist's access-to-information request.

10   Fred Stenson, "Urban v. Rural," *Alberta Views*, May 2008, 30–5.

11   Todd Babiak, "Crop the vote: Urban centres will continue to suffer as long as voter apathy reigns," *Edmonton Journal*, 16 June 2007, H5. See also Les Brost, "Hey, Ed, rope in that rural excess," *Calgary Herald*, 18 February 2008, A10.

12   Lauren Krugel, "Jason Kenney will face 'uphill battle' in bid for Alberta PC leadership: Smith," *Global News*, 5 July 2016, http://globalnews.ca/news/2805263/jason-kenney-will-face-uphill-battle-in-bid-for-alberta-pc-leadership-smith/ (accessed 21 January 2017).

13   Lisac, *Alberta Politics Uncovered*, 79.

14   That farmer is Energy Minister Margaret McCuaig-Boyd, a long-time teacher and educational administrator who has also been involved in a cow-calf operation with her husband on their farm outside of Fairview.

15   Rachel Notley, speech to the Alberta Association of Municipal Districts and Counties Annual Convention, 19 November 2015, https://www.alberta.ca/release.cfm?xID=38870513B27D5-9389-47A7-6D5B664DFEAF3197 (accessed 21 January 2017); quotations at 2 and 5.

16   These quotes are from "Speech from the Throne," *Alberta Hansard*, 29th Legislature, First Session, 15 June 2015, 7, 8.

17   "Speech from the Throne," *Alberta Hansard*, 25th Legislature, Third Session, 18 February 2003, 1, 2 (my italics).

18   "Speech from the Throne," *Alberta Hansard*, 25th Legislature, Fourth Session, 17 February 2004, 4.

19   "Speech from the Throne," *Alberta Hansard*, 26th Legislature, First Session, 2 March 2005, 9.

20   *Rural Alberta: Land of Opportunity*, Report of an MLA Steering Committee, March 2004.

21   Government of Alberta, *A Place To Grow: Alberta's Rural Development Strategy*, February 2005, 1.

22   Government of Alberta, "$100-million development fund will help kickstart innovative rural projects," Media Release, 22 March 2006, https://www.alberta.ca/release. cfm?xID=19611233BBA9A-BA09-4BF7-59F3E0CDD62E9D71 (accessed 21 January 2017).

23   Government of Alberta, Agriculture, "Report on Progress, Alberta's Rural Development Strategy," 2007, http://www1.agric.gov.ab.ca/$Department/deptdocs. nsf/all/csi12110/$FILE/progressreport.pdf (accessed 21 January 2017); see also "Update Report," 2009, at http://www1.agric.gov.ab.ca/$Department/deptdocs.nsf/all/ csi12110/$FILE/2009-Rural-Development-Strategy-Update.pdf (accessed 21 January 2017).

24   "Speech from the Throne," *Alberta Hansard*, 26th Legislature, Fourth Session, 4 February 2008, 4; "Speech from the Throne," *Alberta Hansard*, 27th Legislature, First Session, 15 April 2008, 6.

25   *Rural Alberta: Land of Opportunity*, 3.

26   The Millennium Alberta Rural Incentive Bursary was created with funds from the Canada Millennium Scholarship Fund, established by Parliament in 1998 with a $2-billion endowment, to reduce barriers to post-secondary education over ten years. It was Alberta's choice to designate rural students as the targeted beneficiaries.

27   Conference Board of Canada, "Alberta's Rural Communities: Their Economic Contribution to Alberta and Canada," prepared for Alberta Agriculture and Rural Development, November 2013, http://www1.agric.gov.ab.ca/$Department/deptdocs.nsf/ all/csi12085/$FILE/Alberta-Rural-Update.pdf (accessed 21 January 2017).

28   "Speech from the Throne," *Alberta Hansard*, 27th Legislature, Fifth Session, 7 February 2012, 3.

29   "Speech from the Throne," *Alberta Hansard*, 28th Legislature, First Session, 24 May 2012, 7 (my italics).

30   "Speech from the Throne," *Alberta Hansard*, 28th Legislature, Third Session, 17 November 2014, 4.

31   Government of Alberta, Agriculture and Rural Development, *Rural Economic Development Action Plan: An Economic Pathway for Rural Alberta*, 2014, http://open. alberta.ca/dataset/e7b93667-e6eb-43e2-a9f3-4c726b316ef6/resource/f7ff3b47-3b6e-42b2-ba04-83d0a2e06db5/download/6734329-2014-Rural-Economic-Development-Action-Plan-2014-11-03.pdf (accessed 21 January 2017).

32 In her speech at the swearing-in ceremony for her new government, for example, Rachel Notley noted: "We've built farms and rural communities that weather the toughest storms to support all of our families." See Government of Alberta, "Speech at Swearing-in Ceremony," 24 May 2015, https://www.alberta.ca/release.cfm?xID=38109E386C8C0-0B24-D917-32743CC5B8562069 (accessed 21 January 2017).

33 Rachel Notley, "State of the Province Address," Edmonton, 15 April 2016, https://www.alberta.ca/release.cfm?xID=41590B28C3B56-E600-600A-D5B848FB7DFCCD90, and "State of Province Address," Calgary, 19 October 2016, https://www.alberta.ca/release.cfm?xID=43636B3649E46-D490-C9CB-6CAB1802A1B4F274 (accessed 21 January 2017).

34 Government of Alberta, *Budget 2016, The Alberta Jobs Plan*, 14 April 2016, https://www.alberta.ca/budget-highlights.aspx (accessed 21 January 2017).

35 One good account of the "bitter" conflict between the CCF and the New Party in Alberta—the former more rural and ideological, the latter more urban, labour-based, and interested in electability—is found in Howard Leeson, *Grant Notley: The Social Conscience of Alberta*, 2nd ed. (Edmonton: University of Alberta Press, 2015), ch. 3. See also Alvin Finkel, *Working People in Alberta: A History* (Edmonton: Athabasca University Press, 2012), 163–7; Warren Caragata, *Alberta Labour: A Heritage Untold* (Toronto: Lorimer, 1979), 134–6; Anthony Mardiros, *William Irvine: The Life of a Prairie Radical* (Toronto: Lorimer, 1979), 251–2; and Winston Gereluk's interview with Reg Basken (2003) in the Alberta Labour History Institute's oral history project, at http://albertalabourhistory.org/wordpress/wp-content/uploads/2016/06/Basken.pdf (accessed 21 January 2017).

36 Leeson, *Grant Notley*, 101.

37 Alberta New Democratic Party, Task Force on the Family Farm and the Future of Rural Alberta, *Growth Strategies*, 1987.

38 Amanda Stephenson, "Alberta government hints that more carbon tax relief is coming for farmers," *Edmonton Journal*, 30 December 2016, http://edmontonjournal.com/storyline/alberta-government-hints-that-more-carbon-tax-relief-is-coming-for-farmers (accessed 21 January 2017).

39 Alberta Court of Appeal, Reference Re Electoral Divisions Statutes Amendment Act, 1993, *Dominion Law Reports* 119 (4th Series), judgment issued 24 October 1994.

40 Alberta Electoral Boundaries Commission, *Proposed Electoral Division Areas, Boundaries, and Names for Alberta: Final Report to the Speaker of the Legislative Assembly of Alberta*, June 2010; quotations from the minority position by member Allyson Jeffs at p. 29.

41 See the AAMDC Submission to the Alberta Electoral Boundaries Commission, January 2017, http://www.aamdc.com/archive/miscellaneous/1583-aamdc-submission-to-aebc/file (accessed 21 January 2017); James Wood, "Concern in rural Alberta as electoral boundary commission starts hearings," *Calgary Herald*, 9 January 2017, http://calgaryherald.com/news/politics/concern-in-rural-alberta-as-electoral-boundary-commission-starts-hearings (accessed 21 January 2017); Elise Stolte, "Edmonton angles for one more seat in the legislature," *Edmonton Journal*, 20 January 2017, http://

edmontonjournal.com/news/local-news/edmonton-angles-for-one-more-seat-in-the-legislature (accessed 21 January 2017).

42   Alberta Electoral Boundaries Commission, *Proposed Electoral Division Areas, Boundaries, and Names for Alberta*, Final Report, October 2017, quotations at 14, 27. Legislation to implement the Commission's recommendations was passed in December 2017.

43   *Proposed Electoral Division Areas, Boundaries, and Names for Alberta*, Appendix A, 67.

44   Rachel Notley, Speech to the Alberta Association of Municipal Districts and Counties 2016 Fall Convention, 17 November 2016, https://www.alberta.ca/release.cfm?xID=448528D1C7793-A47E-95DE-7F7827D9F954F9FA (accessed 21 January 2017).

45   Katherine Cramer, *The Politics of Resentment: Rural Consciousness in Wisconsin and the Rise of Scott Walker* (Chicago: University of Chicago Press, 2016), 89, See also "How rural resentment helps explain the surprising victory of Donald Trump," *Washington Post*, 13 November 2016.

46   Cramer, *The Politics of Resentment*, 6. Cramer's account resonates with my own observations in *We Are All Treaty People*, 90–2, 116-18. See also Robert Wuthnow's recent book, *The Left Behind: Decline and Rage in Rural America* (Princeton, NJ: Princeton University Press, 2018).

47   Don Braid, "Rural Alberta meets the government from outer space," *Calgary Herald*, 3 December 2015, http://calgaryherald.com/news/politics/braid-rural-alberta-meets-the-government-from-outer-space (accessed 21 January 2017). The musician quoted is George Canyon.

48   Emma Graney, "Alberta ministers booed over climate change plan by rural leaders," *Edmonton Journal*, 17 November 2016, http://edmontonjournal.com/news/politics/alberta-ministers-booed-over-climate-change-plan-by-rural-leaders (accessed 21 January 2017).

49   Statistics Canada, "Population, urban and rural, by province and territory," 2011, http://www.statcan.gc.ca/tables-tableaux/sum-som/l01/cst01/demo62j-eng.htm (accessed 21 January 2017). See also the survey chapter on Alberta by Lars Hallstrom, Jennifer Stonechild, and Wilissa Reist in the Canadian Rural Revitalization Foundation's *State of Rural Canada 2015*, http://sorc.crrf.ca/ (accessed 21 January 2017).

50   See, for example, Roger Epp, "Off-Road Democracy: The Politics of Land, Water, and Community in Alberta," in *How Canadians Communicate IV: Media and Politics*, ed. David Taras and Christopher Waddell, 259–79 (Edmonton: Athabasca University Press, 2012); Darin Barney, " 'That's No Way to Run a Railroad': The Battle River Branchline and the Politics of Technology in Rural Alberta," in *Social Transformation in Rural Canada*, ed. John Parkins and Maureen Reed, 309–26 (Vancouver: UBC Press, 2013).

V
NOTLEY'S GOVERNING STYLE

A League of Their Own: Alberta's Women Party Leaders

Lori Williams

The 2015 Alberta election was unprecedented in many ways, but particularly with respect to the successes and failures of female political leaders that preceded it. The leaders and events analyzed here include Alison Redford's premiership and resignation, Danielle Smith's party leadership, floor-crossing, and subsequent defeat, and the ascent of Rachel Notley as premier. All raise questions about the challenges and opportunities faced by women in political leadership, both in Alberta and elsewhere.

This analysis will focus on key factors affecting these leaders, including the histories and internal dynamics of their respective political parties, the debates in which they were involved, and their responses to various controversies.[1] The 2015 election highlighted gendered expectations around political behaviour, issues, and personal attributes as amplified in traditional and social media. All this has exposed obstacles and opportunities faced by women in politics, and particularly those in political leadership. These will be used to illuminate the challenges that confront female political leaders, the constraints and possibilities they negotiate, the risks of failure they face, and the innovations that have yielded success.

By focusing on the three Alberta women who came within reach of the premiership, I will trace how some leaders have built winning strategies by combining the lessons of the past with creative approaches to politics, and conclude with some of the challenges that remain.

Challenges and Opportunities for Women in Politics

The world of politics was created by men, and the standards of political practice have historically been defined by male politicians. This means that the role models, practitioners, and norms associated with the notion of a "good politician" are primarily male. Of course, gender stereotypes by their very nature do not necessarily apply to all women and men. However, they do tend to create expectations of male and female political candidates that have significant implications for political success. Political judgments made by voters, contributors, the political community, and the media all tend to focus on and exaggerate counter-stereotypical behaviour, creating pressure to conform to expectations around gender norms.[2]

Stereotypical traits associated with men are also identified with politics; these include strength, toughness, assertiveness, independence, autonomy, competitiveness, decisiveness, self-confidence, aggression, forcefulness, and emotional detachment.[3] Politics rewards adversarial power seeking, ambition, seeking credit for accomplishments, and detached, logical analysis. The hierarchical organization of politics (e.g., within party structures and governments) is also more often associated with masculinity.[4] The language and coverage of politics tends to focus on authoritativeness, aggression, conflict, battles, war (e.g., "war room," "war chest"), and winning.[5] Those considered best suited for political office, and most successful political practitioners, make effective use of stereotypically masculine characteristics.

The stereotypical traits associated with women are less compatible with these traditional understandings of politics. The positives include co-operation, collaboration, orientation toward others, and networking.[6] Research shows that women tend to be consultative, focusing more on finding solutions than getting credit for their accomplishments, and less concerned with their own ambitions than with the impact that a decision has on those affected by it.[7] Some women are uncomfortable with the expectation that they raise their personal profiles or connect their names and ambitions to their initiatives, a factor that may impede their success as political leaders.[8]

Stereotypes about gender-appropriate behaviour, while significant, don't tell the whole story. There are also expectations about which issues are better suited to female and male politicians. Research shows that men are seen as having more affinity with and support for things like national security, foreign affairs, military spending, finance, and free trade. Women, on the other hand, are seen as having more interest and competence regarding issues like health care, education, and social welfare.[9]

This can be an advantage for female candidates in elections or races where issues associated with women's perceived competencies dominate. Leaders, however, are expected to have competence on all issues a government faces, which can make it more difficult for women to contest leadership positions.

Nice, But Not Too Nice . . .

Gender stereotypes do not simply describe masculine and feminine characteristics and issues, they prescribe often unconscious expectations of how men and women ought to behave, and as such are often difficult to identify or counteract.[10] Benevolent sexism is subtle, affirming women's abilities and virtues within traditional or stereotypical parameters, and rewarding or protecting women who conform to them.[11] Conversely, benevolent sexism generates discomfort or negative judgments of women who do not conform. The former sees women as warm, likeable, less threatening and nice—but incompetent; the latter as capable but cold.[12] Those who are less conformist may be evaluated as competent, but less likeable, and labelled with a host of negative epithets. Female political leaders, then, "must be simultaneously perceived as competent and likeable, and these two perceptions may conflict."[13] On the other hand, when they focus on feminine issues, female politicians tend to be perceived as more competent, and this can sometimes be put to political advantage.[14]

Gender stereotypes and norms are reflected and exaggerated in traditional and social media, which tend to emphasize the appearance and personal lives of non-traditional candidates, including women and minorities. A woman's hair, clothing, makeup, weight, wrinkles, voice, sexuality, and relationships are considered newsworthy.[15] Such emphasis on women's appearance can reinforce the belief that their primary value is aesthetic, and divert attention from their intelligence and competence.[16] Women's family status—as opposed to men's—is more often mentioned by the media, raising questions about their ability to balance their political and personal responsibilities. Since scrutiny of political leaders is more intense than for other politicians, the focus on female leaders' personal lives can magnify doubts about their suitability.

Women tend to have less and more limited access to resources conducive to political success. These include money, networks, political contacts, leisure time, and experience in the adversarial culture of traditional politics.[17] Often conducted in a winner-take-all manner, politics focuses on scoring "gotcha" points at the expense of substantive debate.[18] Those who prefer collaboration and co-operation may prefer to work in the background, choosing not to run for office, much less party leadership. Another factor at play is what is often described as the confidence gap: women are more likely to undervalue their suitability to and qualifications for politics, even when they possess comparable qualifications and skills as their male counterparts.[19]

The Players: Alberta's Women Party Leaders

Alberta has seen three women closely contest the premiership, Alison Redford, Danielle Smith, and Rachel Notley, two of whom became premier. In this section, I will connect the hurdles faced by female politicians to the aspirations, challenges, and innovations associated with each of these women, and explore the lessons learned from their experience.

Alison Redford

Alison Redford was elected to Alberta's legislature on 3 March 2008 in the riding of Calgary Elbow, the seat long held by Ralph Klein. Premier Ed Stelmach chose her as his justice minister and attorney general. She came to government with experience as a human rights lawyer and as a policy advisor to prime ministers Joe Clark and Brian Mulroney, and she aspired to rejuvenate the progressive strain of the provincial Progressive Conservative Party. This positioned her to overcome some of the institutional barriers commonly faced by women, as well as the confidence gap. She self-identified as a Peter Lougheed conservative, crediting his mentorship and hearkening back to his government's willingness to invest in the province.

Lougheed's was an activist government; he established human rights legislation, bought an airline to serve Alberta's northern communities, created an oil company (Alberta Energy Company), raised royalties, invested

LORI WILLIAMS

in health care, education, and the arts, and professionalized the civil service. Among Lougheed's political talents was a keen sense of the importance of collaboration and consultation, of constantly communicating with voters in their communities, with riding associations, and with his caucus. Indeed, many of his policy initiatives originated within caucus.[20] Such consultation and networking tools are often associated with women's leadership styles. This, and the fact that Redford claimed to be inspired by Lougheed's leadership, enhanced her appeal to voters hoping for more democratic governance.

By the time Alison Redford rose to political leadership, the commitment and engagement of Lougheed's caucus had given way to indolence and entitlement. PC candidates were primarily seen as party members. During Ralph Klein's premiership most identified simply as members of "Ralph's team," and if their names appeared on campaign signs, they were dwarfed by that of the premier. As members of the "natural governing party," they were largely unaccountable to voters, who tended to focus more on the premier or the party than individual candidates. Some MLAs didn't bother attending legislative sittings or committee meetings, as illustrated by the infamous "do nothing committees" allowing MLAs to pad their salaries without the inconvenience of attending meetings. This culture also permeated cabinet. Many cabinet ministers left the work to their deputies. If they attended cabinet meetings, many arrived unprepared, some not even sober.[21] This may have been the genesis of Redford's apparent disdain for some of her caucus colleagues, and likely fueled her leadership ambitions. She thought Alberta was due for a change, and when Ed Stelmach resigned on 25 January 2011, she entered the race to be the agent of that change.

Redford launched her leadership campaign with the support of outsiders—teachers, nurses, union supporters, women, and even some aligned with other parties. Many joined the PC Party in order to vote for its next leader, and premier. Dubbed opportunists or "two-minute Tories," these supporters won Redford the race. Her strategy appeared to hinge on broadening the support for her policies and her party. Appealing to voters outside the fiscal-conservative base, Redford appeared poised to resurrect the PC's legendary big tent, building a new coalition of progressives and conservatives. She promised a more transparent, accountable government. Many hoped she would exercise the kinds of leadership qualities and embrace issues associated with women and the Lougheed years. The breadth of her support suggested a capacity for building consensus, and she promised action on issues such as health care, education, and social welfare.

However, Redford's ascent to the PC leadership was not a resounding victory. The front-runner in the race was Gary Mar, who led the first ballot with 41 per cent; at 19 per cent, Alison Redford came in a distant second. A second vote was held with a preferential ballot, and while Mar maintained his lead with 43 per cent, Redford jumped to 37 per cent, and Doug Horner came in third with 20 per cent. With Horner out of the race, the second choices marked on his ballots were counted, and Redford pulled ahead with 51 per cent to Mar's 49 per cent. Though Redford won, she was many voters' second choice.[22]

In the 2012 election campaign Redford promised to transform the party from within, a time-honoured PC strategy that had sustained it in power for four decades. Her government was threatened by concerns about the growing debt, reports of intimidation and bullying of health care workers, and publicity around the "do nothing committees." She gestured toward a better future with the "Not Your Father's PC Party" slogan, yet welcomed the endorsement of that party's founder, Peter Lougheed. Many Albertans wanted better from their government, but most had only known one governing party, and were cautious about entrusting the reins of power to neophytes. As election day approached, Danielle Smith's Wildrose Party was rising in the polls, threatening to topple Redford's government. Then a series of missteps derailed their momentum. Already squeamish about the Wildrose Party's social conservatism, voters recoiled at the anti-gay, racially insensitive views expressed by Wildrose candidates. The ensuing controversy was worsened by Smith's refusal to censure these candidates. On 23 April 2012, Redford emerged victorious with 61 seats; she had been on the brink of losing government, but in the end lost only 5 seats. Smith gained 14 seats, winning a total of 17, and so became leader of the Official Opposition.[23]

Redford had become the fourth woman in Canadian history to be voted premier in a general election. Her premiership began with promise as she eliminated pay bonuses for committee work and introduced greater transparency and accountability by requiring the disclosure of some public servants' expense records and salaries. Her rise to power rested on a new coalition drawing support from across the spectrum with promised investments for teachers, union supporters, health-care workers, and universities.

LORI WILLIAMS

The collaborative tone of her campaign tapped into gendered expectations around teamwork and consultation, and most expected this to extend into her government.

Within a year, however, Redford's new-found supporters felt betrayed by a series of broken campaign promises. Facing declines in energy revenues, a so-called "bitumen bubble," Redford cut spending, and worse.[24] She froze wages and suspended the right to arbitration for the province's largest public-sector union, cut university funding by 7.2 per cent, and engaged in negotiation tactics that infuriated teachers and health-care workers.[25] Her imposition of penalties for driving with a blood-alcohol level above .05 angered rural Albertans who didn't have the option of taking a taxi home. And she transgressed gender norms by appearing emotionally detached, overly independent, and self-confident to the point of arrogance.

The austerity imposed on Albertans under Redford's government stood in sharp contrast to the premier's own extravagant use of taxpayers' money. She spent $45,000 for herself and an aide to travel to South Africa for Nelson Mandela's funeral, rather than flying with the prime minister's entourage for a fraction of the cost. As criticism mounted, she persisted in defending her South Africa trip, and when she finally apologized, and only under further pressure said she would reimburse the province, the damage was irreparable. Moreover, she used government planes for non-government travel, excluded caucus members from her flights, and incurred exorbitant expenses, salaries, and severances for her staff, leading Auditor General Merwan Saher to attribute her abuse of government resources to an "aura of power."[26]

Redford's leadership bid had begun with the support of only one caucus member, Art Johnston. This needn't have been an enduring liability, especially since the 2012 election injected new talent into her caucus. But unlike her mentor Peter Lougheed, Redford failed to connect with caucus, thereby severing a crucial source of support. Christy Clark, who also won the leadership of the BC Liberal Party with the backing of only one caucus member, swiftly moved to broaden her support within the party.[27] By contrast, Redford alienated her base, failing to connect with her old caucus, or draw from her new one, depriving her government of considerable talent, insight, and support.[28]

By March 2014 simmering caucus dissent erupted. Len Webber, already planning to leave provincial politics to run for the federal Conservatives, quit, citing Redford's anger. "She's just really not a nice lady," he said. "I cannot work for an individual who treats people poorly."[29] His use of the term "nice lady" echoed a well-documented intolerance of aggression and anger in female politicians. Next, Donna Kennedy-Glans, an associate minister, resigned her position and left the party to sit as an independent, saying her departure was "not just about the leadership," but also about whether change from within the party was possible.[30] And at least ten other MLAs met to express their dissatisfaction with Redford's leadership, threatening to sit as independents.

Two days later, on 19 March 2014, Redford announced that she would resign. She had begun and ended her leadership appealing for support from outside her party and even her province. Her leadership on a national energy strategy (ratified after she left office) yielded national and international support, and was one of her greatest achievements. But it wasn't enough to counter her growing alienation from voters and her party. While she enjoyed some success advocating for Alberta's interests on the national front, dashed hopes led betrayed supporters to lash out.

While gender stereotypes often inhibit women's electoral prospects, in Redford's case, these stereotypes initially worked to her advantage. Studies have shown that gender stereotypes tend to hurt women when they campaign on "masculine issues," but can help them when elections are focused on "feminine issues," or when women's outsider status signals positive change.[31] Redford promised a renewed government and rallied support by pledging improvements on issues where women are often viewed as more competent: education, health care, and social welfare. Voters assessed her as competent and worthy of their confidence in these areas, and felt betrayed and abandoned when she acted against these interests. Many supporters hoped that as a woman and a proponent of Lougheed's legacy, Redford would be a collaborative, consultative leader. Her leadership, however, centred more on ideas and issues, and less on the political foundations and collaboration needed to bring them to life. Initial signs of collaboration and consensus building gave way to a leadership style seen as antagonistic, cold, and dictatorial.

LORI WILLIAMS

Women politicians tend to be perceived as more honest and trustworthy than their male counterparts, and less likely to participate in political corruption.[32] This may have made voters more inclined to embrace Redford's pledge to enhance transparency and accountability. She raised expectations for government support, leadership style, and trust. When she failed to meet these expectations, the censure was doubly harsh; she had reneged on promises *and* violated gender norms. This could at least partly explain why Redford was vilified for her use of government airplanes, when Ralph Klein escaped censure for much worse (including flying a government airplane to Nova Scotia for a golf game). Of course Klein was skilled in employing an elusive "common touch," and was quick to admit mistakes and apologize. Redford lacked such a personal connection, and her apologies, when they were offered at all, were too little, too late. Albertans had grown impatient with the PC's arrogance and entitlement, and had entrusted a woman to govern differently.

In her rise to leadership, Redford managed to navigate the institutional barriers that normally inhibit women's political success. She generated public support to compensate for whatever she lacked in networks and connections, using gender expectations and her outsider status as assets rather than liabilities. And Redford didn't appear to suffer the effects of the confidence gap whereby women self-assess as less qualified than men with similar experience.

As criticism grew, however, the public began to perceive her as arrogant and entitled. In media coverage she wasn't often described as likeable, though many who met her personally found her intelligent, approachable, and even charming. She appeared to focus on competence rather than likeability, leaving little to balance against criticisms of her performance. Media coverage of her personal life was limited, with two notable exceptions. During the leadership race, her mother passed away just before the leaders' debate. Her heartfelt appreciation of her mother's legacy and her determination to continue with the planned debate earned public sympathy and respect. When the issue of flying her daughter and her daughter's friends on government planes emerged, the media coverage was less favourable.

Redford could have benefitted from a more collaborative relationship with the media. She failed to take advantage of opportunities to shore up support through effective communication with her party or with the public.

As she faced a growing barrage of criticism from voters, the media, and her own party, she responded by becoming increasingly isolated, seen in news footage emerging from black-glassed vehicles, or responding abruptly to media queries. She surrounded herself with a revolving door of staff, and had only limited contact with her caucus. During the 2013 floods in Southern Alberta flood, she earned praise from some, but failed to collaborate closely with Opposition leader Danielle Smith, whose constituency included High River, the most devastated area in the province. Redford's response to the flood was eclipsed by Calgary mayor Naheed Nenshi, who was compared to a rock star as he provided continuous updates and reassurances to Calgarians. Redford came to politics without extensive media experience, and this hampered her ability to effectively communicate her leadership or policies through the media. Instead of connecting with potential supporters in her party or the public, she retreated. Redford's leadership became increasingly focused on control, and her caucus feared being seen with members of the media.[33]

Alison Redford was initially a beneficiary of gender expectations. Facing high hopes created by her promises and her gender, her failure raised questions about the prospects for female political leaders. After her departure, in a conversation intended to promote more women in politics, a man closely associated with Redford's campaign suggested that Albertans weren't ready for another woman premier. Redford's defeat, however, owed as much to the PC Party's checkered history as it did to her leadership, as was detailed by Duane Bratt in chapter 2.

Danielle Smith

Danielle Smith rose to the Wildrose Party leadership with a background in economics, politics, and journalism. Her previous experience with elected office was less extensive than in other areas. She was elected to the Calgary Board of Education in 1998, but this board was dissolved by Learning Minister Lyle Oberg eleven months later due to dysfunctional infighting. She worked as a journalist and lobbyist, championing business interests and fiscal conservatism. A longtime PC supporter, Smith became disillusioned with the fiscal record of the Stelmach government and defected to the Wildrose Alliance Party in 2008, ascending to its leadership in 2009. Her communication skills, her public profile, and her laser focus on the

LORI WILLIAMS

governing PCs' culture of entitlement and corruption catapulted her party out of the political wilderness, from a single legislative seat in 2009 into a serious contender in the 2012 election. Smith was media savvy, was often described as telegenic, and received generally positive media coverage.

During the 2012 election campaign, Smith challenged the PC government's history of economic mismanagement and entitlement, and proposed credible alternatives. Polls predicted that she was on the brink of victory when a series of blunders diverted voters' attention away from anger at the PCs to doubts about Wildrose. When public outcry erupted over Wildrose candidate Allan Hunsperger's blogpost claiming gays and lesbians would suffer eternity in a "lake of fire," Smith invoked a libertarian defence of personal freedom, saying that her party "won't be legislating on contentious social issues," and "we accept that people have a broad diversity of viewpoints, but the way we get along is that we focus on the things on which we can agree."[34]

The party's fortunes suffered another blow when Ron Leech, the Wildrose candidate for Calgary Greenway who had previously penned a *Calgary Herald* editorial opposing same-sex marriage, told a multicultural radio station that he could best represent his ethnically diverse constituency because, as a Caucasian, he could speak for the entire community and not any particular ethnic group. When informed of Leech's comments, Smith replied: "I think every candidate puts forward their best argument for why they should be the person who can best represent the community."[35] Hunsperger's and Leech's comments, Smith's responses to them, and her public questioning of climate change were blamed for blowing the Wildrose lead in the polls, and ultimately for losing the 2012 election.

Social conservatism has consistently posed problems for conservative parties at the federal and provincial level. It had been blamed for the failures of the federal Reform and Alliance Parties, and when Stephen Harper won the leadership of the newly united federal Conservative Party, he saw that distancing his party from such issues was key to winning and governing. He imposed strict controls on his caucus, with threats of harsh discipline, and decisively rejected legislating on controversial moral issues. He was criticized for being dictatorial and controlling, but he was effective at containing internal divisions and suppressing socially conservative views.

In an attempt to avoid recurring controversies around social conservatism, Smith sought support for more inclusive policies. In the fall of 2013, with Smith riding high in the polls, Wildrose MLAs voted unanimously at their AGM in favour of equality for gays and lesbians, and against the elimination of Alberta's Human Rights Commission. Her caucus even rejected "conscience rights" for health-care workers that would have allowed them to opt out of providing medical services based on their personal beliefs.[36]

Smith's popularity owed much to her scathing campaign against the "entitled" PCs, by which she steadily eroded the governing party's brand. However, she suffered a setback when Jim Prentice became premier in September 2014. Seeking seats in the legislature for himself and two of his cabinet ministers, Prentice called by-elections in four constituencies for 27 October. Smith overestimated her party's support, and invested heavily in a failed attempt to defeat the new premier in Calgary Foothills. The PCs won all four seats, though by just over 300 votes in Calgary West. Had she funnelled more resources into that race, Smith likely would have picked up a seat. Smith nonetheless valiantly spun the PC sweep, saying it was not a blank cheque, and that Albertans had put Prentice on probation. But internal party divisions began to surface again.[37] At the Wildrose AGM in November, amid doubts about whether she could lead the party to victory, party members voted *against* equal rights for all minority groups regardless of sexual orientation.[38] This reversed the position adopted a year earlier, and exposed an irreconcilable rift between the leader's principles and her party's policy. It was now evident that Smith could no longer contain her party's internal fractures—popularity was too fragile a foundation to sustain internal control. Her leadership was over.

Rather than continue in such an untenable position, or resign as leader, Smith led eight other party members to cross the floor, joining Jim Prentice's PCs on 17 December. This shocked Albertans, along with members of both parties, who remembered Smith's castigation of two other Wildrose MLAs who had defected just three weeks earlier, on 26 November. Smith had vowed there would be no more floor-crossings, and that she would continue to hold the government's feet to the fire. The floor-crossing appeared more opportunistic than principled, violating expectations that women politicians are more trustworthy. It was now Smith's brand that was tarnished. When she ran for the PC nomination in her riding the following March, she was repudiated on the same day the Wildrose Party elected Brian Jean as their new leader.[39] It now appeared that her political career was over.

Though many women politicians struggle to overcome gender stereotypes, the media rely less on such norms when female candidates have an established public profile.[40] Smith's political and journalistic record had established her reputation, and her experience had sharpened her skills as a leader and communicator. She largely escaped the typical focus on female politicians' appearance and personal life, with the exception of those who described her as attractive, young, and telegenic.[41] The one time her personal life became an issue, when a PC volunteer tweeted a question about her support for family policies since she was herself childless, it worked to her advantage. Alison Redford, in a rare show of support, expressed her horror and apologized "woman to woman." Both Redford and Smith were credited for rising above an issue that often plagues political women.[42]

Smith's approach to leadership was widely seen as consultative and conciliatory. Formidable in opposition, she focused on issues and policies, avoiding personal attacks. In contrast to Redford, who was harshly judged for being controlling or angry, Smith demonstrated no real anger in her leadership style.[43] Anger can be a particular liability for female politicians,[44] and Smith's collaborative leadership approach enhanced her public appeal. Unfortunately, it ultimately jeopardized her support. Her search for consensus undermined the strength and decisiveness demanded of political leaders.

Institutional barriers were not a significant factor in Smith's rise to leadership. Her public profile, media presence, and policy background more than compensated for any lack of money or party connections. Soon after she joined the Wildrose Alliance Party, she was recruited to run for the leadership. Party officials recognized that her talent and media profile could improve the party's brand. However, internal party dynamics were a persistent, and eventually fatal, problem. Such divisiveness would have been a challenge for any leader, but was a particular liability given her consultative, collaborative leadership style.

Despite her less-controlling manner, Smith's popularity was a powerful tool for constraining her party's ideologues. Most party members recognized that Smith was their best hope for governing, and supported initiatives to prevent a recurrence of the 2012 "bozo eruptions" (like Hunsperger's and Leech's comments) The ideologues within the Wildrose Party were persuaded to subordinate their principles for a better chance in the next election. However, whenever Smith's poll numbers dipped, her critics began to agitate and erode her support.

Smith's facility with the media was one of her greatest assets. She managed to appear competent and warm, often described as likeable, but also as a capable leader and formidable opponent. During debates and in the legislature, she landed tough questions and challenges without transgressing gender norms. She often smiled while delivering a critique. She was evaluated as nice, but ultimately was too conciliatory, lacking the ability to control her fractious party. This, combined with her stances on certain issues, which seemed to defy gender norms, made it more difficult for voters to trust her with government. Her fiscal conservatism raised doubts about her commitment to health care and education, as her opponents often pointed out. Perhaps the most problematic issue was her failure to protect vulnerable groups.[45] Whether because of her libertarianism or her inability to restrain intolerance within her party, Albertans weren't confident that a Wildrose government would protect the rights of minorities, or could be trusted to advance the interests of all Albertans.

Rachel Notley

Rachel Notley's political roots stretched back to her early childhood. Her father, Grant Notley, became leader of the Alberta NDP in 1968, when Rachel was four, and served in the legislature from 1971 until his death in a plane crash in 1984. Her mother, Sandy Wilkinson Notley, set an example of political engagement, taking Rachel to her first protest when she was ten. Rachel Notley was active in politics while attending Osgoode Hall Law School in Toronto, providing community legal services, co-founding an Osgoode NDP club, and participating in the 1989 federal NDP leadership race. After graduation she advocated for workers seeking compensation in Alberta, and worked for the BC government as a health-and-safety officer and in Attorney General Ujjal Dosanjh's office.[46] She earned a reputation as a gifted communicator, able to make people feel understood, but was also a persuasive advocate, able to find common ground between adversaries.[47]

Notley was elected to the Alberta legislature in 2008, as part of a tiny, four-member NDP caucus that was remarkably effective in opposition.

Moving beyond mere criticism of the government, they proposed better alternatives, and their challenges were often more compelling because they were less negative than other opposition parties. Notley was elected as leader of her party on 18 October 2014, and as premier less than seven months later.

Notley encountered a rare set of opportunities in the lead-up to the May 2015 election, as detailed in the chapters by Melanee Thomas, Duane Bratt, and Keith Brownsey. Capitalizing on every opportunity, she rarely set a foot wrong. She anticipated an early election call and moved quickly to recruit candidates. When she did make mistakes, she was quick to take responsibility and correct them. For example, upon discovering a billion-dollar costing error in the NDP's proposed budget, she immediately acknowledged and fixed the error. When premier Prentice said, "Alberta is not an NDP province," she agreed, stating that "Alberta is not an NDP province. It's not a PC province. It's not a Wildrose province. Alberta belongs to Albertans."[48]

Notley's political dexterity was particularly evident in the televised leader's debate on 23 April. She was articulate and lightning-quick on her feet, demonstrating command of the issues. She managed a rare combination of toughness, competence, and likeability. She smiled as she challenged Prentice's claims, and even winked at the camera. When Prentice claimed that Notley was planning a 20 per cent corporate tax, she interrupted:

Notley: What are you talking about? Our proposed corporate tax rate is 12 per cent. I'm not sure who's briefing you but I just do need to clarify that that's absolutely incorrect.

Prentice: 10 per cent to 12—I know the math is difficult, but 10 per cent to 12 percent is a 20 per cent increase.

Notley: You said a 20 per cent tax, you didn't say increase. I just need to make clear we are not proposing a 20 per cent corporate tax. That would be ridiculous.[49]

Prentice had made an awkward dig at the NDP's fiscal plan miscalculation, but it badly backfired. Twitter exploded with #mathishard and other hashtags ridiculing Prentice's blunder. Rather than objecting to his remarks about math, Notley pivoted to a populist defence against elitism. Later, when the subject of oil and gas royalties came up, she challenged the PC government's treatment of the issue by asserting that "Albertans are always told, 'Don't worry your pretty little heads.' "

The debate played poorly for Prentice, who was seen as elitist, patronizing and sexist, and the PCs dropped in the polls, as Janet Brown shows in chapter 4. In this case, benevolent sexism worked against Prentice. Male politicians are negatively evaluated if they are too harsh or critical of women, because women are perceived as less competitive and less aggressive, and such attacks on them are therefore seen as unfair.[50] Notley herself declined to call Prentice's comments sexist or condescending. When asked about it by reporters she replied that "NDP math means that those who can afford it—wealthy corporations and individuals—would pay 'a little bit more' to ensure that Albertans get the health and education they deserve." She focused on the government's treatment of voters, asserting that "Albertans sometimes feel that they're being talked down to by their government. . . . And I think that's what they're looking to change."[51]

When the media projected that Rachel Notley's NDP would form government on 15 May 2015, Don Martin, in CTV's Calgary studio, pronounced that "she has the royal jelly." She had toppled the PC's nearly forty-four-year dynasty, and jumped from 4 seats in the legislature to 54 of its 87 seats. Following her win, Notley drew on her considerable skills and the experience of others as she got down to the work of governing—a daunting task after more than four decades of PC rule. Her approach was characteristically pragmatic, collaborative, and consultative. At the press conference announcing her Climate Leadership Plan, she shared the stage with some unlikely allies: industry executives, environmental and Indigenous leaders. Notley had drawn from the expertise and won the endorsement of traditional adversaries: Canadian Natural Resources, Suncor, Cenovus, and Shell, along with the Canadian Association of Petroleum Producers—while also securing the support of environmental advocates such as Greenpeace.[52]

Sharing the microphone was also a feature of Notley's leadership when the Fort McMurray wildfire descended on Northern Alberta (described by Kevin Taft and Chase Remillard and Sheridan McVean in their chapters). A mandatory evacuation order displaced almost 90,000 residents who needed information on the availability of services and what was happening to their homes. She updated Albertans with at least two news briefings a day, at which she was joined by various experts, Opposition leader Brian Jean (whose house had been destroyed by the fire), Municipal Affairs Minister Danielle Larivee (who had survived the 2011 Slave Lake fire), Wood Buffalo mayor Melissa Blake, fire chief Darby Allen, and others. She conducted regular telephone town halls with evacuated residents, included Brian Jean in daily briefings, and visited For McMurray personally while limiting media fanfare. She also put social media to effective use. Her leadership was widely praised, including by the leader of the Opposition, whom she had allowed to visit the city during the evacuation. Danielle Smith described Notley's communication during this event as "brilliant," and a welcome contrast to Alison Redford's approach during the June 2013 floods.[53] Notley expressed confidence in the courage, compassion, and generosity of Albertans, and choked back tears when she spoke of the disaster's only two fatalities, killed in a traffic accident while fleeing the fire. She assured Albertans that "we have your backs."[54] Unlike many politicians who crave the limelight, Notley shone a light on Albertans.

On the national stage, Notley promoted interprovincial co-operation in support of a national energy strategy. She rejected anti-federalist rhetoric, presenting herself and her province as a partner and leader, especially on balancing the environment and the economy. Her preference was to work collaboratively with other provinces, but she could also be blunt. At Notley's first Council of the Federation meeting, Saskatchewan premier Brad Wall accused Quebec of trying to veto future projects, criticizing Central and Eastern Canada for taking transfer payments funded by the economies of the West. Notley admonished Wall, and spoke of the importance of getting negotiations back on track rather than "standing in a corner and having a tantrum."[55] She asserted that "relationships among the provinces will only be developed through mature consensus-based dialogue. It's not about showboating."[56] Even at her toughest, she left the door open for co-operation, as seen in her advocacy for pipelines (discussed below).

Notley demonstrated her ability to listen and compromise on a number of issues. One of her campaign promises had been to increase Alberta's minimum wage to $15 an hour, but in response to concerns raised from the business community, she agreed to phase it in more slowly. She promised a royalty review to ensure that Albertans received a fair return from energy revenues, and when the review panel did not recommend an expected increase in royalties, she focused on the proposed improvements in fairness and production incentives.[57]

There have of course been missteps. Perhaps the most damaging was her government's failure to effectively consult and communicate with rural Albertans over Bill 6, the Enhanced Protection for Farm and Ranch Workers Act (discussed in Gillian Steward's chapter). This legislation was intended to bring Alberta in line with the rest of the country and protect farm workers under occupational health and safety and workers compensation legislation, but government representatives made critical errors in meetings with farm groups fuelling fears, distrust, anger, and protests. This was an inexplicable blunder, especially given Notley's childhood roots in rural Alberta and her years of experience with workplace safety and workers compensation. Perhaps so focused on principle, she may have forgotten the importance of process. In response to the backlash, and after further consultation, the bill was amended to clarify that family members and unpaid workers were exempt from the rules.[58] However, the anger in many rural communities has yet to subside, and this will pose a persistent challenge for her government. In another misstep, Notley's decision to ban Ezra Levant's Rebel Media from attending government news conferences—they were not a "journalistic source," as she put it—was criticized for contravening her promises of government accountability. She reversed the decision and apologized within days, saying she had heard from Albertans.[59]

As Notley ascended to the premiership, she appeared to have found the Goldilocks zone for a female political leader: not too tough, not too soft . . . She was depicted as tough and feisty, escaping more pejorative descriptors like "strident" or "angry." She was described in terms that rarely go together for female politicians, including capable, bright, and knowledgeable, while also being approachable, unpretentious, and down-to-earth. She was seen as politically savvy, yet sincere, honest, and trustworthy. She was characterized as capable but compassionate.[60]

As discussed earlier, many women are uncomfortable with the competitive, adversarial cut and thrust of politics, and indeed Notley herself has resisted heckling in the legislature. But she seemed to thrive in debates about ideas and policies, energized by advocating for her beliefs and for Albertans. One of her advisers said, "She just comes right back at you. She is spring loaded to be an effective debater."[61] Notley has performed ably on issues considered soft or feminine, but has defied expectations for women (and NDP leaders) with her support for business, the oil industry, and pipelines. She is in the news on jobs and the economy more often than her finance and labour ministers combined. She clearly has command of a variety of subjects, deftly navigating complex files.

She has faced fewer institutional barriers than most female leaders. Immersed in politics and the party from childhood, her political acumen and connections run deep. Notley does not appear to lack confidence, but her confidence has grown from experience, and she recognizes when advice and support are needed. When she first entered the legislature she was quite intimidated, relying heavily on former leader Brian Mason's experience and presence. She was nonetheless her party's critic on twelve different cabinet portfolios in a lean NDP caucus, giving her a strong foundation in the substantive issues of government.[62]

Notley's ability to communicate through various media has charted new territory. She seems able to reach through the camera to connect with viewers. During the Fort McMurray wildfire, her media presence was sensitive, informative, and reassuring. She has often managed to turn the words and attitudes of others to her advantage, as seen in her responses to Jim Prentice and others. Notley has also skillfully employed the time-honoured strategy of using humour to deflect attacks, and to appear less threatening and more likeable.[63] When Wildrose candidate Rick Strankman invited voters to a pie auction, suggesting they "BYWP (Bring Your Wife's Pie)," Notley quipped, "It's clear he has a sweet tooth, but he needs a wisdom tooth."[64]

Social media has been particularly challenging for Notley and her government. She and female ministers like Marg McQuaig-Boyd have been frequent targets of cyberbullies. Online videos have portrayed gleeful golfers driving their carts into posters featuring Notley's image, and depicted her in the crosshairs of a gun. Although she has often declined to respond to such vitriol, when she has commented she has appealed to Albertans' better natures, saying such behaviour does not represent Alberta.

Rachel Notley's government is noticeably different from its predecessors. This is partly due to her leadership and partly to the composition of her party. She continues to be unpretentious, down to earth, and the antithesis of elitist. For example, at a cabinet retreat in Banff she declined, unlike previous premiers, to occupy the only deluxe room available. A veteran columnist who has analyzed seven Alberta premiers, observed that she earns loyalty and support through competence and warmth. Unlike under previous premiers, including Stelmach and Redford, there is no apparent fear of the leader.[65]

Notley's experience has equipped her well to overcome the confidence gap experienced by prospective female recruits. She understands that women need to be asked to run more than once, and that they need support as they campaign and work in the legislature. The high proportion (47 per cent) of women in Notley's caucus has freed her from some of the resistance faced by other female leaders. This confirms studies that show increased numbers of women in legislative bodies change the way that government business is conducted, creating a different dynamic, one that is "more in touch with life." The difference is seen in commitment to mentorships, the less adversarial tone or culture of government, fewer late-night sittings, and policies that reflect a more diverse range of experience.[66] Indeed, Notley's government has changed the usual schedule of the legislature, setting morning hours so that MLAs would have more time with their families.[67]

Political observers also report a more profound egalitarianism than seen in previous governments. For example, policies for selecting the "best candidate" used to exclude people who were different from those already at the table. In contrast, the composition of boards and committees in Notley's government is more representative of society as a whole. In the past it was common to have female assistants, but in Notley's government women have been hired to top positions, and female ministers have female aides. There is no pressure for female caucus members to be tougher than male colleagues, a common phenomenon where the proportion of females is low.[68]

Notley provides encouragement and support to her caucus, standing on principle but eschewing harsh discipline. For example, when social media exposed compromising images associated with newly elected NDP MLA Deborah Drever, Notley suspended her from the caucus, vowing to review the decision in a year. Drever sat as an independent, but she was not simply left in the political wilderness. She received extensive support in drafting a private member's bill, introduced in the fall of 2015, to protect victims of domestic violence by allowing them to move out of rental accommodation without penalties. When the bill was introduced, Drever shared some of her own experience with abuse that had motivated her to change the law. The bill was unanimously supported, Drever's reputation was at least partly redeemed, and she was welcomed back into the NDP caucus in January 2016. Likewise, Notley's response to Irfan Sabir's mismanagement of the tragic death of a child in "kinship care" was nuanced; she demoted him to a less problematic portfolio and appointed Danielle Larivee to the newly created Department of Children's Services. This restructuring appeared to focus on solving the problem rather than on punishment.[69]

Notley's government has been quite active, motivated by the knowledge that a second term is by no means assured. Her legislative initiatives include reforms in employment law,[70] enhanced protections for students,[71] consumers,[72] patients and health-care workers.[73] Her Climate Leadership plan introduced incentives to reduce greenhouse gas emissions for industry and individuals,[74] but also contained a controversial carbon tax, spurring sustained and widespread criticism. Most notable, however, have been her focus on rehabilitating Alberta's economy and the related pipeline file.

Alberta's economic recovery has been significant; in 2017 it expanded by 4 per cent and was rated the fastest-growing economy in the country.[75] Tens of thousands of jobs have been created since 2015, including in the private sector and the energy industry, while oil prices have significantly increased,[76] and Notley's government has invested in infrastructure and economic diversification. The deficit has become secondary to Albertans' concern for funding social programs like health care and education.[77] However, economists and Albertans agree that unemployment is still too high.[78]

Central to Notley's plan to rehabilitate the economy is the relentless pursuit of pipelines and getting Alberta's resources to market. In March 2017 the Keystone XL pipeline was approved by the US government, which previously had been the most significant impediment to the project. The Trans Mountain pipeline, however, has been the target of persistent challenges. Although the project has faced protests, regulatory delays, and court challenges by municipalities and Indigenous groups,[79] the most significant opposition has come from the BC government. In January 2018, Premier John Horgan raised the possibility of restricting bitumen shipments through the expanded pipeline. Notley stated categorically that he lacked the constitutional authority to do so, empaneling a team of high-profile experts to explore the constitutional options available to both the provincial and federal governments.[80] She also launched a campaign highlighting the economic and environmental benefits of Alberta's and Ottawa's energy and climate policies, openly pressuring the federal government to decisively support the pipeline.

She announced a ban on BC wine on 6 February, a move that captured the attention of Canadians and their political leaders. The initiative was both tough on the BC government and expressive of Notley's concern for the economic and environmental well-being of British Columbians, Canadians, and Albertans. Having shown she was willing to play hardball, and cautious about alienating BC voters, she suspended the ban on 22 February after Horgan referred the question to the courts—a case Notley is confident he will lose. On 12 March she introduced a motion in the Alberta legislature to support the government's fight on behalf of Albertans to ensure that the pipeline is built.

The political uncertainty surrounding the project led Kinder Morgan to announce on 8 April that it was suspending all non-essential activities and spending related to the Trans Mountain expansion project, specifically citing the uncertainty caused by the actions of the BC government and setting a 31 May deadline to establish the certainty necessary for the project to proceed.

On 16 April, Notley introduced Bill 12 (the Preserving Canada's Economic Prosperity Act) authorizing Alberta's environment minister to limit energy shipments to British Columbia. This move invoked the legacy of Peter Lougheed, who restricted energy exports in response to the federal National Energy Program.[81] When British Columbia announced it would challenge Bill 12 in court, Notley quipped, "It's very interesting; on one hand they don't want our oil, on the other hand they're suing us to give them our oil."[82] Throughout, she worked with the federal government to respond to concerns, both in the media and behind closed doors. These initiatives appeared to pay off as polls saw increased support for the pipeline, with a majority of Canadians, including British Columbians, favouring the project.[83] And just before the 31 May deadline set by Kinder Morgan, Finance Minister Bill Morneau announced that the federal government would purchase the pipeline for $4.5 billion, with Alberta promising an additional $2 billion to cover "unforeseen circumstances."[84]

Perhaps primary among Notley's challenges is that despite successes in moving the pipeline and economic files forward, she may face issues with public perception. A Janet Brown poll commissioned by the CBC and conducted from 13 March to 5 April 2018 revealed that Albertans are not happy with the economy or job growth, and, despite the absence of any significant policy proposals, trust Kenney's party over Notley's to manage the economy.[85] This is perhaps not surprising, since the economy has not yet returned to pre-recession levels, and incumbent governments tend to be blamed for lagging economies. Despite her government's investments in infrastructure and economic diversification, directing carbon tax revenues to green initiatives and alternative energy, Albertans think that Notley has not done enough to diversify the economy. Perhaps most surprisingly, Notley's government lags behind the United Conservative Party on files considered Notley's home turf, including education and health care.[86]

Notley is more popular than her party, while the UCP is more popular than Kenney.[87] The poll found that Albertans have more confidence in Kenney and his party's ability to get pipelines built, despite Notley's significant progress. This may relate to Kenney's relentless criticism of the federal government and Justin Trudeau, especially when contrasted with Notley's co-operation with the federal government. It may also illustrate the challenges faced by female leaders. Notley has enjoyed considerable success in being perceived as competent, collaborative, and likeable, but her tenacity, however effective, may not be something voters feel entirely comfortable with. When it comes to traditionally "male" preserves, such as economic management and high-stakes political battles, she may still face challenges to being seen as equal. Her consultation with leaders and experts has laid the groundwork for considerable successes, however this, and her willingness to adopt Jason Kenney's suggestion to restrict energy shipments to British Columbia, may make it more difficult for her to win credit for her pipeline initiatives.

Kenney, leading a newly consolidated UCP,[88] has a long-standing reputation for toughness, as was partly reflected in the CBC poll showing that Albertans trust him over Notley to fight for pipelines and the economy. His attacks on the Alberta government have focused on policy, primarily the carbon tax and the deficit, while he has reserved more personal attacks for Justin Trudeau. This may reflect a recognition on Kenney's part of Trudeau's diminished popularity in Alberta, and of Rachel Notley's popularity. It may also be that he has learned from Jim Prentice not to be too critical of a female leader, particularly Notley.

The CBC poll predated the federal government's 29 May announcement of an agreement to proceed with construction of the Trans Mountain pipeline; this leaves open the possibility that Notley's pivotal role will be recognized by voters. Indeed, Notley's best chance of electoral success continues to hinge on Albertans' personal experiences of economic recovery, her championing of the social programs cherished by voters, and her ability to persuade them that her collaborative, nuanced approach equips her to better promote and protect Alberta's interests.

Lessons

Redford, Smith, and Notley were each able, at least to some degree, to turn what have historically been liabilities into strengths. They managed to navigate around gendered expectations or use them to their advantage in their rise to leadership, and in two cases, to government.

Alison Redford, a capable policy analyst, speaker, and campaigner, was initially able to employ gender norms to build political support for her leadership and her agenda. Like many Alberta premiers, she succumbed to the twin challenge of dwindling oil revenues and growing deficits. When she failed to meet the high expectations created by both her promises and traditional gender expectations, the backlash from voters and her own party was devastating. Her experience illustrates the importance of effective communication, consultation, and party support.

Danielle Smith built a strong public profile over years of experience in the media and as a political advocate. This enabled her to overcome some of the challenges that gendered assessments and institutions can create. Her experience illustrates the challenges faced by the leaders of divided parties, particularly those who practise the collaborative kind of leadership associated with women. The tension between her position on some issues and gender expectations illustrates the challenges posed by embracing counter-stereotypical issues.

Rachel Notley appears to have learned a great deal from her predecessors, managing to bring a new approach to government and avoiding many of the landmines faced by female political leaders. She embraces many stereotypically female characteristics while also managing traits more commonly associated with masculinity by putting her own stamp on them. There aren't many models for such novel political success; Notley has learned from the successes and failures of leaders like Lougheed, Klein, Redford, and Smith, but she has ultimately forged a new path. The best political leaders are innovative, seeing new possibilities and seizing opportunities.

However formidable Notley's talents, many challenges remain. Alberta's urban-rural divide is deepening, as Roger Epp shows in chapter 13, and closer consultation and collaboration with rural communities will have to be a crucial feature of any future government's success. If Notley's policy initiatives bear fruit, and Alberta's economy grows stronger and more diverse, she may have an opportunity to fine-tune her innovative approach to leadership and policy. If not, opposition to things like Bill 6 and the carbon tax, along with the economic perceptions of Alberta voters, may leave future innovations to other leaders inspired by her example.

NOTES

1   This analysis is informed by research on women in politics and power, and based on an examination of historical developments, media coverage, polling data, and interviews with former cabinet ministers, campaign insiders, and veteran political observers, including journalists, columnists, and politically-connected Albertans.

2   Dianne Bystrom and M. C. Banwart, "Framing the Fight: An Analysis of Media Coverage of Female and Male Candidates in Primary Races for Governor and US Senate in 2000," *American Behavioral Scientist* 44, no. 12 (2001): 1999–2013; Elizabeth Goodyear-Grant, *Gendered News; Media Coverage and Electoral Politics in Canada* (Vancouver: UBC Press, 2013), 142, 65; Sylvia B. Bashevkin, *Women Power, Politics; The Hidden Story of Canada's Unfinished Democracy* (Toronto: Oxford University Press, 2009), 42.

3   Brenda O'Neil, "Unpacking Gender's Role in Political Representation in Canada," *Canadian Parliamentary Review* 38, no. 2 (2015), http://www.revparl.ca/english/issue. asp?param=223&art=1643 (accessed 9 August 2016); Goodyear-Grant, *Gendered News*, 110, 142–3; Joris Lammers, Ernestine H. Gordijn, and Sabine Otten, "Iron Ladies, Men of Steel: The Effects of Gender Stereotyping on the perception of Male and Female Candidates are Moderated by Prototypicality," *European Journal of Social Psychology* 39 (2009) 186–95.

4   Carol Gilligan, "Moral Orientation and Moral Development," in *Women and Moral Theory,* ed. Eva Feder Kittay and Diana T. Meyers, 19–23 (Totowa NJ: Rowman and

Littlefield, 1987); Gilligan, "In a Different Voice: Women's conceptions of self and morality," in *The Future of Difference*, ed. Hester Eisenstein and Alice Jardine, 274–317 (New Brunswick, NJ: Rutgers University Press, 1980).

5   This is also reflected in symbols like the ceremonial mace (originally a medieval war club) kept in the custody of the sergeant-at-arms, and the "two swords length" distance between government and opposition benches—each part of our parliamentary heritage. See Linda Trimble and Jane Arscott, *Still Counting; Women in Politics Across Canada* (Peterborough, ON: Broadview Press, 2003), 113; Elizabeth Goodyear-Grant, *Gendered News*, 112.

6   Lammers et al., "Iron Ladies, Men of Steel"; O'Neil, "Unpacking Gender's Role"; Gilligan, "Moral Orientation and Moral Development"; Goodyear-Grant, *Gendered News*, 142–3.

7   Karen Ross, "Women's Place in 'Male' Space; Gender and Effect in Parliamentary Contexts," in *Women Politics and Change*, ed. Karen Ross, 189–201 (New York: Oxford University Press, 2002), 193–4, 201; Susan Delacourt, "Put Off by Parliament: Even strong women MPs find it impossible to play Ottawa's macho game," *Elm Street* (February/March 2001), 58–60; Gilligan, "Moral Orientation and Moral Development."

8   Delacourt, "Put Off by Parliament," 60. Women who've expressed such discomfort include accomplished and powerful cabinet ministers like Anne McLellan, former deputy prime minister and minister of Justice, public safety and emergency preparedness, and natural resources.

9   Manon Tremblay and Linda Trimble, eds., *Women and Electoral Politics in Canada* (New York: Oxford University Press. 2003), 7; Elizabeth Gidengil, "Economic Man—Social Woman? The Case of the Gender Gap in Support for the Canada-US Free Trade Agreement," *Comparative Political Studies* 28, no. 3 (1995): 384–408; Luciana Carraro, Luigi Castelli, Ioana Breazu, Giulia Campomizzi, Antonella Cerruto, Massimiliano Mariani, and Ivano Toto, "Just Ignore or Counterattack? On the Effects of Different Strategies for Dealing with Political Attacks," *European Journal of Sociology* 42, no. 6 (2012): 789–97; Goodyear-Grant, *Gendered News*, 122–3.

10   They sometimes take the form of backhanded compliments, as illustrated by Barak Obama's comment to Hillary Clinton during the 2008 nomination race that she was "likeable enough." Although he was criticized for his comment, the question of Clinton's likeability persisted.

11   Peter Glick and Susan Fiske, "Hostile and Benevolent Sexism: Measuring Ambivalent Sexist Attitudes Toward Women," *Psychology of Women Quarterly* 22, no. 1 (1997): 119–35.

12   Susan T. Fiske, "Managing ambivalent prejudices: The smart-but-cold, and the warm-but dumb stereotypes," *Annals of the American Academy of Political and Social Science* 639 (2012): 3–48.

13   Michèle M. Schlehofer, Bettina Casad, Michelle Bligh, and Angela Grotto, "Navigating Public Prejudices: The Impact of Media and Attitudes on High-Profile Female Political Leaders," *Sex Roles* 65, no. 1 (2011): 69–70.

14   Ibid, 71.

15 Trimble and Arscott, *Still Counting*, 93.

16 Goodyear-Grant, *Gendered News*, 61.

17 Tremblay and Trimble, *Still Counting*, 32.

18 Jacquetta Newman and Linda White, *Women, Politics, and Public Policy: The Political Struggles of Canadian Women* (Toronto: Oxford University Press, 2012), 98, 242; "Delacourt, Put Off by Parliament," 54.

19 O'Neil, "Unpacking Gender's Role."

20 Sydney Sharpe and Don Braid, *Notley Nation; How Alberta's Political Upheaval Swept the Country* (Toronto: Dundurn, 2016), 65. Lougheed bridged Alberta's vexing urban-rural divide "deftly . . . changing not only his suit, but his way of speaking," 150.

21 This information was provided in interviews conducted in 2016 with party insiders on condition of anonymity.

22 Sharpe and Braid, *Notley Nation*, 73–4.

23 Elections Alberta, "Provincial Results," n.d., http://officialresults.elections.ab.ca/orresultspge.cfm?EventId=21 (accessed 9 August 2016).

24 Josh Wingrove, " 'Bitumen Bubble' Means A Hard Reckoning for Alberta, Redford Warns," *Globe and Mail* (Toronto), 24 January 2013, https://www.theglobeandmail.com/news/national/bitumen-bubble-means-a-hard-reckoning-for-alberta-redford-warns/article7833915/ (accessed 9 August 2016).

25 "Alison Redford has Poisoned Labour Relations in Alberta, Union Group Says after Tories Pass Controversial Bills," *National Post* (Toronto), 5 December 2013, http://news.nationalpost.com/news/canada/canadian-politics/alison-redford-has-poisoned-labour-relations-in-alberta-union-group-says-after-tories-pass-controversial-bills (accessed 10 August 2016); Dean Bennett, "Alison Redford spent $3,100 of taxpayers' money to fly daughter's friends on government aircraft," *National Post* (Toronto), 5 March 2014, http://news.nationalpost.com/news/canada/canadian-politics/alison-redford-spent-3100-of-taxpayers-money-to-fly-daughters-friends-on-government-aircraft-but-will-pay-it-back-she-says (accessed 10 August 2016).

26 Merwan Saher, Auditor General of Alberta, "Auditor General Releases August 2014 Special Duty Report on the Expenses of the Office of Premier Redford and Alberta's Air Transportation Services Program," 7 August 2014, www.oag.ab.ca/node/437 (accessed 10 August 2016); Karen Kleiss, "Alison Redford's Abuse of Planes Fuelled by 'Aura of Power,' Auditor Says in Scathing Report," *National Post* (Toronto), 7 August 2014, http://news.nationalpost.com/news/canada/canadian-politics/alison-redford-used-public-resources-inappropriately-and-misspent-millions-auditor-general-says-in-scathing-report (accessed 10 August 2016); Julia Parrish, "Former Members of Redford's Staff Received $1.14m in Severance," *CTV News*, 28 March 2014, http://edmonton.ctvnews.ca/former-members-of-redford-s-staff-received-1-14m-in-severance-1.1750827 (accessed 10 August 2016).

27 Nancy Macdonald, "Christy Clark: The Comeback Kid," *Maclean's*, 11 July 2015, http://www.macleans.ca/politics/christy-clark-comeback-kid/ (accessed 10 June 2016).

28 Don Braid and Sydney Sharpe, interview with author, 30 January 2017.

29   Gary Mason, "One year later, Alison Redford looks back: 'I'm a polarizing figure,'" *Globe and Mail* (Toronto), 20 March 2015, https://www.theglobeandmail.com/news/national/one-year-later-alison-redford-looks-back-im-a-polarizing-figure/article23546195/ (accessed 10 August 2016).

30   Jen Gerson, "Alberta PC Associate Minister Kennedy-Glans Quits in Another Blow to Alison Redford's Already Shaky Leadership," *National Post* (Toronto), 17 March 2014, http://news.nationalpost.com/news/canada/canadian-politics/alberta-pc-associate-minister-donna-kennedy-glans-quits-in-another-blow-to-alison-redfords-already-shaky-leadership (accessed 10 August 2016).

31   Newman and White, Women, *Politics and Public Policy*, 98; Goodyear-Grant, *Gendered News*, 72, 125.

32   Goodyear-Grant, *Gendered News*, 55, 125.

33   Braid and Sharpe interview.

34   James Wood, "Wildrose Candidate Tells Gays in Lady Gaga-Inspired Blog Post: 'You Will Suffer the Rest of Eternity in the Lake of Fire, Hell,' " *National Post* (Toronto), 15 April 2012, https://nationalpost.com/news/canada/allan-hunsperger-wildrose-blog (accessed 10 August 2016); Sharpe and Braid, *Notley Nation*, 77.

35   Jen Gerson, " 'Caucasian Advantage' quip casts shadow over Wildrose campaign despite poll lead," *National Post* (Toronto), 17 April 2012, http://news.nationalpost.com/news/canada/ron-leech-wildrose (accessed 10 August 2016).

36   Colby Cosh, "Out with the Wild, In with the Mild," *Maclean's*, 11 November 2013, 14.

37   "Danielle Smith Replacement Would Be 'Foolish,' Tom Flanagan Says," *CBC News*, 28 October 2014, http://www.cbc.ca/news/canada/calgary/danielle-smith-replacement-would-be-foolish-tom-flanagan-says-1.2815696 (accessed 12 August 2016).

38   Dean Bennett, "Alberta's Wildrose Party Rolls Back on Statement Affirming Equal Rights for All," *Global News*, 15 November 2014, http://globalnews.ca/news/1673873/albertas-wildrose-party-rolls-back-on-statement-affirming-equal-rights-for-all/ (accessed 12 August 2016).

39   Justin Giovanetti, "Danielle Smith Loses PC Nomination Bid, Wildrose Picks New Leader," *Globe and Mail* (Toronto), 27 March 2015, https://www.theglobeandmail.com/news/alberta/wildrose-picks-former-federal-mp-as-new-leader/article23678044/ (accessed 12 August 2016).

40   Linda Trimble and Angelia Wagner, " 'Wildrose Wild Card': Alberta Newspaper Coverage of the 2009 Wildrose Alliance Leadership Contest," *Canadian Political Science Review* 6, no. 2–3 (2012): 197–207, Goodyear-Grant, *Gendered News*, 146.

41   Sonia Verma, "Danielle Smith; 'My Life Will Fall Under the Microscope,' " *Globe and Mail* (Toronto), 12 November 2010, https://www.theglobeandmail.com/news/politics/danielle-smith-my-life-will-fall-under-the-microscope/article1314031/ (accessed 12 August 2016).

42   Karen Kleiss, Cailynn Klingbell, and Darcy Henton, "Smith Discloses Infertility Battle after Tory Tweet,' *Edmonton Journal*, 1 April 2012, https://www.pressreader.com/

canada/edmonton-journal/20120401/281505043187399 (accessed 12 August 2016); Goodyear-Grant, *Gendered News*, 93.

43   Braid and Sharpe interview.

44   Female politicians are particularly vulnerable to a "backlash effect" against women who contravene stereotypes prescribing passive and co-operative feminine behaviour. See Goodyear-Grant, *Gendered News*, 65.

45   Braid and Sharpe interview.

46   Gary Mason, "Notley's Way: How the Alberta premier became determined," *Globe and Mail* (Toronto), 8 May 2015, https://www.theglobeandmail.com/news/alberta/the-alberta-ndps-rachel-notley-she-is-a-child-of-the-party/article24338069/comments (accessed 13 August 2016); "What You Need to Know About Rachel Notley," *Maclean's*, 5 May 2015, http://www.macleans.ca/news/canada/what-you-need-to-know-about-rachel-notley (accessed 13 August 2016); Sharpe and Braid, *Notley Nation*, 89, 95–6.

47   Colby Cosh, "How Rachel Notley became Canada's most surprising political star," *Maclean's*, 21 May 2015, http://www.macleans.ca/politics/how-rachel-notley-became-canadas-most-surprising-political-star/ (accessed 13 August 2016).

48   Sharpe and Braid, *Notley Nation*, 36.

49   "The Alberta Leaders' Debate in 30 Minutes," YouTube video, posted by FactPointVideo, 24 April 2015, https://www.youtube.com/watch?v=5oV5rfzffMc (accessed 13 August 2016).

50   "So, what did we learn from the leaders' debate? Math is hard and Rachel Notley is a winker," *Calgary Herald,* 23 April 2015, http://calgaryherald.com/storyline/ready-to-play-leaders-debate-bingo-of-course-not-you-dont-have-your-card-yet (accessed 13 August 2016); James Armstrong, "Analysis Shows Prentice Took a Beating on Twitter Over #Mathishard," *Global News*, 27 April 2015, http://globalnews.ca/news/1959219/analysis-shows-prentice-took-a-beating-on-twitter-over-mathishard (accessed 13 August 2016); " 'Math Is Difficult': Numbers Dominate Alberta Debate; Alberta Party Leaders Square Off in Lone Televised Election Debate," *Maclean's*, 24 April 2015, http://www.macleans.ca/news/canada/math-is-difficult-numbers-dominate-alberta-debate (accessed 13 August 2016); Sharpe and Braid, *Notley Nation*, 36; Carraro et al., "Just Ignore or Counterattack?"

51   Trevor Howell and James Wood, "Prentice: No Disrespect Intended by 'Math is Difficult' Comment," *Calgary Herald*, 24 April 2015, http://calgaryherald.com/news/local-news/prentice-says-he-wasnt-disrespecting-notley-with-his-math-is-difficult-comment (accessed 13 August 2016).

52   "Alberta's Climate Change Strategy Targets Carbon, Coal Emissions," *CBC News*, 22 November 2015, http://www.cbc.ca/news/canada/edmonton/alberta-climate-change-newser-1.3330153 (accessed 14 August 2016).

53   Smith, then Opposition leader and MLA for flood-ravaged High River, was shunned by then premier Redford. See Don Braid, "NDP Handling of Fire Wins Praise, Even from Danielle Smith," *Calgary Herald*, 17 May 2016, http://calgaryherald.com/news/politics/

braid-ndp-handling-of-fire-wins-praise-even-from-danielle-smith (accessed 14 August 2016).

54   "Alberta Premier Fights Back Tears as she Discusses Fort McMurray Wildfire," *Global News*, 8 May 2016, http://globalnews.ca/video/2687918/albertans-on-mothers-day-are-mourning-those-died-in-wild-fire-notley-tears-up (accessed 14 August 2016); "Rachel Notley to Evacuees: 'Trust Us That We Have Your Backs,' " *Maclean's*, 6 May 2016, http://www.macleans.ca/news/canada/rachel-notley-to-fort-mcmurray-trust-us-that-we-have-your-backs/ (accessed 14 August 2016).

55   Don Braid, "Notley Counter's Brad Wall, Without a Tantrum," *Calgary Herald*, 16 July 2015, http://calgaryherald.com/news/politics/braid-notley-counters-brad-wall-without-a-tantrum (accessed 15 August 2016).

56   "Rachel Notley Accuses Brad Wall of 'Showboating' over Energy Plan; Alberta Premier Says her Saskatchewan Counterpart's Comments are 'Ridiculous and a Bit Naïve,' " *CBC News*, 16 July 2015, http://www.cbc.ca/news/canada/edmonton/rachel-notley-accuses-brad-wall-of-showboating-over-energy-plan-1.3156040 (accessed 15 August 2016).

57   James Wood, "NDP Government to Maintain Current Royalty Structure for Alberta's Oilsands," *Calgary Herald*, 30 January 2016, http://calgaryherald.com/business/energy/live-notley-unveils-royalty-review-report (accessed 15 August 2016).

58   Justin Giovanetti, "Family Farms Exempt from Alberta's Workplace Safety Bill," *Globe and Mail* (Toronto), 8 December 2015, https://www.theglobeandmail.com/news/national/family-farms-exempt-from-albertas-workplace-safety-bill/article27654367 (accessed 16 August 2016); "Alberta's Bill 6 Taught NDP Lesson on Communicating with Farmers," *CBC News*, 22 January 2016, http://www.cbc.ca/news/canada/calgary/agriculture-minister-admits-bill6-mistake-1.3415855 (accessed 16 August 2016).

59   Michelle Bellefontaine, "Rachel Notley Lifts Ban on The Rebel, says it made a mistake," *CBC News*, 17 February 2016, http://www.cbc.ca/news/canada/edmonton/notley-the-rebel-1.3451838 (accessed 16 August 2016).

60   For example, see Gary Mason, "Notley's Way: How the Alberta premier became determined," *Globe and Mail* (Toronto), 8 May 2015, https://www.theglobeandmail.com/news/alberta/the-alberta-ndps-rachel-notley-she-is-a-child-of-the-party/article24338069/ (accessed 17 August 2016), and Paul Wells, "My Name is Rachel Notley: How this Down-to-Earth Politician Capitalized on an Extraordinary Moment in Alberta's History," *Maclean's*, 6 May 2015, http://www.macleans.ca/news/canada/my-name-is-rachel-notley (accessed 17 August 2016); Sharpe and Braid, *Notley Nation*, 45, 96, 101.

61   Wells, "My Name is Rachel Notley."

62   Sharpe and Braid, *Notley Nation*, 99.

63   In Canada this dates back to the women's suffrage movement. In 1914 Nellie McClung staged a satirical mock parliament asking whether men should be allowed to vote. When Agnes Macphail, Canada's first female MP, was taunted by a heckler shouting "Don't you wish you were a man?" she retorted, "Don't you?" See Terence Allan

Crowley, *Agnes Macphail and the Politics of Equality* (Toronto: James Lorimer and Company, 1990). 98.

64 Sharpe and Braid, *Notley Nation*, 31.

65 Braid and Sharpe interview.

66 Karen Ross, "Women's Place in 'Male' Space: Gender and Effect in Parliamentary Contexts," in *Women Politics and Change*, ed. Karen Ross (New York: Oxford University Press, 2002), 198, 200–1.

67 Sharpe and Braid, *Notley Nation*, 161.

68 Braid and Sharpe interview.

69 Carol Gilligan observed a tendency in women to focus more on solutions than punishment. See Gilligan, "Moral Orientation." See also Paula Simons, "Shuffled but not Out; Irfan Sabir Demoted, as Danielle Larivee Takes Over New Children's Services Ministry," *Edmonton Journal*, 20 January 2017, http://edmontonjournal.com/news/local-news/paula-simons-shuffled-but-not-out-irfan-sabir-demoted-as-danielle-larivee-takes-over-new-childrens-services-ministry (accessed 15 May 2017).

70 The changes to employment law include the extension of workers compensation and occupational health and safety protections to agricultural workers, laws to protect workers against harassment and to provide job-protected leaves for illness, caring for a sick family member, bereavement, domestic violence, or attending a citizenship ceremony. These are enshrined in Bill 30: An Act to Protect the Health and Well-being of Working Albertans, and Bill 17: Fair and Family- Friendly Workplaces Act.) UCP house leader Jason Nixon argued against the need for anti-harassment legislation, saying private industry already has policies in place. Later it was revealed that he "fired a woman in 2005 who complained about sexual harassment on a Kelowna worksite." See "UCP house leader Jason Nixon fired woman after sexual harassment complaint," *CBC News*, 12 December 2017, http://www.cbc.ca/news/canada/edmonton/jason-nixon-fired-woman-for-sex-harassment-complaint-1.4444897 (accessed 15 May 2017).

71 Bill 24: An Act to Support Gay Straight Alliances.

72 Consumer protections include restrictions on payday lending.

73 Enhanced protection was provided to health-care workers and patients around abortion clinics by expanding the buffer zone The UCP walked out of the legislature rather than voting on Bill 9.

74 The Custom Energy Solutions Program to promote industrial efficiency announced by Environment Minister Shannon Phillips in May 2018 included $88 million in provincial and federal funds. See Clare Clancy, "Premier Rachel Notley unveils pro-Trans Mountain ads, project means money for roads and hospitals," *Edmonton Journal*, 10 May 2018, http://edmontonjournal.com/news/politics/ndp-spending-1-2-million-trans-mountain-advocacy-campaign-ahead-of-may-31-deadline (accessed 14 May 2018). The Notley government also invested in wind energy and green transit.

75 Chris Varcoe, "Oil price rebound tops list of biggest business stories of 2017," *Calgary Herald*, 2 January 2018, https://www.pressreader.com/canada/calgary-herald/20180102/281513636534843 (accessed 16 May 2018); "Year in Review: Alberta

Premier Rachel Notley touches on province's economy," *Global News*, 1 January 2018, https://globalnews.ca/video/3941078/year-in-review-alberta-premier-touches-on-provinces-economy (accessed 16 may 2018).

76   In mid-May 2018 oil prices hit their highest point since 2013—about US$71/barrel. See Chris Varcoe, "Varcoe; Oil prices rally, but Alberta still waits for liftoff," *Calgary Herald*, 23 May 2018, https://calgaryherald.com/business/energy/varcoe-oil-prices-rally-but-alberta-still-waits-for-liftoff (accessed 23 May 2018).

77   Concerns about the deficit are not as important as opposition to significant cuts in social programs like health and education; 78 per cent of Albertans opposed such cuts, while only 58 per cent thought the budget should be balanced. See Jenn Gerson "The Alberta NDP is probably toast but here's how they could give themselves a fighting chance," *CBC News*, 1 May 2018, www.cbc.ca/news/canada/calgary/alberta-ndp-probably-toast-but-fighting-chance-1.4641852 (accessed 21 May 2018).

78   In April 2018 Alberta's unemployment rate sat at 6 per cent, the highest outside Atlantic Canada, and there were still 28,000 fewer jobs than in June 2015. See Todd Hirsch, "Taking stock of Alberta's labour market," 14 May 2018, available at www.toddhirsch.com/commentary (accessed 21 May 2018).

79   On 24 May 2018, the BC Supreme Court rejected challenges brought by the City of Vancouver and the Squamish Nation. The claims questioned whether there had been proper environmental assessment, and whether the pipeline had had been approved without sufficient Aboriginal consultation, as guaranteed by the Canadian Charter of Rights and Freedoms. See Jason Proctor "Court throws out Trans Mountain pipeline challenge from City of Vancouver and Squamish Nation," *CBC News*, 24 May 2018, www.cbc.ca/news/canada/british-columbia/squamish-nation-taking-fight-against-kinder-morgan-to-court-1.467669 (accessed 5 June 2018).

80   The Market Access Task Force included Peter Hogg, respected nationally for his expertise on constitutional law, Anne McLellan, former deputy prime minister and minister of natural resources, Frank McKenna, former New Brunswick premier, as well as industry representatives and financial and economic experts. Notley's response to the BC and federal governments earned her widespread support, including from key oil industry players. See Reid Southwick, "Premier Notley praised by Alberta's energy industry for tough stance in pipeline dispute," *CBC News*, 15 February 2018, www.cbc.ca/news/canada/calgary/alberta-energy-panel-trans-mountain-1.4537745 (accessed 5 June 2018).

81   Notley announced that "Premier Peter Lougheed took bold action. We will not hesitate to invoke similar legislation if it becomes necessary owing to extreme and illegal actions on the part of the B.C. government to stop the pipeline." In response to the National Energy Program, then premier Peter Lougheed legislated to cut Alberta's oil exports to Ontario by 15 per cent, forcing the federal government to renegotiate the terms of the NEP. See Clare Clancy, "Legislative assembly debates how to push for Trans Mountain progress," *Calgary Herald*, 13 March 2018, https://www.pressreader.com/canada/calgary-herald/20180313/281629600790247 (accessed 5 June 2018).

82   Don Braid, "The weirdness of BC's lawsuit against Alberta," *Calgary Herald*, 22 May 2018, http://calgaryherald.com/news/politics/braid-the-weirdness-of-b-c-s-lawsuit-against-alberta (accessed 5 June 2018).

83   Derrick Penner, "Where court decision lands is key to support of Trans Mountain expansion: Pollster," *Vancouver Sun*, 18 April 2018, https://vancouversun.com/news/local-news/where-court-decision-lands-is-key-to-support-for-trans-mountain-expansion-pollster (accessed 5 June 2018).

84   Kathleen Harris, "Liberals to buy Trans Mountain pipeline for $4.5B to ensure expansion is built," *CBC News*, 29 May 2018, https://www.cbc.ca/news/politics/liberals-trans-mountain-pipeline-kinder-morgan-1.4681911 (accessed 5 June 2018); James Wood, "Alberta ready to pony up $2 billion for Trans Mountain, but details are scarce," *Calgary Herald*, 29 May 2018, https://calgaryherald.com/news/politics/alberta-ready-to-pony-up-2-billion-to-move-trans-mountain-forward-but-details-are-scarce (accessed 5 June 2018).

85   The CBC Road Ahead survey included focus group analysis. One focus group participant perceived no economic recovery: " 'Unfortunately the economy hasn't improved,' he said. 'If the economy improved, I think it would be different feelings, but it hasn't.' " See Brian Labby, "The politics of personality in Alberta—how Notley and Kenney help and hurt their parties," *CBC News*, 1 May 2018, www.cbc.ca/news/canada/calgary/alberta-politics-kenney-notley-leaders-popularity-1.4641898 (accessed 23 May 2018).

86   When asked which party is best able to handle education and health care, the UCP polled 34 per cent (NDP 32 per cent) and 35 per cent (NDP 30 per cent), respectively. See Labby, "The politics of personality."

87   Ibid.

88   Jason Kenney won the leadership of the Progressive Conservative Party, then led a campaign to unite it with Alberta's other major conservative party (and the Official Opposition), the Wildrose Party, winning the leadership of the newly formed party.

Notley and the Beast: An Analysis of the Crisis Communication of Rachel Notley during the 2016 Wildfire

Chaseten Remillard and Sheridan McVean

On 1 May 2016 a small wildfire started southwest of Fort McMurray, Alberta. Wildfires are not unusual for the area; this particular fire was fueled by a combination of dry weather, high winds, and hot temperatures. This time, the combination proved catastrophic. The wildfire continued to grow in size, unpredictability, and power, and it's magnitude and strength earned it the nickname "the beast." By May 3, Fort McMurray faced imminent threat and at 5 p.m. that day a mandatory evacuation of the city was ordered.

As a growing cloud of smoke and flame engulfed the city, nearly 90,000 residents of the city began their exodus. Roads swelled with vehicles whose drivers navigated through walls of burning trees and buildings. Black smoke limited visibility and a hazy, nightmarish landscape prevailed. When, on July 1, the provincial state of emergency was lifted, the fire had raged for 66 days, destroyed 2,400 homes, consumed 590 acres of boreal forest, and caused over $3.5 billion in insurable damage. To date, it is the most expensive disaster on Canadian record.

Almost a year prior, a different type of news story dominated the Albertan public sphere. On 5 May 2015, the Alberta NDP scored an upset victory over the long-serving Alberta Progressive Conservative Party to become the government of Alberta. Leading the Alberta New Democrats was Rachel Notley, subsequently the first NDP premier of Alberta. The May 2016

Fort McMurray wildfire became the first and most significant test of the new government's response to a crisis situation.

In general, crises often act as litmus tests for leadership legitimacy. How a leader responds to crisis can quite literally make or break their career, and in this case, their government. For Notley, the stakes were particularly high. In the early days of her government, important questions remained about its ability to shepherd the province out of an increasingly deep economic recession caused by depressed world energy prices, to address national and international stakeholders around important infrastructure projects such as pipelines, and the potential imposition of new taxes and government royalties on Alberta's energy industry.

During the 2015 Alberta general election, the NDP had campaigned on a policy to review the royalties charged by the Alberta government on oil and natural gas produced in the province. Royalties are similar to taxation, but are premised on the fact that the vast majority of oil and natural gas in Alberta is owned by the provincial government. The government sets the price at which the energy industry is allowed to remove the oil and natural gas. Royalties are charged in addition to corporate or business taxes.

Fort McMurray and the surrounding area, called the Regional District of Wood Buffalo, is the centre of Alberta's oil sands development and a lightning rod for critics of the tar sands, dirty oil, and climate change. Some of these critics saw "justice" in the fact that this area was suffering from the impacts of climate change since it is populated largely by those thought culpable for the effects of fossil fuel development.

Moreover, the vividness of the Fort McMurray fire was not just physical, but also virtual. Captured by smart phones and dash cams, the images of the wildfire streamed out to the world in high definition. The speed and ferocity of the fire and the rapidity of the evacuation had largely locked traditional news sources out of the city, but newsrooms swelled with visual documentation from thousands of embedded citizen journalists. These raw, uncut, and unfiltered first-person narratives of the disaster were visceral, shocking, devastating, and abundant. Countless images, videos, and personal accounts streamed out onto YouTube, Facebook, Twitter, and Instagram, and perhaps unlike any other Canadian natural disaster in history, the Fort McMurray evacuation went viral. Traditional media outlets, such as television network news, used the dark and dramatic video shot and posted on social media by citizens fleeing the wildfire to enhance their own news coverage of the fire.

The sheer magnitude of the fire, the expanded publicity facilitated by the viral nature of the images it produced, and the political climate of a newly established government makes the Fort McMurray fires a particularly unique case of crisis communication, and one that reveals important elements of Rachel Notley's leadership and the impact of social media on public governance. In this chapter, we hope to determine the extent to which the premier's initial personally communicated responses to the Fort McMurray wildfire addressed the visual and online framing of the event as set by social media images and, in so doing, reinforced the mandate and legitimacy of her premiership.

To do so, we consider three distinct sources of data: the images of the Fort McMurray evacuation, as recorded on several widely viewed YouTube videos posted during or immediately after the evacuation; the public comments posted to news stories that either incorporated or linked to footage from those privately produced videos; and Premier Notley's first five press conferences and updates that occurred during the first three days after the mandatory evacuation was ordered.

We conclude that in her crisis communication, Notley used an effective strategy to emphasize "bolstering" and "corrective action" messages.[1] Furthermore, although the narrative of the fire, as set by online images and commentary, framed the fire differently than Notley and her government did, her crisis communication efforts implicitly addressed many of those alternative frames, and did so in a manner that emphasized collaborative action and positive outcomes.

Setting the Stage for Crisis: The Importance of Initial Communications

Our contention is that the initial organizational communication responses to a crisis situation can be very enlightening. Because public and media interest is so focused on the crisis, the initial communications messages from the organization deemed responsible can reveal both expected organizational characteristics and those that otherwise could have remained hidden. In other words, organizations dealing with the pressure of a crisis tend to make or break their public responses early on. Early organizational communication missteps or misstatements can reveal unintended negative organizational characteristics and cause long-term reputational issues. Conversely, successful crisis communication typically expands from timely, appropriate, and well-measured organizational responses early on in the crisis and reinforces existing key points of legitimacy related to that organization.

In those instances when a politician or leader speaks about the scope, severity, impact of a crisis and the mitigation strategy by which they hope to bring it under control, those statements function to define for the public what the crisis is and how it is best managed. By framing the crisis as such, successful crisis communication endeavours to set the agenda for the news coverage of a crisis.

Making the Crisis Meaningful: Agenda-Setting and Crisis Communication

Agenda-setting is a well-established and highly studied form of media effect.[2] Substantial research over the last forty years has shown that the prominent agenda set by the media influences the expressed agenda of the public that consumes that media.[3] Importantly, agenda-setting is not propagandistic, for "the press may not be successful much of the time in telling people what to think, but it is stunningly successful in telling its readers what to think about."[4] So, for example, during an election, the media may not tell the voters how to vote, but the media will set the agenda of what is important to "think about" when voting.[5] Those policy issues given most attention by the media predictably become the expressed policy priorities for the public who have consumed that media. So, voters who watch a particular news channel or read a particular newspaper during an election will not have their voting decision directly determined by such coverage, but rather will rank the top issues of the election in alignment with the news coverage they consumed.

Although crisis communication literature uses a different vocabulary than agenda-setting, both share a central concern with message framing and communication effects. In general, two paradigms in crisis communications theory have been dominant in the public relations literature over the past two decades: Benoit's image restoration theory and Coombs's situation crisis communication theory.[6] Benoit considered communication messages during crisis situations and defined five broad categories that organizations employ to repair their corporate images: denial, evasion of responsibility, reducing the offensiveness of an event, corrective action, and mortification (apology). Two key premises of Benoit's theory are that an organization must be believed by a relevant audience to be responsible for an act (he claims that the perception is important, not the reality); and that the act be considered offensive.[7]

On the surface, natural disasters, such as wildfires caused by lightening, would not be seen by a company or organization or individual as responsible. The Fort McMurray wildfire was started by human activity rather than by a lightning strike,[8] but police stated they were unable to identify a specific organization or individual who caused the wildfire. However, the evacuation of Fort McMurray and surrounding communities was very much a government action, with the Regional District of Wood Buffalo responsible for mandatory first evaluations and the Alberta government responsible for subsequent mandatory evacuations. As is discussed later in this chapter, social media chatter around the initial mandatory evacuation generated speculation on the causes of the wildfire as well as questions about the need for the evacuation. For this reason, and despite the fact that Benoit's work was published more than two decades ago and, at that time, he envisioned his theory as one designed for corporations, we will discuss his types of crisis communication messages and assess their applicability to the Fort McMurray wildfire.

In creating situation crisis communication theory, Coombs utilized and added to Benoit's strategies by distinguishing between strategies intended to change perceptions of the crisis and strategies intended to change perceptions of the organization experiencing the crisis. He also defined *diminishment strategies* as messaging intended to reduce the negative effects of the crisis or the organizational control over the crisis, and *rebuilding strategies* as messaging intended to improve the organization's reputation.[9] In addition, Coombs connects Bernard Weiner's attribution theory with crisis communication. Attribution theory posits that people have a need to search for the causes of events, in this case, crisis events. In other words, people want to identify a cause for a crisis event and attempt to determine who is responsible for it.[10]

For these reasons, situation crisis communication theory directs a three-step process for communications managers in crisis situations to determine communication messages and responses that are appropriate to the individual crisis situation. First an assessment is made of organizational responsibility for creating the crisis as viewed by stakeholders and/or the public and if the organization is a victim, if an accident caused the crisis, or if the crisis was preventable by the organization. Next the crisis history of the organization is reviewed according to two measures: consistency—if the organization experienced similar problems/crises in the past—and distinctiveness—how well the organization has generally treated stakeholders/ people in the past.[11]

Coombs notes other factors that are important when organizations select crisis response strategies: stakeholder and public assessment of organizational credibility—composed of the expertise and trustworthiness of the organization—and the prior reputation of the organization.[12] He cites comments from other crisis experts that during a crisis, the organization must both establish control and show compassion.

In addition, believability of the organization is important, and the speed with which the organization can disseminate its communications messages helps increase believability, assuming stakeholders and the public will actually accept what the organization is stating in its communication messages. Coombs also points out that challenges to an organization and its messages can occur when a stakeholder or credible third party calls the organization's actions or messages into question.[13]

Thus, what Coombs adds to Benoit's categorization is the importance of responsiveness, context, and organizational legacy. Crisis communication messaging must be understood in the context of the specific crisis and in relation to the legacy of the organization communicating about that crisis. Messages may need to be adapted to accommodate or address alternative framings of the crisis, or existent public perceptions of the organization. Thus, timeliness, or the act of "stealing thunder" as Arpan and Roskos-Ewoldsen describe it, is an important consideration in successfully framing a crisis.[14] Stealing thunder is the voluntary and proactive disclosure of potentially damaging information by an organization seen as responsible for a crisis situation. In Arpan and Roskos-Ewoldsen's research findings, an organization was rated as more credible when it proactively steals thunder than when it does not.

Moreover, as Boin and his colleagues point out, this decision-making task for government is determined not only "by crucial leadership decisions but, to a considerable extent, also by the institutional context in which crisis decision making and implementation take place."[15] Wildfires in Alberta are frequent; between 2006 and 2015, Alberta experienced an average of 1,500 wildfires per year.[16] Additionally, initial responses to wildfires are generally the responsibility of local municipal governments. Moreover, the Alberta government uses well-established and tested disaster management protocols and has experienced significant previous disasters involving wildfires and floods. In May 2011, for example, a wildfire burnt through the town of Slave Lake; like the Fort McMurray wildfire, the Slave Lake wildfire was also propelled by strong winds. In Alberta's government emergency management circles, the experience of the Slave Lake wildfire became embedded in the "how to" manual for fighting urban wildfires in the province.

The institutional context in which the Fort McMurray wildfire began was that the local government in the Regional District of Wood Buffalo, and not the Alberta government, were engaged in the sense-making and decision-making tasks about the wildfire. Once the wildfire grew in size and became a crisis, the Alberta government also had to move through these critical tasks of sense-making, decision-making, meaning-making, before eventually declaring that the wildfire was under control. However, given that the fire had been identified as a crisis already, and that a well-established decision-making architecture was in place for fighting such fires, our analysis focuses on the meaning-making task that Premier Notley engaged in during her initial news conferences. Certainly, the Alberta government was responsible for the "on-the-ground" fighting of the Fort McMurray wildfire, and Premier Notley and her government made strategic choices to that effect, but what did they then communicate to Albertans and Canadians to make those choices meaningful? This question is at the heart of both agenda-setting and crisis communication literature, as it is the role of leadership in a crisis to "impute meaning to the unfolding crisis in a way that their efforts to manage it are enhanced." If Notley failed to do this, her actions and "decisions will not be understood or respected."[17]

In a crisis situation, leaders and spokespeople have the opportunity, through press conferences and news releases, to attempt to shape the agenda originally set by the media, and in doing so, to frame the crisis in a manner strategic to both the resolution of the crisis and the benefit of themselves and their organization.

In the three days that followed the announcement of the mandatory evacuation of Fort McMurray, Premier Notley held five separate news conferences. Typically each news conference update began with opening comments from the premier, followed by updates from non-elected government officials, and then a media question-and-answer period. To us, the opening comments for the initial wildfire updates are a particularly rich set of data for the following reasons: these comments were directly from Premier Notley and not filtered; the content of these comments were not set by the media (as questions from the media in the media question-and-answer component of the update could shape the discussion); and having the video record of the initial comments provided the ability to measure the length of the comments and sort the comments by subject category. Such content analysis enabled us to quantify what was prioritized in Premier Notley's communicative management and agenda-setting of the crisis.

Seeing the Crisis Online: Social Media and a New Age of Crisis

Simultaneous to Notley's news conferences, during the opening days of the crisis, an abundance of images and videos of the evacuation and wildfire became available through social media and other online sources. These images generated both a visual narrative of the evacuation and a growing online commentary on the wildfire, which in turn generated both supportive and skeptical discourses of the crisis.

Recently, scholars of agenda-setting have turned their attention to the impact of images of crises on public opinion, and the recalling of previous crises such as 9/11, Hurricane Katrina, and the Deepwater Horizon oil spill.[18] In these studies, the type and frequency of news images were found to impact the recollection of the crisis event. In other words, the choice and repetition of news images functions to shape the public's collective memory

CHASETEN REMILLARD AND SHERIDAN MCVEAN

of an event. As Miller and LaPoe conclude, "society's visual saturation is an important area of study because visuals can affect the way audiences respond to or prioritize responses to a crisis."[19]

The power of images as a visual agenda-setting agent is amplified in moments of crisis for several reasons. First, audiences have a higher level of exposure to crisis coverage than regular news coverage. In general, audiences consume crisis information at higher rates than regular news.[20] This higher rate of exposure is a result not only of extended coverage often related to crisis situations, but also new digital technology. The internet enables people to tailor their news diet and to search out information that is of interest to them.[21] In times of crisis, audiences are therefore able to find and consume even more information across multiple news sources and through social network streams.

The highly affective impact of crisis images is a second reason why visual agenda-setting is so powerful. In general, shocking imagery increases an audience's attention to and consumption of news.[22] Also, generally speaking, images function as important mnemonic aids and can stand as iconic representations for entire political events.[23] Images can, as well, stimulate immediate and long-term emotional reactions to events, and "audiences respond to media messages using the same dimensions of emotions used in responding to real-life experiences."[24]

In comparison with regular news images, images of crisis are more engaging and more threatening. However, despite the impetus of photojournalists to capture distinctive and unique images of crises, and a marked increase in the public's appetite for images of crisis, some contend that even these images are conventional.[25] Wright describes how images of disaster follow predictable narratives within the news, and that these characteristic images of disaster facilitate easier editorial decisions, aligning with audience expectations to "numb down" audience reaction: "the repetitious use of 'TV codes' and the reporting of disasters according to predetermined formulae has a numbing effect on the audience."[26] Therefore, although viewer ratings of news broadcasts increase, Wright questions whether or not news audiences have mentally "switched off," even in the face of disaster.[27]

Here, once again, the impact of digital technology amplifies the power of images to function as agenda-setting agents. Advances in technology and the ubiquity of internet coverage now make the transmission of digital images easy. As a result, social media content and internet news is becoming more image rich. Moreover, the ease with which high-quality images can be distributed on contemporary digital networks means that audiences can easily monitor a crisis situation through continuous news updates and also watch it in real time as it unfolds. Importantly, these images of contemporary crises are not always vetted or curated through traditional news agencies. As such, these images function differently than traditional news images, as they triangulate the crisis from a multitude of citizen perspectives. The handheld smart phone in everyone's pocket acts as a phalanx of embedded photojournalists. The imagery it captures is raw, immediate, personal, and palpable.

Moreover, the instantaneous, interactive, dialogic, and global characteristics of social media enable images to not only broadcast crises outside the parameters of traditional reportage, but also to stimulate and facilitate public debate and discussion around the meaning, direction, and consequences of the crisis. In other words, the capture and dissemination of crisis images through social media creates both a visual agenda-setting function, but also a dialogic and public agenda-setting one as well.

The internet, and by extension social media, has long been heralded, or feared, as a new public sphere. Since social media commentary is readily available and not controlled by editorial decisions to the extent that mainstream media is, some predict that social media comments can potentially enable minority opinions more voice than traditional news media.[28] In terms of crisis situations, such alternative voices may set an agenda that quite starkly contrasts that of official proclamations. This poses an interesting question: To what extent should leadership monitor and respond to such frames and make sense of the crisis in relation to this visual narrative and the consequential agenda it initiates, as set by social media commentary?

As an aside, Marland has written about the use of branding and marketing techniques in government and politics, particularly in regards to the Canadian federal government.[29] We believe that the sudden growth of the Fort McMurray wildfire severely restricted the Alberta government's ability to brand or use the marketing techniques described by Marland in its early communication. The widespread availability of social media images, as described in the previous section, provided the context in which the crisis was subsequently understood in a way not planned or prescribed by Premier

CHASETEN REMILLARD AND SHERIDAN MCVEAN

Notley or her government. And she had very little time to plan prior to her first news conference on the wildfire.

Method

Typically, agenda-setting effects are measured through a comparison of two distinct metrics, a quantitative content analysis of media content related to an event (e.g., an election, a policy change) and a quantitative or qualitative survey of audience opinions or recollections of that same event.[30] The impact of the agenda-setting effect, therefore, is understood normatively, and these quantitative results are considered robust in terms of both generalizability and predictability. Our approach is different. Since we seek to analyze the extent to which the potential agenda-setting effects of images and social media commentary shaped the crisis communication of Premier Notley, we compare the content of images associated with the Fort McMurray wildfire, the content of comments associated with online news stories of the crisis posted during the opening days of the wildfire, and the content of Notley's first five press conferences.

Content coding for the image set was facilitated through the use of Google Images. Using the search term "Fort McMurray wildfire," a set of 150 images was collected. Once gathered, the images were coded inductively. This enabled us to approach the data without preconceived categories, and instead to let meaningful categories emerge from the data.

Inductive content coding was also used to develop meaningful content themes from the comments of two online news stories related to the wildfire, posted by the CBC on 4 and 5 May 2016.[31] Although only a small sample of the vast amount of coverage the wildfire garnered, these news stories provide an insight into the emergent public response to the fire. The content of all comments posted to the two stories during the same time period as the initial five Notley news conferences, were collected as well. An initial open coding and word count was conducted; secondary coding then provided us a "means of describing the phenomenon, to increase understanding and to generate knowledge."[32]

A similar process was used to code the content of Premier Notley's addresses. We selected Notley's statements from the official updates held at the Emergency Operations Centre.[33] They were available on the "YourAlberta"

YouTube channel, which is maintained by the government-run Alberta Public Affairs Bureau. The premier's initial comments from the first five government updates were coded inductively. The length of the premier's initial comments in these updates ranges from 3:00 minutes in the first update (the shortest) to 11:37 minutes in the fifth update (the longest of the five under study). During the third update, the Honourable Danielle Larivee, then the provincial minister of municipal affairs, made the initial comments instead of Premier Notley, as the premier was visiting the wildfire area and therefore unavailable.

Given that these updates were consisted of speeches delivered by Notley, we used time rather than word count as our unit of measurement. This enabled us to account for emphasis expressed through the form of delivery, pacing, and non-verbal communication. By measuring the time the premier took to relay her messages we were able to remark on what the performative salience of each of her points were.

Findings

From the content coding of the visual data, commentary data, and the Notley press release data, we found several contrasting agendas. The visual data emphasized the evacuation, the scope and severity of the fire, and the urban context in which it took place. The online comments prioritized support and concern for those impacted, and the causes and magnitude of the fire. Importantly, the commentary also emphasized negative emotions, conspiracy theories related to the fire's cause, and judgment of those impacted by the fire as responsible or deserving of the fire because of their association with so-called dirty oil. In Notley's updates, she set an agenda that emphasized governmental and intergovernmental actions to address the evacuation and magnitude of the fire; she also offered support and sympathy for those impacted, and thanked first responders and industry for their efforts.

Seeing the Beast: The Visual Agenda

The visual data was categorized according to eight content codes: evacuation (28 per cent); scope and severity (23 per cent); urban fire (17 per cent);

forest fire (10 per cent); rural fire (3 per cent); destroyed property (10 per cent); and first responders (9 per cent).

Evacuation (28 per cent) was the most prevalent image code. Evacuation images showed cars moving in long lines, often in front of or between large walls of flames. The images were variously composed; some were screen shots from dash cams and smart phones. Others were shot from a distance, revealing the number of vehicles, and by implication, people impacted by the fire. Overall, the evacuation code showed the size, speed, and embodied experience of those fleeing the fire.

Scope and severity images were comprised of several different visual representations of the fire, and these account for 23 per cent of the images. Some were aerial or satellite images of the fire, which documented its geographical enormity. Others consisted of maps, which again distilled the size and scope of the fire. Finally, still others depicted eerily beautiful vistas that present the landscape at a distance and the fire encompassing the horizon or plumes of smoke rising into the sky. These images all express the uncontrollable magnitude of the fire and do not specifically address the displacement of people.

Urban fire (17 per cent), forest fire (10 per cent), and rural fire (3 per cent) collectively account for 30 per cent of the images; as such they comprise the largest category of images. However, it was still important for us to differentiate the contexts in which the fire was pictured. Each of the "fire" categories depicts flames or smoke, or both, without a visual representation of evacuation, but they do so in different contexts. Urban fire images depict fire consuming or threating buildings, residential homes, and businesses. Forest fire images show trees and forests engulfed in flames. And rural fire images depict pasturelands or agricultural fields in flames, or under threat of flames.

The last two coded categories of visual data are destroyed property (10 per cent) and first responders (9 per cent). Images coded as "destroyed property" show the aftermath of the fire. These images show burned cars, furniture, or homes. Images coded "first responders" depict any first responder in the act of conducting their job during the fire.

Overall, when the top three categories of images are considered together, the visual agenda of the fire is evacuation, magnitude, and urban destruction.

The Beast Online: The Social Media Agenda

The textual data gathered from the comments sections of two news stories associated with the fire during the first few days of the crisis generated eleven different content categories: support (24 per cent); cause of fire (22 per cent); magnitude of fire (8 per cent); fire management (10 per cent); government distrust (9 per cent); judgment and mockery (9 per cent); evacuation (4 per cent); negative emotions (8 per cent); positive emotions (3 per cent); first responders (3 per cent); and media control and bias (2 per cent).

The support code was the most prevalent of all eleven content codes. Comments associated with that category included statements of empathy and sympathy for the people impacted by the fire. These included calls and suggestions for donations, as well as statements of solidarity and caring. The support code is differentiated from the positive emotion code in that the later captured statements of gratitude, thanks, and positive outcomes. In other words, "positive emotion" was a code we used to demark, typically, comments by people who had been impacted by the fire.

Interestingly, despite a dominant agenda set by the visual data, evacuation was a minor component of comment content. The code "evacuation" was used to categorize comments that referenced the logistics and undertaking of the evacuation. Instead, causes of fire was the second most discussed topic in the commentary of the news stories. The list of causes discussed in the commentary section ranged from arson to climate change. Of the causes listed or discussed, natural causes (30 per cent) was the most frequently cited. The fire's natural causes were speculated to include warmer than usual weather, lighting storms, and high winds, for example. Almost equally present in the discussion of causes was a category we labelled "conspiracy" (24 per cent). Conspiracy causes ranged from the coming of the apocalypse to tailing ponds. The unifying element of this code was expressed in the assumption that the fires were caused by mismanagement, malfeasance, or malice. The fires were positioned as a result of wrongdoing.

Finally, climate change was categorized as its own separate cause category within the data because some comments framed climate change as a natural (albeit human-initiated) cause of the fire as it resulted in unseasonably high temperatures and low precipitation. Others, however, cited climate change as a direct result of petroleum extraction and use. These

CHASETEN REMILLARD AND SHERIDAN MCVEAN

comments tended to align with the tone and intent of the conspiracy code, however they maintained a more implicit culpability.

After looking at both the conspiracy theme and those comments related to climate change that implicated the oil sands as a contributor to global climate change, we observed that a significant amount of online commentary placed both implicit and explicit blame for the fire on the oil sands industry. These types of comments were reinforced by the code "judgment and mockery" (9 per cent), which included comments that framed the fire as retribution for working in the oil industry, or supporting the oil industry. These types of comments often made a karma connection that assumed that Fort McMurray was getting "what it deserved" because it had benefited from the extraction of "dirty oil."

This sentiment also aligns with comments coded as "government distrust" and "media control and bias," both of which voice skepticism about the truthfulness of the government and the media. Implicit in these comments is the suspicion that the whole story is not being shared with the public, and often, as with the more conspiratorial comments, an underlying sense that the fire was a result of an industry blunder or cover-up.

Finally, many comments expressed overt negative emotions associated with the fire. These "negative emotion" comments included fear, sadness, depression, shock, and horror. Although constituting only 8 per cent of the commentary content, these negative emotions reinforce the power of images to generate strong affective impacts on viewers.

Notley's Response: The Premier's Agenda

The content gathered from the first five government updates generated nine different categories: evacuation (23 per cent); scope and magnitude (16 per cent); support and sympathy (14 per cent); government actions, assessments, and plans (14 per cent); inter-government co-operation (13 per cent); motivation and gratitude (7 per cent); first responders (5 per cent); industry co-operation (4 per cent); and fire prevention (1 per cent).

The two most prevalent codes in Notley's updates were predictably related to the evacuation of Fort McMurray and the scope and magnitude of the fire. The impact and logistics of the fire on Fort McMurray and its residents constituted nearly 40 per cent of the total time of Notley's speech.

These codes included topics such as instructions to evacuees, updates on the fire's position, and statements about where evacuees were currently being housed.

Unlike the previously discussed content, government and inter-government actions featured prominently in Notley's speeches. The codes "government actions, assessments, and plans" and "inter-government co-operation" collectively comprise nearly a third of Notley's speaking time, accounting for 27 per cent of the total. These codes included statements about government decisions, explanations about implementing a state of emergency, details about how government agencies were assessing the safety of key infrastructure elements, and the premier's personal plans to visit different locations or meet with different stakeholders.

The codes "support and sympathy" and "motivation and gratitude," which both express positive emotional messages or material and emotional support for those directly impacted by the wildfire, or Albertans in general, combined to account for 21 per cent of the Notley updates. We continued to differentiate these codes, as the term "support and sympathy" denote statements or actions that have occurred and that are material or emotional in nature. By contrast, the code "motivation and gratitude" captures comments that are unifying in nature, such as "we are strong and will overcome this," as well as statements of thanks to specific individuals, groups, or agencies.

Nearly equally represented in the content of Notley's updates were industry and first responders. This content was categorized in the codes "industry" and "first responders," respectively. The first responders code was used to categorize comments related to the efforts and progress of various first responders, police, fire fighters, and emergency medical services in their collective efforts to fight the fire and provide support for citizens. The industry code specifically refers to the oil industry and those companies that have operations in the region impacted by the fire. Those of Notley's comments that were coded "industry" included statements of co-operative actions, updates on the support companies provided to evacuees, and the status of employees impacted by the evacuation order.

Taming the Beast: Trends in Notley's Crisis Communication

Our primary finding is that Notley's updates frame the wildfire crisis in a predictable manner that emphasizes "bolstering" and "corrective action" messages, as outlined by dominant theories of crisis communication. However, her updates did not fully address the alternative agendas set by the visual and online narratives of the wildfire. In avoiding certain points of the visual and online agendas, Notley was better able to emphasize a cohesive, collaborative, and positive response the fire.

When the content of Notley's speeches are considered from the perspective of dominant crisis communications strategies, her communication followed a predictable pattern. The premier primarily used what Benoit has labelled "bolstering messages," meaning she stressed positive aspects, for example by thanking the firefighters and emergency workers responding to the fire, as well as thanking the work of other governments and the energy companies with operations in the area. Overall, the tone of her speeches was positive, as the prevalence of the codes "support and sympathy" and "motivation and gratitude" reflect.

The premier also used what Benoit has termed "corrective action" messages, which state specific actions the government was or would be doing to help make the situation better and to support evacuees. Although the scope and magnitude of the fire was a prevalent content category of Notley's statements, as it was in both the visual and the online commentary content, details of the wildfire's spread were nearly always framed by Notley in relation to efforts to fight the fire and mitigate its negative impacts on citizens and property. This emphasis on action is reflected in the high prevalence of content that detailed the various government and intergovernmental actions taken.

Moreover, Notley also addressed the actions of both first responders and the energy industry in their efforts to combat the fire. In considering the role of government during crisis situations as what Boin and his co-authors describe as "meaning-making," the premier actively generated a narrative of collaboration between government, industry, and first-response agencies. She also heralded firefighters, police, and emergency response personnel as superheroes fighting against "the beast." She consistently praised the energy industry's contributions during the initial and subsequent evacuations. She discussed the work of municipal and local leaders, and she outlined her government's actions and plans. Taken together, nearly 40 per cent of the entire content of her updates was dedicated to chronicling the different actions, agents, and collaborative efforts undertaken to stop the fire and keep people and property safe. Furthermore, over the course of the five news conferences, the premier changed from expressing only sympathy for the evacuees in the first two conferences to providing more information and reassurance to evacuees during the three subsequent addresses. This underscored the government's determination to take action to further and deepen its support of the evacuees.

Notley emphasized both "bolstering" and "corrective action" messages, and set an agenda that was both positive in tone and anchored in action. Her key messages were rooted in positive emotions, concrete and corrective actions, co-operation, and progress. Thus, although Notley did not specifically address the shocking visual nature of the fire, which in the visual content was expressed through images of fiery escape, expansive horizons of smoke, and urban destruction, she was able to combat that visual agenda through her own agenda of sustained and collective action and positive, motivational, and gracious sentiment.

A major category of the online commentary agenda was the causes of fire. The premier made no comments about the cause of the wildfire, although she did slightly discuss fire prevention (1 per cent). Similarly, despite the significant distrust in the government voiced in the online content, Notley did not attempt to justify or defend the mandatory evacuations and did not mention the possibility that the government may have done a better job preventing wildfires. In this way she avoided altogether any discussion of culpability in her updates. Again, through an emphasis on bolstering and corrective action, Notley set an agenda that did not prioritize looking backward at causes, but rather focused on current actions aimed at improving and mitigating the situation. So, while the government took no responsibility for anything related to the start of the wildfire or the initial mandatory evacuation, the frequency of the news conferences and the premier's comments at the news conferences demonstrated that the government was taking action to deal with the wildfire situation and the plight of the evacuees.

CHASETEN REMILLARD AND SHERIDAN MCVEAN

Finally, Premier Notley seized an opportunity to emphasize collaboration, gratitude, and co-operation with the oil industry. Her promises to re-evaluate royalties and carbon taxes convinced most Albertans that her government would strike a more adversarial role with oil industry than previous governments. To some, this was a benefit, as it showed that the Notley government would strike a seemingly more responsible path in terms of carbon emissions and environmental oversight. To others, such policy changes could only deepen the growing recession in Alberta and stymie economic growth. The online commentary raises this debate in the content coded in the category "judgment and mockery" and the conspiratorial elements of the "causes of fire," which include such things as industry pollution or the connection between industry, global warming, and increased wildfires. In other words, albeit in a more extreme, insensitive, and vitriolic manner, some of the sentiments raised in the online commentary speak to the very issues that propelled Notley to power and made her a controversial figure in relation to the oil industry. In not addressing the causes of the fire, and through emphasizing the responsible actions of the oil industry, Notley once again emphasized messages that were both "bolstering" and "corrective." In so doing, she unified Albertans as a collective and avoided potentially divisive topics of culpability.

Putting the Beast to Rest

"The beast" raged for over sixty days, destroyed homes, and displaced thousands. Images of the fire generated powerful emotions and brought the shock and horror of the event to countless smart phones, tablets, and television screens. Online commentary and social media enabled citizens to comment and question the events of the fire. Premier Notley, new to power, faced an unparalleled test of her leadership. But in those opening days of the crisis, through consistent and purposeful crisis messaging, Notley set the agenda of the fire in terms of government action and co-operation and positive support and sympathy. Although she did not explicitly address some of the most prevalent concerns raised by the narrative set by online images and commentary, her emphasis on "bolstering" and "corrective action" messages aligned with crisis communication best practices and enabled her to set an agenda that reinforced her leadership style and capacity.

NOTES

1   William L. Benoit, "Image repair discourse and crisis communication," *Public Relations Review* 23, no. 2 (1997): 177–86.

2   Maxwell McCombs and Donald Shaw, "The agenda-setting function of the mass media," *Public Opinion Quarterly* 36, no. 2 (1972): 176–87.

3   Ibid.; see also Shanto Iyengar and Donald Kinder, *News that matters: Television and American opinion* (Chicago: University of Chicago Press, 1987), and Kimberly Goss and Sean Aday, "The scary world in your living room and neighborhood: Using local broadcast news, neighborhood crime rates, and personal experience to test agenda-setting and cultivation," *Journal of Communication* 53 (2003): 411–26.

4   Bernard C. Cohen, *The Press and Foreign Policy* (Princeton, NJ: Princeton University Press, 1963), 13.

5   McCombs and Shaw, "The agenda-setting function of the mass media."

6   See Benoit, "Image repair discourse," and Timothy Coombs, *Ongoing crisis communication: Planning, managing, and responding* (Thousand Oaks, CA: Sage, 2015).

7   Benoit, "Image repair discourse," 178.

8   Nia Williams, "Humans probably caused the Fort McMurray Wildfire: Police," *Reuters*, 14 June 2016, http://www.reuters.com/article/us-canada-wildfire-cause-idUSKCN0Z02OO (accessed 22 November 2016).

9   Coombs, *Ongoing crisis communication*, 147.

10 Timothy Coombs, "Attribution theory as a guide for post-crisis communication research," *Public Relations Review* 33, no. 2 (2007): 135–9.

11 Ibid., 137.

12 Coombs, *Ongoing crisis communication*.

13 Ibid.

14 Laura Arpan and David Roskos-Ewoldsen, "Stealing thunder: Analysis of the effects of proactive disclosure of crisis information," *Public Relations Review* 31, no. 3 (2005): 425–33.

15 Arjen Boin, Paul Hart, Eric Stern, and Bengt Sundelius, *The politics of crisis management: Public leadership under pressure* (Cambridge: Cambridge University Press 2005), 12.

16 Alberta Agriculture and Forestry, "Wildfires 10-Year Average," 15 April 2015, https://wildfire.alberta.ca/resources/historical-data/documents/Wildfires10YearAverage-Mar08-2017.pdf (accessed 14 August 2018).

17 Boin et al., *The politics of crisis management*, 13.

18 Shahira Fahmy, Sooyoung Cho, Wayne Wanta, and Yanghoi Song, "Visual agenda-setting after 9/11: Individual emotion, recall and concern about terrorism," *Visual Communication Quarterly* 13, no. 1 (2006): 4–15; Andrea Miller and Victoria LaPoe, "Visual Agenda-Setting, Emotion, and the BP Oil Disaster," *Visual Communication*

Quarterly 23, no. 1 (2016): 53–63; and Andrea Miller and Shearon Roberts, "Visual agenda-setting and proximity after Hurricane Katrina: A study of those closest to the event," *Visual Communication Quarterly* 17, no. 1 (2010): 31–46.

19   Miller and LaPoe, "Visual Agenda-Setting," 53.

20   Ibid.

21   David Taras, *Digital Mosaic: Media, Power, and Identity in Canada.* (Toronto: Toronto University Press, 2015).

22   Silvia Knobloch, Matthais Hastall, Dorf Zillmann, and Coy Callison, "Imagery effects on the selective reading of Internet newsmagazines," *Communication Research* 30, no. 1 (2003): 3–29.

23   David Perlmutter, *Photojournalism and foreign policy: Framing icons of outrage in international crisis* (Westport, CT: Greenwood, 1998).

24   Fahmy et al., "Visual agenda-setting after 9/11," 8.

25   See Andrew Mendelson, "Effects of novelty in news photographs on attention and memory," *Media Psychology* 3 (2001): 119–57, and Terence Wright, "Collateral coverage: Media images of Afghan refugees, 2001," *Visual Studies* 19, no. 1 (2004): 97–112.

26   Wright, "Collateral coverage," 100.

27   Ibid., 101.

28   Roger Silverstone, "Finding a Voice: Minorities, Media and the Global Commons," *Emergences: Journal for the Study of Media & Composite Cultures* 11, no. 1 (2001): 13–27.

29   Alexander J. Marland, *Brand Command: Canadian Politics and Democracy in the Age of Message Control* (Vancouver: UBC Press, 2016).

30   See most notably McCombs and Shaw, "The agenda-setting function of the mass media."

31   "Fort McMurray special May 5th, 2016," YouTube video, posted by Canadian Broadcasting Corporation, https://www.youtube.com/watch?v=jfsXF4v3Zeo, and "Fort McMurray special, May 4, 2016," YouTube Video, posted by Canadian Broadcasting Corporation, https://www.youtube.com/watch?v=Xn2ydiQctus&t=50ls.

32   Satu Elo and Helvi Kyngas, "The qualitative content analysis process," *Journal of Advanced Nursing* 62, no. 1 (2007): 111.

33   These are online as follows: "Fort McMurray Wildfire Update #1 – May 3, 2016 at 5 pm," YouTube video, posted by YourAlberta, https://youtu.be/Wp9rhagUcUM; "Fort McMurray Wildfire Update #2 – May 4, 10:15 am," YouTube Video, posted by YourAlberta, https://youtu.be/kX8um8SYKiY; "Fort McMurray Wildfire Update #3 – May 4, 2016 at 3:15 pm," YouTube Video, posted by YourAlberta, https://youtu.be/9Xp7o3-dQ_4; "Fort McMurray Wildfire Update #4 – May 5, 2016 at 11:20 am," YouTube Video, posted by YourAlberta, https://youtu.be/B8UJ-OLBsZA; and "Fort McMurray Wildfire Update #5 – May 5, 2016 at 6:05 pm," YouTube Video, posted by YourAlberta, https://youtu.be/Z_-9oOW9Uuo (all urls accessed 22 November 2016).

VI

ALBERTA'S FUTURE
POLITICAL SYSTEM

What's Past is Prologue:
Ontario 1990 and Alberta 2015

Graham White

Commentary on the results of the 5 May 2015 Alberta election often began with words like "stunning upset," "totally unexpected," and "unprecedented." Indeed, anyone who predicted, even a few weeks earlier, that Rachel Notley's New Democrats would form a majority government would have been dismissed as seriously delusional. Yet an NDP majority it was. And "totally unexpected" certainly applied to a convincing majority victory by a party which in the previous election hadn't even managed 10 per cent of the vote, electing fewer than a handful of MLAs.

But as for unprecedented . . . Was it?

The 2015 election was by no means the first in Alberta to see a third party come out of nowhere to claim a smashing electoral victory. In 1921, the United Farmers of Alberta (UFA) ousted the Liberal government, going from 3 seats to 38, a majority in the 61-seat House. In turn the UFA suffered a similar—in fact worse—fate in the 1935 election, losing every one of its seats as the Social Credit Party, which hadn't existed until a few months before the election, took all but 7 of the legislature's 63 seats.

Given the social, economic, and demographic changes that have transformed the province since the Great Depression, 1921 and 1935 rate as close to prehistoric so far as contemporary Alberta is concerned. Surely the surprise accession to power in modern-day Alberta of a (to be sure, moderate) left-wing NDP, when the party had never come remotely close to winning power in the province, was truly unprecedented.

In Alberta it was, but a generation earlier an eerily similar election brought an equally surprised and unprepared NDP government to power—in Ontario, of all places. In recent decades the NDP has formed the government in British Columbia, Saskatchewan, Manitoba, Yukon, and Nova Scotia, but in each instance the NDP had already been a major contender for power, so while its electoral victories in those provinces may have been noteworthy, they were not unexpected. By contrast, the 1990 Ontario election brought to power a provincial NDP that had never come close to winning an election, though its vote share was consistently higher than that garnered by its Alberta brethren.[1]

This chapter is an exercise in comparison, on the presumption that even unique political developments are better understood in comparison with similar situations. Given my limited expertise in Alberta politics, the object of the chapter is not to make pronouncements about the early days of the Notley government. My hope, rather, is that juxtaposing the early experiences of the Notley-led NDP government with those of the Ontario NDP a generation before will generate questions and insights that will enhance the understanding of those who study and participate in Alberta politics. It may even be of wider relevance to the study of newly elected social democratic governments in Canada, regardless of whether their ascent to power was unexpected.

The focus here is not on the policy directions adopted or avoided by the Notley government, in large part because it will be some time before the political and substantive success of the NDP's policy decisions can be evaluated (including their staying power under subsequent governments of different stripes). Instead, significant emphasis is placed on transition, the oft-times mysterious process by which newly elected political parties take over the reins of power and prepare themselves to govern. The chapter employs a broad understanding of "transition," one that encompasses not just the brief period between election and swearing in (when the formal transition team typically disbands), but also the early political and administrative decisions taken by the new government. Transitions can be done well or badly, but either way they are critically important in rendering a neophyte government into an effective one. Arguably, the Ontario NDP government never fully recovered from its rocky transition.

GRAHAM WHITE

Alberta is not Ontario

Lest it be thought that this chapter is little more than an exercise in Central Canadian hubris—the implicit message being that Ontario had done it all before so that there was nothing new or interesting about the Alberta NDP's ascension to power—let me make it clear that while striking similarities are evident, the two cases also exhibit extensive, significant differences. And that intriguing as the Ontario comparison may be, what transpired in Alberta in 2015 was very much *sui generis* and worthy of study of its own accord, as indeed this book demonstrates. In addition, of course, there is value in knowing what the Notley government learned from the experiences of the Ontario NDP—especially their mistakes—as it took power.

First and foremost, of course, Alberta in 2015 was a very different place than Ontario in 1990, not just in the context of politics but also in terms of the two provinces' economics and of socio-demographic profiles. Both economies were in serious decline when the NDP came to power, but the depth of the Ontario recession did not become clear for some time after the election, whereas Alberta's economic woes had been obvious for some time prior to the election. As well, the economic downturn in Alberta was almost entirely due to a precipitous decline in world prices for oil and gas and was far more severe than what Ontario experienced in 1990 (though, to be sure, it was that province's worst economic slump since the Depression), which was primarily a function of problems in the manufacturing sector, compounded by high interest rates.

Politically, substantial differences are evident as well. Leaving aside the conceptual and empirical morass into which comparisons of provincial political cultures often fall, sharp contrasts mark the two provinces' party systems. While the 2015 Alberta election saw the end of forty-four years of Conservative rule, and while it was only five years before the Ontario election of 1990 that forty-three years of Conservative rule came to an end, it would be a mistake to assume too much similarity. For much of their time in office the Alberta Tories enjoyed massive, overwhelming majorities in the legislature, often with a small, enfeebled opposition. Alberta was a classic one-party dominant system, with support for other parties, including distinctively Albertan parties such as Wildrose, constantly waxing and waning. In Ontario, the Conservatives were clearly in control during their long reign but (other than in the 1950s) had to contend with numerically and politically strong opposition parties. This reflects the primal reality that since the early 1960s Ontario has had a stable three-party system. Relatedly, in recent decades, including during the long Conservative period, Ontario has experienced repeated episodes of minority government. Alberta, by contrast, has never known a minority government.[2]

When Bob Rae's New Democrats came to power in 1990, some may have thought that a new political balance among the parties would ensue, but no one expected either the Liberals or the Conservatives to disappear. Otherwise put, the essential stability of the three-party system was not in doubt. By contrast, if the highly fluid political situation faced by the Notley government in its early days has solidified for the next election, the medium- and long-term future for the Alberta party system is opaque. This topic is discussed in the next chapter by Anthony Sayers and David Stewart.

Among the political imponderables—and this is yet another contrast with the earlier Ontario situation—are the prospects that the Alberta NDP can maintain the level of support it received in May 2015. The more than four-fold jump in the party's vote share—from under 10 per cent to more than 40 per cent—was nothing less than remarkable, but can the party retain it, let alone build on it? To be sure, the Ontario New Democrats came to power in 1990 by virtue of a substantial boost in their electoral fortunes, but the increase they enjoyed was far less dramatic: from about 25 per cent in 1987 to just under 38 per cent.

In the legislative realm, an important difference is the nature and effectiveness of the opposition faced by the two NDP cabinets. The Rae government in Ontario faced some fifty-six members of the opposition, many of whom were able, experienced ex-ministers. Although Rachel Notley's cabinet looked across the chamber at thirty-three opposition MLAs, only a handful of the Progressive Conservative members had experience in government.[3]

Of the good many further political differences that could be explored, two deserve at least passing mention. First, the substance and the tenor of federal-provincial relations have long been starkly different, with of course correspondingly different and important implications for provincial politics. Second, nothing that occurred during Bob Rae's premiership (or that of any other Ontario premier for that matter) approaches in scale and significance—including in the political realm—the catastrophic Fort McMurray fire (see the previous chapter by Chaseten Remillard and Sheridan McVean), which kept Premier Notley front and centre for the duration of the most destructive episode in provincial history.

A final difference: Rachel Notley is unlikely to be a candidate for the leadership of the Liberal Party of Canada.

Surprised and Unprepared

The Alberta NDP under Rachel Notley had aspirations to win power, but this was expected to take some time. As Melanee Thomas describes in her chapter, the NDP plan built on its small but effective four-MLA caucus. For the 2015 election the party had identified a small number of ridings it believed it could win; in turn, this broader base would serve as the springboard to victory one or two elections down the road. Even the most optimistic party operatives could hardly conceive of an election outcome producing dozens of NDP MLAs and a majority government. From the outset it was clear that the election was going badly for the ruling Conservatives, that the Wildrose Party was struggling to recover from the devastating mass defection of nine of its MLAs—including its leader, Danielle Smith—just five months earlier, and that Notley and the NDP were attracting widespread support. Still, according to journalists Sydney Sharpe and Don Braid, it was just over a week before voting day that the party's internal polling convinced an astounded Notley that the NDP would win. Notley immediately realized that nothing had been done by way of transition planning, and so she directed that top priority be devoted to it.[4]

If the Alberta New Democrats had barely a week of pre-election transition planning, at least they had begun the process before the votes were counted. As in Alberta in 2015, the Ontario election of 1990 began badly for the governing party—in this instance the Liberals—and it continued downhill as the campaign progressed. Nor were the Progressive Conservatives doing much better; they had a new, inexperienced leader and the party was still in disarray after its humbling fall from power in 1985. By contrast, the NDP was attracting big and supportive crowds in ridings where it had previously been all but irrelevant. Although the NDP had formed the Official Opposition following the 1987 Ontario election, unlike in Alberta, little optimism existed in the party about a possible path to power. Bob Rae had privately decided to resign after the election and leading MPPs did not run.[5] Although things were going remarkably well for the NDP, and despite internal poll numbers pointing to an NDP victory, top party officials seemed unable to contemplate forming a government.[6] According to Rae's memoirs, even on election day "we began to prepare for the *possibility* of a transition to government."[7]

That the Ontario NDP experienced a difficult transition owed a good deal to the party's lack of attention to the possibility that it would be called on to govern. The NDP was hardly unusual in this regard; in Canada parties that see themselves far from power typically pay little heed to transition planning, in part because it can seem a poor use of scarce organizational resources and in part because they fear being portrayed as arrogant or out of touch in media accounts that fail to appreciate the importance of transition planning. Indeed, the Rae government's predecessor, the Liberal government of David Peterson, had come to power five years earlier having done no transition planning whatsoever before the election.[8]

At the same time, the bureaucracy also bore significant responsibility for the inadequacies of the NDP transition. In terms of preparation for a possible change in government, the bureaucracy was caught almost as flatfooted as the NDP. Very little work had been done in anticipation of a transfer of power from the Liberals to the NDP or Progressive Conservatives. Moreover, once the results were in, significant elements in the senior ranks of the Ontario bureaucracy failed not only to appreciate that the NDP's goals and approaches differed substantially from those of the Liberals, but also to accommodate the needs of the new government.[9]

A Good Time or a Long Time?

At the first meeting of the BC NDP cabinet following the 1972 provincial election, which brought the party to power for the first time, Premier Dave Barrett put a key question to his ministers:

> Were we there for a good time or a long time? Under that umbrella, we discussed whether we were really going to make fundamental changes in British Columbia, or whether we

GRAHAM WHITE

should try to hang on for another term, rationalizing that we'd get the job done next time around. We agreed unanimously to strike while the iron was hot. Our government represented the first real break from the traditional power base in the province. We were free and unfettered to roam in new directions. We were impatient to do something decent and honest and human. It was going to be a good time for the ordinary people of British Columbia.[10]

No political party wins power and immediately plans on being defeated in the next election. At the same time, a party that comes to office with an agenda significantly outside the mainstream needs to address the issue of whether it will be a one-term government, especially if an unusual confluence of political circumstances contributed substantially to its electoral victory. And if the probabilities suggest that it will indeed be a one-term government, what can it do to produce, in Barrett's apt phrase, a "good time"—substantial, lasting political and policy change?

To be sure, nothing—neither victory nor defeat—is assured in politics. If, as Harold Wilson famously put it, a week is a long time in politics, five years is an eternity. Incumbency at the local level and control of the machinery and financial clout of government have served many parties seeking re-election well. Nonetheless, the very strong likelihood was that the Ontario NDP was destined to be a one-term government. This is not a retrospective judgement based on the dire economic straights Ontario faced in the early 1990s, much of which was unfairly blamed on the NDP. Rather, it should have been clear from the outset that the Ontario NDP victory in the 1990 election owed a great deal to an unlikely-to-be-repeated alignment of political factors. The NDP benefitted extensively from favourable vote splits, which allowed them to win a comfortable majority—74 of 130 seats—on less than 38 per cent of the vote. The potential for growth was very limited; in the next election, the New Democrats might hope to win at most 3 or 4 of the seats that had escaped them in 1990. By contrast, the party had managed to win between a dozen and a score of rural or semi-rural ridings (depending on how one counted them), often by slim margins, that it had no business winning, having never been competitive in them and lacking all but the most rudimentary campaign organization. Many, if not all, of these ridings were unlikely to return to the NDP fold come the next election.[11]

The Ontario NDP leadership, both government and party, would have been keenly aware of these hard political realities, and they would have known that this pointed to the likelihood of a one-term NDP government (the deep animosity between the NDP and both the Liberals and the Progressive Conservatives, as well as the ideological gap between them, rendered improbable the prospect of a minority NDP government). However, it seems that the Rae government never seriously confronted the practical questions of only holding power for one term.

What about their compatriots in Alberta twenty-five years later? As Anthony Sayers and David Stewart indicate in the next chapter, the future of Alberta politics would entail either long-term consolidation of the right or continued division, each with very different electoral implications for the NDP. Duane Bratt writes in his chapter that he would not be surprised to see the complete demise of the Progressive Conservative Party.

According to Brian Topp, chair of the Alberta NDP's transition team and subsequently Premier Notley's chief of staff, Barrett's challenge to his cabinet—"a famous exchange in Western NDP history"—was directly addressed by the new Alberta government. Notley's conclusion was that the way Barrett had framed the issue was "a false choice"—that it was important to do what the party had been elected to do (noting "we're condemned to be ourselves") and that this was the key to re-election.[12]

Of course, no government can guarantee that its capstone policies won't be reversed by its successors. Many of the principal policy initiatives of the Barrett NDP remained in place throughout the long tenure of the right-wing Social Credit Party, but most of the Ontario NDP's signature policies did not survive long under the Mike Harris Progressive Conservatives.

The Alberta Transition

Keith Brownsey's chapter provides a far more detailed account of the NDP transition in Alberta than is offered here. Still, in contrasting the Alberta experience with what happened in Ontario twenty-five years earlier, a few points warrant attention.

The Alberta transition team enjoyed a significant advantage over its Ontario predecessor in terms of its key members' previous government experience. Chair Brian Topp had served as deputy chief of staff to Saskatchewan premier Roy Romanow, and he had worked with other NDP governments so he knew the governmental ropes. Another member, John Heaney, had similar experience working for BC premier Mike Harcourt, and still others knew their way around government (as opposed to politics more generally). In contrast, while the members of the Ontario NDP transition team were all highly experienced politicos, not one had significant experience in government; as a result, they not only faced a steep learning curve but also lacked understanding and appreciation of the role of the public service.[13]

Topp points out that "the Alberta transition team did not have the luxury that some other Western NDP transitions had of thinking about its work for a year or more." Paradoxically, this turned out to be a blessing in that the transition "had the virtue of not being overthought." Especially in light of the premier's decision, in part to secure "supply" (i.e., authorize spending) to meet the legislature only six weeks after the election, "the brutal lack of time" forced the transition team to focus only on urgent tasks. Policy issues, for example, would be addressed by the premier and the new cabinet rather than in the transition process.[14]

The transition team relied heavily on the often substantial briefing books prepared by previous Western NDP transition teams. No attempt was made to duplicate their detailed analyses, however; rather the Alberta team distilled their contents into a "to do" list—a checklist of essential tasks. As this suggests, the Alberta transition was firmly located within the rich traditions of the Western Canadian NDP; the transition team did not seek out documentation on either the Ontario NDP transition or the much more recent NDP transition in Nova Scotia. Indeed, the Notley government sought to emulate not only Western NDP traditions but also prominent elements of Alberta history. In this vein, the first Throne Speech explicitly linked the government's aspirations and approaches to those of governments and parties in earlier eras—the founding Liberal government, the United Farmers of Alberta, the Socreds, and even, in their early days, the Progressive Conservatives.[15]

The transition team did touch base with most former NDP premiers, including Bob Rae, as well as other senior party officials, primarily from the West. Topp's former colleagues in the Romanow-era Premier's Office provided significant advice and encouragement, as did Romanow himself. Former Saskatchewan deputy premier Pat Atkinson provided mentoring and counsel to newly appointed ministers and to government MLAs.

The Ontario experience had little if any direct influence on the work of the transition team. The need to focus on the "irreducible minimum" left no time for academic sources on transitions, such as David Zussman's *Off and Running*[16] or the book that David Cameron and I wrote about transitions in Ontario, *Cycling into Saigon*, which examined what went wrong with the 1990 NDP transition and why the 1995 Progressive Conservative transition was so successful.[17] However, once in office, the Rae experience, in Topp's words, "did colour some of what we did in Alberta."[18] According to Topp, this influence could be seen in three different ways. (As discussed below, in political terms the Alberta NDP handled its first budget more adroitly than did the Ontario NDP, but this does not seem to have been as a result of a conscious decision to proceed differently.)

First, the Notley government had "a much lighter touch in shaking up the public service" than was the case in Ontario, since it was "less inclined to see them as opponents."[19] (The crucial topic of relations with the bureaucracy is examined in the next section of this chapter.) Second, Notley and her government understood that it was essential that the public saw them keeping their promises. The Alberta NDP government would avoid fundamental policy reverses, such as the Rae government's decision to abandon one of their central policy commitments, public auto insurance, which not only engendered a serious public credibility gap but also enraged party activists.[20] Third, noble as it may have been in the early 1990s to devote significant time and energy to constitutional issues, the political lesson was the need to "stick to your knitting"—that is, to give prime attention to dealing with the economic shocks that had rocked Alberta as a result of the decline in natural resource prices. Here Notley enjoyed an advantage not open to Rae. As premier of Ontario, Rae had to play a central role in the Meech Lake and Charlottetown processes, but Notley has not had to deal with such mega-constitutional issues, with their potential to create divisiveness on the home front. She has of course been deeply engaged in pipeline politics marked by bitter conflict with British Columbia and sometimes uncertain relations with Ottawa, but her strong advocacy of Alberta's resource

GRAHAM WHITE

industries carries substantial political benefits. (See Deborah Yedlin's chapter in this volume for analysis of this contentious issue.)

An important early decision for Notley concerned the size of her cabinet, and in this she took a very different approach than Rae in 1990. Against advice from NDP elder statesman and former Saskatchewan premier Allan Blakeney, who advocated beginning with a very small cabinet, Rae's initial cabinet numbered twenty-seven. In retrospect, Rae recognized that "I should have followed [Blakeney's advice]. . . . I listened instead to others who encouraged me to make the cabinet as inclusive as possible, and give people a chance to learn on the job."[21] For her part, Notley chose to heed the political advice of both her transition team and Roy Romanow, who favoured a small cabinet.

Beginning with a small cabinet brought significant political advantages: it permitted Notley to appoint people she knew, it sent a message to the rest of caucus that they were being given the opportunity to demonstrate their abilities, and it limited the challenges of staffing ministers' offices. In addition, according to Brian Topp, it made for a cabinet that was small enough to actually deliberate on decisions and thereby, in line with Notley's predisposition, establish a culture of deliberation in cabinet that would persist even when cabinet would expand.[22] Partly on the basis of his experience as a deputy minister in Ontario, Cabinet Secretary Richard Dicerni also recommended that Notley keep her first cabinet small for administrative reasons: the caucus included few experienced decision-makers and she faced too many unknowns when it came to prospective ministers.[23] Notley did not repeat Rae's mistake; her first cabinet consisted of only a dozen, including herself. (Three years later, the cabinet had grown substantially, to twenty, though this was still significantly fewer than the numbers in some Progressive Conservative cabinets; when she resigned Alison Redford, for example, had twenty-nine ministers.)

Whether a new government's first budget marks the end of the transition process is a question that need not concern us here. What is of interest is the significant contrast between the first budgets put forward by the Ontario and Alberta parties.[24] Overall, the numbers were similar: both entailed deficits of roughly $10 billion on spending of a little over $51 billion; in both cases, these were record high deficits.[25] Both budgets elicited severe criticism from the business community, though nothing in Alberta matched the spectacle of stock brokers and accountants screaming in protest on the lawn of the Ontario legislative building. Indeed, the Alberta NDP handled the politics of its first budget far more adroitly than had their Ontario counterparts in 1991.

Ontario treasurer Floyd Laughren inherited a structural deficit of roughly $8 billion from his Liberal predecessors, so that in some ways his first budget was less radical than status quo.[26] It did not of course appear that way at the time, given that the Liberals had claimed (quite wrongly) that they had delivered a balanced budget the previous year and the New Democrats were projecting a $10 billion deficit. The Ontario NDP government naively assumed that the budget's positive features, which were obvious to them, would be equally obvious to the public. They weren't, and the NDP immediately plunged 20 to 25 per cent in the polls, a reverse from which they never recovered.[27]

In Alberta the NDP brought in former Bank of Canada governor David Dodge—surely the antithesis of a wild-eyed economic radical—to review the province's infrastructure needs and financing. Not surprisingly in light of the pervasive infrastructure deficit that had plagued Alberta for some time, Dodge recommended a substantial increase in capital spending.[28] Citing his advice, when Minister of Finance Joe Ceci brought down his 2016 budget he boosted infrastructure spending by 15 per cent, which amounted to an additional $4.5 billion (front-end loaded) over the course of a five-year capital plan.[29] The budget pledged to avoid public sector layoffs and it projected 10,000 new infrastructure-based jobs in each of the first two years of the capital plan. Overall, although his budget was palpably more of a departure from previous fiscal policy than was Laughren's, Ceci avoided saying anything as inflammatory as Laughren's well-intentioned boast that, faced with a choice between fighting the deficit and fighting the recession, he was proud to fight the recession.[30] To be sure, Ceci's first budget engendered significant criticism, but the party did not experience anything like the drop in popularity that beset the Ontario NDP in the wake of its first budget.[31]

The public-relations disaster that accompanied their first budget was an important but was by no means the only instance of a phenomenon the Ontario NDP government experienced to a far greater degree than its later Alberta counterpart. Having come to office largely because of the negative reaction against its Liberal predecessor, the Rae government lacked a broad base of popular support for even its modestly left-wing policies. At the same time, pent-up demand for thoroughgoing change among the party faithful led to unrealistic expectations as to what an NDP government could and should achieve. When those expectations weren't met, the extra-parliamentary wing of the party was not shy about expressing its dissatisfaction. The sense among party activists that the Rae government was betraying its *raison d'être* was evident in the title of a book that two long-time NDP militants published while the Rae government was still in office: *Giving Away a Miracle: Lost Dreams and Broken Promises and the Ontario NDP*.[32] Rae may have been indulging in hyperbole but he conveyed the contradictory pressures his government faced when he reflected that "the left felt my brain had been captured by Bay Street and Bay Street thought I was some kind of Maoist."[33]

Tension, oft-times serious tension, between the parliamentary and extra-parliamentary wings of the NDP (and the CCF before it) has been a perennial theme of Canadian politics. While the Alberta NDP has not been immune to criticism from party activists about the pace and scope of change, it has not had to endure anything like the internal party dissension that hamstrung the Ontario NDP government, perhaps because the Alberta party's base is so much smaller and less militant than that of the Ontario NDP. As well, despite facing as bleak a fiscal situation as Rae, Notley has not repeated his probably fatal mistake of enraging previously supportive public-sector unions by breaking collective agreements and imposing wage and salary cuts on public servants. Criticisms from Alberta NDP supporters have been muted, even in instances where Notley reversed previous party positions on the oil sands and pipelines.

Relations with the Bureaucracy

As mentioned above, lack of preparation on the part of the bureaucracy and its failure to understand the NDP's aspirations and approaches contributed to the party's problematic transition in Ontario in 1990. However, a good deal more than inadequate bureaucratic preparation and understanding marked the transition and subsequent developments. Few if any of the New Democrats in the new government—or the transition team for that matter—had more than a rudimentary knowledge of how government worked. Bob

Rae himself remarked that "there is probably no worse training in the world for becoming premier than spending a career in opposition"—in large part because of the reluctance of senior bureaucrats to share information with opposition politicians, especially NDP politicians.[34] Many NDP ministers and political staff had considerable policy expertise but a common attitude among them, at least at the outset, was that policy was all and that once policy was developed and decided, administrative issues were just "plumbing."

Ignorance was of course a problem, but far more intractable was the deeply rooted negative attitudes toward the bureaucracy among many in the Ontario NDP. A reasonable expectation might be that the NDP and the bureaucrats would be natural allies, in that both believe in activist, interventionist government. However, profound mistrust often trumped such potential affinities. Many in the NDP saw the senior bureaucracy as an integral part of "the establishment" that they had been fighting for so long, and they expressed concern that their policies and priorities would be sabotaged by hostile civil servants. "We all have copies of *A Very British Coup*" was how one senior NDP figure put it.[35]

Not everyone in the new government harboured such dark views about the bureaucracy. Some understood and accepted the division of responsibilities between politicians and bureaucrats, while others, if wary of bureaucratic foibles (they had all watched *Yes Minister*), recognized that they needed the bureaucrats more than the bureaucrats needed them.[36] Rae himself early on sought to signal that his government respected the bureaucracy, telling the press "I've been called the son of many things, but I'm the son of a professional civil servant. And I understand well their sense of professionalism and their sense of public service."[37]

Accordingly, the NDP did not begin their term with a purge of deputy ministers, though Rae found himself under pressure to remove Cabinet Secretary Peter Barnes.[38] Over time, however, Rae's views of the bureaucracy became less sanguine, and changes were made to the senior mandarinate, generating disquiet in the bureaucracy.[39] In particular, two years into the mandate Rae replaced Barnes with his key political advisor, Principal Secretary David Agnew, a move widely criticized as politicizing the public service. Thus the New Democrats were not the only ones expressing mistrust and ill feeling; it was not so much that some senior public servants

GRAHAM WHITE

spoke disrespectfully of their political masters, but rather that many in the bureaucracy were uneasy with the NDP's style and approach.[40]

From the outset, a far different tenor characterized relations between the Notley government and its senior officials. Several factors were at play. First, the Progressive Conservatives had not endeared themselves to the bureaucrats. According to veteran legislative reporter Graham Thomson, years of politicization and intimidation had taken a toll on public service morale. Noting that one of Alison Redford's first acts as premier had been to sack nine deputy ministers, Thomson quotes Premier Jim Prentice on his frustration at finding "shockingly high" turnover and widespread de-moralization among senior bureaucrats: "I was surprised when I stepped in as premier the extent to which [the civil service] needed repair work. . . . People had been cowed. . . . [My weekend briefing material was] five or six hundred pages of basically information and no advice. People were fearful of providing advice" (Thomson 2016: 310).[41] Prentice moved to address the problem, making some progress before his defeat, but for many in the bu-reaucracy the Progressive Conservative defeat and the arrival of the NDP was a welcome event. Second, Prentice's key move in attempting to revive the public service was to bring in as cabinet secretary Richard Dicerni, who had been his deputy when he was industry minister in Ottawa. As a highly experienced and well-respected bureaucrat, Dicerni was a good choice. And in terms of working with the new NDP government he was a fortuitous choice, for he had been a deputy minister under Bob Rae and was known and respected by senior New Democrats.

Third, whereas the Ontario bureaucracy was as unprepared for a tran-sition to an NDP administration as was the NDP itself, the Alberta public service, under Dicerni's direction, had engaged in serious transition plan-ning and was able to move quickly and effectively to support the new gov-ernment. Finally, a great many of the newly elected NDP MLAs—ministers included—had so little experience of government that they had few precon-ceived ideas about the public service, positive or negative. Few exhibited the jaded attitudes and overt hostility towards the bureaucracy that character-ized so many in Rae's caucus and cabinet.

With so much churn in the senior levels of the Alberta bureaucracy, none of the deputy ministers had gone through a transition-planning ex-ercise as deputies (given the strong possibility of a Wildrose victory in the

2012 election, extensive transition planning had taken place but few of those involved at a senior level remained). Dicerni assigned key deputies to analyze the platforms of both the Wildrose and the NDP, and he shared the analysis with the entire deputy cadre. He also mapped out a calendar of activities and decisions that the new government would face in its first six to eight weeks and a personal transition schedule for meetings that would be necessary with the new premier and his or her team.

Dicerni did not specifically ask Premier Prentice for permission to engage in dialogue with the opposition parties, though he believes it would have been granted had he done so, considering Prentice's understanding of the need for strong, professional government administration. He did, however, let it be known that he would be receptive to phone calls from opposition representatives and did engage in what he terms "constructive dialogue" with them. Ground rules for these discussions included an agreement that there would be no exchange of documents—indeed, there would be nothing on paper—and that discussions would be limited to "framework matters."[42]

Within minutes of the TV networks declaring an NDP majority, Dicerni received a phone call from Topp to set up a meeting the following day. Dicerni also spoke with the premier-elect. Early meetings between Dicerni and Topp concentrated on "fundamentals" such as the size of cabinet, decision-making processes, and the like. As well, overview discussions were held on the platform commitments the government wished to pursue. (As was the case with "Agenda for People," the platform of the Ontario NDP in 1990, Notley's manifesto, "Leadership for What Matters," was not developed with any sense that it might actually need to be implemented. However, at least "Leadership" was a coherent platform of policy initiatives. By contrast, "Agenda for People" was, according to two NDP insiders, no blueprint for governing; rather it was "mostly a compilation of demands that had been articulated in the daily Question Period over the previous year . . . little more than an election ploy".[43])

Three main briefing sessions were organized for Notley: on the overall budgetary/financial situation, on climate change and possible policy responses to it, and on health issues, in terms of both policy and financing. The transition process also included a review of the deputy minister cadre. Notley and Topp made it clear that they supported continuity in the public service—one of the party's campaign pitches had been to vote NDP for a stable government—and no deputies were fired. The NDP believed, with good reason given their strong showing in Edmonton, that, overall, the public service welcomed the advent of the new government. Still, it was recognized that not all those in the senior ranks of the public service would be comfortable with the policies and approaches of their new political masters or appropriate for implementing their agenda. Dealing with such officials, however, was left in the non-partisan hands of Cabinet Secretary Dicerni. Subsequently, as in Ontario, some deputies who were found not to be up to the job were reassigned.

As mentioned, although Rae kept Cabinet Secretary Peter Barnes in place for two years, when he did eventually replace him, he generated widespread criticism within the bureaucracy and elsewhere for appointing his key political aide to the top position in the public service.[44] To avoid a similar situation by ensuring a smooth, non-partisan transition when he left (and also to lighten his load), Dicerni brought in as associate cabinet secretary Marcia Nelson, a career bureaucrat who had served as deputy minister in three Alberta departments, following more than a dozen years in the Ontario public service, including during the Rae administration. When Dicerni retired in April 2016, Notley confirmed her faith in the bureaucracy by appointing Nelson cabinet secretary.

Conclusion

To repeat: Alberta is not Ontario. It should therefore not be surprising that beyond some striking similarities in their unexpected electoral victories (and the dire economic conditions they inherited) significant differences are evident in the early days of the first NDP governments to rule the two provinces. The Alberta transition went far more smoothly and proved far more effective than its Ontario predecessor, reflecting better bureaucratic planning and a significantly higher level of government experience among members of the transition team. Both during and after the transition, the Alberta public service had more positive perceptions of the politicians, while the politicians were more trusting of the public service.

In other areas, such as the size of the first cabinet and the "good time/ long time" question, the government of Rachel Notley chose a different path than the Rae government followed. To a limited extent this was because the Alberta NDP consciously applied the lessons that had emerged from the Ontario experience, but for the most part it was because the context in which the Alberta party operated, such as the influence of Western-Canadian NDP tradition, differed significantly from that of its Ontario predecessor.

Occasional superheated rhetoric aside, neither the election of Bob Rae's New Democrats nor their time in office marked anything like a major turning point for Ontario. If anything, it was the 1995 election of Mike Harris and his "Common Sense Revolutionaries"—in large measure a reaction against the NDP government—that set Ontario politics on a new, neo-conservative course. Even though, save in labour legislation, the policies adopted by the Rae government were close to, if not within, the Ontario mainstream, precious few survived more than briefly after the Harris Conservatives came to power. Perhaps the one lasting legacy of the Rae government—evident to this day—has been the widespread perception that it was simply incompetent and hence that successive NDP leaders and teams lack the ability to govern.

Jim Morrison warned that "the future's uncertain but the end is always near." Even if, as currently seems likely, the Notley government goes down to defeat at the approaching election, it will be some time before its legacy is clear. Will a stable, competitive, polarized party system emerge in Alberta? Whether the Alberta NDP establishes itself as a long-term, credible contender for power will depend to a substantial degree on the right's ability to remain unified. However, the NDP in Alberta will not have to deal with the image of ineptitude that burdens the Ontario NDP. Opposition to the Notley government has largely focused on policy and ideology; attacks on its competence have been no more frequent or effective than those encountered by other governments.

The Bard of Avon was undoubtedly right that the past is prologue, yet he would never claim that stories beginning in a similar fashion necessarily end in similar ways. Twenty-five years on, the Rae government appears as an intriguing but essentially minor blip in the course of Ontario history. While the Notley government may suffer the same short-term fate as its Ontario predecessor, the remarkable outcome of the 2015 election and the NDP's record in office suggest a substantial, long-lasting impact on Alberta politics.

Notes

In addition to the secondary sources cited below, this chapter draws on not-for-attribution interviews conducted by David Cameron and myself for our 2000 book *Cycling into Saigon*, and on a small number of not-for-attribution interviews I conducted with political figures in Alberta. In addition, I wish to record my thanks to former Alberta cabinet secretary Richard Dicerni and to Brian Topp, former chief of staff to Premier Notley, for agreeing to on-the-record interviews. All direct quotations and paraphrases of their observations are taken from these interviews, which are cited below. The judgements about Alberta politics reflect information and opinion gleaned from the editors and contributors to this book, but they are not responsible for my interpretations.

1   In 1943 the NDP's predecessor, the Co-operative Commonwealth Federation, won thirty-four seats, only four fewer than the victorious Conservatives. Within two years, however, the CCF had fallen to a poor third place; by the late 1960s through to the 1980s, the Ontario NDP was garnering a respectable 20 to 29 per cent of the vote but, save in the minds of its most optimistic supporters, remained far distant from power.

2   A comparison of the provinces' political cultures, party systems, and voting tendencies can be made by contrasting Cameron D. Anderson, "Ontario," with Anthony M. Sayers and David Stewart, "Alberta," both in *Big Worlds: Politics and Elections in the Canadian Provinces and Territories*, ed. Jared J. Wesley (Toronto: University of Toronto Press, 2016). For an analysis of the Ontario party system in the Rae era, see Robert Williams, "Ontario Party Politics in the 1990s: Comfort Meets Conviction," in *The Government and Politics of Ontario*, ed. Graham White, 5th ed. (Toronto: University of Toronto Press, 1997).

3   Rae's caucus had seventeen MPPs who had previously sat in the legislature (almost all of whom became ministers), whereas Notley had but three returning MLAs plus herself. However, while Rae's caucus had more legislative experience, it had the same experience in government as Notley's: zero.

4   Sydney Sharpe and Don Braid, *Notley Nation: How Alberta's Political Upheaval Swept the Country* (Toronto: Dundurn, 2016), 45–6.

5   Bob Rae, *From Protest to Power: Personal Reflections on a Life in Politics* (Toronto: Viking, 1996), 120.

6   To some extent this may have reflected the quite reasonable concern that the NDP might win a plurality but not a majority of seats and find itself out in the cold as the Liberals and the Conservatives formed a governing alliance or coalition.

7   Ibid., 125 (emphasis added).

8   See David R. Cameron and Graham White, *Cycling into Saigon: The Conservative Transition in Ontario* (Vancouver: UBC Press, 2000), 20. The 1985 election produced an ambiguous result: 52 Conservatives, 48 Liberals, and 25 New Democrats. Several weeks of negotiations among the parties produced a Liberal-NDP alliance that led to a Liberal government. It was thus only three weeks after the election (but more than a month before the Liberals were sworn in) that a Liberal transition team was assembled.

9   Ibid., 33–7.

10   Dave Barrett and William Miller, *Barrett: A Passionate Political Life* (Vancouver: Douglas and McIntyre, 1995), 61.

11   Some of the MPPs elected from rural and semi-rural Ontario, such as Elmer Buchanan, who proved an extraordinarily able minister of agriculture, were first-rate members; others, however, were barely adequate local representatives. This further reduced the likelihood that the party would retake their ridings.

12   Brian Topp, interview with author, 3 February 2017.

13   Cameron and White, *Cycling into Saigon*, 28.

14   Topp interview.

15   "Speech from the Throne," *Alberta Hansard*, 29th Legislature, First Session, 15 June 2015, 7–8.

16   David Zussman, *Off and Running: The Prospects and Pitfalls of Government Transitions in Canada* (Toronto: University of Toronto Press, 2013).

17   Cabinet Secretary Richard Dicerni suggested to the deputy ministers that they read both Zussman's *Off and Running*, which focuses on transitions at the federal level, and *Cycling into Saigon*. How widely these tomes were read and what, if any, influence they may have had is impossible to gauge.

18   Topp interview.

19   Ibid.

20   See Thomas Walkom, *Rae Days: The Rise and Follies of the NDP* (Toronto: Key Porter, 1994), ch. 5.

21   Rae, *From Protest to Power*, 134.

22   Topp interview.

23   Richard Dicerni, interview with author, 23 January 2017.

24   October 2015 saw an interim budget, with some holdovers from the (unpassed) final Prentice budget; this discussion refers to the first budget with the full NDP stamp on it, released in April 2016.

25   The deficit of at least one budget during the Conservative government of Bill Davis was of similar magnitude to that of the first Rae budget in percentage terms, but the dollar figure was much lower.

26   Walkom, *Rae Days*, 99.

27   See Chuck Rachlis and David Wolfe, "An Insiders' View of the NDP Government of Ontario: The Politics of Permanent Oppositions Meets the Economics of Permanent Recession," in *The Government and Politics of Ontario*, ed. Graham White, 5th ed. (Toronto: University of Toronto Press, 1997), 344. On the first Ontario NDP budget, see Walkom, *Rae Days*, 98–104. Walkom was a Queen's Park reporter with a doctorate in economics.

28   David A. Dodge, "Report to the Government of Alberta on the Development, Renewal and Financing of the Government's plan for Spending on Capital Projects to 2019," Bennett Jones LLP, 19 October 2015.

29   Alberta Department of Finance, *Fiscal Plan* (Edmonton: Department of Finance, 2016), 43–56.

30   Walkom, *Rae Days*, 98.

31   A survey of 900 Albertans conducted shortly after its release found that 40 per cent of respondents approved ("strongly" or "somewhat") the budget, with 43 per cent disapproving; the balance were "not sure." This was substantially better than the response to the last Redford budget (24 per cent approving; 57 per cent disapproving). Data from "Janet Brown Opinion Research/Trend Research". My thanks to Melanee Thomas, John Santos, and Janet Brown for these data.

32   George Ehring and Wayne Roberts, *Giving Away a Miracle: Lost Dreams and Broken Promises and the Ontario NDP* (Oakville: Mosaic Press, 1993).

33   Rae, *From Protest to Power*,197.

34   Ibid., 130.

35   See Cameron and White, *Cycling into Saigon*, 34. *A Very British Coup* was a television drama about a decidedly leftist British government destroyed by the establishment through illegal and underhanded means with the connivance of the civil service.

36   *Yes Minister* was a British comedy of the 1980s, closely based on real-life situations, in which a hapless minister repeatedly fell victim to the stalling and obfuscation of his bureaucrats.

37   Quoted in Cameron and White, *Cycling into Saigon*, 33.

38   Rae, *From Protest to Power*, 129.

39   As Rae put it in his memoirs, "my views about the government and civil service changed dramatically as a result of my experience. There were, in fact, layers upon layers of internal politics and cronyism within the public service. It was impossible for much of the bureaucracy to escape the inevitable consequences of having been an integral part of forty-two years of Tory governments." This from Rae, *From Protest to Power*, 130.

40   Cameron and White, *Cycling into Saigon*, 36.

41   Graham Thomson, "The Civil Service: Can it Adapt?" *Alberta Views* 19, no. 1, (January/February 2016): 31.

42   Dicerni interview.

43   Rachlis and Wolfe, "An Insiders' View," 360n8.

44   Many in the Ontario public service who worked with Agnew found him to be highly professional and non-partisan, but in politics perception routinely trumps reality.

Out of the Blue: Goodbye Tories, Hello Jason Kenney

Anthony M. Sayers and David K. Stewart

The 2015 Alberta election ended a Progressive Conservative regime that by 25 August 2014 had continuously held power longer than any other party in Canadian history. The reign, begun in 1971, came to an end amid a declining economy and a party in disarray. The last years of the dynasty were dominated by competition between the PCs and the right-wing Wildrose opposition that had reduced the traditional left-wing opposition of Liberals and New Democrats to, respectively, third- and fourth-placed parties in the legislature. The rise of the Rachel Notley–led New Democrats from fourth to first is therefore one of the most remarkable election results in Canadian history.

Upon their defeat the Tories confronted an existential crisis, as no party that has lost power in Alberta has ever returned to government. Third in size in the Alberta legislature and lacking a permanent leader following the election-night resignation of Jim Prentice, the party struggled to be heard and to rebuild its organization. In March 2017 party members chose a leader, former Conservative MP Jason Kenney, committed to merging with the Wildrose. They then endorsed such a merger by referendum in July to establish the United Conservative Party. On 28 October Kenney, the last PC leader, was elected the first leader of the UCP. Rarely in Canada or elsewhere has a party with such a storied past been willing to vote itself into oblivion.

The lead-up to the devastating 2015 election had been a roller coaster for the Tories. The Conservative Party dynasty had long rested on its sensitivity to changing political dynamics through its use of open leadership contests and a willingness to adjust its policies to appeal to a plurality of Albertan voters. The party moved leftward at the 2012 provincial election in response to the Wildrose threat and continued to use royalty revenues to support heavy government spending in search of electoral support. This centrist strategy collapsed in 2015 with the election of the more populist New Democrats as the governing party and the right-wing Wildrose as Official Opposition, albeit with fewer votes than the PCs.

For a party that had not experienced electoral defeat since 1967, the result was catastrophic. The notion of parties alternating in office is not part of the Alberta experience, and with no history of a defeated party returning to power, the Progressive Conservatives faced a grim situation. Kenney capitalized on this fear and along with others pressed the narrative that vote-splitting on the right had allowed Albertans to elect the NDP by mistake. A merger with Wildrose would deliver government to the new party and remove the "ideological" New Democrats from power. The previous merger of the federal Progressive Conservatives and the Canadian Alliance, which had delivered government to the new Conservative Party of Canada, was offered as a model.

A merger would require the disbanding of both parties, turning the post-Prentice leadership race into a referendum on the future of the PCs. It was widely known that Kenney supported such a move and his success is evidence of support for a merger among those who voted in the contest. The construction of the UCP ended the "big tent" strategy that had made the Tories one of the most successful political machines in Canada and confirmed Kenney's centrality to the merger process.

We begin our analysis of the end of the Tory dynasty by describing the political attitudes of Albertans and the degree to which their values are conservative. We then move to a discussion of leadership selection within the PC Party and the factors that led to its defeat in 2015. From there we trace how electoral defeat led to the formal dissolution of the party. We conclude that the decision to disband the PCs and merge with the Wildrose was a political choice, not a requirement. Despite having received more votes than the Wildrose, the Tories catastrophized the 2015 election defeat and gave up on the option of trying to return to power on their own. Jason Kenney took full advantage of this narrative. The creation of the UCP sets the stage for more polarized party competition in Alberta.

ANTHONY M. SAYERS AND DAVID K. STEWART

Political Values in Alberta

It is important to understand what Albertans think about politics.[1] Many have noted there is a decidedly individualistic tinge to Alberta politics expressed as the notion of personal freedom.[2]

As Table 17.1 demonstrates however, Albertans are not as individualistic as some have suggested. There is solid support, for example, for the value of generalized health care and social programs that assist those in need.

Stereotypes notwithstanding, voters in Alberta appear broadly supportive of a substantial role for the state with respect to government spending. Table 17.2 shows that when asked, they take a decidedly expansionist view of the preferred extent of government activity, with overwhelming majorities favouring a role for the state in ensuring living standards, adequate housing, and rent controls. They are not as keen on the sorts of public auto-insurance schemes found in some other provinces. These attitudes are shaped in part by the strength of the economy and the royalty revenues that allow government to deliver high levels of public goods and services without having to demand matching levels of personal taxation.

An expansive view of government activity may not necessarily translate into unfettered support for spending and budget deficits, but it does suggest that the former Progressive Conservative government and its successor, the New Democrats, have read the public mood correctly. Boom times in Alberta allow governments additional room to keep spending high while maintaining the lowest tax regime of any province, but this approach creates difficulties when the good times end. Managing this shift in circumstances remains a key feature of Alberta politics.

Albertans' suspicion of overt individualism and support for robust state spending captures the peculiarity of a province with a distinctive history that favours self-reliance and yet which finds itself with a government able to collect supernormal levels of revenue through a booming resource sector. Government restraint may have little appeal, and individual preferences are shaped without the need to internalize the policy trade-offs (notably about taxes and spending) common elsewhere.

Despite its centrality to the economy, Albertans are clearly uncomfortable with the power of the energy industry. As Table 17.3 shows, about three-quarters of them believe the industry has too much political influence

Table 17.1. Individualism

ATTITUDINAL STATEMENT	2008 % SUPPORT	2012 % SUPPORT	2015 % SUPPORT
Government regulation stifles drive	48%	48%	64%
Most unemployed could find jobs	71%	60%	60%
Those willing to pay should get medical treatment sooner	43%	39%	46%
A lot of welfare and social programs unnecessary	30%	29%	41%

Sources: NRG Research and Research Now. See endnote 1 for further information.

Table 17.2. Preferred Extent of Government Activity

ATTITUDINAL STATEMENT	2008 % SUPPORT	2012 % SUPPORT	2015 % SUPPORT
Government should ensure decent living standard	73%	73%	79%
Government should ensure adequate housing	78%	76%	77%
Government should limit amount of rent increases	76%	71%	76%
Government should take over auto insurance	46%	38%	41%

Sources: NRG Research and Research Now. See endnote 1 for further information.

Table 17.3. Oil, Gas, and the Environment

	2008 % SUPPORT	2012 % SUPPORT	2015 % SUPPORT
Oil and gas companies have too much say in provincial politics	69%	68%	75%
Increase royalties on natural gas and oil	56%	59%	71%
Alberta should slow pace of oil sands development	53%	39%	40%
Alberta needs to take firm action to combat global warming	82%	75%	76%
Tough environmental standards should take precedence over employment	58%	53%	49%

Sources: NRG Research and Research Now. See endnote 1 for further information.

and that royalties are too low. The effects of the recession after 2009, which were still felt in the lead-up to the 2012 election, and then the 2014 drop in oil prices that hurt the provincial budget, can be seen in a willingness to countenance fewer controls on the growth of the oil sands in recent years. Yet this support is not without reservation: three-quarters of our respondents continue to favour action on global warming and about half want tough environmental standards.

Table 17.4 reveals that Albertans are not particularly socially conservative. Most see moral issues as largely a matter of individual choice. This tends to run counter to the view that repeatedly electing a Progressive Conservative government is evidence of a commitment to conservative social values.

Populism remains an important part of Albertan political culture (see Table 17.5). From the United Farmers of Alberta through to Social Credit, the Tories, and even the New Democrats, Alberta has been friendly to parties and leaders adept at appealing to popular sentiment against large institutional forces, whether they are business or the federal government. The strength of populism is reinforced by the royalty roller coaster, which requires taxpayers to fairly share the pain regularly inflicted by swings in government revenues. Klein's folksy charm, Stelmach's background on the farm in Northern Alberta, and Redford's ability to suggest that the Wildrose did not share the values of most Albertans were key elements in the construction of recent PC majority governments. Similarly, Notley's deep links to Alberta—her father having died in a plane crash while leader of the provincial NDP—no doubt helped her cause.

As seen in Table 17.6, Western alienation is another powerful strand in Albertan political culture. It seems that while Albertans are willing to countenance a strong provincial state that provides public goods and services at high levels, they take a dim view of the national state in Ottawa, which they see as beyond their control.

The views of Albertans might surprise many Canadians.[3] Albertans are not particularly individualistic and in general they are supportive of extensive government spending, an attitude made easier by long periods in which supernormal royalty payments allow governments to avoid passing costs on to taxpayers. Provincial voters are concerned about the environment, not

Table 17.4. Social Conservatism

	2008 % SUPPORT	2012 % SUPPORT	2015 % SUPPORT
Abortion is a matter between a woman and her doctor	76%	80%	84%
Gays and lesbians should be allowed to marry	62%	75%	77%

Sources: NRG Research and Research Now. See endnote 1 for further information.

Table 17.5. Populism in Alberta

	2008 % SUPPORT	2012 % SUPPORT	2015 % SUPPORT
Trust ordinary people more than experts	58%	54%	70%
Solve problems if government is brought back to grassroots	75%	75%	73%
Need government to get things done with less red tape	86%	85%	90%

Sources: NRG Research and Research Now. See endnote 1 for further information.

Table 17.6. Western Alienation in Alberta

	2008 % SUPPORT	2012 % SUPPORT	2015 % SUPPORT
Alberta is treated unfairly by the federal government	46%	42%	56%
Alberta does not have its fair share of political power in Canada	56%	57%	65%
The economic policies of the federal government seem to help Quebec and Ontario at the expense of Alberta	65%	62%	79%
Because parties depend on Quebec and Ontario Alberta usually gets ignored in national politics	70%	66%	80%

Sources: NRG Research and Research Now. See endnote 1 for further information.

particularly attached to conservative social values, and willing to limit the rate of oil and gas development.

More deeply, the political culture of Alberta remains heavily shaped by the uncertainties and conceits that flow from the boom and bust cycles of the oil and gas sector. These cycles highlight tensions with the federal government and Central Canadian economic and political rhythms, thereby making Alberta appear distinctive. Confirmed as it is by extraordinary levels of long-term economic and population growth, this sense of distinctiveness has provided fertile ground for the development of a populist streak in provincial politics.

Albertans generally favour governments and political leaders capable of protecting an enviable quality of life by keeping taxes low, retaining high levels of government spending, and protecting the province from outside forces that might bring this magical circumstance to an end. Long-term Tory success rested on choosing leaders and policies sensitive to these underlying political realities. The post-Redford leadership race of 2014 was an opportunity to renew this dynamic to ensure continued electoral success.

Leadership

Leadership has been central to party politics in Alberta, with party leaders, especially premiers, essentially defining their parties for voters. Yet all PC leaders since Klein have struggled to connect with Albertans. At the same time, there has been intense competition within the party as to where it should locate itself on the political spectrum given rapid economic and social change along with the traditional challenges of managing the Alberta economy. This has been expressed in the character of leadership contests.

The rules for selecting leaders in 2006 and 2011 reflected a willingness to open the party to changing social forces in an effort to cement its role as the party of the people.[4] Anyone with five dollars could attend a polling station in their local riding, purchase a membership, and have a say in choosing Alberta's next premier. Table 17.7 shows that Albertans came out by the thousands to participate in these events—and both times defeated the candidate favoured by the party establishment. The party went on to win consecutive majority governments.

Table 17.7. Voter Mobilization at Tory Leadership Contests

YEAR	VOTERS	MOBILIZATION*
2006	144,289	34.61
1992	78,251	17.80
2011	78,176	15.60
2014	23,386	4.12

* Leadership voters as a proportion of the number of Albertans who voted for the Tories at the most recent provincial election.

Sources: Data compiled by the authors from media reports of party voting, and "Election Results" reports from Elections Alberta.

Some elements of the Conservative party were unhappy with this populist approach, arguing that it allowed "two-minute-Tories," mainly from the left, too much influence over leader selection.[5] The 2014 leadership race doubled the price of membership, abandoned voting in local communities, and got rid of the rules that allowed both Stelmach and Redford to win. Table 17.7 records the resulting collapse in party mobilization and the lack of populist appeal in the race that selected Mr. Prentice.

The selection of Jim Prentice as party leader and effectively Alberta's sixteenth premier on 6 September 2014 was a triumph for the party establishment and the overwhelming majority (forty-six) of MLAs who backed him. But, as seen in Table 17.8, the 2014 race lacked the competitive drive of past races that had signalled the centrality of the party to Alberta politics. It was the least dynamic of any of the post-Lougheed leadership races. Prentice dominated the contest. He raised $2,661,201 and spent all but $24,151 of that. Second-placed Ric McIver spent $484,029, and third-placed Thomas Lukaszuk $336,338. This dominance prevented growth in party membership that had attended past, competitive PC leadership contests.

The party chose to use a phone poll (cheap and plagued with technical issues) in place of in-person voting, thereby reducing the excitement—and popular engagement—generated when members vote face-to-face in their constituencies. It doubled the cost of membership and instituted a cut-off that ensured that no one could join and vote on the day of the election. Keeping the process open until the final vote had been a source of great energy and engagement in previous races. Unsurprisingly, Prentice's strength

ANTHONY M. SAYERS AND DAVID K. STEWART

Table 17.8. Competitiveness of Tory Leadership Contests

	1992	2006	2011	2014
Leader's Vote Share	31%	30%	41%	77%
Number of Candidates	9	8	6	3
Party Caucus Support for Winner	63%	16%	3%	83%

Sources: Source: Data compiled by the authors from media coverage of party leadership campaigns.

in terms of support from caucus and financial resources expressed itself in an overwhelming first-round win. The number voting fell by two-thirds compared with the two previous races.

The apparent coronation of Jim Prentice meant limited disruption to the party but was also evidence of a clear retreat from the dynamic, open populism of previous leadership contests. The selection of a prominent former federal Conservative cabinet minister also complicated the traditional PC claim to be the defenders of Alberta's interests in the federation. Indeed, it highlighted the odd dynamics that resulted from dealing with a governing party in Ottawa that had strong support in Alberta. There was no easy way of playing the Western alienation card used so effectively when Liberals governed from Ottawa, or even during the latter part of the Mulroney government, which led to the formation of the Reform Party.

A Perfect Storm

The election of Jim Prentice to the Tory leadership brought apparent stability to provincial politics. The Conservatives launched a series of initiatives designed to turn the page and place the party on course for a subsequent election win. Yet the massive collapse in the price of oil across 2014 became a crisis that relentlessly drove government action and, along with continued change across the political system, threatened to overwhelm the party and its new leader.

The collapse of oil prices quickly worsened the government's fiscal situation. Along with long-term weakness in natural gas prices, Alberta's major natural resources were now selling cheaply and delivering much less in the way of royalties.[6] Changes in the structure of the economy and royalty revenues further complicated the fiscal situation. Whereas natural gas had accounted for up to 80 per cent of government resource royalties a decade earlier, the more volatile and complex revenues from oil production now contributed this proportion. Because of this flip, the rapid decline in the price of a barrel of oil from over $100 to the mid-$50-dollar range had an outsized effect on government revenues.

At his first press conference in September, Premier Prentice was at pains to talk about renewal. The main policy thrust of his speech was to highlight the need to engage the United States with other provinces to ensure market access for oil and gas. The emphasis was on improving the delivery of government services—health care and education in particular—while containing costs, with a promise of more new schools.[7] On 27 October 2014, less than two months after winning the leadership, Prentice was able to celebrate four by-election wins, including his own in Calgary-Foothills.[8]

The $7-billion shortfall in the 2015 budget resulting from reduced resource revenues soon came to dominate Tory strategy. In early December, Prentice and his new finance minister, Robin Campbell, announced a seven-member cabinet committee chaired by the premier to oversee the development of the 2015 provincial budget. As well, the government introduced a series of measures to reduce spending.[9] The government seemed in full crisis mode as it came to realize the depth of the fiscal challenge and the threat that oil and gas prices posed to its future.

On 17 December, Prentice and the now former Wildrose leader Daniel Smith appeared at a press conference to announce that she and eight of her colleagues (more than half the Wildrose caucus) were crossing the floor to join the Tories—this in addition to the two other Wildrose MLAs who had crossed in November of 2014. This created a governing-party caucus numbering 72 in a chamber of 87 MLAs. Despite outward appearances, news leaked that the floor-crossing had created deep tensions among the members of the PC caucus, worn as they were by a history of fierce Wildrose criticism in the legislature.[10] Anger among remaining Wildrose MLAs and ordinary party members was palpable. New NDP leader Rachel Notley, who had replaced Brian Mason on 18 October, joined Liberal leader Raj Sherman and Wildrose MLAs in characterizing the move as a "backroom deal" that amounted to a "betrayal of democracy."[11]

As the Prentice government attempted to come to terms with the new fiscal realities, its budget committee commissioned a survey of Albertans seeking suggestions for tax and spending changes to help manage the budget shortfall. The survey revealed that on the tax side, 71 per cent favoured raising tobacco taxes, 69 per cent corporate taxes, and 58 per cent a graduated personal tax to replace the single tax rate. Half rejected the reintroduction of health-care premiums while respondents were about evenly divided on implementation of a provincial sales tax. Given its storied place as part of the "Alberta Advantage," this last is perhaps the most remarkable result of the survey. On the spending side, respondents wanted to protect front-line health care (75 per cent) and education (70 per cent), with around 40 per cent favouring infrastructure spending in these areas.[12]

In a radio discussion on the budget in early March, Mr. Prentice suggested that Albertans "look in the mirror" for an explanation of the dire fiscal circumstances facing the province, sparking widespread condemnation for his failure to assign any of the blame to four decades of Tory rule. Opposition parties once again blasted the government for being out of touch.[13] At the same time, and despite the results of the survey, the government rejected the idea of raising corporate taxes, citing advice from economists that it would reduce employment. The government introduced a budget on 26 March that moved slightly away from the single tax rate on income; increased alcohol and tobacco taxes; brought in a new tax to support health care; reduced or eliminated planned increases in spending across government (with protection for some infrastructure spending in healthcare and education); and announced future changes in methods for saving resource revenue.

The wisdom of allowing Wildrose MLAs to join the party took a hit when on 28 March three of them, including Danielle Smith, lost PC nomination battles. Then the party's decision to eliminate Jamie Lall from the nomination in Chestermere-Rocky View in favour of former Wildrose MLA Bruce McAllister caused an outcry.[14] At the same time, and as if to highlight the continued vitality of the party, 55 per cent of the 8,738 voting Wildrose members elected former federal Conservative MP Brian Jean to lead the party.[15] Jean promised to campaign on the Alberta Advantage of lower taxes. With David Swann having replaced the exiting Raj Sherman as

Liberal leader in early February, each of the four major parties had experienced leadership change. Alberta politics was in flux.

On 7 April the government called an early election for 5 May 2015, ignoring the fixed-election legislation that scheduled the next election between March and May 2016.[16] The decision to call an early election was widely criticized, not only for ignoring the legislation but because with the non-Tory parties competing for second spot, voter turnout would be low.[17] The government's introduction of a relatively tough budget gave their opponents, two with recently elected new leaders, the raw materials to argue that the four-decade-old regime was out of touch with Albertans: this set the course for the subsequent election.

The 2015 Election Campaign

Despite their long dominance, the Tories faced challenging economic conditions and rapid social and political change. Regular turnover in leadership and internal tensions, most notably in light of the success of the Wildrose to its right, threatened the party. A new leader added another element of uncertainty. Despite massively outspending its opponents, a retreat from the populism that had sustained it for four decades, coupled with a series of damaging events, undercut its support.

The Tories appeared dominant at the start of the campaign. The Liberals were on the wane, Wildrose had been decimated by floor-crossings, and the fourth-placed New Democrats led by recently elected Rachel Notley held just four seats.[18] As Table 17.9 makes clear, a recovery in PC fundraising gave party members reason for optimism, although the rise of the NDP suggests donors had come to see them as a viable challenger to the Tories.

The 2015 PC budget proposed tax hikes on individuals, an additional child supplement for low-income families, and cuts to public-sector employment. It was aimed squarely at the Wildrose, which had cornered the low-tax, small-government policy terrain.[19] The Liberal and New Democrat platforms both aimed leftward.[20] New Democrats emphasized change with stability, highlighting Notley as a leader in the mold of Peter Lougheed. Only the NDP would "fight for Alberta families." The floor-crossing was held to be evidence that change could not be achieved by voting for a party—the Wildrose—closely aligned with the Tories.[21]

Table 17.9. Electoral Cycle Funding 2012–15 ($)

	2012	2013	2014	Q1 2015	CAMPAIGN
PC	2,331,592	2,865,669	5,625,669	825,318	3,373,733
WR	2,793,895	3,074,072	3,085,982	355,091	1,169,470
LIB	478,795	447,826	396,796	110,764	156,048
NDP	864,046	775,152	999,834	406,883	1,635,991

Sources: "Financial Disclosure" reports from Elections Alberta.

In contrast to the Tories' proposed budget, major NDP policies were consistent with the preferences expressed by Albertans in the government's survey of voters.[22] The NDP promised to reverse spending cuts to health care and education, fund daycare, introduce a progressive income tax aimed at the top 10 per cent of earners, raise corporate taxes, and rethink royalties. They promised to balance the budget by 2017 and to scrap a proposed Tory health levy while enhancing democratic transparency by banning union and corporate donations to political parties and strengthening oversight of government.[23]

New Democrats managed to capture the populist ground vacated by the Tories and forced the PCs to fight a two-front war, the most difficult for a centrist party.[24] To make matters worse, the PC campaign was tarnished by scandals and interventions that only served to make the party and its supporters appear entitled and out of touch, while at the same time NDP campaign mistakes were overlooked.[25] The 23 April leaders' debate confirmed Notley's appeal, Prentice's awkwardness, the third-place position of the Wildrose, and the irrelevance of the Liberals.[26]

In a post-election survey conducted by Abacus Research, 93 per cent of respondents identified change rather than support for the NDP and "cooling on Jim Prentice" rather than "warming to Rachel Notley" as critical to their vote. Sixty-seven per cent felt the leaders' debate was a crucial moment in the campaign, with 58 per cent seeing leadership as generally important.[27] Women favoured the NDP more than men did, as did young over older voters, patterns that were reversed for the Tories but less strongly so for Wildrose. Voters with more education and city folk also favoured the NDP, with Edmonton the heartland of the party's victory.[28]

The collapse of the Tory vote was key to the NDP victory. An overwhelming majority of New Democrat supporters remained loyal, but only 49 per cent of Tory voters stuck with the party, with nearly a third of defectors heading to the NDP. Nineteen per cent of those who had supported the Wildrose in 2012 moved to the NDP, as did 62 per cent of Liberals. Tellingly, 55 per cent of non-voters in 2012 chose to support the NDP in 2015.[29]

While the arrival of Jim Prentice initially boosted the Tories, his handling of the floor-crossing, the budget process, and the decision to call an early election cast doubt on his intuitive feel for Alberta politics. This was confirmed by the election campaign. The Tories ran an underwhelming campaign that failed to reset the widespread sense among voters that is was time for a change, while the NDP managed to present a leader and a set of policies that played to the populist dynamics of Alberta politics.

The Death of a Dynasty: The End of the Progressive Conservative Association of Alberta

In Canada, and in especially Alberta, leaders are important. Alberta politics has been described as "leadership politics,"[30] and the race for a new leader to replace Prentice became a contest to define the party. In this contest, the party returned to the leadership convention model that had not been used in Alberta since the election of Don Getty as PC leader in 1986. The decision to return to a convention, it turned out, was consequential.

Primaries afford more opportunities for outsiders to participate. In both 2006 and 2011, the primary model had elected leaders who were not the choice of the party elite and were seen as moving the party more to the left. In reflecting on his experiences as a leadership candidate in both of those races, Ted Morton lamented that the primary "rules have facilitated the growth of a second conservative party by pushing disillusioned Blue Tories into the Wildrose party."[31] Essentially, the involvement of less "conservative" voters, particularly after an inconclusive first ballot, led to the election of a leader who was not reflective of the aspirations of many party activists. Former leadership candidate and deputy premier Doug Horner raised much the same point in discussing these changes to the leadership selection model. As he explained to the CBC in May of 2016, "I think it's time

ANTHONY M. SAYERS AND DAVID K. STEWART

we stopped electing premiers and started electing the leader of our party."[32] For many in the party there was dissatisfaction that candidates who were not favoured by party regulars were advantaged by primary selections, and that such elections "appear to have transformed the PC party into a centre left coalition party."[33] The easy victory of Prentice in a more closed primary model did little to diminish such concerns. One of the other elements critical to understanding the evolution of the Progressive Conservative Party is the enhanced importance of candidate organizations in the convention model. Leadership conventions place a greater premium on these organizations as campaign teams attempt to determine the outcome not by persuading voters at a convention to support them, but by electing delegates predisposed to support them. This battle has been well described as "trench warfare," and the viciousness that accompanied such battles in 1986 was one of the reasons the PCs moved to their successful primary model in 1992.[34] This battle proved dramatically one-sided in 2017.

Reports in the month leading up to the March 2017 leadership race suggested that after elections in 80 of 87 constituencies, Kenny had 977 delegates and his opponents only 199.[35] These numbers proved quite prophetic as Jason Kenney, the only candidate favouring a union with the Wildrose, was elected with 1,113 of the 1,476 votes cast. Kenney's organizational dominance could also be seen in candidate expenditures: he spent over $1.5 million on the campaign while the total spent by his opponents came in under $300,000.

The leadership contest initially attracted a wide range of people with elected experience and it appeared there would be a competitive election to decide the future of the party. The candidates ranged from PC MLA Sandra Jansen, a candidate very much associated with the progressive side of the party, and (as we have seen) former federal Conservative cabinet minister Jason Kenney, a candidate directly associated with social-conservative beliefs and a desire to lead the PCs into a merger with the Wildrose that could end the splitting of votes many Conservatives credited with electing the NDP in 2015. But the race exposed serious internal tensions as to how best to proceed. The decision to continue to pursue a centrist strategy was quickly eschewed as Kenney rode a steamroller of support into the delegate selection meetings that resulted in the election of a huge majority of pro-merger delegates and drove a number of his opponents out of the race.

Sandra Jansen not only left the leadership race, but just over a week later, after claiming to have been harassed by Kenney supporters, she crossed to the New Democrats. As Jansen departed, she strongly critiqued the direction in which she saw Kenney taking the PCs, suggesting that "I don't believe there has been anything moderate or pragmatic being offered or even discussed by the people intent on taking over the Progressive Conservative Party of Alberta."[36] Barely two months later, former St. Albert MLA Stephen Khan withdrew from the race after also lamenting the desire to destroy the venerable PC Party. As he explained, he had been the target of ugly attacks; he also stated that he had "entered this race because I believed the PC army would show up. But what I've seen is that there are more federal Conservative/Reformers and Wildrosers who want to tear down and destroy our party than there are PCs who want to save it."[37] Khan endorsed Richard Starke, another PC MLA, who continued in the race and who Khan described as a "true Progressive Conservative."[38]

The battle for the future of the PCs continued with some opponents of the potential merger calling on the party's board in February to disqualify Kenney from the race because his intent was to harm the PC brand. A disqualification was not forthcoming, and the race continued to its inevitable outcome. Kenney, with the endorsement of former Conservative prime minister Stephen Harper and an incredibly well-financed organization, cruised through the delegate selection process, which utilized a first-past-the-post method to elect delegates in each constituency. Thus, even a slim plurality at the delegate selection meetings could produce a solid swath of Kenney delegates, and the two remaining candidates could not stop Kenney from turning the March convention into a virtual coronation.[39] Kenney scrutineers lined the registration desks at the convention, and the floor of the convention was solidly in his favour. When Starke in his speech called on the party to avoid association with the Wildrose and its social conservatism he was booed.[40] The Kenney campaign maintained its momentum as interim federal Conservative leader Rona Ambrose seconded his nomination.

With more than 75 per cent of the voting delegates opting for Kenney and his merger strategy, the PC Party seemed to be celebrating its demise. The party rejected the opportunity to return to the "big tent" politics that served it so well for so long and instead emphasized ideological similarities with Wildrose, endorsing a strategy to pursue a formal merger with their

ANTHONY M. SAYERS AND DAVID K. STEWART

former opponents. The elected delegates ensured that the Alberta tradition of a defeated government never returning to power continued by placing the PCs on a path to formal dissolution. A number of prominent Progressive Conservatives were uncomfortable with the decision, with former deputy premier and leadership candidate Thomas Lukaszuk tearing up his membership card and party president Katherine O'Neill stepping down from her position and speculating about the need for a more moderate option.[41] Kenney's success in this race, despite perceived opposition from members of the party's executive, were described by some as a "hostile takeover" of the PCs.[42]

The forces calling for the dissolution of the PC Party eventually fulfilled Kenney's goal, and in May they reached an agreement with the Wildrose to combine, though with the negative experience of the floor-crossings of 2014 in mind, the decision was made to allow party members to vote on the party's future. A vote was scheduled for July of 2017 with a simple majority needed to move the party along the path to merger. Wildrose rules required a 75 per cent vote in favour of the move.[43] Prominent federal Conservatives such as former prime minister Stephen Harper and former interim leader Rona Ambrose spoke out in favour of the merger; the move to unite subsequently proved unstoppable. Despite some initial speculation that the unity proposals might be defeated, they were overwhelmingly endorsed by members of each party. With turnouts below 60 per cent in both cases, 23,466 of the 24,598 Wildrosers who voted endorsed the merger, as did 25,692 of the 27,060 PC members.[44] With some rules for participation uncertain, it is unclear how many people participated in both parties.

The road was now clear for the final drive: the selection of a leader for the new UCP. Some dissent remained. Richard Starke, the runner up to Kenney in the March 2017 PC leadership race, refused to join the new party and another PC MLA, Rick Fraser, entered the leadership race for the upstart Alberta Party.[45] He was joined by Stephen Mandel, a former Edmonton MLA who had served as a cabinet minister under Jim Prentice. Mandel went on to win the leadership contest.[46]

Former party leaders Jason Kenney and Brian Jean both entered the UCP leadership race. Reverting to a primary process, albeit one with a cut-off date a week before voting opened, Kenney demonstrated that he could win in the more open format. More than 100,000 members were eligible to participate and almost 62,000 were registered to vote in the October contest. Kenney defeated Jean almost 2 to 1, attracting 35,623 votes to Jean's 18,336.[47] Interestingly, the votes received by Kenney fell well below the totals received by those winning the PC primaries in 1992, 2006, and 2011, suggesting the new party could not quite attract the levels of participation the Progressive Conservatives had managed through open primaries. Kenney went on to win a December by-election, becoming the first elected MLA for the new party.

Conclusion

Selecting a new leader became a choice among possible futures for the Tories. Ending the Progressive Conservative Party was not the only option available following its 2015 election defeat. The party decided not to treat the defeat as part of a normal political process, as other parties do, and attempt to return to power, but rather to catastrophize the loss. Dropping the open primary system for leader votes in 2014 and 2017 strengthened the hand of the party's unhappy right wing and weakened the Tories populist appeal. The selection of Jason Kenney was an emphatic answer in favour of the myth of the inevitable death of party regimes in Alberta and the narrative that the NDP government was an accident caused by vote-splitting on the right. The rightward turn this and the merger with the Wildrose entailed reverses the logic of the 2012 and 2015 elections. Rather than seeing the Wildrose as the major challenger, Kenney and those who voted for him fashion the New Democrats as the enemy. Losing a centrist "big tent" party such as the Tories is likely to increase the polarization of Alberta politics over the coming years.

The view that governing parties that lose office struggle to regain lost ground was facilitated by the politics that followed the 2015 election. The Tories faced challenges in raising money. The NDP government and the Wildrose opposition (still stinging from the floor-crossing) moved quickly to end the corporate donations on which the PCs had become dependent. Those on the right of the PC Party, unhappy with what they saw as its leftward drift over recent elections, viewed unification with the Wildrose as a means of recreating the voting bloc that allowed Ralph Klein to win huge

ANTHONY M. SAYERS AND DAVID K. STEWART

Table 17.10. Opinion Distribution by Party Supporters 2008–15

ISSUE AREA	NDP	PC	WILDROSE
Individualism	.25–.44	.41–.60	.61–.70
Active Government	.74–.87	.58–.62	.49–.62
Environment	.76–.85	.51–.57	.43–.50
Social Conservatism	.14–.19	.21–.40	.34–.60
Populism	.59–.80	.66–.79	.78–.89
Western Alienation	.42–.71	.50–.75	.74–.81

Sources: NRG Research and Research Now. See endnote 1 for further information.

electoral victories. A new party would be more right wing and skirt the historical legacy of no former governing party having ever regained office.

An examination of voter attitudes in 2008, 2012, and 2015 makes clear that moving in this direction was a political choice, not a requirement. Voter attitudes reported earlier in this chapter reveal that Albertans are not as conservative as many assume.[48] Table 17.10 uses responses to attitudinal questions reported earlier to construct a scale for six issue areas in which 1 indicates strong affinity for the matter while 0 equates to no support. It displays the clear distance between the NDP and the Wildrose and the centrality of the Tories. Only on the populism scale is there any overlap between the Wildrose and the NDP. On all other issues, the distance between the two parties is striking. Equally striking is the more centrist location of PC voters, who almost invariably fall between their two opponents. In comparison to the NDP voters, PC voters were more individualistic, less supportive of an activist government, less pro-environment, more socially conservative, more populist, and more likely to take positions associated with Western alienation. In comparison to Wildrose voters, PC supporters were less individualistic, more supportive of an activist government, more pro-environment, less socially conservative, less populist, and less likely to give responses demonstrating Western alienation. This is largely what one would expect of a "big tent" party. What this suggests is that space existed for the PCs to peel unhappy NDP voters away in a subsequent election.

In opting for the "unite the right" strategy, Tories chose to destroy the most electorally successful party in Canadian history. While there is now a clear right-wing alternative to the NDP, the strategy comes with its own challenges. As Abacus Research found, despite the fact that the combined 2015 vote total of the PCs and the Wildrose eclipsed the NDP, 73 per cent of respondents suggested they could support the New Democrats in future elections if they performed well.[49] In 2012 the PCs secured re-election by successful portraying the Wildrose as too far right and out of touch with Albertans.[50] They attracted a substantial number of voters who in 2008 had supported the NDP or the Liberals.[51] Many of those who voted PC in 2008, 2012, and 2015 held positions closer to NDP voters than to Wildrose voters. Disillusioned NDP voters from 2015 might well have found moving to the PCs in the next election—had the party continued to exist—relatively easy, as many did in 2012. A move to the more right-wing UCP may be more difficult for these voters to contemplate, even if they are unhappy with the NDP government.

These concerns are reinforced by the refusal of some prominent former PC members and MLAs to join the UCP. Of the nine PC MLAs who took seats in the Alberta legislature following the 2015 election, one is now an NDP cabinet minister, one is a member of the Alberta Party, and another remains resolutely apart from the UCP caucus. The loss of a third of the caucus and the concerns raised about the policy choices attributed to the UCP suggest that combining the PC and Wildrose vote from 2015 is neither simple nor inevitable. The success of the UCP's polarizing strategy depends on the structure of the provincial party system, including the positioning of the NDP and whether there is a viable centrist party. It will be interesting to watch how Alberta political culture responds to these new arrangements.

The challenge for the UCP is to hold on to as many of the more moderate PC voters as possible while also attracting repentant NDP supporters. For this to succeed they will need to portray the NDP as an ideologically fixated party well out of the province's mainstream. The Prentice-led PCs were, of course, unsuccessful in this approach in 2015. The other option is to depict the NDP government as unworthy of re-election because of their management of the provincial economy and the absence of a pipeline despite the NDP's efforts to create "social licence" for oil and gas exports. This will to some degree depend on energy prices and economic recovery. Both factors are beyond the control of the UCP.

The NDP will likely respond with a campaign like that waged by the PCs against the Wildrose in 2012—that is, by portraying the UCP as promoting values that are inconsistent with those of most Albertans. In pursuit of this goal an emphasis on identifying the UCP as the carrier of "social conservatism" will become the priority of the government. It is not clear what the outcome of the next election will be, but the party system in Alberta is likely to be more polarized if the alternative to the NDP is not a "big tent" party such as the Progressive Conservatives. There is no future for "Tories" in Alberta.

NOTES

1 Data for this analysis is drawn from surveys of eligible Albertan voters taken in the week following the 2008, 2012 and 2015 provincial elections. For 2008 and 2012, NRG Research conducted 1500 random phone interviews stratified by region and gender. The 2015 survey was based on an on-line panel of 1505 randomly drawn from the Research Now panel and stratified by age, gender. The same attitudinal and demographic questions were asked in each survey.

2 Jared J. Wesley, *Code Politics: Campaigns and Cultures on the Canadian Prairies* (Vancouver: UBC Press, 2011).

3 David K. Stewart and Anthony Sayers, "Albertans' Conservative Beliefs," in *Conservatism in Canada*, ed. James Farney and David Rayside (Toronto: University of Toronto Press, 2013).

4 David Stewart and Anthony Sayers, "Leadership Change in a Dominant Party: The Alberta Progressive Conservatives, 2006," *Canadian Political Science Review* 3, no. 4 (2009): 85–107; David Stewart and Anthony Sayers, "Breaking the Peace: The Wildrose Alliance in Alberta Politics," *Canadian Political Science Review* 7, no. 1 (2013): 73–86.

5 Ted Morton, "Leadership Selection in Alberta, 1992–2011: A Personal Perspective," *Canadian Parliamentary Review* 26, no. 2 (2013): 31–8, http://www.revparl.ca/english/issue.asp?param=215&art=1533 (accessed 22 January 2018).

6 Government of Alberta, "Economic Dashboard: Oil Prices," 2018, http://economicdashboard.alberta.ca/OilPrice; see also US Energy Information Administration, "Natural Gas," 2018, https://www.eia.gov/dnav/ng/hist/rngwhhdm.htm (both accessed 22 January 2018).

7 Dean Bennett, "New Alberta Premier Jim Prentice shrinks cabinet, appoints 2 Outsiders," *CTV News*, 15 September 2014, https://www.ctvnews.ca/politics/new-alberta-premier-jim-prentice-shrinks-cabinet-appoints-2-outsiders-1.2006954 (accessed 22 January 2018).

8 "Alberta byelections swept by Jim Prentice's Progressive Conservative Party," *CBC News*, 27 October 2014, http://www.cbc.ca/news/canada/calgary/alberta-byelections-swept-by-jim-prentice-s-progressive-conservative-party-1.2815059 (accessed 22 January 2018).

9   Trevor Robb, "Alberta Premier announces new seven-member budgetary Committee," *Edmonton Sun*, 14 December 2014, http://edmontonsun.com/2014/12/15/alberta-premier-announces-new-seven-member-budgetary-committee/wcm/98f09da9-be9b-425c-b2c2-32b385ffa31e (accessed 22 January 2018).

10 Gordon Thomson, "Smith's Defection from Wildrose Party a blow to democracy," *Edmonton Journal*, 18 December 2014, http://edmontonjournal.com/news/politics/thomson-smiths-defection-from-wildrose-party-a-blow-to-democracy (accessed 22 January 2018).

11 Notley, who garnered 70 per cent of the 3,589 votes cast, easily defeated two other candidates. Quotes from Karen Kleiss, "Nine cross floor to PCs; Wildrose MLAs make history with mass exodus," *Edmonton Journal*, 18 December 2014, http://edmontonjournal.com/news/politics/from-the-archives-nine-cross-floor-to-pcs-wildrose-mlas-make-history-with-mass-exodus (accessed 22 January 2018).

12 Finance Alberta, "Alberta's fiscal situation Budget 2015 and beyond: What We Heard," 2015, http://finance.alberta.ca/publications/budget/budget2015/Budget-2015-Consultation-Report.pdf (accessed 22 January 2018).

13 Jason Franson, "Prentice's 'look in the mirror' comment 'insulting' to Albertans, rivals say as backlash spreads," *National Post* (Toronto), 5 March 2015, http://nationalpost.com/news/politics/prentice-tells-alberta-to-look-in-the-mirror-for-the-reason-bloody-drastic-cuts-are-needed-in-the-province (accessed 22 January 2018).

14 "McAllister appointed as PC candidate after party disqualifies opponent," *CTV News*, 29 March 2015, https://calgary.ctvnews.ca/mcallister-appointed-as-pc-candidate-after-party-disqualifies-opponent-1.2303331 (accessed 22 January 2018).

15 Cypress-Medicine Hat MLA Drew Barnes was second with 3,502 votes, and former Strathcona County mayor Linda Osinchuk third with 444 votes, out of a total of about 25,000 members. See "Brian Jean elected new leader of Wildrose Party," *CBC News*, 28 March 2015, http://www.cbc.ca/news/canada/edmonton/brian-jean-elected-new-leader-of-wildrose-party-1.3013900 (accessed 22 January 2018).

16 See David K. Stewart and Anthony M. Sayers, "Prentice needs a miracle: Alberta PCs abandoned populist traditions," *Winnipeg Free Press*, 5 May 2015, https://www.winnipegfreepress.com/opinion/analysis/prentice-needs-a-miracle-302525021.html, and Rachel Maclean, "Alberta Budget 2015: 5 things you need to know," *CBC News*, 26 March 2015, http://www.cbc.ca/news/canada/calgary/alberta-budget-2015-5-things-you-need-to-know-1.3011244 (both accessed 22 January 2018).

17 Erika Stark, "Nenshi takes Tories to task for 'early' election," *Calgary Herald*, 8 April 2015, http://calgaryherald.com/news/local-news/nenshi-takes-tories-to-task-for-early-election; Rob Brown, "Alberta election 2015: The real race is for 2nd place," *CBC News*, 7 April 2015, https://www.cbc.ca/news/elections/alberta-votes/alberta-election-2015-the-real-race-is-for-2nd-place-1.3024277 (both accessed 22 January 2018).

18 Kent Hehr and Darshan Kang indicated in 2014 that they would run for the federal Liberals, Raj Sherman resigned as party leader and MLA in January 2015, and Laurie Blakeman chose to run for the Liberal, Green, and Alberta Parties in the provincial election. See Brown, "Alberta Election 2015"; James

Wood, "Kent Hehr will seek the federal liberal nomination in Calgary Currie," *Calgary Herald*, 18 July 2014, http://www.calgaryherald.com/news/ Kent+Hehr+will+seek+federal+liberal+nomination+Calgary+Centre/10038440/story. html; Chris Varcoe, "Sherman resigns as Liberal leader," *Calgary Herald*, 26 January 2015, http://calgaryherald.com/news/politics/raj-sherman-resigns-as-alberta-liberal-leader; Mariam Ibrahim, "Laurie Blakeman to run as candidate for Liberals, Greens and Alberta Party," *Edmonton Journal*, 13 March 2015, https://web.archive.org/ web/20150527205357/http:/www.edmontonjournal.com/Laurie%2BBlakeman% 2Bcandidate%2BLiberals%2BGreens%2BAlberta%2BParty/10887325/story.html (accessed 22 January 2018).

19   See both parties' election platforms: Progressive Conservative Party of Alberta, "The Prentice Plan: Choose Alberta's Future," 2015, https://www.poltext.org/sites/poltext. org/files/plateformes/prenticeplan.pdf (accessed 6 August 2018), and Wildrose Party, "Standing Up For Albertans," 2015, https://www.poltext.org/sites/poltext.org/files/ plateformes/standingupforalbertans.pdf (accessed 22 January 2018).

20   See Alberta Liberal Party, "Trusted Leadership for all Albertans," 2015, https://www. poltext.org/sites/poltext.org/files/plateformes/ab_liberal_platform.pdf, and Alberta NDP "Leadership for What Matters" 2015, https://www.poltext.org/sites/poltext.org/ files/plateformes/alberta_ndp_platform_2015.pdf (both accessed 22 January 2018).

21   See "Alberta's NDP 2015 Election Ads," YouTube video, posted by FactPointVideo, 28 April 2015, https://www.youtube.com/watch?v=8zKZ7RP93Lc (accessed 22 January 2018).

22   "Alberta election 2015: Platform planks of the 4 main parties," *Global News*, 4 May 2015, https://globalnews.ca/news/1978342/alberta-election-2015-platform-planks-of-the-4-main-parties/ (accessed 22 January 2018).

23   Alberta NDP, "Leadership for What Matters."

24   See Giovanni Sartori, "European Political Parties: The Case of Polarized Pluralism," in *Political Parties and Political Development*, ed. Joseph LaPalombara and Myron Weiner, 137–76 (Princeton: Princeton University Press, 1966) and Sartori, *Parties and Party Systems: A Framework for Analysis* (Cambridge: Cambridge University Press, 1976); see also Richard Johnston, *The Canadian Party System: An Analytic History* (Vancouver: UBC Press, 2017), 6.

25   Don Braid, "Just how scary is Rachel Notley?" *Calgary Herald*, 29 April 2015, http:// calgaryherald.com/news/politics/braid-just-how-scary-is-rachel-notley; "Jim Prentice defends PC candidate Mike Allen convicted of soliciting prostitute," *CBC News*, 29 April 2015, http://www.cbc.ca/news/elections/alberta-votes/jim-prentice-defends-pc-candidate-mike-allen-convicted-of-soliciting-prostitute-1.3054410; Dave Lazzarino, "Corporate business leaders warn of risks to Alberta NDP government," *Edmonton Sun*, 1 May 2015, http://edmontonsun.com/2015/05/01/corporate-business-leaders-warn-of-risks-to-alberta-ndp-government/wcm/51511789-8e62-4606-931e-a4761b21fca4; and Karen Kleiss, "NDP misses by a year on balanced budget calculation," *Edmonton Journal*, 21 April 2015, http://edmontonjournal.com/news/local-news/ndp-misses-by-a-year-on-balanced-budget-calculation (each accessed 22 January 2018).

26 Darcy Henton, "Fiery debate as Alberta's political leaders clash over health, corporate taxes and jobs," *Calgary Herald*, 23 April 2015, http://calgaryherald.com/news/politics/albertas-political-leaders-clash-in-televised-debate; Rick McConnell, "Alberta leaders debate: Poll suggests NDP's Rachel Notley won," *CBC News*, 24 April 2015, http://www.cbc.ca/news/elections/alberta-votes/alberta-leaders-debate-poll-suggests-ndp-s-rachel-notley-won-1.3047233; Forum Research, "NDP take dramatic lead in Alberta," 24 April 2015, http://poll.forumresearch.com/post/275/majority-government-seen-in-wake-of-debate/ (each accessed 22 January 2018).

27 Bruce Anderson and David Coletto, "Alberta's election was more about change, less about the NDP, say voters," Abacus Data, 17 May 2015, http://abacusdata.ca/albertas-election-was-more-about-change-less-about-the-ndp-say-voters (accessed 22 January 2018).

28 Bruce Anderson and David Coletto, "No regrets about election outcome, say Albertans in new poll," Abacus Data, 14 May 2017, http://abacusdata.ca/no-regrets-about-election-outcome-say-albertans-in-new-poll/ (accessed 22 January 2018).

29 Ibid.

30 See David K. Stewart and Keith Archer, *Quasi-democracy: Parties and Leadership Selection in Alberta* (Vancouver: UBC Press, 2000).

31 Morton, "Leadership Selection in Alberta," 31.

32 Michelle Bellefontaine, "Alberta PC party ends one member, one vote system to choose leaders," *CBC News*, 7 May 2016, http://www.cbc.ca/news/canada/edmonton/alberta-pc-party-ends-one-member-one-vote-system-to-choose-leaders-1.3572040 (accessed 22 January 2018).

33 Morton, "Leadership Selection in Alberta," 38.

34 Stewart and Archer, *Quasi-democracy.*

35 Lorne Gunter, "Jason Kenney unstoppable in pursuit of leadership of the Progressive Conservatives," *Edmonton Sun*, 13 February 2017, http://nationalpost.com/news/canada/graham-thomson-spoiler-alert-jason-kenney-will-win-the-alberta-pc-leadership-race-but-what-happens-next (accessed 20 January 2018).

36 Quoted in Michelle Bellefontaine, "Alberta MLA Sandra Jansen leaves PCs, joins NDP Caucus," *CBC News*, 17 November 2016, http://www.cbc.ca/news/canada/edmonton/alberta-mla-sandra-jansen-leaves-pcs-joins-ndp-caucus-1.3855868 (accessed 22 January 2018).

37 Quoted in Paula Simons, "Stephen Khan quits PC leadership race," *Edmonton Journal*, 26 January 2017, http://edmontonjournal.com/news/politics/paula-simons-stephen-khan-quits-pc-leadership-race (accessed 22 January 2018).

38 Ibid.

39 David Cournoyer, "Delegate election rules make it easy for Kenney to win," *Daveberta—Alberta Politics*, 22 November 2016, http://daveberta.ca/2016/11/jason-kenney-unite-alberta-party/ (accessed 21 January 2018).

40 James Wood, "Kenney sweeps to victory at PC leadership Convention," *Calgary Herald*, 18 March 2017, http://calgaryherald.com/storyline/pc-leadership-convention-candidates-make-closing-arguments-before-voting-begins (accessed 22 January 2018).

41 See James Wood, "Longtime members of Lougheed's PCs planning to 'cut up' their memberships," *Calgary Herald*, 17 February 2017, https://www.pressreader.com/canada/calgary-herald/20170217/282999694597231, and Kim Trynacity, "Former Alberta PC president to help organize political centre," CBC News, 16 June 2017, http://www.cbc.ca/news/canada/edmonton/former-alberta-pc-president-to-help-organize-political-centre-1.4165374 (both accessed 22 January 2018).

42 Helen Pike, " 'It's a hostile takeover': Alberta experts, politicos react to the United Conservative Party," *Metro News*, 18 May 2017, http://www.metronews.ca/news/calgary/2017/05/18/experts-political-react-united-conservative-party-alberta.html (accessed 21 January 2018).

43 Dean Bennett, "Alberta Progessive Conservatives, Wildrose strike merger deal," *Toronto Star*, 18 May 2017, https://www.thestar.com/news/canada/2017/05/18/alberta-pcs-wildrose-strike-tentative-deal-to-merge-sources-say.html (accessed 22 January 2018).

44 Dean Bennett, "Alberta PCs and Wildrose vote to merge as United Conservative Party," *CTV News*, 22 July 22 2017, https://www.ctvnews.ca/politics/alberta-pcs-and-wildrose-vote-to-merge-as-united-conservative-party-1.3514601 (accessed 22 January 2018).

45 Jane Schwartz, "Former PC leadership contender won't join the New United Conservative Party," *Calgary Herald*, 24 July 2017, http://calgaryherald.com/news/local-news/former-pc-leadership-contender-wont-join-the-new-united-conservative-party (accessed 22 January 2018).

46 James Wood, "Alberta Party leadership race to feature three contenders," *Calgary Herald*, 15 January 2018, http://calgaryherald.com/news/politics/alberta-party-leadership-race-likely-to-feature-three-contenders (accessed 22 January 2018); Emma Graney, "Former Edmonton Mayor Stephen Mandel wins Alberta Party Leadership," *Edmonton Journal*, 27 February 2018, http://edmontonjournal.com/news/politics/alberta-party-leadership-vote-closes-winner-to-be-announced-tuesday-night (accessed 28 May 2018).

47 James Wood, "Kenney wins big in UCP leadership race, fires warning shot at NDP," *Calgary Herald*, 29 October 2017, http://calgaryherald.com/news/politics/kenney-wins-big-in-ucp-leadership-race (accessed 22 January 2018).

48 David K. Stewart and Anthony Sayers, "Albertans' Conservative Beliefs," in *Conservatism in Canada*, ed. James Farney and David Rayside (Toronto: University of Toronto Press, 2013).

49 See Colby Cosh, "How Rachel Notley became Canada's most surprising political star," *Macleans*, 21 May 2015, http://www.macleans.ca/politics/how-rachel-notley-became-canadas-most-surprising-political-star/ (accessed 22 January 2018), and Anderson and Coletto, "No regrets about election outcome."

50 See Tom Flanagan, *Winning Power: Canadian Campaigning in the 21st Century* (Montreal and Kingston: McGill-Queens University Press, 2014).

51 David K. Stewart and Anthony M. Sayers, "Breaking the Peace: The Wildrose Alliance in Alberta Politics," *Canadian Political Science Review* 7, no. 1 (2013): 73–86.

APPENDICES

Appendix 1. Alberta Voter Turnout, 1975–2015

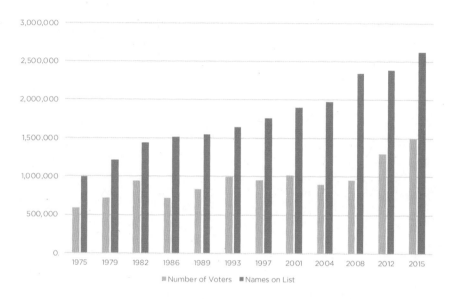

Sources: Candidate Summary of Results. Report of the Chief Electoral Officer on the 5 May 2015 Provincial Election. Edmonton: Chief Electoral Officer, 11 April 2016, 36.

Appendix 2. Party Votes in the 5 May 2015 Alberta Provincial Election (87 seats)

PARTY	TOTAL VOTE	VOTE (%)	SEATS
AFP	72	0.00%	0
LIB	62,153	4.20%	1
AP	33,221	2.20%	1
SC	834	0.10%	0
CP-A	182	0.00%	0
GPA	7,215	0.50%	0
NDP	604,518	40.60%	54
PC	413,610	27.80%	10
WRP	360,511	24.20%	21
IND	5,932	0.40%	0
Total	1,482,316	100%	87

Voter Turnout (%): 56.74
Number of Polls   7141

Sources: "Voter Turnout (1979-2015)." Report of the Chief Electoral Officer on the 5 May 2015 Provincial Election. Edmonton: Chief Electoral Officer, 11 April 2016, 35–36.

Appendix 3. Non-Renewable Resource Revenues Tables, 2005-6 to 2017-18 (current dollars)

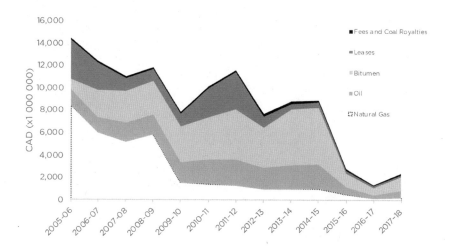

Sources: Alberta Treasury Board and Finance, Fiscal Plan Tables, 2005-6 to 2017-18, and Alberta Budgets, 2005-6 to 2017-18.

Appendix 4.A GDP Expenditure-Based, 2005-16

GDP EXPENDITURE-BASED (X $1,000,000)

YEAR	CANADA	BC	AB	SK	MB	ON	QC	NB	NS	PEI	NL
2005	1,079,835	143,116	124,296	32,432	38,382	423,243	234,642	23,905	31,720	4,550	16,083
2006	1,120,854	150,052	133,496	33,464	39,293	438,080	240,854	24,565	32,491	4,664	16,466
2007	1,164,057	157,834	141,943	35,268	41,007	450,039	249,012	25,459	33,551	4,752	17,650
2008	1,201,030	162,382	147,028	37,102	42,748	464,401	255,751	26,336	34,546	4,887	17,963
2009	1,209,948	162,911	146,758	37,884	43,163	466,543	259,559	26,558	34,809	4,974	18,778
2010	1,248,739	167,714	152,039	39,046	44,154	482,061	267,920	27,317	35,688	5,137	19,378
2011	1,273,984	171,479	158,102	39,941	45,609	489,514	272,174	27,386	36,445	5,206	19,725
2012	1,294,103	174,894	163,585	41,002	46,751	495,042	274,769	27,459	36,925	5,205	19,974
2013	1,315,785	178,467	169,822	41,916	47,546	501,462	278,313	27,703	37,067	5,236	20,233
2014	1,342,760	182,732	175,214	42,666	48,188	512,093	282,720	27,941	37,441	5,269	20,371
2015	1,369,766	189,033	177,840	43,182	48,675	526,160	284,666	28,374	37,749	5,324	20,625
2016	1,400,951	194,770	179,972	43,660	49,793	539,771	291,541	28,898	38,213	5,472	20,745

Sources: Statistics Canada. Table 36-10-0222-01 (formerly CANSIM 384-0038). Accessed 9 June 2018.

Appendix 4.B Canadian Provincial Per Capita Expenditure-Based Spending, 2005-16

GDP EXPENDITURE-BASED PER CAPITA (IN CURRENT DOLLARS)

YEAR	CANADA	BC	AB	SK	MB	ON	QC	NB	NS	PEI	NL
2005	33,491	34,110	37,420	32,643	32,574	33,784	30,951	31,957	33,820	32,956	31,271
2006	34,413	35,376	39,018	33,724	33,200	34,599	31,559	32,946	34,643	33,830	32,249
2007	35,395	36,783	40,393	35,196	34,478	35,258	32,370	34,154	35,881	34,505	34,673
2008	36,126	37,334	40,889	36,469	35,690	36,049	32,951	35,263	36,913	35,218	35,115
2009	35,980	36,936	39,890	36,611	35,714	35,894	33,092	35,413	37,102	35,552	36,340
2010	36,722	37,554	40,733	37,136	36,164	36,700	33,788	36,275	37,882	36,258	37,125
2011	37,096	38,114	41,713	37,456	36,968	36,907	33,989	36,247	38,588	36,143	37,569
2012	37,240	38,470	42,153	37,754	37,393	36,906	33,981	36,284	39,076	35,877	37,941
2013	37,431	38,881	42,477	37,939	37,568	36,993	34,143	36,658	39,305	36,061	38,364
2014	37,787	39,327	42,648	38,073	37,620	37,433	34,434	37,023	39,737	36,110	38,553
2015	38,227	40,265	42,571	38,175	37,575	38,156	34,484	37,634	40,093	36,269	39,002
2016	38,631	40,938	42,483	38,012	37,776	38,620	35,033	38,155	40,283	36,609	39,119

Sources: Statistics Canada. Tale 36-10-0222-011 (formerly CANSIM 384-0038). Accessed 9 June 2018.

Appendix 4.C Provincial Population. 2005-17

PROVINCIAL POPULATION, 2005-17

YEAR	CANADA	BC	AB	SK	MB	ON	QC	NB	NS	PEI	NL
2005	32,242,364	4,195,764	3,321,638	993,523	1,178,296	12,527,990	7,581,192	748,044	937,899	138,064	514,315
2006	32,570,505	4,241,691	3,421,361	992,302	1,183,524	12,661,566	7,631,873	745,609	937,869	137,865	510,584
2007	32,887,928	4,290,988	3,514,031	1,002,048	1,189,366	12,764,195	7,692,736	745,407	935,071	137,721	509,039
2008	33,245,773	4,349,412	3,595,755	1,017,346	1,197,774	12,882,625	7,761,504	746,855	935,865	138,764	511,543
2009	33,628,571	4,410,679	3,679,092	1,034,782	1,208,589	12,997,687	7,843,475	749,954	938,194	139,909	516,729
2010	34,005,274	4,465,924	3,732,573	1,051,425	1,220,930	13,135,063	7,929,365	753,044	942,073	141,678	521,972
2011	34,342,780	4,499,139	3,790,191	1,066,349	1,233,728	13,263,544	8,007,656	755,530	944,469	144,038	525,037
2012	34,750,545	4,546,290	3,880,755	1,086,018	1,250,265	13,413,702	8,085,906	756,777	944,943	145,080	526,450
2013	35,152,370	4,590,081	3,997,950	1,104,825	1,265,588	13,555,754	8,151,331	755,710	943,049	145,198	527,399
2014	35,535,348	4,646,462	4,108,416	1,120,639	1,280,912	13,680,425	8,210,533	754,700	942,209	145,915	528,386
2015	35,832,513	4,694,699	4,177,527	1,131,150	1,295,422	13,789,597	8,254,912	753,944	941,545	146,791	528,815
2016	36,264,604	4,757,658	4,236,376	1,148,588	1,318,115	13,976,320	8,321,888	757,384	948,618	149,472	530,305

Sources: Statistics Canada. Table 17-10-0005-01 (formerly CANSIM 051-0001). Accessed 9 June 2018.

Appendix 5. Alberta Provincial Revenues and Expenditures, 2007-17 (billions of current dollars)

YEAR	REVENUES	EXPENDITURES	SURPLUS/DEFICIT
2007	35,332	33,149	2,183
2008	38,571	37,003	1,568
2009	31,661	36,375	-4,714
2010	33,964	38,712	-4,748
2011	35,589	38,994	-3,405
2012	40,263	41,149	-886
2013	38,612	38,006 (5,209)	606* (1,287)
2014	44,354	40,432 (6,599)	3,922* (2,677)
2015	49,481	48,366 (6181)	1,115* (6,118)
2016	45,015	51,097	-6,082
2017	42,938	54,859	-13,424

* Indicates borrowing from Alberta Sustainability Fund. Withdrawals from the provincial stability fund are not included as revenues.

Sources: Alberta Treasury Board and Finance, Alberta Provincial Budget 2007-17.

Appendix 6 Alberta Provicial Government Per Capita Health Expenditure, 2008–17 (current dollars)

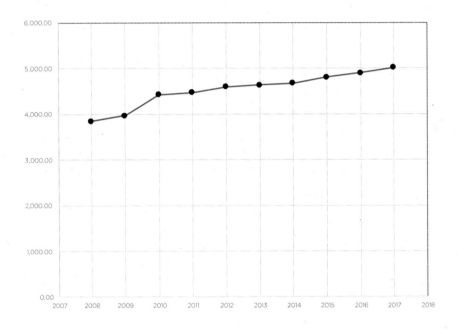

Sources: Canadian Institute of Health Information, National Health Expenditure Data Tables.

Appendix 7. Alberta Provincial Government Health Expenditure, 2008–17 (millions of current dollars)

YEAR	MILLIONS OF CURRENT DOLLARS (2008–17)	PERCENTAGE CHANGE
2007	12,377.80	
2008	13,811.80	11.58525748
2009	14,584.90	5.597387741
2010	16,504.30	13.16018622
2011	16,950	2.700508352
2012	17,839.40	5.24719764
2013	18,508.50	3.750686682
2014	19,211.90	3.800416025
2015	20,077.10	4.503458794
2016	20,825.80	3.729124226
2017	21,711.90	4.254818542

Sources: Canadian Institute of Health information, National Health Expenditure Trends Data Tables.

CONTRIBUTORS

DUANE BRATT is chair of the Department of Economics, Justice and Policy Studies at Mount Royal University. His is author, most recently, of *Canada, the Provinces and the Global Nuclear Revival* and co-editor of *Readings in Canadian Foreign Policy*. He is seen and heard regularly on TV and radio.

JANET BROWN is principal of Janet Brown Opinion Research, and has been tracking public opinion in Alberta for more than twenty-five years. She has managed research projects for all levels of government and numerous private-sector organizations. She regularly provides political commentary in the news media.

KEITH BROWNSEY teaches in the Department of Economics, Justice and Policy Studies at Mount Royal University. He has served as a consultant to governments and has co-edited *The Provincial State in Canada* and *Executive Styles in Canada: Cabinet Structures and Leadership Practices in Canadian Government*, among other works. He is currently writing a book on the Ontario Progressive Conservatives.

BRAD CLARK teaches broadcasting at Mount Royal University, where he is chair of the Journalism and Broadcasting Program. For many years he was a national reporter for CBC Radio, covering the oil and gas industry. His doctoral dissertation from Charles Sturt University in Australia was on TV coverage of Indigenous peoples in Canada.

ROGER EPP teaches in the Department of Political Science at the University of Alberta. A former dean, he currently serves as director of UAlberta North. His books include *We are All Treaty People: Prairie Essays* and *Roads Taken: The Professional Life, Scholarship and the Public Good*.

RON KNEEBONE is director of the Master of Public Policy Program in the University of Calgary's School of Public Policy. He is co-author of two well-known textbooks in economics and has served as an advisor to provincial and municipal governments.

SHERIDAN McVEAN teaches at Royal Roads University in Victoria and has been a consultant to governments and corporations for over thirty years.

CHASETEN REMILLARD teaches communication at Royal Roads University. A specialist in visual communications, he has published studies on artist Bill Reid, hockey art, and the Alberta oil sands, among other topics. He is currently completing a book on the visual communication of homelessness in Canada.

PETER MALACHY RYAN teaches public relations at Mount Royal University. Together with Patrice Dutil he received the J. E. Hodgett's Award from the Institute of Public Administration of Canada for article of the year in 2013, and together with Susan Ormiston and Greg Elmer he received a Gemini Award (now called the Canada Screen Award) for "Best Cross Platform Project" for coverage of the 2008 federal election.

JOHN B. SANTOS is project manager at Janet Brown Research. He also has an MA in political science at the University of Calgary, where he studied public opinion and electoral behaviour.

ANTHONY M. SAYERS teaches in the Department of Political Science at the University of Calgary. His research deals with major political institutions, including political parties, elections, federalism, parliaments, and Alberta provincial politics. He is currently working on a co-authored book with David K. Stewart entitled *Change in Alberta Politics*.

GILLIAN STEWARD was a former editor-in-chief of the *Calgary Herald* and she writes a regular column on Western politics for the *Toronto Star*. She teaches a course on journalism and war at Mount Royal University.

DAVID K. STEWART teaches in the Department of Political Science at the University of Calgary. He has published in the areas of provincial politics, Canadian politics, and political parties. His most recent book is *Conventional Choices: Maritime Leadership Politics*. He is currently working on a co-authored book with Anthony M. Sayers entitled *Change in Alberta Politics*.

RICHARD SUTHERLAND teaches in the Department of Economics, Justice and Policy Studies at Mount Royal University. He has published in the areas of cultural industries, policy, and media regulation. In particular, his work has focused on the music industry in Canada and government policies.

KEVIN TAFT was an Alberta Liberal MLA from 2001 to 2012 and leader of the Opposition from 2004 to 2008. He has a PhD in business and is the author of four books, including *Shredding the Public Interest* and, most recently, *Oil's Deep State*.

DAVID TARAS holds the Ralph Klein Chair in Media Studies at Mount Royal University. He is the author, most recently, of *Digital Mosaic: Media, Power and Identity in Canada*. He has served as an advisor to the Alberta government on national unity and as an expert advisor to the House of Commons Standing Committee on Canadian Heritage. He is a frequent media contributor.

MELANEE THOMAS teaches in the Department of Political Science at the University of Calgary. She is the co-editor, most recently, of a collection entitled *Mothers & Others: The Role of Parenthood in Politics* and she is currently working on a project on women premiers in Canada. She is a frequent media contributor.

GRAHAM WHITE is professor emeritus of political science at the University of Toronto. He is the author or editor of thirteen books, including *Inside the Pink Palace: The Government and Politics of Ontario* and *Cycling into Saigon: The Conservative Transition in Ontario*. He is also a former co-editor of the *Canadian Journal of Political Science* and a past president of the Canadian Political Science Association.

LORI WILLIAMS teaches in the Department of Economics, Justice and Policy Studies at Mount Royal University. She specializes in women and politics, law and bioethics, and political philosophy. She is frequently interviewed in the media.

JAMES WILT is a freelance journalist based in Winnipeg, Manitoba. He holds a journalism degree from Mount Royal University and is currently studying for his master's degree in geography at the University of Manitoba. He has written for CBC Calgary, Vice Canada, *Fast Forward Weekly*, and *Alberta Oil*, among other news organizations.

DEBORAH YEDLIN was an investment analyst with Goldman Sachs before embarking on a career as a journalist. She was until recently a business columnist for Post Media. She is chancellor of the University of Calgary.

JENNIFER ZWICKER is director of health policy at the University of Calgary's School of Public Policy. She holds a cross-appointment in the Department of Kinesiology and has a PhD in neurophysiology from the University of Alberta. She is co-chair of the Canadian Science Policy Centre.

INDEX

Edmonton, AB, 8, 10, 15, 19–20, 23, 25–27,
   37, 41, 44–45, 52, 60–61, 132, 140–41, 149,
   152–53, 160, 174, 181, 192, 213, 217, 219, 250,
   252, 254, 258, 260, 271–73, 275–82, 284–88,
   294–97, 301, 303, 305–8, 310–11, 393, 411, 415
Edmonton Journal, 29, 40
Edmonton Sun, 29
Edmonton-Glenora, 61
Edmonton-Gold Bar, 61
Edmonton-Highlands-Norwood, 118
Edmonton-Strathcona, 60
Edmonton-Whitemud, 45–46
education, 19, 26, 42, 59, 69, 175, 228, 232,
   234, 235, 238, 240, 241, 242, 243, 273, 295,
   298, 299, 300, 301, 309, 321, 323, 324, 326,
   332, 334, 339, 341, 350n77, 351n86, 408,
   409, 411. *See also* post-secondary; teachers;
   universities
Eggan, David, 221
EKOS, 81–82, 86–87, 94–96, 98
elections
—Alberta: 1935, 21, 377; 1944, 54n1; 1971, 1, 10,
   17, 18, 33, 37, 40, 46, 47, 148, 211, 212, 213,
   303, 399; 1975, 148, 427; 1982, 47, 151, 427;
   1986, 30, 47, 271, 303, 427; 1989, 46, 47, 427;
   1993, 19, 20, 23, 30, 31, 40, 46, 47, 98, 231,
   427; 1997, 20, 47, 98n2, 427; 2000, 98n2, 427;
   2004, 30, 36, 38, 47, 79, 98, 427; 2008, 30, 37,
   38, 41, 47, 57, 59, 69, 79, 104, 107, 108, 111–21,
   126, 128, 140, 141, 212, 300, 322, 332, 418,
   419n1, 427; 2012, 1, 4, 19, 30, 31, 36, 39–41,
   42, 43, 46, 47, 56n32, 57, 60, 66, 79, 81, 88,
   89, 91, 92, 96, 97, 98, 100n23, 104, 107, 111,
   116, 122–31, 133, 138, 139, 140, 141, 296, 297,
   301, 324–25, 329, 331, 391–92, 400, 427; 2015,
   1, 2, 3, 4, 5, 10, 11, 16, 17, 18, 19, 30, 31, 33,
   35, 36, 43, 45, 46, 48, 49, 50–52, 53, 57–73,
   75–76n28, 79–80, 81, 84–86, 88–89, 90, 91,
   92–93, 94, 95, 96, 97, 98, 103, 104, 105, 106,
   107, 108, 109, 110, 111, 130, 132–39, 140, 141,
   161, 165, 183, 198, 209, 212, 213, 215, 216,
   222, 223, 232, 248, 250, 253, 263, 264, 271,
   285, 297, 305, 306, 319, 333, 353, 354, 377,
   379, 380, 381, 383–84, 392, 394, 399, 400, 403,
   410, 411–12, 413, 416, 418, 419, 427, 428;
   Calgary Municipal 2010, 39, 132; Edmonton
   Municipal 2013, 132
—federal: 1988, 79, 98n2; 1993, 98n2; 1997,
   98n2; 2000, 98n2; 2004, 98n2, 99n6, 116;
   2006, 62, 98n2, 99n6; 2008, 62, 129; 2011,
   122, 217; 2015, 75n28, 88, 89, 92, 93, 96,

109–10, 132, 133, 140, 249, 252;
   Ontario 1990, 9, 378, 379, 380, 381–82, 383,
   392
Elections Alberta, 51, 248, 252
Electoral Boundaries Commission Act, 304–5
electoral redistribution, 10, 304–6
Elzinga, Peter, 26
Emergency Operations Centre, 363
emissions, 159, 165–74, 176, 177, 182, 198,
   200, 201, 205, 219, 260, 339, 371. *See also*
   greenhouse gases
Enbridge, 193, 196, 198–201, 261
Energy Diversification Advisory Committee,
   161
Energy East Pipeline, 196–97, 198, 204
Energy Efficiency Advisory Panel, 161
Energy Efficiency Alberta, 173
energy industry, 2, 3, 5, 6, 24, 27, 28, 31, 33, 43,
   64, 147–62, 168, 178, 180, 191–206, 230, 239,
   261, 293, 298, 303, 307, 339, 350n80, 354,
   369–70, 401. *See also* oil
Energy Information Agency, 196
energy policy, 2, 3, 5–6, 27–28, 147–62, 168, 173,
   177, 179, 180, 191–206, 230, 260, 262, 294,
   298, 302, 304, 326, 335, 340, 350n79, 80, 81
Enoch Cree Nation, 258
environment, ix, 27, 31, 118, 159, 167, 169, 175,
   183, 200, 402, 403, 417. *See also* climate
   change; global warming
Environment Canada, 155
Environment Policy, 3, 29, 33, 154, 155, 157,
   176, 178, 197, 198, 199, 200, 222, 248, 259,
   261, 282, 285, 298, 304, 335, 340, 371, 402,
   403, 417
Environmentalism, ix, 28, 33, 43, 159, 161, 177,
   192, 194–95, 196, 199, 200, 260–61, 262, 303,
   334
Epp, Roger, 8, 19, 293–315, 343
Equalization, 22,
Ermineskin, Randy, 258–60
Ermineskin Cree Nation, 258
Established Program Financing, 235
Europe, 170, 177, 255
Evans, Iris, 26
Executive Council, 45, 212–15, 218–20, 224
expenditure, 8, 228, 232, 233, 234, 238, 240, 241,
   242, 243, 244n8, 274, 285, 430, 431, 433, 434,
   435. *See also* spending
Explorers and Producers Association of
   Canada, 179
Exxon, 168, 170